THE WISDOM AND
BUSY MOTHERS F

Breads . . . pancake. . . . . vegetables . . .
omelettes . . . meat . . . fish . . . poultry . . . pasta . . . pastry . . .
regional American and international dishes . . . dishes for meat
lovers and for vegetarians . . . dishes for those on special diets
. . . dishes to satisfy the most hearty appetites and to tempt the
most picky eaters . . . old standbys for new cooks and new
ideas for old pros.

WHOLE
FOODS
FOR THE
WHOLE
FAMILY

LA LECHE LEAGUE® INTERNATIONAL, the world's foremost
authority on breastfeeding and producer of the million-copy
best-seller WOMANLY ART OF BREAST FEEDING, is also
deeply committed to advising and encouraging women in family management. La Leche League® research and experience
have pointed out the need to translate the principles of good
nutrition into menus and recipes that provide a well-balanced
diet with a variety of foods for the whole family.

WHOLE FOODS
FOR
THE
WHOLE
FAMILY

Edited by
Roberta Bishop Johnson

La Leche League® International Cookbook

A PLUME BOOK

PLUME
Published by the Penguin Group
Penguin Books USA Inc., 375 Hudson Street, New York, New York 10014,
U.S.A.
Penguin Books Ltd, 27 Wrights Lane, London W8 5TZ, England
Penguin Books Australia Ltd, Ringwood, Victoria, Australia
Penguin Books Canada Ltd, 2801 John Street, Markham, Ontario, Canada L3R
1B4
Penguin Books (N.Z.) Ltd, 182-190 Wairau Road, Auckland 10, New Zealand

Penguin Books Ltd, Registered Offices: Harmondsworth, Middlesex, England

Published by Plume, an imprint of New American Library, a division of Penguin
Books USA Inc.

BOOKS ARE AVAILABLE AT QUANTITY DISCOUNTS
WHEN USED TO PROMOTE PRODUCTS OR SERVICES. FOR
INFORMATION PLEASE WRITE TO PREMIUM MARKETING DIVISION,
PENGUIN BOOKS USA INC., 375 HUDSON STREET, NEW YORK,
NEW YORK 10014

PUBLISHED BY ARRANGEMENT WITH LA LECHE LEAGUE INTERNATIONAL.
THE ORIGINAL EDITION WAS PUBLISHED SIMULTANEOUSLY IN CANADA BY
LA LECHE LEAGUE INTERNATIONAL.

 REGISTERED TRADEMARK—MARCA REGISTRADA

LA LECHE LEAGUE AND ⬆ ARE REGISTERED TRADEMARKS OF LA LECHE
LEAGUE INTERNATIONAL, INC.

Library of Congress Cataloging in Publication Data

Main entry under title:

Whole foods for the whole family.
        Originally published : Franklin Park, Ill.: La Leche
League International, 1981

        Includes index.
    1. Cookery (Natural foods)   I. Johnson, Roberta Bishop.
TX741.W47   1984   641.5'637   84.2128
ISBW 0-452-25503-1

FIRST PLUME PRINTING, MAY, 1984

    5 6 7 8 9 10 11

PRINTED IN THE UNITED STATES OF AMERICA

Editor: Roberta Bishop Johnson

Associate Editors:
Bryanna Clark
Helen Henning Palmer
Lois Lake Raabe
Norene Schulenberg
Jean Baker White

Art Editor: Lois Lake Raabe
Layout: Lois Lake Raabe and Roberta Johnson

Director of Testing: Janice Smith
Director of Typists: Kathleen White

Kids' Cookbook
Editor: Helen Palmer
Illustrators: Eileen Dudley
Mary Lumens O'Donoghue

Chief Indexer: Marcia Casais
Copy Editor: Judy Savage

Editorial Assistants:

Karen Barclay
Barbara Bahun
Barbara Dick
Beth Elmore
Joann S. Grohman
Pat Jensen
Margaret MacPherson
Karen Nelson
Diana Reardon
Brenda Santer

Ronnie Barhite
Marcia Casais
Mary Recktenwald Chesney
Jan Foulk
Janice Hartman
Carol Lewis
Barbara Becker Nelson
Renny Northrop
Janet Repucci
Judy Savage

Protein and Calorie Count: Jan Foulk
Assistant Indexers: Brenda Santer
Helen Palmer
Cover Design: Roberta Johnson and Eileen Dudley
Cover Illustrator: Eileen Dudley
Calligraphy: Karen Williams Burdette
Cookbook Illustrators: Eileen Dudley
Mary Lumens O'Donoghue

Contents

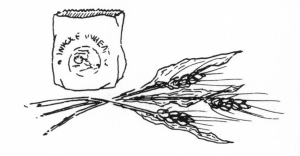

Foreword

Whole Foods for the Whole Family is testimony to the fact that volunteer-ism, reportedly on the wane, is indeed alive and well among La Leche League mothers.

But, volunteer though she is, the editor, Roberta Bishop Johnson, is a real pro. Roberta, an at-home wife and mother, was the volunteer editor for LLLI's first cookbook, *Mother's In the Kitchen*, and has gone on to work on cookbooks for other volunteer organizations. She is well-read on the subject of nutrition, and she's also a superb cook.

Working from home, Roberta created the editorial concept of the cook-book, then developed a workable procedure for enlisting, training and coordinating the talents of many widespread LLL volunteers. An attrac-tively designed flyer sent to LLL members brought floods of mail from enthusiastic LLL mothers with over 7,000 recipes and offers to help edit, type and test recipes. Responses came from coast to coast in the United States and Canada and trickled in from other parts of the world as well. Under Roberta's efficient and gentle guidance, the far-flung staff of 28 editorial assistants, 56 typists and 1,400 testers condensed the 7,000 recipes to a select 900. It was a volunteer effort right up to the final typing for the printer. Even the illustrations, calligraphy, layout and indexing were done by volunteers.

The recipes represent many different kinds of foods selected for good nutrition as well as taste. No junk foods or highly processed items are included. These days different family members' diets often require spe-cial cookbooks—low salt, low calories, whole grain, meatless, etc. *Whole Foods for the Whole Family* is unique; it includes all these specialties under one cover. Meat-eaters and vegetarians alike will be pleased. And, whether you are a beginning cook or an old hand, the variety is such that one of the editors commented, "We offer plenty to satisfy the novice and to give something new to the pro."

It's really quite a book and a tribute to these La Leche League mothers. We are proud of them and we know you'll love the cookbook they have produced.

Edwina Hearn Froehlich
Founding Mother and
Member of LLLI Board of Directors

Preface

In 1956, seven special women founded La Leche League to promote better mothering through breastfeeding. Many women, seeking help with breastfeeding their children, asked about the "magic foods" which would produce abundant milk. La Leche League research and personal experience pointed up the need for a good well-balanced diet with a variety of foods for the breastfeeding mother. These nutrition principles were explained at the LLL meetings for new mothers. However, we noticed that although most women knew about a good diet they were unsuccessful in translating the principles into menus and recipes. In addition, we LLL leaders encouraged mothers of new babies to plan meals ahead so that they would not have to neglect a fussy baby in order to prepare dinner.

We saw the need for a cookbook which would meet our needs, and in 1964 I began to collect and test recipes. The cookbook *Mother's In the Kitchen*, published in 1971, evidently met a need. La Leche League International has sold almost 200,000 copies.

Mother's In the Kitchen was far ahead nutritionally in 1964–68 when we were collecting recipes. We devoted half of the book to protein-rich main meals rather than the usual desserts. (And we wondered if putting yogurt and wheat germ in our book would brand us as food faddists!)

Now it is time for a new cookbook. The whole country has grown in nutrition consciousness and thoughtful LLL mothers are at the forefront with new ideas. These LLL mothers love their families enough to learn how to feed them well. However, they also value their time with their families so they don't want to spend unnecessary time in the kitchen. Many have developed clever methods and time-saving recipes which they have shared with us.

The purpose of this cookbook is to allow you to feed your family well, planning your preparation and cooking time around the needs of your family. It is not a cookbook of magic milk-producing recipes nor a whole book of recipes for using excess breast milk—although many have presumed so when they have heard about the cookbook.

We bring this collection to you with a great deal of love—for our families, for La Leche League, and for those families which may share our gleanings and in turn be enriched.

Gather your family into the kitchen and cook with joy.

Roberta Bishop Johnson

the Whole Foods Ideal

Whole Foods for the Whole Family is a cookbook for families who wish to eat whole foods processed as little as possible. All ingredients in the recipes are presumed to be whole grain and natural, with minimal processing and without artificial preservatives. Therefore, not every recipe will repeat these specifications. Ideally, all fruit and vegetables will be fresh, grown without dangerous sprays and chemicals. However, we are aware that supplies and availabilities of unsprayed fruit and vegetables may be limited; each consumer will have to decide whether or not to wash, scrub or discard the skin or peeling. We would prefer that the skin or peeling would be eaten if possible, but leave the decision to you.

We have included recipes using nitrate- and nitrite-free bacon and sausage because food suppliers are beginning to respond to consumer demand, and nitrite-free foods are becoming more readily available. Also, many families now grow their own pork and would like to have recipes. We are especially proud of our sausage and salami recipes which will help a family satisfy a desire for these well-loved foods in a homemade way.

All flours, grains and pasta are whole grain.

All oils and nut butters are without added sugar, hydrogenated fats or preservatives such as BHA and/or BHT.

Our recipes use butter, rather than margarine, because butter is essentially natural and can be made at home. Oil may be whipped into it to add unsaturated fat.

Carob chips, shredded coconut and canned fruit are assumed to be unsweetened when specified in our recipes.

Cheeses are natural cheeses, rather than processed cheese food.

Dry milk powder in recipes is non-instant.

Fruits and vegetables are to be fresh, if possible, with frozen as second choice. Any canned or frozen fruits should be unsweetened, packed in water or their own juice.

Although artificially sweetened desserts are not necessary in a good diet, many families have become accustomed to eating desserts. We have carefully chosen dessert recipes which use a minimum of sweeteners, and rely instead upon enhancing the natural sweetness of the ingredients. In most recipes, alternative sweeteners are listed to allow for the preference of each family.

1

Protein and calorie counts are calculated using the average or medium size items such as potatoes, onions, eggs, tomatoes, etc. Ground beef is figured as average fat hamburger. If several ingredients are listed as alternatives, the first was used for the protein/calorie calculation. All optional ingredients listed along with the other ingredients thus: (optional) are included in the protein and calorie calculation. Optional ingredients listed under the heading *Optional* were not included in the calculation. In some cases the protein/calorie count is given with toppings or garnish, if used, to be added to the total.

References used for calculating the protein and calorie values were standard: *Composition of Foods*, U.S. Department of Agriculture Handbook No. 8, and *Food Values of Portions Commonly Used*, Bowes and Church. A few items not found in these standard sources were researched from *Laurel's Kitchen*, Robertson et al.

Protein and calorie counts are given for the total recipe since appetites and serving sizes vary widely from family to family and time to time.

Because of the many alternative ingredients offered in many recipes, our cookbook will serve as a useful transition to more healthful recipes using greater amounts of whole foods as the family's tastes change. The many options and alternatives also allow for the optimum use of a bountiful harvest or an inexpensive supply of a particular item.

We also list our ingredient measurements in cups to make it easier to measure foods bought in bulk, pre-cooked, home-canned, frozen, or dried.

Since many families are concerned about eating well but economically, we have included a wide selection of meatless or less-meat meals, concentrating especially upon those which are similar to familiar dishes.

We recognize that availabilities of whole foods vary widely. For some families, cooking with whole wheat flour means finding a supermarket which carries a name brand package; for others it means buying whole wheat grain and having it ground; for others, it means growing the wheat and custom grinding it fresh for each baking. We have designed our book to be useful to you wherever you are in this supply chain.

RBJ

Breakfasts

ALTERNATIVES TO THE RUN-OF-THE-MILL BREAKFAST

1. tuna sandwich
2. cold chicken
3. toasted cheese sandwich
4. bread pudding or rice pudding
5. leftover meatloaf
6. oatmeal muffins
7. burritos-tortillas, beans and cheese
8. egg salad on toast
9. hamburger sandwich
10. creamed tuna on toast
11. Welsh rarebit
12. individual pizzas
13. cottage cheese on a.cantaloupe or honeydew melon section
14. yogurt and your favorite fruit whirled in blender
15. 1 C. yogurt and a sliced banana, add crushed graham cracker

Claudia Scattergood   *Bonnie Irvin*
Toutle, Washington   *Hudson, N. Carolina*

BREAD SPORNGE
(spornj)

For each serving:
1 t. **butter**
1 slice **bread**
1 or 2 **eggs**
dash of **salt** (to taste)
2 slices **bacon**, fried
   and crumbled

Melt butter in skillet. Break bread in small pieces and add to skillet, stirring until golden. Add remaining ingredients and scramble until set but not dry.

Quick and easy for children to make. Uses up all odd scraps of bread.

PROTEIN: 12.4 grams; CALORIES: 277   *Mae Seib*   *Sandie Koenig*
Columbus, Wisconsin   *Waterton, Wisconsin*

HEALTHFUL BREAKFAST "DANISH"

1 C. **cottage cheese**
¼ to ½ C. chopped **dates**,
   figs or prunes
¼ C. **nuts** and **seeds**
1 t. to 1 T. **honey**
½ t. ground **cinnamon**
grated **orange peel**

whole grain **bread** or English
   muffins

Mix cheese spread ingredients together. Spread on bread. Place on cookie sheet. Broil until bubbly.

PROTEIN: 35.5 grams; CALORIES: 547 + bread
Lois Lake Raabe
Easton, Connecticut

THREE BEARS PORRIDGE
(With Extra Special Options)

½ C. cracked **wheat**
½ C. rolled **oats**
¼ C. dry **milk powder** (optional)
½ t. ground **cinnamon**
¼ C. **raisins**
3 C. boiling **water** or
  scalded milk
honey to taste

Add dry ingredients to boiling water (or milk) in saucepan. Stir until thoroughly mixed. Bring back to a boil. Reduce heat and simmer, covered, for 10 to 15 minutes, or until desired consistency. Add honey to taste.

Our Three Bears book has Mama Bear making porridge with "honey and a pinch of cinnamon and two pawfuls of raisins in it," so this recipe sounds like the real thing. Our children love it.

PROTEIN: 26.7 grams; CALORIES: 673 + honey

Cathy Strahan
North Bend, Oregon

Optional:
¼ C. **dried fruit** (such as
  dates, etc.)
¼ C. chopped **apple**
¼ C. **bran**
¼ to ½ C. **wheat germ**
2 T. **nutritional yeast**
2 T. soy **flour** or soy grits
½ C. **sunflower seeds**
2 **eggs**

Any of these may be added to the above porridge, if desired. Combine the ingredients and cook as you would for Three Bears Porridge. Then stir in eggs, cover and let stand 1 to 2 minutes.

Variation: Any combination of **grains** may be substituted for oats and cracked wheat. Vary the porridge each time you make it, or make a large batch ahead of time for convenience. *Adjust cooking time* to the grains used, cooking for the amount of time required by the longest-cooking grain you use. See table (p. 292).

BANANA OATS
(A Perfect First Cereal)

½ C. rolled **oats**
1 C. **milk**
½ ripe **banana** (optional)
½ C. **milk** (optional)

Grind rolled oats in a blender or processor until finely ground. Mix ground oats in heavy saucepan with 1 C. milk. Bring to a boil. Reduce heat and simmer 4 minutes, stirring often. Remove from heat. Cover and let stand 5 minutes.

If desired, blend banana and ½ C. milk in blender or processor until frothy. Stir into cooked cereal. This was my baby's first cereal and is still his favorite four years later—I just don't grind the oatmeal as finely.

PROTEIN: 19.4 grams; CALORIES: 472

Marlene Fairbairn
Mississauga, Ont., Can.

A Helpful Suggestion: If you make the baby's cereal with milk instead of water, then it is not necessary to add more milk as a topping. This way the cereal is "thick enough to stay on an upside-down spoon" when the baby wants to feed him- or herself and starts waving the spoon around.

ROASTED GRAIN BREAKFAST CREAM CEREAL

1 to 1½ C. **grains** (wheat, rice, millet, rye, barley, oats)
5 to 6 C. **water**
1 t. **salt**

Toppings:
milk
raisins, nuts or chopped apple (optional)
butter (optional)

Wash and clean whole grains, if necessary. Drain and dry. Roast grains in a cast-iron skillet over medium-high heat, stirring constantly until lightly browned (about 1 to 2 minutes, depending on the grain). Or roast in large quantity in a 300° oven until lightly browned, using a large baking pan. Blend or process roasted grains until as fine as flour.
Bring water and salt to a boil. Slowly sprinkle in grain flour, stirring constantly until well mixed. Reduce heat, if necessary, to prevent boiling over. Continue cooking and stirring for the amount of time indicated in the Grain Cooking Table (p. 292). Serve with your choice of topping(s).   *PROTEIN: 16 grams; CALORIES: 400 + topping*

Karima Khatib
Paris, France

Milk Soup. Substitute **milk** for the 5 to 6 C. water. Scald the milk. Add 1 **egg** to 1 C. grain flour (which may be unroasted, if desired) and 1 t. salt. Stir to form lumps. Drop "lumps" into scalded milk, stirring constantly until soup thickens. Add ¼ C. (or less) **honey** and serve topped with a sprinkling of ground **cinnamon**. This is nutritious, quick and just as tasty cold as it is hot.

Wanda Rezac
Marlboro, Massachusetts

MUESLI

3 C. rolled **oats**
1 C. rolled **rye**
1 C. **bran**
1 C. **sunflower seeds**
1 C. **sesame seeds**
1 C. unsweetened, shredded, dried **coconut**
1 C. unsalted **soybean nuts**

Optional toppings:
chopped fresh **fruit** (apples, bananas, strawberries, etc.)
dried **fruit** (raisins, dates, etc.)
milk or yogurt
honey

Mix all the ingredients together. Store in an air tight container in a cool, dry place. Serve with desired toppings.
Any combination of nuts, seeds, and grains can be used. This is the combination which my family finds most satisfying. In fact, my children prefer this over the sweetened, cooked granolas. We also find it very satisfying because our hunger does not return as quickly as with other cereals.

Jan Foulk
Elwin, Illinois

PROTEIN: 182.7 grams; CALORIES: 4181
¼ C. = P.: 5.1 gms; C.: 116

CHEESY GRAINS

1 C. cooked **grains**
½ C. grated Swiss **cheese**
seeds (sesame or sunflower)

For a quick, high-protein breakfast or lunch, put grains and cheese in a buttered pan. Stir constantly over low heat until cheese melts. Top with seeds.   *P.: 33.6 gms.; C.: 572*

Lois Lake Raabe
Easton, Connecticut

SCRAMBLED EGGS

1 T. **butter** or oil
2 **eggs**
1 to 2 T. **milk**, cream or water
pinch of **salt**

Optional:
grated, crumbled or cubed **cheese**
small pieces of leftover **meats**
   (bacon, sausage, chicken,
   turkey, ham or beef)
sauteed or leftover **vegetables**
sliced, sauteed **mushrooms**
chopped **tomatoes**
cooked, shredded or cubed
  potatoes
leftover cooked **brown rice**
herbs

Melt butter in frying pan. Combine eggs with milk and salt. Beat until smooth and well blended. Pour egg mixture into heated pan. Allow to set a little, then stir frequently until eggs are done to your liking.
Have your choice of additions at room temperature or warmer. Add when you beat the eggs, or when you begin stirring the eggs in the pan.

PROTEIN: 13.5 GRAMS; CALORIES:274

Many LLL Contributors

Omelette. Follow directions for Scrambled Eggs above, but do not stir. When eggs begin to set, push with a spatula toward center of pan; tilt to allow unset eggs to reach pan surface. (Repeat this procedure if many eggs are used.) When almost completely set, add any of the optional ingredients to one side of the omelette. Loosen around the edges with a fork or spatula. Carefully fold omelette over the filling. Serve immediately.

For a fluffy omelette, separate eggs. Beat yolks with milk and cream. Whip whites until stiff but not dry. Fold whites into yolk mixture. Cook as above, or bake in a 375° oven until done. Do not fold. Check often to avoid over-baking.

BAKED EGGS

2 C. **white sauce** (p. 251)
1 C. grated **cheese**
sliced **mushrooms** (optional)
6 to 8 **eggs**
chopped, fresh **herbs** for garnish

Stir cheese into hot white sauce, reserving some cheese for topping. Saute mushrooms and add to white sauce, if you wish. Pour sauce into a rectangular baking dish. Break eggs into sauce in an orderly arrangement. Sprinkle with herbs and cheese. Bake at 350° for about 20 minutes.

PROTEIN: 90.2 grams; CALORIES: 1811

Jan Dallman   Monica Kelly
Jonesboro, Georgia   Longview, Texas

EGGS IN A BASKET

Line sections of muffin tins with squares of **biscuit dough** (p. 123). Break an **egg** into each one. Bake 10 to 15 minutes at 400°.

P.: 9.4 gms.; C.: 191   Geni Wixson
Germantown, Maryland

If, when you are hard-cooking eggs, you realize you don't remember how long they have been cooking and are tempted to over-cook just to be sure, test an egg by removing it from the water and spinning it on the counter. If the center is firm, it will spin easily. If it wobbles, the center is still liquid and needs more cooking.

JIFFY RICE PUDDING

1 C. cooked **brown rice**
½ C. **cottage cheese**
½ C. plain **yogurt**

Optional:
honey
mashed **banana**
raisins
unsweetened, shredded **coconut**
ground **cinnamon**
ground **nutmeg**

For "instant" Rice Pudding, mix cooked rice, cottage cheese and yogurt. Sweeten with a little honey or mashed banana, if desired. Add other optional ingredients to taste. This is good for breakfast, dessert or snack.

PROTEIN: 25 grams; CALORIES: 370

Lois Lake Raabe
Easton, Connecticut

CHEESE BREAD FOR BREAKFAST

2 T. **water**
2 C. grated Longhorn **cheese**
1 **egg**, beaten
6 slices **bread** or toast
dash of **salt**
dash of **pepper**

Bring water to a boil in 8" fry pan. Over low heat, add cheese. Stir until melted. Stir in egg and cook until white sets. Spoon out and spread on bread. Season to taste. Try different cheeses.

This has always been my favorite breakfast when I visit my grandmother, who now serves it to my daughter. It is a recipe handed down through my grandmother's Scotch-Irish family.

PROTEIN: 75.4 grams; CALORIES: 1360

Cheryl M. Dennis
Reading, Pennsylvania

GOETTA
(Getta)

6 C. **water**
1 T. **salt**
1 lb. ground **beef**
1 lb. bulk **pork sausage**
2 **bay leaves**
1 C. finely chopped **onion**
2½ C. pin **oats** (steel cut oats)
bacon drippings

Bring water and salt to a boil. Break up beef and add to water. Cut up sausage and add to water with bay leaves and onion. Cook for 15 to 20 minutes. Stir in pin oats and cook over low heat for 50 minutes more until thickened, stirring frequently to prevent sticking. Pour into loaf pans and chill until firm. Slice ¼ to ½ inch thick and fry in bacon drippings.

Goetta is delicious fried with eggs. It is a short version of what my grandmother made for her 10 children, using whole hog's head with the eyes removed, and cooking it all day for the meat. It is a Cincinnati area specialty. Some prefer to use all cooked pork. If pin oats are hard to find, use regular rolled oats.   PROTEIN: 183 grams; CALORIES: 4176   Donna Vore
Springboro, Ohio

FRUIT-CHEESE TOAST

¼ C. **butter**
3 **eggs**
3 T. **milk**
8 slices whole grain **bread**
3 oz. cream **cheese**, softened
1 **apple**, pear or banana
½ t. **lemon juice**
¼ C. **raisins**
honey (optional)

Heat oven to 450°. Melt butter in a jelly roll pan in oven, and spread evenly. Beat 2 whole eggs and one egg white with milk. Dip bread in egg mixture, coating both sides, then put bread in buttered pan. Bake for 5 minutes. Mix cream cheese and remaining yolk. Chop fruit and add lemon juice and raisins. Remove bread from oven. Turn and spread each slice with cheese mixture and top with fruit. Bake 5 more minutes or until cheese is set and fruit is tender. Drizzle with honey if desired.

This is a super way to use up stale ends of bread. Everyone from toddler to house-guest enjoys it!

Becki Findley
Charleston, West Virginia

PROTEIN: 49.2 grams; CALORIES: 1718 + honey

MARTY'S BREAKFAST BURRITOS

flour tortillas (p. 168)
scrambled **eggs**
grated **cheese**
taco sauce (optional)

Warm tortillas till pliable in a covered frying pan over medium heat. Put a serving of eggs in each tortilla and top with cheese. Fold over tortilla and serve. The hot eggs will melt the cheese. My husband, Marty, developed this delicious change of pace breakfast. Excellent things result when "Father's in the Kitchen."

Alice Stefanic
Kalispell, Montana

ORANGE RICE AND SPICE BREAKFAST

1 C. brown **rice**
2 C. **water**
dash of **salt**
milk to cover rice
½ C. dry **milk powder**
¼ C. **honey**
1 t. ground **cinnamon**
¼ t. ground **allspice**
¼ t. ground **nutmeg**
¼ C. ground **nuts**
1 T. grated **orange peel**
½ C. **raisins**
orange slices (optional)

Mix rice, water and salt in saucepan. Bring to a boil, stir once, reduce heat and cover. Simmer for approximately 35 minutes or until rice is cooked. Add liquid milk to cover rice. Stir in remaining ingredients. Cook over medium heat until thoroughly heated. Garnish with orange slices for a special touch. Serves 4.

Christina Pinkerton
Loveland, Colorado

P.: 45.2 gms.; C.: 1589 + milk and orange slices

Rice and Raisins. For a simpler dish, just cook rice with water and raisins. Serve with milk and honey (optional).

My family loves this and it satisfies a hungry tummy.

Julie Delaplane
Anderson, Indiana

Pancakes & Waffles

NUTTY FRUITY FRENCH TOAST

½ C. **peanut butter**
½ C. chopped **raisins** or
  apricots
2 T. **apricot** preserves
dash **cinnamon**
12 slices whole grain **bread**
2 **eggs**
½ C. **milk**
2 T. **butter**

Combine peanut butter, fruit, preserves and cinnamon. Spread six slices of bread with this mixture. Top with remaining bread. Beat eggs and stir in milk. Dip each sandwich in this mixture, draining off excess liquid. Melt butter in skillet and saute sandwiches over medium heat, turning to brown both sides. Serve warm. *Wanda Byars*

PROTEIN: 83.6 grams; CALORIES: 2306 *Norman, Oklahoma*

FREEZER FRENCH TOAST / PANCAKES

I make up a whole loaf of bread into French Toast, freeze the slices individually on a baking sheet and then put them back in the bread bag. When you need some for a fast breakfast, just pop in the toaster. Pancakes can also be made in advance and frozen, separated by waxed paper. They're easily reheated in an oven, under a broiler, or in a toaster. Works great for us new mothers. *Janet Roy*
Manitouwadge, Ont., Canada

PANCAKES OR WAFFLES

3 C. **LLL Baking Mix** (p. 123)
2 C. **milk** or water
2 **eggs**

Beat together all ingredients just until mixed (can use blender). Bake on hot griddle (375°) until bubbles appear, turn over and bake until no steam comes out.

Makes 18 3" pancakes

Waffles. Use 2 to 4 eggs. Separate the eggs, beating the yolks into the batter. (If you're in a hurry you can use whole eggs, as for pancakes.) Bake in a hot greased waffle iron until steam no longer escapes. Makes 18 4" waffles. *PROTEIN: 75.7 grams; CALORIES: 2017*

BASIC WHOLEGRAIN PANCAKES

2 C. **milk** or soy milk
1 to 3 **eggs**
2 t. **baking powder**
½ t. **salt**
2 C. **flour**: any combination of
   whole wheat, rye, soy, oat,
   millet or buckwheat; rolled
   oats, wheat or rye; bran,
   wheat germ or cornmeal

Optional:
up to ¼ C. **honey**, maple
   syrup, molasses or brown
   sugar
up to ¼ C. **oil**, melted butter,
   or other fat

In a large bowl, place milk, eggs, baking powder, salt and optional honey and oil. Mix well. Add flour and/or grain, beating only until large lumps disappear. Batter may also be mixed in blender and poured onto griddle directly from the blender. Batter may be made the night before; store in a covered container in the refrigerator.

Cook on a lightly greased skillet or griddle over medium-high heat (375°). Turn when small bubbles appear. Remove when they stop steaming. Freeze extras and heat in toaster for snacks or busy mornings. Makes about 16 4" pancakes.

PROTEIN: 55 grams; CALORIES: 1210

Buttermilk, Sour Milk or **Yogurt Pancakes.** Omit milk and baking powder. Add 2 C. **buttermilk**, sour milk or yogurt and 1 t. **baking soda.** Yogurt may need a little thinning with milk or water. Sour milk may be made by adding 2 T. vinegar or lemon juice to 2 C. milk.

Orange Pancakes: Use 2 C. **orange juice** in place of buttermilk.

Flavor Choices: Add any of these to either Basic or Buttermilk Pancakes:

1 t. **vanilla**
up to 2 T. **nutritional yeast**
1 t. grated **orange peel**
extra dry **milk powder**
¾ C. unsweetened **applesauce**
½ C. unsweetened, shredded
   coconut
¼ C. **carob powder**
up to 1 t. ground **cinnamon** or
   nutmeg

up to 2 t. ground **coriander**
1 C. **blueberries** or other berries
½ C. chopped **nuts** or seeds
up to 1 C. **raisins**, dates or other
   dried fruit
1 C. chopped **apples** or other fruit
1 T. **protein powder**
½ C. grated **cheese**

Pancake Toppings: butter, maple syrup, applesauce, yogurt, sour cream, whipped cream, mashed fruit, bananas, cottage cheese, warm honey, peanut butter, fruit butter, homemade jams or jellies, cream cheese, ricotta cheese . . .

Many LLL Contributors

PEANUT BUTTER PANCAKES

Follow the Basic Wholegrain Pancake recipe using 1½ C. whole wheat flour and ½ C. wheat germ for the flour. Use ¼ C. honey and ½ C. **peanut butter** in place of the oil. Good topped with yogurt and bananas!

PROTEIN: 110.1 grams; CALORIES: 2557

Terri Gaffney
Dayton, Ohio

WHOLE WHEAT BANANA PANCAKES

Follow the Basic Wholegrain Pancake recipe using 1¼ C. whole wheat flour and ¾ C. wheat germ for the flour. Use 1½ T. brown sugar, 3 eggs and no oil. Add 1¼ t. **vanilla**, ¼ t. **lemon juice**, ¾ C. chopped **banana** (about 1½ bananas) and ¾ C. chopped **nuts**.

PROTEIN: 103.7 grams; CALORIES: 2374   Marsha Wilson
Jefferson City, Missouri

RICE PANCAKES

Follow the Buttermilk Pancake recipe using 4 **eggs**, separated. Beat the egg whites until stiff with a pinch of **cream of tartar**. Use 2 C. brown rice **flour**, 2 T. **honey** and 2 T. melted **butter**. After mixing the batter, fold in the beaten egg whites.   PROTEIN: 60.7 grams; CALORIES: 1690

Mary Jo Johnson
Shavertown, Pennsylvania

BUCKWHEAT PANCAKES

Follow the Buttermilk Pancake recipe using 2 eggs, 2 t. brown sugar and 2 T. oil. Use ½ C. unbleached white flour, ½ C. whole wheat flour and 1 C. **buckwheat flour**. Our Sunday morning treat!

PROTEIN: 47 grams; CALORIES: 1257   Nancy O'Bosky
Visalia, California

RICE CAKES

1 **egg**, well beaten
⅓ C. **milk**
2 t. grated **onion**
2 C. cooked **rice**
¼ C. **flour**
salt and **pepper** to taste
1½ t. **baking powder**
1 t. **sugar** or honey

Combine egg with milk and onion. Stir in rice. Combine remaining ingredients and add to rice mixture, mixing slightly. Drop by tablespoons onto hot griddle. Cook until brown, then turn and brown second side. Makes 10 to 12 cakes.
This is a Southern folk recipe.

PROTEIN: 20.7 grams; CALORIES: 1937   Jocelyn Butler
Washington, D.C.

SOURDOUGH WHOLE WHEAT PANCAKES

1 C. **sourdough starter** (p. 164)
1 C. whole wheat **flour**
1 T. **honey** or sugar
1 **egg**, beaten
2 T. **oil** or melted butter
½ C. **milk**
½ t. **salt**
½ t. **baking soda** dissolved in
   1 T. **water**

For **Waffles:** Add 2 T. more oil.

Mix all ingredients except soda with the starter. Heat a griddle or skillet to 375°. Just before cooking, fold dissolved soda into batter. If batter seems thick, dilute with lukewarm water. Bake as for ordinary pancakes, making them 3 to 4". Makes about 12 small pancakes.

PROTEIN: 36.5 grams; CALORIES: 1004

Brenda Strand   Diane M. Wickham
Fessenden, North Dakota   Elma, New York

COTTAGE CHEESE PANCAKES
(Blender Method)

½ C. whole wheat **flour** or rolled oats
1 C. **cottage cheese** or tofu
4 **eggs**
⅓ C. **milk** (approximately)

Optional:
¼ t. **salt**
½ t. **vanilla**
1 T. **wheat germ**
½ t. **baking soda** (if cottage cheese is very sour)

Combine all ingredients except milk in blender and process at medium speed until smooth. Add milk until batter is like medium-thick pancake batter. Bake as for ordinary pancakes on a lightly greased skillet or griddle over medium high heat until brown on both sides. Serve hot with fresh fruit, jam, hot applesauce or butter and cinnamon-sugar. A delicious change! Makes about 25 3" pancakes. *PROTEIN: 66.1 grams; CALORIES: 808*

Many LLL Contributors

PUFFED OVEN PANCAKE

3 T. **butter** for baking

Batter:
6 **eggs**
1½ C. **milk**
1½ C. whole wheat **flour** (pastry or sifted flour)

Optional:
1 t. **vanilla**
¾ t. **salt**
dash ground **nutmeg**
¼ t. ground **cinnamon**

Preheat oven to 450°. Place butter in a 4½ to 5-quart baking dish. Any pan will do as long as it has sides no higher than 3". A 12 to 14" cast iron skillet or paella pan works well, or you can use 2 or 3 eight-inch skillets. Place pan in oven and let butter melt (but not burn!) while the oven heats up.

Meanwhile, whirl the eggs in blender at high speed 1 minute, then add milk and slowly add flour. Whirl 30 seconds more. (Or beat eggs until thick and lemon-colored with a whisk, mixer or rotary beater, then beat in milk and flour.) Immediately pour batter into hot pan and bake 10 minutes. Lower heat to 350° and bake 10 minutes more, or until puffed and well browned on the edges. Serve this deceptively easy dish to family or guests, who should be ready and waiting at the table, and sit down to enjoy it hot with sugar and lemon juice, fresh fruit, jam or preserves, cinnamon-sugar, syrup or honey. Also good with bacon and sausage. *PROTEIN: 74.1 grams; CALORIES: 1626*

This recipe can be reduced, using proportions of 1 egg, ¼ C. milk, ¼ C. flour and ½ T. butter (1/8 t. salt, if used) per person.

Fruit Puffed Pancake. Lay **apple** slices or other fruit in pan before pouring in the batter. Sprinkle with a little **cinnamon-sugar** just before it's finished, if desired.

Arline Ferguson
Coldwater, Michigan

Shirley McLaughlin
Hillside, Illinois

Buckwheat Crepes. Follow the recipe for Swedish Pancakes, adding ½ C. **buckwheat flour** and omitting ½ C. whole wheat flour. Omit ¾ C. milk and add ¾ C. **yogurt**. Use 1 T. melted butter, but no sugar, salt, spices or vanilla. Fill with anything from herring in sour cream to maple syrup!

Linda McConnell
Regina, Sask., Canada

SWEDISH PANCAKES
(Crepes)

3 **eggs**
1¼ C. **milk**
¾ C. whole wheat **flour**
¼ t. **salt**

Optional:
2 t. to 3 T. melted **butter**
1 T. **honey**
1 t. **cinnamon**
½ t. **nutmeg**
½ t. **coriander**
½ t. **vanilla**

Beat eggs until thick and lemon colored. Stir in milk and sift   dry ingredients. Add to egg mixture, beating until smooth. (Or mix all ingredients together in blender.) Batter will be thin. Allow to sit 1 hour or more before using. For each crepe, pour about ¼ C. batter into a lightly greased 8" skillet over medium-high heat, swirling over bottom to make a thin pancake. Turn only once. Fold each finished crepe in quarters. Keep warm in oven or store in freezer or refrigerator. Not only everyday fare, but good for company! Roll up after filling with cottage cheese, fruit, cream cheese, ricotta, whipped cream, syrup, jam, leftover meat or whatever else strikes your fancy.

PROTEIN: 41.1 grams; CALORIES: 735

Many LLL Contributors

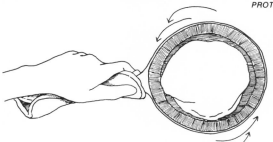

MAKE-AHEAD RAISED WAFFLES OR PANCAKES

1 T. **yeast**
¼ C. warm **water**
½ t. **salt**
1 to 2 T. **honey** or sugar
1½ C. warm **milk** or
    ½ C. dry milk powder and
    1½ C. warm water
2 to 3 **eggs**
¼ C. **oil** or melted butter
2 C. whole wheat **flour**
½ to 1 C. chopped **nuts**, seeds
    or fruit (optional)

Dissolve yeast in water, adding salt and honey. Beat in remaining ingredients with rotary beater. Let sit in covered 3-quart container in refrigerator overnight. In the morning, let it come to room temperature, then pour into preheated waffle iron. (If you forget to make this the night before, let it rise in a warm place 30 to 40 minutes before cooking.) Makes 5 8" waffles.

Yeast waffles are flavorful, tender and soft rather than hard and stiff.

PROTEIN: 67.6 grams; CALORIES: 2104

Variations:

#1 Omit 1 C. whole wheat flour and add 1 C. **wheat germ, rye flour, buckwheat flour**, rolled **oats** or **cornmeal**.

#2 Raised Pancakes. Use only 1 T. oil and bake as for ordinary pancakes.

Sandy Naylor   *Mary W. Bell*   *Jane David*   *Kathy and Eric Johnson*
Ft. Eustis, Virginia   *Springfield, Virginia*   *Niles, Michigan*   *Champaign, Illinois*

BASIC WHOLEGRAIN WAFFLES

2 to 4 **eggs**, separated
1½ C. **milk**
¼ to ½ C. **oil** or melted butter
1 to 2 T. **brown sugar**, heated
  honey or maple syrup
  (optional)
2 t. **baking powder**
½ t. **salt**
2 C. **flour**: whole wheat or any
  combination of whole wheat,
  rye, buckwheat, soy or
  triticale flour; cornmeal,
  bran or wheat germ

Beat egg whites until stiff. In a large bowl, beat yolks with milk. Add remaining ingredients, beating after each addition. Fold in beaten egg whites. Pour into lightly greased pre-heated (medium-hot, 375°) waffle iron and bake until it stops steaming. Makes about 5 round waffles.

If you're in a hurry, use whole beaten eggs, but waffles won't be quite as light. Freeze leftovers and heat in the toaster for snacks or quick breakfasts.   *P.: 61.2 gms.; C.: 1784*

Buttermilk, Sour Milk or Yogurt Waffles. Omit the milk and 1 t. baking powder. Add 1½ C. **buttermilk**, sour milk or yogurt and ½ t. **baking soda**. Make your own sour milk by adding 2 T. lemon juice or vinegar to 2 C. milk.

Fruit Waffles. Substitute **fruit juice** for the buttermilk.

Flavor Choices: Add any of these to Basic or Buttermilk Waffles:

¼ to ½ C. chopped **nuts**
½ C. unsweetened **applesauce**
½ t. ground **cinnamon**
¼ t. ground **ginger**
1/8 t. ground **mace**
½ C. **granola**

1 T. **nutritional yeast**
1 T. **bran**
1 t. **vanilla**
½ t. ground **cloves**
½ t. ground **nutmeg**
1 C. sliced **bananas** or other fruit

Toppings: honey-cinnamon-butter, raisins, nuts, apricot jam or any of the Pancake Toppings
  Many LLL Contributors

UNCOOKED PINEAPPLE TOPPING

2½ C. unsweetened, crushed
  pineapple, with juice
1½ t. **vanilla**
a generous dash of ground
  cinnamon

Put about ¼ cup pineapple and juice in blender. Add vanilla and cinnamon and blend until smooth. Mix in with rest of the pineapple and juice.

This is a good *sugarless* topping. It could also be used on breakfast **porridge** or over **crepes**.

Barbara Creighton
Ernest, Pennsylvania

PROTEIN: 2.5 grams; CALORIES: 372

APPLE SAUCE

4 **apples**, peeled, cored and
   chopped
1 C. **water**
1½ t. **cinnamon**
½ t. **nutmeg** (optional)

Bring all ingredients to a boil in a covered 1-quart saucepan. Simmer, uncovered, for about 15 minutes, stirring often to break up the apple chunks. Remove from heat and pour into blender. Blend until smooth.

PROTEIN: 1.4 grams; CALORIES: 362

Apple Butter. Cook on low heat in slow cooker or in oven, until applesauce is thickened. To test, place spoonful on a plate. It is done when no watery ring forms around the edge of the applesauce.

This will keep in the refrigerator for several weeks, but if your family uses it on pancakes, muffins and toast, it won't last that long!

Linda Bozack
Ridgecrest, California

APPLE BUTTER

12 C. **apple cider**
8 lbs. ripe **apples**
1 t. ground **cloves**
2 t. ground **cinnamon**
½ t. ground **allspice** (optional)
dash of **salt**
honey or brown sugar to taste

In 16-qt. kettle, rapidly boil cider, reducing volume by half. Meanwhile, wash, quarter and core apples. Add to the reduced cider with spices and cook until mushy (about 1 hour). Put through food mill or strainer. Return to low heat or slow cooker. Simmer 1 to 2 hours, until thick. (A circle of liquid does not form around a spoonful placed on a plate.) Add honey or sugar to taste. Heat to simmering (185 to 210°). Stir to prevent sticking. Pack hot butter to ¼" of jar top. Process in boiling water bath for 15 minutes or process at 5 pounds pressure for 5 minutes.

An old-fashioned specialty with timeless appeal.   *P.: 9.9 gms.; C.: 3348 + honey*

Karen Myers   *Diane Gates*
Butler, Pennsylvania   *New Paris, Pennsylvania*

BERRY-YOGURT SAUCE

1 C. **berries** (blueberries,
   boysenberries,
   cranberries or other)
1 C. boiling **water**
honey to taste
1 C. plain **yogurt**

Combine berries, water and honey and bring to a boil. Drain liquid and use as a drink. To the cooked fruit, add yogurt. Mix well. Serve with **pancakes**.

PROTEIN: 12.9 grams; CALORIES: 230 + honey

Papaya Sauce. Substitute mashed pulp of 1 ripe **papaya** for cooked berries.

Dot Buck
Lahaina, Maui, Hawaii

FRUIT "SYRUP"

1 T. **cornstarch**
1 C. unsweetened **fruit juice**
   (apple, grape, etc.)
1 t. **sugar** or honey (optional)

Mix cornstarch into juice. Add sugar, if desired. Bring to a boil, stirring until thickened. (In microwave oven, cook on HI about 1½ minutes.) Serve hot over pancakes.

Some families prefer a syrup rather than a fruit or yogurt topping, and this fills the bill.

PROTEIN: .3 grams; CALORIES: 170

Cinnamon Apple Syrup. Make **apple juice** "syrup". After the syrup is thickened, add 2 to 4 medium **apples**, diced, and ½ t. ground **cinnamon**. Cook until fruit is tender. Try other **fruits**, such as pears, peaches or strawberries.

Deirdre Eiler   *Paulette Muccianti*
Renton, Washington   *Palatine, Illinois*

BLUEBERRY JAM

4 C. fresh **blueberries**
   or other fruit
¼ to ½ C. **honey** or sugar
2 T. (envelopes) unflavored
   gelatin
¼ C. **orange juice**

Puree blueberries in blender. Add sweetener to taste. Bring to a boil in 2-qt. saucepan. Boil rapidly, stirring constantly, for 1 minute.

In a small bowl, sprinkle gelatin over juice. Let stand 1 minute. Add to blueberry mixture and heat, stirring until gelatin is completely dissolved, about 3 minutes. Remove from heat. Let stand 5 minutes, skimming off foam with a spoon. Ladle into jars. Cover and cool slightly before refrigerating. Freeze for long-term storage.

PROTEIN: 16.8 grams; CALORIES: 666

Janet Colbrunn
Hudson, Ohio

FRUIT TOPPING OR PUDDING

2½ to 3 C. unsweetened,
   crushed or pureed **fruit**
   (fresh; canned, drained;
   frozen, thawed)
2 to 3 T. **arrowroot** or
   cornstarch
honey to taste (optional)
ground **cinnamon** to taste
   (optional)

Blend arrowroot into fruit. Add honey and cinnamon to taste. Cook in 1½-quart pan for 5 to 7 minutes, stirring constantly, until mixture thickens. Serve on **pancakes, waffles** or **toast**. Refrigerate the leftovers. Fruit spread on pancakes makes a nutritious snack for a hungry toddler.

If frozen fruit needs to be thawed, heat slowly with 2 T. **water**. When fruit is warmed, mix arrowroot with ¼ C. cold **water** and stir into fruit. Cook until thickened.

Fruit Pudding. Add 1 C. **fruit chunks** before cooking as directed. Serve warm or cold.

Pegi Phillips-Sapp   *Jacki Glover*   *Lisa Johnson*
Fayette, Missouri   *Calgary, Alberta, Canada* *Austin, Texas*

LOW METHOXYL PECTIN JAMS AND JELLIES

Low methoxyl (L.M.) pectin, obtained from the inner rind of citrus fruit, has the distinct advantage of jelling fruit, not with sugar, but with calcium in the form of (tasteless) di-calcium phosphate.

Making jams and jellies with these ingredients is simple and fast; two pints can be made in about 10 minutes. The initial investment for 8 oz. L.M. pectin and 1 oz. di-calcium phosphate is reasonable considering that it lasts on the shelf indefinitely and provides enough jell for 32 to 48 pints of fruit. (Order from Walnut Acres, Penns Creek, PA 17862 or other sources which may carry it).

A **calcium solution** is needed to jell the fruit. Combine ½ t. di-calcium phosphate with 1 C. water in a small jar. Store indefinitely in the refrigerator until needed. Shake well immediately before using.

The L.M. pectin can be added by sprinkling it on the fruit, as in the following recipes, or by combining it with water or sugar before adding it to the fruit, as described below.

Pectin Solution. Put 2 C. very hot water in blender, turn onto low speed, and add 2 T. L.M. pectin all at once. Blend on high speed for several minutes, or until pectin is dissolved. Store in refrigerator until needed. Measure and add in jelled form.

Pectin-Sugar. Omit honey. Mix ¼ C. sugar with dry pectin. Add to hot fruit and proceed as directed.

Any amount of fruit or juice can be used; for each cup of fruit or juice, add ½ t. L.M. pectin (or 1 C. pectin solution) and 1 t. di-calcium phosphate solution. A small sample of the finished jam or jelly can be chilled. If it is not firmly set, add more pectin while the fruit is still hot. Increase the pectin in future batches using the same kind of fruit.

If some separation occurs during refrigeration, occasionally pour off as much of the liquid as possible. The separation and shorter refrigerator storage time are a small price to pay for having delicious jams and jellies without a lot of sweetener!

L.M. PECTIN JAMS

4 C. **fruit**, fresh or frozen (thawed), slightly mashed
¼ C. **honey** (optional)
2 t. **L.M. pectin** or ¼ C. pectin solution
4 t. **calcium solution**, well shaken

Bring the fruit and juices resulting from the mashing to a simmer in a heavy saucepan. Add honey if desired. Sprinkle the pectin evenly over the fruit and stir well, using a wire whisk if the pectin clumps. Shake the calcium solution well and add 4 t. to the hot fruit. Stir well; remove from heat and pour into hot sterilized jars. Refrigerate for up to 3 weeks. For longer storage, either freeze in suitable containers or can by processing pints for 10 minutes in a boiling water bath.

Variation: Soak 1 C. dried apricots or peaches overnight in a mixture of 2 C. orange juice and 2 C. apple juice. Use all of this mixture to replace the fruit called for in the recipe above; mash or blend the fruit and proceed as directed.

L.M. PECTIN JELLIES
(from concentrates)

12 oz. grape or apple juice **concentrate**, thawed
¾ C. **water**
1 t. (slightly rounded) **L.M. pectin** or ½ C. plus 1 T. pectin solution
2¼ t. **calcium solution**, well shaken

Combine concentrate and water in a heavy saucepan over medium heat. When mixture is about 100°, sprinkle on the pectin evenly. Stir well until liquid simmers. Use a wire whisk if pectin clumps. Add the well shaken calcium solution and stir thoroughly. Remove from heat and pour into hot sterilized jars. Store as in jam recipe.

Variation: For a fruity pancake or yogurt syrup increase the liquid by adding 1 C. fruit juice (drinking strength) of the same flavor and proceed as directed. Using orange juice concentrate makes a different, zesty syrup by this method.

LEKVAR (PRUNE BUTTER)

dried prunes
water

Put prunes in saucepan and add water to about 1" above the prunes. Bring to a boil and simmer for 20 minutes. Drain (reserving juice), cool and pit. Blend in small batches with a little juice, or process until thick jam is formed.

Use on pancakes or in peanut butter and "jelly" sandwiches in place of the jelly. It's excellent on whole grain buttered toast, and delicious on yogurt. My mother spread it on Hungarian crepes, rolled them up, put them in a buttered casserole and warmed them in the oven for 20 minutes.

The reserved juice that remains may be strained and added to other fruit juice for a breakfast drink.

Variation: Substitute **dried apricots** for the prunes.   *Sharon Falatovics*
Michigan City, Indiana

DRIED FRUIT JAM

2 C. **dried fruit** (prunes, figs, apricots, dates, pears, peaches and apples)
1¼ C. unsweetened **fruit juice** (pineapple, orange or apple)
1¼ C. crushed fresh **pineapple** (or unsweetened canned, undrained)

Cover dried fruit with juice and soak overnight in the refrigerator. Mix in food processor or blender with the crushed pineapple and its juice. Refrigerate or freeze.   *P.: 8.6 gms.; C.: 1082*

Delicious as a spread on waffles or warm whole grain bread.

Topping. Freeze until slushy.
Slush. Freeze, liquefy with additional **liquid:** juice, milk or water.

June Friesen   *Ronnie Barhite*   *Jane David*   *Elinor Wilson*
Altona, Man., Canada   *Medina, New York*   *Niles, Michigan*   *Washington, D.C.*

BASIC WHOLEGRAIN MUFFINS

2 C. whole wheat **flour**
1 t. **baking soda**
¼ C. **brown sugar** or honey
1 t. ground **cinnamon** (optional)
1/8 t. ground **cloves** (optional)
½ t. **salt**
½ C. **raisins**
1 **egg**, beaten
1 C. **buttermilk**, yogurt or
   sour milk
3 T. **oil** or melted **butter**

Mix all dry ingredients thoroughly, including raisins. Make a well in the center and add egg, milk and oil. Mix only until dry ingredients are moist. Fill greased muffin pans half full and bake at 375° for about 15 minutes. Good hot or cold. Makes 12 to 16 muffins.

Store-bought cakes and cookies may be things of the past, so now we try to bring goodness to our desserts. One fast, easy way is by serving muffins. This is a favorite.

PROTEIN: 48.9 grams; CALORIES: 1757

Nancy Morrison Karen Barclay
Hamilton, Ontario, Can. Connelsville, Pennsylvania

Variations:
#1 Omit raisins. Add 1 C. **blueberries** or chopped fruit.
#2 Add **nuts** or seeds, if desired.
#3 Omit 1 C. or more whole wheat flour and replace it with rye, soy or triticale **flour**, rolled **oats** or oat flour, **wheat germ** or **bran**.
#4 Omit baking soda and buttermilk. Add 2 t. **baking powder** and 1 C. **milk**.

DATE NUT MUFFINS

1½ C. boiling **water**
1½ C. chopped **dates**
1 **egg**
2 T. **oil** or butter
¾ C. **wheat germ**
¼ C. dry **milk powder**
2 t. **baking powder**
1 C. whole wheat **flour**
½ C. chopped **nuts**

Pour water over dates. In a separate bowl, mix egg and oil. Combine dry ingredients and stir into egg mixture. Add nuts and dates; stir just until moistened. Pour into greased muffin tins and bake at 400° for 15 to 20 minutes. Makes 16 muffins.

A delicious, moist muffin which uses dates as the only sweetening. Dates have essentially the same nutritional value as raisins, so these muffins are high in iron.

PROTEIN: 81.7 grams; CALORIES: 2617 Mary Whelan Bell Lori Morrison
Springfield, Virginia Mississauga, Ontario, Can.

ORANGE MUFFINS

4 C. whole wheat **flour**
2 T. **baking powder**
1 t. **salt**
1½ t. ground **cinnamon**
2 **eggs**
½ C. **oil**
¼ to ½ C. **honey**
1 to 2 T. grated **orange peel**
2 C. **orange juice**

Combine dry ingredients. In a large bowl, mix together eggs, oil, honey, orange peel and juice. Stir liquid into dry ingredients just until moistened.

Pour into greased muffin tins and bake at 400° for 20 minutes. Makes 20 to 24 muffins. These freeze and reheat with good results.

PROTEIN: 81 grams; CALORIES: 3266

Kristi Towns
Littleton, Colorado

CARROT SPICE MUFFINS

1½ C. whole wheat **flour**
1 t. **baking soda**
1 t. **baking powder**
½ t. **salt** (optional)
½ t. ground **cinnamon**
¼ t. ground **nutmeg**
1/8 t. ground **ginger**
1/8 t. ground **allspice**

⅓ C. **honey** or brown sugar
1 **egg**
½ C. **sour milk** or yogurt
⅓ C. **oil** or melted butter
½ t. **vanilla**
1½ C. grated **carrots**
½ C. **raisins**
½ C. chopped **nuts**

Measure dry ingredients into a large bowl. Mix wet ingredients in another bowl with carrots, raisins and nuts. Add to dry mix, stirring only until flour is moistened. Place in greased muffin tins and bake for 15 minutes at 400°. This makes delicious, moist muffins. Enjoy them at breakfast or anytime. Makes 16 to 18 muffins.   *PROTEIN: 43.5 grams CALORIES: 2440*

Cathy Grant   Marion Bueche   Margaret J. Doner
Richmond, B.C., Canada   Gray, Sask., Canada   Kitchner, Ont., Canada

RHUBARB MUFFINS

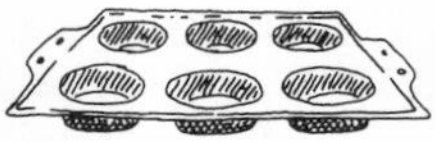

⅓ C. **honey**
¼ t. **salt**
3 T. **butter** or oil
2 **eggs**, beaten
¾ C. **yogurt**, sour milk
  or buttermilk
1 t. **vanilla**
2 C. whole wheat **flour**
½ C. **wheat germ**
1 t. **baking soda**
3 C. chopped **rhubarb**,
  fresh or frozen

Blend honey, salt and butter. Add eggs, yogurt and vanilla; beat well. Stir in flour, wheat germ and baking soda, and blend just until moistened. Fold in rhubarb. Fill paper-lined muffin cups ¾ full. Bake at 375° for 20 to 25 minutes. Makes 18 to 20 muffins.

A quick way to use rhubarb. Yummy!   *PROTEIN: 77 grams; CALORIES: 2426*

Meg VanderHart
Cedar Rapids, Iowa

NO SUGAR, NO HONEY MUFFINS
(Blender Method)

1 **apple**, peeled and cored
9 pitted **prunes**
9 pitted **dates**
2 small **bananas**
3 **eggs**
¼ C. **butter**, softened
1 t. **vanilla**
1 t. **salt**
¼ C. **orange juice**
1½ C. whole wheat **flour**
½ C. **sunflower seeds**
1 C. rolled **oats**
½ C. chopped **walnuts**
⅓ C. dry **milk powder**
2 t. **baking powder**
1 t. **baking soda**
⅓ C. unsweetened, shredded
  coconut

Blend the apple, prunes and dates. Add bananas, eggs, butter, vanilla, salt and juice, and blend. In a bowl, mix together the rest of the ingredients. Pour blender mixture over dry ingredients and mix well. Pour into greased muffin cups; bake at 350° for 20 to 25 minutes. Makes 1½ to 2 dozen muffins.

I bought a no honey, no sugar muffin in the health food store. I liked the taste but not the price. I took the list of ingredients, added a little knowledge about protein complementarity, and made my own muffins.   *PROTEIN: 92.2 grams; CALORIES: 3240*

Barb Muehlhausen
Schaumburg, Illinois

MOLASSES MUFFINS

1 C. rolled **oats**
¾ C. **sunflower seeds**
1 C. **wheat germ**
½ C. soy **flour**
1 C. whole wheat **flour**
½ C. dry **milk powder**
½ C. **sesame seeds**, ground
1 t. **salt**
2½ t. **baking powder**

½ C. **oil**
1 C. **molasses**
1½ C. **milk**
2 **eggs**

Optional:
2 T. **nutritional yeast**
½ C. **raisins**

Stir dry ingredients together. Blend wet ingredients and mix into dry, just until moistened. Bake in greased muffin tins at 375° for about 18 minutes. Makes 24 muffins.

Other flours, seeds, nuts, granola and fruit may be substituted as desired.   PROTEIN: 152.1 grams; CALORIES 4492

Helen Riley
Lawton, Oklahoma

Suellen Slater
Westboro, Massachusetts

PINEAPPLE MUFFINS

2 C. whole wheat **flour**
2 t. **baking powder**
½ t. **salt** (optional)
¼ C. **butter**, softened
¼ C. **brown sugar** or honey
1 **egg**, beaten
¾ C. (8½ oz.) unsweetened, crushed **pineapple** with juice
1 C. chopped **nuts** or less (optional)

Sift together flour, baking powder and salt. Cream butter, sugar and egg. Combine with flour mixture and pineapple; stir until just moist. Fill muffin tins ⅔ full and bake at 400° for 20 to 25 minutes. Makes 12 muffins.

PROTEIN: 53.8 grams; CALORIES: 2262

Variation: Omit ½ C. flour, add ½ C. **bran.**   PROTEIN: 45.8 grams; CALORIES: 2062

Pineapple Nut Bread. Bake in a greased 9 x 5 x 3" loaf pan at 350° for 50 minutes.

Barbara Parker
Raleigh, North Carolina

Karen A. Lijek
Detroit, Michigan

Cindy Garrison
Canonsburg, Pennsylvania

WHEAT GERM MUFFINS

⅓ C. melted **butter**
⅓ C. **honey**
2 **eggs**
½ C. dry **milk powder**
1 C. **wheat germ**
¾ t. **baking powder**
¼ t. **salt**
½ t. **almond extract**
1 t. **vanilla**
½ C. slivered **almonds** or sunflower seeds
½ C. **raisins**
½ C. shredded, unsweetened **coconut** (optional)

Put all ingredients into a bowl and mix with a fork until well blended. Pour into paper-lined muffin tins and bake at 350° for 25 minutes. Makes 10 to 12 muffins.

This recipe is very easy and great for breakfasts and lunch box snacks. The little ones call them cupcakes!

PROTEIN: 61.4 grams; CALORIES: 2584

Maureen Onstott
Jacksonville, Florida

Shannon Stieglitz
Norcross, Georgia

VARIATION OF SIX WEEK MUFFINS

2 C. boiling **water**
5 C. **bran**
5 C. whole wheat **flour**
5 t. **baking soda**
1½ t. **salt** (optional)
2 t. ground **cinnamon** or pumpkin pie spice (optional)
1 C. **wheat germ**
1 C. **oil**
1 C. **honey**, molasses or brown sugar
4 **eggs**, beaten
4 C. **buttermilk** or yogurt
1 C. **dates, raisins**, chopped **apples** (optional)

Pour boiling water over 2 C. of bran. In another bowl, sift flour, soda, salt and spice. Add wheat germ and rest of bran; combine with wet bran. Stir until moist; add oil, honey, eggs, buttermilk and optional fruit. Pour into well-greased muffin tins. Bake at 400° for 15 to 20 minutes. Keep in refrigerator to use as needed. Bring a batch to a friend upon the birth of her baby.

PROTEIN: 188 grams; CALORIES: 6756

Rindalee M. Skimina   Nancy Hart   Susan Meintz Maher
Highland, Indiana   Libertyville, Illinois East Lansing, Michigan

APPLE MUFFINS

2 unpeeled **apples**, chopped
½ C. **honey** or brown sugar
1 **egg**, beaten
¼ C. **oil** or melted butter
1 C. **milk**
1¾ C. whole wheat **flour**
½ to 1 t. ground **cinnamon**
½ t. **salt**
2 t. **baking powder**
¼ C. **wheat germ**

Put chopped apples in a bowl and pour honey over them. In a large bowl, mix together the egg, oil and milk. Sift in flour, cinnamon, salt and baking powder. Add wheat germ and stir just enough to moisten. Fold in apples. Bake in greased muffin cups at 400° for 20 to 25 minutes. Makes 12 to 16 muffins.

PROTEIN: 54.4 grams; CALORIES: 2283

Sandra Osgood   Doris I. Falconer
Marietta, Georgia   Bismarck, North Dakota

OATMEAL MUFFINS

¼ C. soy **flour**
¾ C. whole wheat **flour**
1½ t. **baking soda**
½ t. **salt**
1 C. rolled **oats**
1 **egg**
1 C. **buttermilk** or yogurt
2 T. **honey** or sugar
3 T. **oil** or butter
½ t. ground **cinnamon** (optional)

Optionals:
Add ½ C. of *one* of the following:
 raisins
 currants
 chopped **apples**
 dried **fruit**
 1 C. fresh or frozen **blueberries**

Combine dry ingredients. Beat together egg, buttermilk, honey and oil. Add to flour mixture, stirring just to moisten. Fold in one optional ingredient if desired. Fill greased muffin tins ¾ full. Bake at 425° for about 10 minutes. Makes 12 muffins.

These muffins are extremely tender, soft and flavorful. They are a favorite at morning LLL meetings, where refreshments are served in order to save toddlers' appetites for lunchtime. *PROTEIN: 48.1 gms.; CALORIES: 1379*

Many LLL Contributors

Lunches

PACHADI PITA POCKETS

Pachadi (Yogurt Salad)
  2 C. plain **yogurt**
  2 medium **tomatoes**, diced
  1 t. hot green **chili pepper**,
    minced (seeds removed)
  ¼ C. minced **onion**
  ¼ C. chopped, fresh **parsley**
  1 t. ground **mustard seed**
  ½ t. ground **cumin**
whole wheat **pita bread**
Monterey Jack **cheese**, grated
avocado, mashed

Stir together ingredients for Yogurt Salad. If fresh chili is unavailable, canned ones will do (adjust quantity to taste).

Spread avocado inside pita bread, add cheese, and spoon in Pachadi.

Because it is rather spicy, this sandwich is not suited to most children's taste. For little ones, fill pitas with avocado and grated cheese.

This recipe stirs fond memories of the Mt. Vernon, Virginia, LLL Group. The hostess made delicious pita bread, and we brought various stuffings to sample and share. Many of us have since moved near and far, added new babies to our families, and become LLL Leaders. Each time I make these sandwiches, I'm reminded of the LLLove that brought us together and the friendships that endure, even though it's so hard to keep in touch.   *Janet Repucci*
Yogurt Salad—P.: 30.6 gms.; C.: 410   *Hopkinton, Massachusetts*

TACOS

Filling:
1 medium **onion**, chopped
2 stalks **celery**, chopped
2 C. coarsely grated **zucchini**
  (optional)
oil
1½ lbs. ground **beef**
1 C. **tomato sauce**
½ t. ground **cumin**
½ t. **marjoram**
2 C. **beans** (kidney or pinto),
  cooked and drained (optional)
½ t. **salt** (or less)
dash of **pepper**

20 **tortillas** (p. 168), baked or fried
  and folded in half

2 chopped fresh **tomatoes**
1 chopped **green pepper**
2 C. shredded **lettuce** or sprouts
2 C. grated **cheese** (Colby or
  Cheddar)

Saute onion, celery and zucchini in small amount of oil. Brown and drain beef. Add rest of ingredients. Simmer 15 minutes. To serve: fold tortillas in half. Fill with meat mixture. Top with desired garnishes.

PROTEIN: 304.8 grams; CALORIES: 4795

Frances Andrusiak   Lynn Wannberg
Winnipeg, Manitoba, Can. Sewell, New Jersey

TACOS / CHALUPAS / TOSTADAS

8 to 12 **tortillas** (p. 168)
2 to 3 T. **oil**
3 C. cooked **pinto beans**
½ to 2 t. **chili powder**
½ to 1 t. ground **cumin**
1 clove **garlic**, minced
1¼ C. grated sharp **cheese**
½ C. chopped **lettuce** or spinach
¾ C. chopped **tomatoes**
1 oz. (½ C.) **alfalfa sprouts**
¼ C. chopped **onion**

Fry tortillas briefly in oil. Mash beans with seasonings and ¼ C. cheese. Spoon bean mixture onto tortillas. Fold up. Serve, garnished with cheese and vegetables. Or top with cheese, warm in oven at 350° for 5 to 10 minutes, and garnish with vegetables.

PROTEIN: 106.2 grams; CALORIES: 2096

Janet Jendron   *Sharon Bish*
Columbia, S. Carolina   *Oklahoma City, Oklahoma*

Fran Vasi
Barstow, California

QUESADILLAS
(kay-sa-dias)

1 recipe **flour tortillas** (p. 168)
1 lb. Cheddar **cheese**, grated
1 **jalapeno pepper**, thinly sliced
4 **tomatoes**, thinly sliced
1 **green pepper**, diced
1 **onion**, thinly sliced
oil

Place cheese on half of each tortilla; top with the various vegetables. Roll tortilla up to encase filling. Fry in hot oil, ½ minute per side. Drain on paper towels and serve immediately.

PROTEIN: 181.5 grams; CALORIES: 4293

Variation #1: Use the firm stone-ground **corn tortillas**, cover the top of each tortilla with cheese, then vegetables, and bake in 350° oven for 10 minutes, or until cheese bubbles. Cut into quarters to serve.

Claudia Scattergood   *Julie Delaplane*
Toutle, Washington   *Anderson, Indiana*

Variation #2: Substitute diced, cooked **meat** of your choice for half the cheese. Add 2 T. **taco sauce** or hot sauce, if you wish.

Junie Hostetler
Tucson, Arizona

BEANS IN PITA

Filling:
4 C. cooked **garbanzo beans**
  or other beans
2 to 4 cloves **garlic**, minced
1 t. *each* ground **coriander** and
  cumin *or* basil and marjoram
1 T. chopped **parsley**
dash of **cayenne pepper**
4 T. **lemon juice** or orange juice
whole grain **pita** or other bread

Toppings:
½ C. shredded **lettuce**
¼ C. chopped **tomatoes**
½ C. sliced **cucumber**
¼ C. chopped **onion**
4 oz. (½ C.) **sprouts**
1 small **apple**, chopped
½ C. plain **yogurt** or grated cheese

Mix and heat filling ingredients. You may mash the mixture or leave it intact. Stuff into pita. Serve with topping ingredients. These are sort of "Middle Eastern Tacos." They are delicious, high in protein and inexpensive!

PROTEIN: 96.6 grams; CALORIES: 1690 + pita

Laurie Carroll   *Sharon Bish*
Suttons Bay, Michigan   *Oklahoma City, Oklahoma*

CHICKEN AND WALNUTS IN PITA

3 to 4 T. **milk**
8 oz. **cream cheese**, softened
⅓ C. chopped **green pepper**
¼ C. chopped **walnuts**
2 C. cooked, chopped **chicken**
1 T. **lemon juice**
1 T. grated **onion**
½ t. dry **mustard**
½ t. **thyme**
alfalfa sprouts

Add milk to cream cheese; mix until creamy. Add remaining ingredients except sprouts. Cut **pita bread** into halves or quarters; add filling. Top generously with the alfalfa sprouts. May be made the night before.

PROTEIN: 135.7 grams; CALORIES: 1625 + pita

Ann Corcoran
South Bend, Indiana

CHICKEN AND PEPPER FILLING FOR PITA BREAD

1 **chicken breast**, boned and chopped (about 1 lb.)
1 clove **garlic**, minced
1 T. **oil**
1 T. **cornstarch**
½ C. cold **water**
2 T. **soy sauce**
¼ t. crushed **red pepper** (optional)
⅔ C. chopped **pepper** (red or green)
¼ C. coarsely chopped **peanuts** (optional)

Cook chopped chicken and garlic in oil over medium-high heat until it browns. In a bowl, combine cornstarch, water, soy sauce and crushed pepper. Stir into the chicken and continue cooking until thick and bubbly. Add chopped pepper and nuts. Cover and cook until peppers are tender-crisp. Makes about 2 cups. PROTEIN: 106.5 grams; CALORIES: 1038

Patty Holtz
Geneva, Illinois

GREEK FILLING FOR PITA BREAD

1½ lbs. ground **beef**
1 medium **onion**, chopped
1 T. **wheat germ**
1 T. **sunflower seeds**
1 **bay leaf**
1 T. dried **mint**
2 t. **oregano**
2 T. plain **yogurt**
6 whole wheat **pita bread**

Brown beef and onions; drain. Add wheat germ, seeds and herbs. Simmer 30 minutes. Just before serving, add yogurt. Serve in pita bread with a cucumber-tomato salad or a vinegar-and-oil tossed salad.

PROTEIN: 130.5 grams; CALORIES: 4980 + pita

Marilynn Berry
Lawrenceville, Georgia

VEGETARIAN REUBEN SANDWICH

1 slice **bread** (rye or whole wheat), toasted
1 t. **mayonnaise** (p. 48)
¼ C. **sauerkraut**
1 oz. **cheese** (Swiss, Provolone, etc.), sliced
5 small **mushrooms**, sliced

Spread toasted bread lightly with mayonnaise. Add layers of mushrooms, sauerkraut and cheese slices. Heat in broiler or microwave oven until cheese melts.

PROTEIN: 11.7 grams; CALORIES: 214

Mary K. Brieser
Geneseo, Illinois

SHRIMP AND CHEESE FILLING

1 C. medium **shrimp**, cooked and halved
¼ C. thinly sliced **celery**
¼ C. chopped **onion**
1 T. **butter**
2 t. whole wheat **flour**
¼ t. **marjoram**
½ t. **worcestershire sauce**
dash of **hot pepper** (optional)
¼ C. grated Swiss **cheese** (or other cheese)
¼ C. dry **white wine** or white rice vinegar
1 T. chopped, fresh **parsley**

Saute vegetables in butter 5 minutes. Blend in flour and seasonings. Add cheese and wine. Stir until thick. Mix in shrimp and parsley. Heat through and spoon into **pita bread**. Makes 1¼ C.

PROTEIN: 28.3 grams; CALORIES: 398 plus pita

Patty Holtz
Geneva, Illinois

SUPER SUMMER TUNA

6½ oz. **tuna**, drained
2 hard-cooked **eggs**, chopped
1 C. cooked shell **macaroni** or alphabet noodles
3 T. **mayonnaise** (p. 48) and/or **yogurt** to moisten
¼ t. **salt**
dash of **pepper**
dill weed to taste

Mix all ingredients. Serve on whole grain **bread**, garnished with **lettuce** and **sprouts**, or in **avocado** halves.

PROTEIN: 78.4 grams; CALORIES: 1051

Lois Lake Raabe
Easton, Connecticut

HAM, EGGS AND SPROUTS IN PITA BREAD

3 C. cubed **ham**, chicken or turkey
2 hard-cooked **eggs**, chopped
1 stalk **celery**, chopped
½ C. **pickle relish**
½ C. **mayonnaise** (p. 48)
2 t. prepared **mustard** (½ t. dry)
4 oz. **alfalfa sprouts**
1 medium **tomato**, cut in wedges

6 pieces **pita bread**, halved

Mix all ingredients except sprouts and tomatoes. Layer ham mixture with a thin layer of sprouts and a tomato wedge inside halves of pita bread. Many children who aren't used to sprouts, eat them and like the crunchiness.

PROTEIN: 204.1 grams; CALORIES: 4266

Patty Holtz
Geneva, Illinois

SURPRISE HAM'N CHEESE

½ lb. **ham**, cubed, or tuna
½ lb. sharp **cheese**, diced
⅓ C. minced **onion**
½ C. chopped **olives**
3 T. **mayonnaise** (p. 48)
½ C. **chili sauce**

4 to 6 **buns**

Mix all ingredients together. Spread in buns. Wrap individually in aluminum foil. Bake at 425° for 12 to 15 minutes. Or wrap in waxed paper and warm in microwave oven.

PROTEIN: 129.8 grams; CALORIES: 2660

Patricia Schulte
Sterling Hts., Michigan

This mixture keeps for several days and is a favorite for Easter leftovers. Children like tiny buns which are more their size.   *Carol Kubic*
Newbury Park, California

HAM SALAD

cooked **ham** or chicken
celery
onions
pickles
bread crumbs (optional)
horseradish to taste
mayonnaise (p. 48) to taste
wheat germ

Chop meat, vegetables, and bread crumbs in food processor, meat grinder or with knife, until fine. Mix together with remaining ingredients until desired consistency is obtained.

A nice way to lighten ham sandwiches.
Jean Kremer
Anna, Ohio

HEART SANDWICH MEAT

1 beef **heart**, washed
4 whole **cloves**
4 whole **allspice**
1 t. **salt** (or less) per qt. of **water**
½ t. **pepper**
⅓ C. **vinegar**
1 medium **onion**, sliced
1 **bay leaf**

Put trimmed heart in slow-cooker. Cover with water; add remaining ingredients. Cook, covered, on *low* overnight. Cool in broth, drain and refrigerate. Slice thinly.
PROTEIN: 123.8 grams; CALORIES: 2058

Arla Crosier
Yakima, Washington

MEAT SPREAD

1 C. leftover **meat** (beef, ham, chicken, turkey or chicken livers)
1 C. chopped **celery**, onion or other vegetables (cooked or raw)
2 to 3 T. **mayonnaise** (p. 48) or plain yogurt
dash *each* of **salt, pepper** and **garlic powder**
1 to 2 T. **wheat germ** (optional)

Chop meat finely by hand or in blender or food processor. Blend meat and vegetables. Add mayonnaise, seasonings and wheat germ, if used. It will keep longer if you use cooked vegetables. Serve on **bread** or **crackers**.
PROTEIN: 58.8 grams; CALORIES: 691

Lynn Rudin
Babylon, New York

Gerry Chamberlain
Cedar Falls, Iowa

Jacqueline Croft
Elmira, New York

Ann Feligno
Geneva, New York

CHEESE SPREAD

4 to 5 oz. any firm **cheese**, grated
½ to 1 T. cold **water**, milk or yogurt

Optional:
2 T. **worcestershire sauce**
1 t. prepared **mustard**
½ C. **mayonnaise** (p. 48)
4 oz. chopped **pimentos**
½ C. chopped **walnuts**
1 T. chopped dill **pickle**
1 to 2 T. minced **onions**

Blend in food processor or blender, or with fork, until smooth. Serve with crackers, in sandwiches or as a dip for raw vegetables.
PROTEIN: 28.8 grams; CALORIES: 458

Many LLL Contributors

CHICKEN LIVER PATE

½ lb. chicken **liver**
½ C. sliced **carrot**
½ C. sliced **onion**
3 T. **oil**
2 cloves **garlic**, minced
2 t. **soy sauce**
2 T. **butter**
¼ t. **pepper**
¼ t. **sage**

Optional:
leftover **meat** or cooked bacon, instead of part of the liver
1 hard-cooked **egg**
mayonnaise (p. 48)
chopped, fresh **parsley**
¼ t. *each* **thyme** and **marjoram**
1 T. **brandy**

Saute vegetables in oil until soft. Place liver in pan. Cover. Steam until liver is no longer pink inside, 8 to 10 minutes. Puree contents of pan with the remaining ingredients in a blender or food processor until smooth. Chill. Yields about 1¼ cups.

This spreads smoothly for sandwiches or crackers. It keeps in the refrigerator about a week, but does not freeze well.

PROTEIN: 48.3 grams; CALORIES: 951

Barbara Becker Nelson
Eugene, Oregon

TOASTY TOFU

2 thin slices **cheese** or
 ½ C. grated cheese
1 slice tofu ¼" thick
1 T. chopped green **onion**
dash **salt**
dash **pepper**
1 t. **lemon juice**

Optional
dash **worcestershire sauce**
dash tamari **soy sauce**
dash **tabasco sauce**

Place cheese on griddle or pan with superslick finish. Cook over medium heat until melted and crisp around the edges. Place tofu slice on cheese and sprinkle with onions, lemon juice and seasonings of your choice. Top with more cheese. Turn and grill the cheese until golden. Cheese should be slightly larger than tofu slice so that the cheese edges meet and melt together, making a seal. Blot oil which melts from cheese to reduce calories. Good hot or cold. Makes a good travel food.

PROTEIN: 16.4 GRAMS; CALORIES: 250

Roberta Bishop Johnson
Champaign, Illinois

Crispy Cheese. Use only the cheese, plus any options if you choose. Cheese may be cooked as crispy as you wish. Turn to brown on both sides. Allow to cool; cut into squares or snack-size pieces.

"HOT CHEESE"

1 C. grated **cheese** (Cheddar or Swiss)
½ C. **cottage cheese**
2 T. **mayonnaise** (p. 48)
¼ C. chopped **nuts** or seeds
paprika to taste (optional)
curry powder to taste (optional)

3 slices whole grain **bread**

Mix the cheese spread ingredients together. Spread on bread; cut into shapes, if you wish. Place on cookie sheet. Broil until cheese melts.

PROTEIN: 55.6 grams; CALORIES: 1112

Lois Lake Raabe
Easton, Connecticut

Soups

SOUP STOCK

vegetable peels and trimmings
a few fruit trimmings, such as
  apples, pears, or lemon or
  orange peels
leftover bones, chicken necks
  and livers, etc. (optional)
water or vegetable cooking
  water, to cover
a few sprigs parsley
1 or 2 bay leaves
peppercorns to taste
other seasonings to taste,
  such as:
  salt, marjoram, thyme, cayenne pepper, sage, oregano,
  basil, garlic powder
¼ C. lemon juice or vinegar,
  if bones are used

Collect vegetable scraps, and optional bones, in plastic containers or
bags in refrigerator or freezer until
you have at least 2 quarts. (Omit
corncobs, sausage; use cabbage
family very sparingly to avoid strong
flavors.) Combine all ingredients in 3
to 4-qt. pot, choosing seasonings to
taste (sage and thyme are good with
chicken; basil and bay with beef).
Bring to a boil; simmer several
hours. Strain; discard solids. Adjust
seasoning; cool; put in freezer containers.

This method is so simple, and
you'll feel so good about using up all
those discards. Use for any recipe
needing stock, or simmer with rice
or noodles for a quick lunch.

Stock-As-You-Go. If you are out of stock, put leftovers, with some parsley
sprigs, celery leaves, and perhaps a sliced onion, in a cheesecloth bag,
and simmer along with your soup ingredients. When soup is ready, remove and discard the bag.

Baby-Food Stock. When baby starts eating finger foods but you have
your freezer full of pureed foods, add them to homemade soup stock with
other ingredients.

Karen Wedman   *Caroline Seligman*   *Debra J. Baird*   *Joanne Wilhelm*
Blueberry Mt., Alta., Canada   *De Kalb, Illinois*   *Platte City, Missouri*   *Brookfield, Wisconsin*

BEEF STOCK

2 lb. (or more) meaty beef bones
2 T. oil, if needed
½ t. *each* marjoram and thyme
1 T. chopped, fresh parsley
1 bay leaf
¼ C. vinegar
1 medium onion, quartered,
  unpeeled
8 C. cold water, and/or cooking
  water from vegetables
leftover gravy from beef roast
  (optional)

In Dutch oven, sear bones (if uncooked) in oil. Add remaining ingredients and bring to a boil over medium-high heat. Simmer 2 hours or
more. Remove bones and meat; reserve meat for later use. Strain stock
and discard vegetables. May be frozen in 1 or 2 C. containers until
needed.

Ellie Gasior
Vincentown, New Jersey

CHICKEN STOCK

4 to 5 lbs. **chicken** parts, whole
chicken, or leftover roast
chicken parts or carcass
1½ medium-large **onions**, sliced
9 **peppercorns**
2 T. **parsley**, fresh or dried
generous ½ T. **rosemary**
2 or 3 pinches **sage**
1 or 2 pinches **thyme**
1 **bay leaf**
1 t. **celery seeds**

Optional:
1 to 3 **carrots**, chopped
1 or 2 stalks **celery** with
leaves, chopped
1 t. **salt**

In 6-qt. kettle, bring all ingredients to a boil in cold water to cover; simmer 3 hours or more. Remove bones to colander to drain (save the broth that drains off). Remove and reserve larger pieces of meat (not tiny bits from necks or backbones, or you may get too many small bones mixed in). If using whole chicken or meaty chicken parts, remove chicken when meat is tender; reserve meat and return skin and bones to pot for longer simmering, then discard skin and bones. Discard bay leaf. Boil broth vigorously until reduced to about 6 or 7 cups; strain, if desired, and discard solids. Chill; remove fat. You may now make chicken soup, adding reserved meat, vegetables, rice, noodles, etc., or save the broth for other recipes. Good to have on hand, frozen in 1 or 2-cup containers.

This recipe, without the optional ingredients, was developed for someone who was on a special diet, but everyone loves it. This is strong stock, so thin with water. Chicken backs make the tastiest stock. Strength and flavor will vary if whole chicken or leftovers are used.

Turkey Stock. Substitute a **turkey carcass**, plus any leftover meat bits. Use the same seasonings, or substitute:

2 **green onions**, tied in a knot
or like a pretzel
1 stalk **celery**
1 dry, whole **red pepper** (optional)

Marcia Casais
Chatham, New Jersey

Susan Wallace
Nacogdoches, Texas

OVERNIGHT ONION SOUP

4 large **onions**
8 C. chicken or beef **stock**
small **bay leaf** (optional)
whole grain **bread**, 1 thick
slice per person
grated **cheese** (Swiss
or Parmesan)

PROTEIN: 23.6 grams; CALORIES: 328
+ bread & cheese

Slice onions into thin rings. Put in slow-cooker and cover with broth. Add bay leaf. Cover and cook on low about 24 hours. Before serving, ladle into heavy bowls; cover each slice of bread with cheese. Broil until cheese melts. Float a slice of bread in each bowl.

Rhoda Taylor
Duncan, B.C., Canada

Diana Reardon
Dallas, Texas

VEGETABLE SOUP

10 C. **liquid:** 2 C. or more beef, chicken or vegetable stock; liquid from soaking beans; plus water to make 10 C.
1 C. chopped **celery**
1 or 2 **onions**, chopped
1 small **green pepper**, chopped
2 T. **oil**, if no meat is added
2 small **zucchini**, diced (about 2 C.)
1 C. sliced or diced **carrots**
1 or 2 large **potatoes**, unpeeled diced
2 C. **peas**
1 to 2 C. **corn**
1 or 2 C. shredded **cabbage**
2 or 3 C. cut-up **tomatoes**

Optional:
1 C. dried **beans**, soaked overnight in water to cover, or dry lentils or split peas
¼ to ½ C. **barley**
½ C. raw **brown rice** (1 C. cooked)
1 C. cooked **bulgur wheat**
½ C. small **macaroni**, uncooked
½ C. **alfalfa sprouts**
1 C. (or more) any raw or cooked **vegetables**
bits of leftover **meat** or small chunks of raw stewing beef
½ t. **salt** (or less)
seasonings to taste:
basil, paprika, bay leaf, thyme, pepper, sherry, garlic paste (see below), **miso** (see below), **tabasco sauce, worcestershire sauce, marjoram**

Combine all ingredients, except cabbage, tomatoes, macaroni, sprouts and leftovers, in 8-qt. pot. Bring to a boil; simmer, covered, 1 to 2 hours or longer, adding remaining ingredients for last 30 to 45 minutes. Check occasionally and add a little boiling water if necessary. Discard bay leaf, if used. Stir in garlic paste or miso, if desired. Makes 6 qts. or more. Recipe may be halved. Fewer vegetables may be used, if you prefer.

PROTEIN: 47.3 grams; CALORIES: 1058

Slow-Cooker Method: Cook soup in slow-cooker on high for 6 hours. You may have to reduce quantities to fit cooker.

Garlic Paste for Vegetable Soup.

1½ t. minced **garlic** (about 6 cloves)
¼ t. **salt**, or to taste
2 T. **basil**
1 T. **oil**
¼ C. **tomato paste**
¼ C. grated Parmesan **cheese**

Press garlic into salt to form a smooth paste. Stir in 1 t. basil and ½ t. oil. Repeat until all basil and oil are used. Mix in tomato paste and cheese; cover and refrigerate until ready to use. Mix ½ C. of soup liquid into paste and then stir into soup. Steep 20 minutes.   *P.: 11.8 gms.; C.: 292*

Vegetable-Miso Soup. When soup is finished, mix ⅓ C. rice miso or barley **miso** with ½ C. warm **water**. Add to soup and heat through, but do not boil. Nice addition to a vegetarian vegetable soup.   *P.: 56.8 gms.; C.: 1352*

Terrie Sewall   *Barbara Fore*   *Sharon Bish*
Fond du Lac, Wisconsin   Mason, Michigan   Oklahoma City, Oklahoma

BUTTON SOUP
(First Cousin of Stone Soup)

Broth:
3 lbs. **short ribs** of **beef**, or
  2 lbs. stewing beef and a
  soup bone
8 C. cold **water**
1 C. chopped **onion**
1 C. chopped **celery**
1½ t. **salt**
dash of **pepper**
1 **bay leaf**
1 **green pepper**, quartered
  and seeded (optional)

Vegetables:
½ C. **lima beans**
½ C. chopped **carrots**
4 C. **tomatoes**
¼ C. **brown rice** or barley
½ C. **corn**
½ C. **peas**
½ C. **string beans**
½ C. chopped **green pepper**

Optional:
½ to 1 C. *each:*
  **cabbage, mushrooms, potato,
  turnips, parsley, sweet potato,
  spinach,** etc.
¼ to ½ C. **lentils**, split peas
  or soaked dried beans

Combine broth ingredients in a 6-qt. pot; simmer 2 to 3 hours. Strain broth; discard vegetables and bay leaf. Cut meat from bones and return to broth. Add limas, carrots, tomatoes and rice (also any soaked dried beans, potatoes or turnips). Simmer 30 minutes, or until tender. Add remaining ingredients. Simmer 15 minutes. Makes 5 quarts. May be doubled.

Choose vegetables to suit your family, but tomatoes are important. My mother called this "vegetable soup" and used only a soup bone. My husband likes the meat. My children have named it "Button Soup" after the folktale in which a miser is tricked into making enough soup for the whole town—using just one button.

With no optionals—P.: 193.7 gms.; C.: 4192

*Judy Halter
Great Falls, Montana*

STONE SOUP

1 large **soup pot**
1 to 1½ C. **water** per serving
½ t. **salt**, or to taste
(no stone)

As in the children's story, the most important ingredients are not supplied by the cook. Each guest brings one ingredient. As guests arrive, fill the pot with water, add salt and any ingredients requiring long cooking. Bring to a boil, then return to simmer. Each guest decides how long before meal time to add her ingredient. Before serving, remove any bones and correct seasonings. Bread or crackers, raw vegetables or fruit complete an easy and delicious meal for a crowd.

Chapter meeting at your house? HRE session? Family gathering?

*Penny Geis
Salina, Kansas*

CHICKEN NOODLE SOUP

2½ to 3-lb. whole **chicken**
2 C. **water**
½ lb. **carrots**, chopped
1 medium **onion**, chopped
4 or 5 stalks **celery**,
   chopped
1 T. **butter**
8 C. **water**
6 to 8 oz. **noodles** (p. 170)
½ to 1 t. **salt** (or less)
dash of **pepper**

Place whole chicken in baking pan with 2 C. water; bake 2 hours, uncovered, at 325°. Cool chicken (reserving broth), and discard skin and bones. Saute vegetables in butter in 4 or 5-qt. pot until golden. Add broth from baking pan and 4 C. water. Add remaining water to baking pan; bring to a boil on top of stove, stirring up cooked bits from pan; add this water to pot with chicken meat. Bring to a boil; simmer 1 hour or longer. Add noodles 20 minutes before serving. Season to taste. Makes about 14 C.

My 3-year-old son Billy calls this "carrot stew"—the carrots are his favorite part! He never tires of it.   *PROTEIN: 175.4 grams; CALORIES: 1744*

Susan J. Barnes
N. Granby, Connecticut

CHICKEN FINOLA
(Chicken Soup with Greens)

3 to 4-lb. **chicken**, cut up and
   skinned
water to cover, or part chicken
   broth
½ to 1 t. **salt**
2 T. thinly sliced, fresh
   ginger root (1 t. ground)
   (optional)
3 C. **greens** (spinach, bok choy
   or Swiss chard leaves),
   cut in half, fresh or frozen

Simmer chicken with seasonings for 45 minutes, or until almost tender. Add greens to top of chicken. Cook 15 minutes longer, or until chicken is done.

This recipe from the Philippines is traditionally given to new mothers as a benefit to mother and nursing baby. Leftover chicken may be removed from bones and sliced into thin strips for a quick cold lunch.

PROTEIN: 177.2 grams; CALORIES: 1192   *Linda Rullan*
Urbandale, Iowa

GREEN SOUP WITH RICE

1 medium **onion**, sliced
4 T. **butter**
4 C. chicken **broth**
½ t. **salt** (or less)
½ C. **brown rice** or triticale
1 lb. **spinach**
½ C. **milk**
2 **eggs**, beaten
1 T. **lemon juice**
dash of **pepper**

Brown onion in butter. Add broth, salt and rice. Simmer, covered, 50 minutes or until rice is tender. Add spinach and simmer 6 to 8 minutes. Process in blender or food processor until smooth. Combine milk and eggs. Add a few tablespoons of soup to egg mixture (to avoid curdling), then stir egg mixture into soup. Heat through. Add lemon juice and pepper. Thin with extra **milk** or **broth**, if desired. Makes about 6 C.

PROTEIN: 49.3 grams; CALORIES: 1268

Arla Ford
Creston, Iowa

EGG DUMPLINGS

1 C. whole wheat **flour**
2 t. **baking powder**
2 or 3 **eggs**, or 3 or 4 yolks
water, as needed

Combine flour, baking powder and eggs, and mix until liquid is absorbed. Add water as needed to achieve doughy consistency. Drop by spoonfuls into boiling soup or stew; lower heat and cook, uncovered, for 10 minutes, then covered for 10 minutes. Delicious with **chicken soup**.

PROTEIN: 28.4 grams; CALORIES: 566

Helen Palmer
Edgewater Park, New Jersey

QUICK EGG DROP SOUP

4 C. **broth** (chicken or
   vegetable)
½ C. **noodles** (pastina or
   alphabet)
1 **egg**, beaten
½ t. **salt**
2 T. grated Parmesan **cheese**
   (optional)

Bring broth to boil. Sprinkle pasta in slowly, so that boiling does not stop. Cook until tender. Reduce heat below boiling point; drop beaten egg in by teaspoonfuls, stirring constantly. Do not return to boil after adding egg. Makes about 5 C.

PROTEIN: 29.2 grams; CALORIES: 410

Lois Lake Raabe
Easton, Connecticut

LENTIL SOUP

2 C. dried **lentils**, or 1 C.
   lentils and 1 C. split peas
1 C. chopped **onion**
1 C. chopped **green pepper**
¼ C. **oil** (olive or salad)
2 T. whole wheat **flour**
several large **tomatoes**, or 1 to
   2 C. spaghetti sauce (p. 199)
2 C. chopped **carrots**
1 C. chopped **celery**
pinch of **pot herbs** (or mixture
   of dried marjoram, thyme and
   parsley)
8 C. **water**, or ham, beef or
   turkey stock

Optional:
ham bone, roast beef or turkey bone,
   or leftover bits of ham, sausages
   or frankfurters
1 C. (or more) shredded **spinach**
   or cabbage
½ C. **brown rice**
1 or 2 **bay leaves**
1 or 2 cloves **garlic**, minced
½ t. **salt** (or less)
dash of **pepper**

Simmer onion and green pepper in oil until soft. Add flour and cook until bubbling (do not brown). Add remaining ingredients. Simmer in 5-qt. pot for at least 1 hour, in a slow-cooker for 4 to 6 hours on high, or in pressure cooker for 15 minutes. Remove bones and bay leaves, if used, returning any meat to pot. Makes 4 to 5 quarts.

PROTEIN: 127.1 grams; CALORIES: 2385

Jeri Bradshaw   *Bonnie James Walther*
Riverside, New Jersey   *Houston, Texas*

CHICKEN CORN SOUP

6 C. chicken **broth**
2 C. cubed, cooked **chicken**
2 C. cubed, unpeeled **potatoes**
2 C. **corn**
1 medium **onion**, finely chopped
handful of chopped, fresh
   parsley
4 hard-cooked **eggs**, diced
½ t. **salt**
dash of **pepper**

Combine all ingredients except eggs, salt and pepper in a 4-qt. pot. Bring to a boil and simmer until potatoes are tender. Add eggs; season to taste.

This soup has as many versions as there are Pennsylvania Dutch families.   *P.: 136.7 gms.; C.: 1436*

Ann Barley
Brogue, Pennsylvania

CORN SOUP

leftover **ham hock**
3 C. (or more) **water**
3 (or more) **potatoes**, peeled
   and quartered
4 or 5 **tomatoes**, cut in chunks
1 medium **onion**, chopped
2 stalks **celery**, chopped
4 or 5 **carrots**, chopped
½ head green **cabbage**, chopped
   or shredded
4½ C. **corn**

Cut meat from ham bone and add with bone to water. Add vegetables in order given; simmer until all vegetables are soft. Makes 14 C.

This soup will be somewhat thick and creamy. I add no seasonings because the ham is usually salty enough, and flavors the soup. This is a good dish for a new mother or a sick friend to enjoy.   P: 86.7 G C : 1613

Connie B. Comeaux
New Iberia, Louisiana

CHEESY CORN CHOWDER

1 large **potato**, peeled and
   diced
2 C. boiling **water**
1 **bay leaf**
¼ t. **sage**
½ t. **cumin**
3 T. **butter**
1 **onion**, chopped
3 T. whole wheat **flour**
1¼ C. **milk**, buttermilk or cream
¼ t. ground **nutmeg**
1½ to 2 C. grated Cheddar **cheese**
2 C. **corn**, fresh or frozen

Optional:
4 to 5 T. dry **white wine** or
   rice vinegar
2 t. nutritional **yeast**
chopped **chives**, parsley or
   pimento for garnish

Cook potato, bay, sage, and cumin in water until barely tender, 15 to 20 minutes. Saute onion in butter until tender; blend in flour. Off heat, gradually add milk, stirring constantly. Stir milk mixture and corn into potatoes and water. Add nutmeg and simmer gently for 10 minutes. Add cheese and stir until it melts. Stir in any optional ingredients.

We like cornbread with the soup.

PROTEIN: 71.9 grams; CALORIES: 1767

Margaret Keyes
St. Charles, Missouri

CREAM OF MUSHROOM SOUP

3 to 4 C. medium **white sauce** (p. 251), made with **milk**, or part milk and part chicken **broth**
12 oz. fresh **mushrooms**, chopped
2 T. chopped **onion** (optional)
ground **nutmeg** and **thyme** to taste

Make white sauce, first sauteing mushrooms and onions in butter. Simmer, stirring, until soup thickens. If desired, stir in extra **milk** to achieve desired consistency. Garnish with nutmeg or thyme.

Freeze leftovers in 1-cup containers and substitute for canned mushroom soup in recipes.

PROTEIN: 41.8 grams; CALORIES: 1385

Sally Eldred
Vestal, New York

MY HUSBAND'S CLAM CHOWDER ◦

2 doz. cherrystone **clams**
3 strips nitrite-free **bacon**, cut up
2 C. chopped **celery**
1 C. chopped **onion**
1 C. chopped **carrot**
2 lbs. **potatoes**, diced
6 large, ripe **tomatoes**, peeled and chopped
2 C. chicken **broth**
4 C. **water**
½ t. **salt** (or less)
dash of **pepper**
4 t. **thyme**

In heavy 5-qt. pot, fry bacon. Stir in vegetables, except tomatoes. Shuck and chop clams, adding juice to pot; reserve clams. Add tomatoes, liquids and seasonings; simmer 4 hours. Add clams 5 to 10 minutes before serving.

PROTEIN: 102.4; CALORIES: 1814

Susan Edwards
St. Thomas, Virgin Islands

ZUCCHINI-POTATO SOUP

2 or 3 medium **zucchini**
2 or 3 medium **potatoes**
2 small **onions** (1 large)
4 C. **broth** (chicken or vegetable)
1 clove **garlic**, minced
½ t. **salt** (or less)
dash of **pepper**
¾ C. plain **yogurt**, to garnish
dill weed or curry powder to taste

Slice vegetables. Simmer in broth with garlic, salt and pepper until tender. Puree in blender in batches. Serve hot or cold, garnished with a large dab of yogurt, and dill or curry. Freezes well. For a change, use ½ bunch **broccoli** or ½ lb. **spinach** in place of zucchini.

This is one of our favorite summer-picnic soups, served cold, with a **salad** and fresh **bread**, though it's just as delicious hot, eaten in front of the fire in winter. *P.: 29.5 gms.; C.: 503*

Lois Lake Raabe
Easton, Connecticut

NEW ENGLAND CLAM CHOWDER

3 C. minced **clams**
(reserve drained juice)
5 or 6 slices nitrite-free
bacon, or 4 or 5 oz. minced
salt pork
1 medium **onion**, chopped
1 C. **clam juice**
2 to 4 C. chopped **potatoes**
1½ C. **milk**, light cream or
half-and-half
2 or 3 C. regular or skimmed
milk
2 T. **butter**
sprinkle of chopped, fresh
parsley
½ t. **salt** (or less)
dash of **pepper**
½ to 1 C. chopped **celery**
(optional)

Fry bacon or salt pork and reserve. Add onion to 2 T. of bacon fat. Cook until soft. Add juice drained from clams plus additional 1 C. clam juice. Add potatoes and cook 15 to 20 minutes until tender. Add remaining ingredients, except bacon. Heat until just hot enough to serve. Do not overheat or boil, or clams will toughen. Crumble bacon over top.

PROTEIN: 147.4 grams; CALORIES: 2060

Judy Good   *Pat Guilmette*
Columbus, Ohio   *Albuquerque, New Mexico*

SLOW-COOKER FISH CHOWDER

1 to 1½ lbs. white **fish**
(cod, halibut or perch)
2 stalks **celery**, chopped
2 **carrots**, sliced
1 medium **onion**, chopped
2 T. **butter**
2 C. **clam juice**
1 C. chicken **stock**
1 C. **water**
2 to 4 medium **potatoes**, cut
in chunks
1 C. dry **milk powder**
or 1 C. fresh milk

Optional:
1 t. **rosemary**
2 to 6 slices nitrite-free
bacon, fried and crumbled
1 C. diced, mixed **vegetables**
(leftover or frozen)
1 **bay leaf**

Saute celery, carrots and onion in butter. Put in slow-cooker; add remaining ingredients, except milk. Cover and cook on low for 4 to 8 hours. Remove fish and cut into chunks. Uncover pot and stir in milk and fish. Cover and cook 45 minutes longer.

Non-slow-cooker Method: Saute vegetables as above. Blend in remaining ingredients, except milk. Cover and simmer 20 minutes. Stir milk and water together; add to soup and heat until just hot.

PROTEIN: 144.3 grams; CALORIES: 1432

Emmy Eaton
Thurmont, Maryland

POTATO SOUP

8 medium **potatoes**, diced
1 medium **onion**, chopped
1 to 3 **carrots**, grated
1 stalk **celery**, chopped
8 C. **water**, or part water and
  part chicken stock
1 C. **milk**
2 T. **butter**
½ t. **salt**
dash of **pepper**
2 T. chopped, fresh **parsley**,
  to garnish

Optional:
4 to 8 slices nitrite-free
  bacon, cooked, drained and
  crumbled; or 2 to 6 sliced
  frankfurters or cooked sausages;
  or 1 C. cubed, leftover meat
1 or 2 **bay leaves**
1½ C. shredded **spinach**
½ to 1 C. grated Cheddar **cheese**

Cook potatoes, onion, carrot and celery in water, covered, for 45 minutes. Stir in remaining ingredients except cheese. Simmer gently 15 minutes. Add cheese, if you wish, and heat, stirring, until cheese melts. Garnish with parsley. Makes about 14 C.

PROTEIN: 29.2 grams; CALORIES: 1081

Carol Hoefler
Zanesville, Ohio

Charlotte Bridges
Otterville, Missouri

TOMATO SOUP

4 large **tomatoes** (2½ C. chopped)
2 slices **onion**, or more
¼ small **green pepper** (optional)
1 **carrot** (optional)
½ t. **salt**
dash of **pepper**
2 C. thin **white sauce** (made with
  stock, water, or milk)

Seasoning Choices:
1 **bay leaf**, ¼ t. ground **cinnamon**
  and a dash of ground **cloves** or
  allspice
Or choice of:
  **basil, parsley, thyme, marjoram,
  garlic, oregano**

Peel fresh tomatoes easily by plunging into boiling water for 20 to 60 seconds, then removing skin. Chop, process or blend all vegetables together. Add seasonings and simmer 10 minutes until vegetables are tender. If you wish a fine texture, you may process or strain through food mill. Stir mixture into white sauce, pouring very slowly to avoid curdling. Reheat. Makes 5 cups.

PROTEIN: 29.6 grams; CALORIES: 819

Tomato Rice Soup. Add ½ to ¾ C. cooked brown **rice**. Some of the rice may be processed with the tomatoes, if you wish.

Tomato Vegetable Soup. After mashing or blending tomatoes, add 1 or 2 C. other **vegetables** and/or cooked dried **beans**. Simmer until everything is tender. Add leftover vegetables just to heat through.

Ruth Chaney
Appleton, Wisconsin

Susan Ratner
Cincinnati, Ohio

Brenda Wilson
Carlyle, Sask., Canada

HAMBURGER SOUP OR STEW

1 lb. ground **beef**
1 **onion**, chopped
1 **green pepper**, cut in strips
1 C. cubed **potato**
1 C. sliced **carrot**
½ C. diced **celery**
½ C. shredded **cabbage**
3 to 4 C. sliced **zucchini**
4 C. cut up **tomatoes**
  or tomato sauce
¼ C. **brown rice** or barley, or
  1 C. macaroni or noodles
1 **bay leaf**
½ t. **thyme** or oregano
¼ t. **basil**
½ t. **salt** (or less)
dash of **pepper**
6 C. (approximately) **water**, for
  soup consistency

Optional:
1½ t. **soy sauce**
¼ C. **lentils**
¼ C. dried **split peas**
leftover **vegetables**

Brown meat with onion in a 5-quart pot. Drain. Add vegetables. Bring to a boil. Add rice and seasonings. Add any or all the optional ingredients and up to 6 C. water, depending on thickness desired. Bring to second boil, cover and simmer 1 hour, or until rice is tender. Add more water if necessary. Serve sprinkled with **grated cheese**.

This recipe is easy, nutritious and great to have in the freezer. It's good to give to help out new moms, even little ones can eat it with their fingers or from a spoon.

PROTEIN: 102 grams; CALORIES: 1418

Carol Stratton
Holyoke, Colorado

ITALIAN ESCAROLE SOUP

Meatballs:
1 lb. ground **beef**
2 **eggs**
½ t. chopped, fresh **parsley**
¼ to ½ C. **wheat germ**
¼ to ½ t. **salt** (or less)
dash of **pepper**

Soup:
1 lb. **escarole**
8 C. homemade chicken **broth**
1 lb. cooked **white kidney beans**
3 C. cooked **brown rice**
1 T. **tomato paste**

Combine meatball ingredients. Shape into very small balls (not more than 1 T. of meat each) and brown in skillet. Set aside. Cook escarole in small amount of water for about 5 minutes. Drain (liquid may be saved for another soup) and cut in small pieces; add to chicken broth with beans, rice, tomato paste and meatballs. Simmer about 1 hour. Serve with Parmesan **cheese** to sprinkle on top.

Very tasty and nutritious. It's one of the Italian recipes that is rarely written down, and is really a meal in itself. *PROTEIN: 148.6 grams; CALORIES: 2439*

Carol Ann Lott
Absecon, New Jersey

JOAN'S ORIGINAL MINESTRONE

1 C. **lentils**
water to cover
1 **onion,** chopped
2 C. **tomatoes,** whole and
  peeled, with juice
7 or 8 C. **water**
2 T. chopped, fresh **parsley**
1 T. **basil**
1 T. **oregano**
2 cloves **garlic,** minced
½ t. **salt** (or less)
dash of **pepper**
1 C. **barley**
2 C. *each* **green beans,** cooked
  kidney beans and cooked
  garbanzo beans
4 stalks **celery,** cut in chunks
2 or 3 peeled **carrots,** cut
  in chunks
1 small **zucchini,** sliced
  (optional)
1 C. elbow **macaroni** or other
  small pasta (optional)
½ C. grated Parmesan **cheese**
  (optional)

In a 7 or 8-qt. pot, cook lentils in water until tender (30 to 60 minutes). Add onion, tomatoes, 4 C. water, parsley and seasonings. Bring to a gentle boil; add barley. Simmer about 1 hour. Add remaining vegetables and 3 to 4 C. water. Bring to a boil; add macaroni slowly, so boiling does not stop. Reduce heat and simmer at least 30 minutes longer. Garnish with Parmesan cheese. Makes 6 quarts.

Start early in the day, so that flavors blend—just stir occasionally. This is easy to make in stages between nursings, reading stories, putting on bandaids and sometimes even sweeping the floor! A complete meal—and delicious!

PROTEIN: 157.3 grams; CALORIES: 2973

Joan D'Alessandro
Kent, Washington

TZATZIKI
(Authentic Greek Cucumber Soup or Salad)

4 C. plain **yogurt** (for soup) or
  2 C. (for salad)
2 large **cucumbers,** peeled
2 or 3 cloves **garlic,** minced
1 T. wine **vinegar**
1 T. **water**
2 T. olive **oil** (optional)
2 T. **walnuts**
dash of **salt**
dash of **pepper**
½ T. **dill weed** (or more)
cherry tomatoes and **mint leaves**
  (optional)

Place garlic, vinegar, water, oil, and half the walnuts in blender. Blend until very smooth. Add rest of nuts. Blend until they are finely chopped. Pour into non-metal bowl. Add salt, pepper and ¼ t. dill weed. Chop or grate cucumbers. Gently stir cucumbers and yogurt into mixture. Adjust seasonings. Refrigerate for 1 to 48 hours or more. Garnish with remaining dill, cherry tomato "roses" and mint leaves, if desired. Keeps well for summer snacking.

PROTEIN: 52 gms.; C.: 968 *Roberta Bishop Johnson*
Champaign, Illinois

COLD CUCUMBER SOUP

2 to 4 medium **cucumbers**
4 C. plain **yogurt** or buttermilk
1 to 2 small **onions** or scallions
¼ C. chopped, fresh **parsley**
1 t. **dill weed**
½ t. **salt** (or less)
dash of black **pepper**

Quarter cucumbers. Puree all ingredients in batches in the blender. Chill for at least 4 hours. Serve garnished with dill, a sprig of parsley, and/or a paper-thin slice of cucumber. PROTEIN: 52.9 grams; CALORIES: 661

*Lois Lake Raabe
Easton, Connecticut*

GAZPACHO

1 medium **cucumber**
1 medium **onion**
1 **green pepper**
1 large **tomato**
8 C. **tomato juice**
6 T. **oil**
4 T. wine **vinegar**, or lemon juice or part of each
1 t. **sugar** or honey
½ t. **worcestershire sauce**
½ t. **salt**
dash of **pepper**
2 cloves **garlic**, minced
2 T. finely chopped, fresh **parsley**

Optional:
5 or 6 slices whole wheat **bread**
8 to 12 **ice cubes**

Garnishes: **croutons, yogurt** or **sour cream**; chopped **avocado, tomato, green pepper, onion, cucumber, parsley, zucchini, eggs, celery, cauliflower, radishes, cheese, sprouts,** cooked **bacon**

Finely chop cucumber, onion, green pepper and tomato. Combine all ingredients, except garnishes, in large bowl. Mix well. Cover and refrigerate overnight. Serve cold with one or more garnishes. Makes 10 C. or more.

To use immediately, blend tomato juice, oil, onion, vinegar and seasonings in blender with bread and ice, adding ice cubes one at a time. Add all chopped vegetables with other garnishes at the table.

The easiest gazpacho: blend all solids, cubed instead of chopped, in blender with 2 C. tomato juice. Stir in more tomato juice to desired consistency.

This colorful soup is nutritious, delicious and low in calories. Keeps well for several days in refrigerator. Summer favorite—great for picnics! Try it in a thermos.

P.: 26.3 gms.; C.: 1290 + garnishes

*Kathi Ambrose
Kingston, New York*

*Marian Baker
Riverton, Wyoming*

*Barbara J. Maletz
Ridgewood, New Jersey*

VALENTINE SOUP
(Borscht)

1 large **onion**, chopped
2 stalks **celery**, chopped
2 T. **oil** or butter
3 or 4 **potatoes**, cubed
3 or 4 **carrots**, sliced
4 C. **stock** (beef or vegetable)
4 large **beets**, grated, with
    tops, chopped, or 1 lb. cooked
2 T. **vinegar**
½ t. **salt** (or less)
dash of **pepper**

Optional:
yogurt or sour cream
cottage cheese

Saute onion and celery in oil in a 5-qt. pot until soft. Add potatoes, carrots and stock to cover. Bring to a boil; reduce heat and simmer until vegetables are nearly soft, about 15 minutes. Add beets; cook 15 minutes (or about 3 minutes, if beets are already cooked). Add vinegar and seasonings; cook 1 minute. Garnish with yogurt and/or cottage cheese for more flavor and nutrition.

Garnishes also cool soup a bit for children. Makes 6 C.

This is borscht or beet soup, but my kids called it Valentine Soup after I cut the potatoes into heart shapes one Valentine's Day.

PROTEIN: 30.7 grams; CALORIES: 944

Marie Tobaben
Warren, Michigan

THE UNCANNED CONDENSED SOUP

Basic White Sauce (thick):
3 T. **butter** or oil
3 T. **flour**
¼ t. **salt** (or less)
dash of **pepper**
1¼ C. **liquid**, milk or stock

Melt butter or oil in saucepan. Stir in flour and seasonings. Cook over medium heat until bubbly. Add liquid slowly, stirring with wire whisk to prevent lumps. Cook until thick. Makes 1 C. or 1 can of condensed soup. PROTEIN: 13.8 grams; CALORIES: 600

Tomato Soup. Use **tomato juice** for the liquid. Add dashes of **garlic** and **onion powder, basil** and **oregano.**

Mushroom/Celery/Chive Soup. Saute ¼ C. chopped **mushrooms, celery** or **chives** and 1 T. minced **onion** in butter before adding flour.

Cheese Soup. Add ½ C. grated **cheese** after the liquid. Stir until melted.

Chicken Soup. Use **chicken broth** for half or all the liquid. Add ¼ t. **poultry seasoning** or **sage.**

Use any sauteed vegetables or liquid combinations you choose. Be creative—much better than store-bought soups.

Janet Dow
Janesville, Wisconsin

Barbara Becker Nelson
Eugene, Oregon

Bryanna Clark
Union Bay, B.C., Canada

Eileen Wason
Sarasota, Florida

CREAMY SOUP

2 T. finely chopped **onion**
2 T. **butter**
2 T. whole wheat **flour**
3 to 3½ C. **milk**, or part milk
  and part chicken stock or
  vegetable cooking liquid
1½ to 2 C. chopped **vegetables**
  (leftover or frozen), such as
  corn, potato, carrots, green
  beans, peas, celery, or any
  combination
¼ t. **celery salt** or celery
  seeds (optional)
½ t. **salt**
dash of **pepper**

Optional:
5 slices nitrite-free **bacon**, cooked
  and crumbled
1 C. cubed **ham**
½ to 1 C. chopped, cooked
  chicken
6 oz. to 1 lb. **salmon**, tuna, shrimp
  or crabmeat, or a combination
⅓ to 2 C. grated **cheese** (Monterey
  Jack or Cheddar)

Saute onion (and celery if used) in butter until tender. Remove from heat, blend in flour; gradually add milk, stirring constantly. Cook over medium heat, stirring constantly, until mixture boils and thickens. Simmer 3 minutes. Add vegetables, seasonings and any optional ingredients, except cheese. Cook until all vegetables are tender. Add cheese and cook, stirring, until cheese is melted. If you use the smaller amount of cheese, you may reserve it for a garnish, if you prefer. Makes 5 to 6 C.   *P.: 34.4 gms.; C.: 967*

Rea Standridge
Sugar Land, Texas

MY PEANUT SOUP

1 medium **onion**, chopped
2 stalks **celery**, chopped
¼ C. **butter**
3 T. whole wheat **flour**
4 C. strong chicken **stock**
2 C. smooth **peanut butter**
1½ to 2 C. **milk**
1 C. chopped or whole
  roasted **peanuts**

In a 3-qt. pot, simmer onions and celery in butter for 10 minutes. Turn up heat and brown. Remove from heat and stir in flour. Add chicken stock gradually; heat, stirring, until blended, smooth and hot. Puree stock, peanut butter and milk in blender, or food processor, in 3 batches. Chill, *or* heat gently. Serve garnished with peanuts. Makes about 2 quarts.

The peanut-milk combination is an excellent source of protein. If you can get fresh (raw or unhomogenized) milk, use the top cream in place of some of the milk. Roasting your own raw peanuts (1 hour on cookie sheet at 275°) adds even more flavor.   *PROTEIN: 201 grams; CALORIES: 4712*

Roberta S. Rogers
Newport News, Virginia

CREAM OF CELERY SOUP

leaves, ends and trimmings
   from 1 bunch **celery**, chopped
1 (or more) small **onion**, chopped
½ C. **water**
2 C. thin **white sauce** (p. 251)
1 C. (or more) **milk** (optional)

Bring celery, onion and water to a boil. Simmer until just tender. Puree in blender or food processor. Add more water, if needed, to make 2 C. Stir in white sauce; heat to boiling point. Thin with additional milk, if needed. If celery yields more than 2 C. puree, add another cup of white sauce for each cup of puree.

This uses all the celery pieces that I used to throw away (can't imagine I was that wasteful). After you've washed the celery and made your soup, you have the stalks ready to fill with **cottage cheese, peanut butter** or whatever you like for a nutritious snack.   PROTEIN: 29.8 grams; CALORIES: 804

Sally Eldred
Vestal, New York

BEAN SOUP

1 or 2 C. dried **beans** (lima,
   white, navy, pinto, lentils,
   split peas, or a mixture of
   different kinds)
6 to 8 C. **water**, *or* 1 ham bone
   and 1 or 2 T. vinegar for
   ham stock
1 large **onion**, chopped
1 or 2 cloves **garlic**, minced
1 to 3 **carrots**, sliced or
   chopped
2 or 3 (or more) stalks **celery**,
   chopped
1 or 2 C. peeled, chopped
   tomatoes

Optional:
2 C. **stock** (vegetable or
   chicken)
1 large **green pepper**, chopped
1 C. **ham** or other leftover meat
1 C. **green beans**
1 C. small **noodles**
½ C. mashed **potatoes**
½ t. **salt** (or less)
seasonings to taste:
   thyme, bay leaf, basil, parsley,
   pepper, marjoram

Soak beans (except lentils or split peas) overnight in water to cover. Saute onion and garlic in butter until transparent. If using ham stock, drain beans (save the liquid for another soup). Combine beans, liquids and raw vegetables, except tomatoes, in a 5 or 6-qt. pot; simmer, covered, until beans are tender. Add tomatoes, meat and seasonings; cook 30 minutes longer. If you wish, add noodles and cook until tender; or thicken soup by mashing some of the beans or adding mashed potatoes. Makes about 3 quarts.

To make **ham stock**, put ham bone and vinegar in a pot and cover with water. Bring to a boil; simmer 1 to 2 hours; or cook 12 to 24 hours in a slow-cooker on **low**. Discard bone, reserving bits of meat for soup.

PROTEIN: 46 grams; CALORIES: 824

Catherine King   Rojean Loucks   Patt Hagge   Susan Althof
Mt. Holly, New Jersey   Assaria, Kansas   Clinton, Iowa   Youngstown, New York

SPLIT PEA SOUP FOR BUSY MOTHERS

1 lb. **split peas**
1 **onion**, chopped or sliced
3 to 6 **carrots**
2 to 3 stalks **celery**, or tops
  from 1 bunch
1 **bay leaf**
1 clove **garlic**, minced
  (pinch of garlic powder)
dash of **cayenne pepper** (optional)
¼ t. **thyme**
8 to 10 C. **water**
½ t. **salt** (optional)

Optional (*one* of the following):
  2 C. chicken **stock**
  a **turkey carcass**
  a **ham bone**
  leftover **ham**
  ¼ lb. **salt pork** or bacon

Put all ingredients in a soup kettle or 5-qt. slow-cooker (leave 1 to 1½" for boiling room). Simmer, covered, for 3 to 4 hours. Or cook in slow-cooker for 8 to 10 hours on **low**, 3 to 4 hours on **high**. About half an hour before serving, remove meat and bones, and put soup through a food mill or processor. Return soup and meat bits to pot; add salt, if desired, and serve hot. Add **milk** to cool soup, if you wish. Makes 10 to 12 C. This is a great recipe for busy mothers. Assemble in the morning while you are getting breakfast; or if you forget, then start before naptime in the afternoon. I like to use the slow-cooker because it doesn't boil over. If this is one of those days when the baby wants to nurse very frequently, maybe Daddy could put the soup through the mill when he gets home.

PROTEIN: 111.2 grams; CALORIES: 1765 + milk   Nadine Bowlus
Jackson, Mississippi

Curried Pea Soup. For a different flavor and consistency, cut all vegetables into small dice, use 1 C. **peas** and 8 C. chicken **broth**. Substitute 1 t. **curry powder** and **black pepper** to taste for seasonings. Add ¼ C. **soy flakes** (optional). Cook on top of the stove about 45 minutes, until peas are tender, but do not puree.

Jean Baker White
Van Buren, Maine

Vegetarian Pea Soup. Omit meat, stock or bones. For a complete protein, add 1 C. **barley** or other grain, or serve with whole grain **bread**. If you wish, add 6 oz. grated **cheese** (Gruyere, Swiss, Jack or Cheddar) before serving.

Donna More   Stacy Laputz
Toms River, New Jersey   Long Beach, California

SPANISH BEAN SOUP

1 lb. dried **garbanzo beans**
  (chick peas)
5 medium **carrots**, chopped
5 medium **potatoes**, chopped
1 medium **onion**, chopped
2 pinches string-type **saffron**
  (½ t. powdered)
ham bones (preferable, but
  optional)
1 C. **ham** chunks (optional)
water to cover

Soak beans overnight in about 6 C. water. Add other ingredients and cook until all are tender (beans may take up to 4 hours). Check occasionally and add water if necessary so that beans are covered. Remove bones. Very tasty with **cornbread**.

My mother has been making this soup as long as I can remember. The recipe has been in our family for nearly 40 years; my uncle learned it from a restaurant in Ybor City, a mostly Cuban section of Tampa, Florida. Although the saffron is important to the soup's character, it *is* expensive, so you may omit it or substitute less expensive Mexican saffron.

Carol Pritchard
PROTEIN: 128.7 grams; CALORIES: 2384   San Jose, California

Salads &
Salad Dressings

BASIC VINAIGRETTE DRESSING

¼ C. **vinegar** or lemon juice
2 t. tamari **soy sauce**
1/8 t. dry **mustard**
1/8 t. **garlic powder**
1/8 t. black **pepper**
¼ t. *each* **basil** and **oregano** *or*
   mint and dill weed
½ t. **celery salt** (optional)
5 T. olive **oil**

Place vinegar in measuring cup. Add soy sauce, seasonings and oil. Stir well and refrigerate several hours before using.

PROTEIN: 1 gram; CALORIES: 639

1 T. = P.: o gms.; C.: 46

Chris Mulford
Swarthmore, Pennsylvania

Ellen Wadyka
Somerville, New Jersey

Patty Holtz
Geneva, Illinois

Barbara Bahun
New Carlisle, Ohio

ITALIAN SALAD DRESSING

1⅓ C. **oil**
½ C. **vinegar**
¼ C. grated **cheese**
   (Romano or Parmesan)
2 t. **salt**
1 t. **onion salt** or celery salt
½ t. **pepper**

½ t. dry **mustard**
¼ t. **paprika**
1 clove **garlic**, minced

Optional:
4 slices **bacon**, fried and chopped
⅓ C. **green olives**

Mix all ingredients and pour into glass jar. Refrigerate several hours and shake well before using. Store in refrigerator.   *PROTEIN: 8.9 grams; CALORIES: 2757*

1 T. = P.: .3 gms.; C.: 81

Vicki Ruggiero
Mankato, Kansas

Chris Fletcher
Alexandria, Indiana

Suzie Owen
Van Nuys, California

HONEY FRENCH DRESSING

½ C. **oil**
½ C. **lemon juice** or
   cider vinegar
1 large **onion**, grated
¼ C. **water**
⅓ C. **catsup** (p. 252)
2 to 4 T. **honey**

¼ t. **salt**
½ t. **celery seed**
½ t. prepared **mustard**
½ t. **garlic powder**
½ t. **onion powder**
1 t. **paprika**

Put all ingredients into a jar, cover and shake well. Store in refrigerator and shake before use.   *PROTEIN: 4.7 grams; CALORIES: 1284*

1 T. = PROTEIN: .1 gram; CALORIES: 30

Julie Griffin
Springfield, Ohio

Judy Heininger
Vadnais Hts., Minnesota

Ruth Chaney
Appleton, Wisconsin

Rindalee M. Skimina
Highland, Indiana

BACON SWEET AND SOUR DRESSING

4 slices nitrite-free **bacon**
2 T. chopped **onion**
2 to 4 T. **honey**
¼ C. **vinegar**
½ C. **water**
1 C. **Italian salad dressing**

Fry bacon until crisp. Drain and crumble. Saute onion in drippings until tender. Discard all but 1 T. drippings. Add honey, vinegar and water. Bring to a boil. Cool. Combine all ingredients. Mix well. Chill. Shake before using. Makes 2 C.

PROTEIN: 9.7 grams; CALORIES: 1994
1 T. = P.: .3 gms.; C.: 62
Suzie Owen
Van Nuys, California

RUSSIAN SALAD DRESSING

1 C. **oil**
¼ C. **honey**
½ C. **catsup** (p. 252)
½ C. **vinegar**
2 T. **worcestershire sauce**

¼ C. finely minced **onion**
¼ t. crumbled **oregano** leaves
¼ t. **dill weed**
¼ t. **savory**

PROTEIN: 4.1 grams; CALORIES: 2427
1 T. = PROTEIN: .1 gram; CALORIES: 58

Pour all ingredients into a quart jar and shake well. Chill. Shake before using. Keeps well refrigerated.
Frances Bauer
Pontiac, Michigan

LOW-CAL BLENDER DRESSING

1 C. low-fat **cottage cheese**
½ C. **buttermilk** or yogurt
2 T. **vinegar**
½ t. **garlic powder**
½ t. **celery seed**

½ t. **paprika**
¼ t. **pepper**
¼ t. **salt**
½ t. **onion powder**

Optional:
¼ to ½ C. **mayonnaise**
1 t. **dill weed**

Put all ingredients in a blender and blend until smooth.
PROTEIN: 32.8 grams; CALORIES: 220 *1 T. = P.: 1.3 gms.; C.: 8*
Laurie Owens
Cincinnati, Ohio

TOMATO SALAD DRESSING

1 C. cider **vinegar**
¼ C. **honey** (or less)
1 C. **oil**
2 C. **tomato sauce**
½ t. **paprika**
2 cloves **garlic**, split
1 T. chopped **onion** (optional)
1 t. **celery seed** (optional)
salt and **pepper**, if needed

Boil vinegar and honey together for 1 minute. Combine with oil, tomato sauce, paprika, garlic, salt and pepper. Mix well and store in a covered non-metal container in the refrigerator. Makes 4¼ C.

PROTEIN: 8 grams; CALORIES: 2470
1 T. = P.: .1 gms.; C.: 36

Mary Westra
White Bear Lake, Minnesota
Adrienne Archambault
Dauphin, Manitoba, Can.
Jan Cooper
Vicksburg, Michigan

BLENDER MAYONNAISE

2 **eggs**, at room temperature
2 T. **lemon juice** or cider vinegar
¼ t. **salt**
1 t. dry **mustard**
1¼ C. **oil**

Optional:
1 T. **parsley** and 1 t. **dill weed**,
  or ½ t. paprika
  or 1 to 2 T. **honey**

Combine all ingredients except oil in blender at high speed for 1 minute. Slowly and gradually add oil. For a different flavor, add one of the optional ingredients. Refrigerate in a non-metal container.

PROTEIN: 13.2 grams; CALORIES: 2656

Jean Kremer *Anna, Ohio*	*Barbara Wortham* *Garland, Texas*	*Betsy Ennis* *Wilmington, N. Carolina*	*Denise Parker* *Ridgecrest, California*

YOGURT-MAYO DRESSING

2 C. plain **yogurt**
1 C. **mayonnaise** *or*
  part cottage cheese
1 t. **dill weed**
1 t. freshly-ground **pepper**
½ t. dry **mustard**
½ t. **paprika**
½ t. **garlic powder**

Mix all ingredients. Use as a salad dressing, or as a dip for fresh vegetables.

PROTEIN: 27.9 grams; CALORIES: 1922
1 T. = P.: .6 gms.; C.: 40

Lois Lake Raabe
Easton, Connecticut

TARTAR SAUCE

1 C. **mayonnaise** or
  yogurt-mayo dressing
1 T. minced **onion**
2-4 T. chopped **pickle** or
  relish

Mix all ingredients. Serve with fish.

PROTEIN: 7 grams; CALORIES: 1374
Many LLL Contributors

BLEU CHEESE DRESSING AND DIP

1 to 1½ C. plain **yogurt**
¼ to ½ C. crumbled **bleu cheese**
½ C. **mayonnaise**
1 T. Parmesan **cheese**
1 t. **vinegar**
1/8 t. **pepper**

Optional:
½ C. **milk**
1 to 2 cloves **garlic**, minced
½ C. **sour cream**
3 T. finely minced **onion**
¼ t. **thyme**
¼ t. **oregano**

Mix together all ingredients and store. For different flavors, add one or more of the optional ingredients. Refrigerate several hours before using. Dressing keeps well in refrigerator for several weeks.

Good on spinach and mushroom salads.

PROTEIN: 27.8; CALORIES: 1180
1 T. = P.: 9 gms.; C.: 41

Dip: Omit optional milk and use the mixture as a fresh vegetable dip.

Pam Patrick *Huntsville, Alabama*	*Marian Smith* *Endwell, New York*	*Diane Spenny* *Chicago, Illinois*	*Nancy Pittman* *Roseburg, Oregon*

CREAMY CAESAR SALAD DRESSING

1 C. **mayonnaise**
juice of 2 large **lemons**
1 t. **salt**
1 t. **pepper**
2 T. **worcestershire sauce**
¾ C. grated Parmesan **cheese**
¼ C. **water**
¼ t. **garlic powder**

Combine all ingredients. Chill. Delicious on romaine lettuce with coddled eggs and croutons.

PROTEIN: 27.9 grams; CALORIES: 1934
1 T. = PROTEIN: .7 grams; CALORIES: 51

Susan C. Huml
Great Lakes, Illinois

1000 ISLAND DRESSING

1½ C. **mayonnaise**
3 T. **catsup** (p. 252) or
 chili sauce
1½ T. **relish**
1 small **onion**, minced
½ t. **pepper**
2 T. **lemon juice**
½ t. **salt**

2½ C. plain **yogurt**

Optional:
1 T. chopped **green pepper**
1 hard-cooked **egg**, chopped
1 T. chopped **pimento**
1/8 t. **garlic powder**

Stir the ingredients together well, adding yogurt last. For flavor variations, add one or more of the optional ingredients. Allow to chill at least 4 hours before serving. *PROTEIN: 37.3 grams; CALORIES: 2906*

Jean Baker White
Van Buren, Maine

BUTTERMILK SALAD DRESSING

½ C. **mayonnaise**
½ C. **buttermilk**
½ t. **parsley flakes** (dry)
¼ t. **garlic powder**
¼ t. **onion powder**
½ t. seasoned **salt** *or* ¼ t.
 salt, dash pepper and
 dash paprika

Combine all ingredients. Refrigerate.

 This recipe is an attempt to match the flavor of the commercial ranch-type dressing.

PROTEIN: 6.2 grams; CALORIES: 856
1 T. = P.: 1.4 gms.; C.: 54

Gael M. Chaney
Martinsville, Virginia

Green Salads

SALAD BAR SUGGESTIONS

Greens:
lettuce (Ruby, Endive,
   Romaine or Iceberg)
spinach
watercress

Additions:
carrots, grated or sliced
cabbage, shredded red or green
radishes, sliced
celery, sliced
green or **red pepper**, sliced
cauliflower florets
zucchini, sliced
broccoli florets
cucumbers, sliced
red beets, shredded
black olives
mushrooms, sliced
summer squash, sliced
tomatoes, sliced (or cherry)
parsley, chopped
sprouts
apple, chopped
raisins

Protein Power:
almonds, sliced
walnuts, chopped
seeds (sesame or sunflower)
tuna
chick peas (garbanzos)
cheese wedges
eggs, hard-cooked, sliced
meat strips
poultry strips

Toppings:
lemon wedges
dressings (see Salad Dressings
   in this section)

Nutritious Hint:
When thinning young tender plants
in the vegetable garden, bring them
in to toss into your salad. All of the
"greens" family, young beets, young
corn stalks, etc., may be used.

Kathy Siddons   *Donita Tompkins*   *Marcie Chancey Jones*   *Sylvia Carruth*
Manchester, Connecticut   *Fayetteville, Arizona*   *Snellville, Georgia*   *Wilmore, Kentucky*

CALICO COTTAGE CHEESE SALAD

2 C. **cottage cheese**

Any combination of the
   following to total 4 C.:
peas
chopped **celery**
minced **onion**
sliced **carrots**
chopped **cucumber**
chopped **chives**
chopped **tomato**
chopped **broccoli**
chopped **nuts**
sunflower seeds

Combine ingredients of your choice
and add to cottage cheese. Mix well.
   Serve this on a bed of **lettuce** with
whole grain bread for lunch, or with
a hearty soup or stew for a cold
weather treat.

Sharon Kuhnau
Selah, Washington

LAYERED SALAD

1 head **lettuce**, shredded
2 red or green **peppers**, chopped
1 C. sliced **celery**
1 C. chopped red or green **onion**
2 C. **peas**, fresh or frozen

Optional:
1 C. cooked **garbanzos** or
  other beans
1 C. sliced, fresh **mushrooms**
4 to 6 hard-cooked **eggs**, sliced
1 to 2 **tomatoes**, sliced
½ C. sliced **water chestnuts**
1 C. sliced **black olives**
½ C. **sunflower seeds**
  or chopped nuts

Dressing:
3 C. **yogurt-mayo dressing** (p. 48)

Toppings:
½ C. grated **cheese** (Parmesan or
  Cheddar)
1 T. **wheat germ**

Layer salad vegetables and any optionals in deep bowl or oblong pan.
Spread dressing completely over
top of salad. Sprinkle with toppings.
Cover and refrigerate for 4 to 24
hours. *PROTEIN: 78.8 grams; CALORIES: 2573*

Dale Blumen   *Chrisanne Forsythe*
Newport, Rhode Island *Sandwich, Illinois*

Tess' Glory Day Salad. Add 1 head **cauliflower** and 1 bunch **broccoli**, both
in florets, to salad. Thoughtful neighbors brought this salad to the house
after my godmother's funeral. I named it for her. *Polly M. Denton*
Eden Prairie, Minnesota

GAZPACHO SALAD

2 **cucumbers**, sliced or diced
½ t. **salt**
12 to 15 **mushrooms**, sliced
4 **green onions**, sliced
½ C. chopped, fresh **parsley**
5 **tomatoes**, diced
1 **green pepper**, chopped

Optional:
½ lb. Swiss **cheese**, grated
2 to 4 hard-cooked **eggs**, sliced
1 C. **ham** or meat strips

1 C. **basic vinaigrette dressing**
  (p. 46) with 1 t. **basil**

Layer all ingredients (in a glass bowl
if possible, for a lovely visual effect).
Pour dressing over. Chill 4 hours or
longer.

PROTEIN: 21.9 grams; CALORIES: 1077

Connie Kaiser   *Jane O'Loughlin*
Pocatello, Idaho   *Alexandria, Virginia*

ORIENTAL BROCCOLI SALAD

2 lbs. fresh **broccoli** florets
½ lb. **mushrooms**, sliced
2 C. **mung bean sprouts**

Dressing:
⅓ C. **oil**
⅓ C. **vinegar**
2 t. **catsup** (p. 252)
½ t. **salt** (or less)

Steam broccoli for 2 minutes. Mix with mushrooms and sprouts. Pour
dressing over salad. Refrigerate until cold. *PROTEIN: 24.5 grams; CALORIES: 903*

Cindy Horne
Great Falls, Montana

ORANGE ROMAINE SALAD

1 head romaine **lettuce**
2 **oranges**, peeled
a few rings of purple **onion**

Dressing:
¼ C. **oil**
2 T. **orange juice**
2 t. **vinegar**
pinch of dry **mustard**
¼ t. **salt**

Tear romaine into bite-sized pieces. Section oranges. Toss romaine, oranges and onion. Mix dressing ingredients and pour over salad, tossing well. Chill in refrigerator for several hours to blend flavors. This is a colorful salad that dresses up any meal. PROTEIN: 12.7 grams; CALORIES: 793

Margaret MacPherson
Hudson, Massachusetts

WILTED SALAD

1 lb. fresh **dandelion greens**, spinach or mixed lettuce
1 to 2 **onions**, chopped
2 to 3 T. **oil**
½ t. **salt** (or less)
2 to 3 T. **seeds** (sesame or sunflower

Optional:
1 C. sliced **radishes**
1 large **tomato**, diced

Gather dandelion greens early in spring before they bloom. Clean greens well. Place in bowl (with radishes and tomatoes, if desired). Cook onion in oil over low heat until very brown. Add salt and seeds, stirring until hot. Pour over salad. Serve immediately. PROTEIN: 17 grams; CALORIES: 591

Carol Tag   *Karima Khatib*
Springfield, Missouri   *Paris, France*

KOREAN SPINACH SALAD

1 lb. fresh **spinach**, torn
4 hard-cooked **eggs**, sliced
2 C. **bean sprouts**
¾ C. sliced **water chestnuts**
½ lb. nitrite-free **bacon**, cooked and crumbled

Optional:
½ C. chopped **green onion**
1 medium **tomato**, chopped
¾ C. **croutons**
2 T. diced **red bell pepper**
3 oz. Cheddar **cheese**, grated
1 T. **seeds** (sunflower or sesame)
1 tart **apple**, chopped
1 to 2 **oranges**, chopped

Dressing:
⅓ C. **catsup** (p. 252)
1½ t. **worcestershire sauce**
2 to 4 T. **honey**
½ C. **oil**
2 T. **vinegar**
½ t. **salt** (or less)

Mix washed spinach with rest of salad ingredients and any optionals you wish. Just before serving, toss mixed dressing into salad. PROTEIN: 87.7 grams; CALORIES: 4609

Barb Staffeldt
Plainfield, Illinois

Linda Desmarais   *Wendy Marks*
Chicopee, Massachusetts   *Canoga Park, California*

SUSAN'S COLE SLAW

1 head **cabbage**, shredded
1 **carrot**, grated
1 to 2 **apples**, chopped
½ C. chopped **dates** or raisins
2 to 3 T. **sunflower seeds**

Optional:
½ C. chopped **celery**
½ C. chopped **green pepper**
½ C. unsweetened, crushed **pineapple**
½ C. grated Cheddar **cheese**
½ C. chopped **nuts**
1 to 2 **oranges**, chopped
½ to 1 C. unsweetened, shredded **coconut**

Dressing:
yogurt-mayo dressing (p. 48)
without herbs, *or*
4 T. honey
3 T. wine or cider vinegar
2 T. oil

Toss all salad ingredients. Mix in dressing. Chill.

To make a clown face for children, top with shredded carrot hair, raisin eyes, apple peel nose and apple slice mouth.

PROTEIN: 26.5 grams; CALORIES: 1048

Susan Mansfield   *Pat Zee*   *Marcia Hahn*
Vincentown, New Jersey   *Glassboro, New Jersey*   *Hesston, Kansas*

TUNA-MACARONI SLAW

¾ C. (4 oz.) uncooked **macaroni**
15 oz. **tuna**, rinsed and drained
3 C. finely grated **cabbage**
½ C. chopped **celery**
1 C. sliced **carrots**
1 **bell pepper**, diced
1 medium **onion**, finely sliced
½ C. (4 oz.) grated Cheddar **cheese**
1 C. **Italian dressing** (p. 46)
3 T. **mayonnaise** (p. 48) (optional)
4 **green olives**, sliced (optional)

Cook macaroni. Rinse in cold water and drain. Mix with tuna, vegetables and cheese in a large bowl. Pour dressing over salad. Toss well. Refrigerate ½ hour. May serve as is or add mayonnaise and toss well. Garnish with olives, if desired.

Whether served as a salad or main course, it's always a hit at a picnic or LLL dinner.

PROTEIN: 173.3 grams; : CALORIES: 3267

Michele Nicosia
Warrensburg, Missouri

SUMMER SALAD
(For Anytime)

½ lb. whole wheat **pasta**, cooked and drained
½ C. chopped **celery**
2 to 4 T. chopped **onion**
2 C. or more of any of the following:
carrots, cabbage, cheese, green peppers, cucumbers, hard-cooked **eggs, tuna, sprouts,** etc., in chunks or sliced

Dressing:
yogurt-mayo dressing (p. 48)
½ C. **cottage cheese**

Combine salad ingredients. Toss dressing in lightly. Chill.

This is a good salad to make on a hot morning and refrigerate until dinner time. It's attractive and versatile.

PROTEIN: 58.9 grams; CALORIES: 1295

Linda Gagne   *Casey Goldblat*   *Cherie Wolfe Parsons*
Rockwood, Michigan   *Fords, New York*   *Morgan Hill, California*

CUCUMBER SALAD

3 **cucumbers,** peeled and chopped
2 **tomatoes,** chopped
1 C. diced Swiss **cheese**
1 C. diced **ham**
¼ C. chopped **onion**

Dressing:
 ½ C. Italian dressing (p. 46)
 ¼ C. **milk**
 2 T. **honey**
 1 C. **mayonnaise** (p. 48)

Topping:
1 T. grated Parmesan **cheese**

Mix salad ingredients. Blend dressing ingredients until smooth, and combine with salad. Sprinkle grated Parmesan cheese over the top.

PROTEIN: 79.1 grams; CALORIES: 3287

Janet Glover
Russiaville, Indiana

POTATO SALAD

6 medium **potatoes,** boiled
¼ C. minced mild **onion**
1 C. **cottage cheese**
¼ C. chopped **chives**
¼ C. **mayonnaise** (p. 48)
⅓ C. plain **yogurt**
1 t. **salt** or less
freshly ground **pepper**
ground **cayenne pepper**

Slice potatoes thinly. Put ⅓ of the potatoes in a bowl and cover with ⅓ of each of the other items. Repeat twice. Cover and refrigerate for 12 to 24 hours. When ready to serve, toss well.

Refrigeration allows the flavors to blend and results in a delicious, unusual potato salad. *P.: 48.8 gms.; C.: 1174*

Karen Lakamp
Beardstown, Illinois

VEGGIE-POTATO SALAD

5 medium **potatoes,** cooked
4 hard-cooked **eggs**
¼ C. **mayonnaise** (p. 48)
¼ C. plain **yogurt**
½ t. **salt** (or less)
1 T. **celery seed**
1 T. **paprika**
1 T. chopped **chives**
2 T. chopped, fresh **parsley**

2 C. **vegetables** (any combination of the following):
 chopped fresh **spinach**
 chopped **sweet** or **dill pickle**
 sliced **green olives**
 chopped raw **zucchini**
 chopped **celery**
 chopped **alfalfa sprouts**
 chopped **green onion**
 chopped **cucumber**

Dice potatoes and eggs, and mix together. Add mayonnaise, yogurt, seasonings and your choice of vegetables. The raw things give this salad a special crispness. Kids will love it if you make a face on top with egg slice eyes, pimento mouth and a pickle nose.

P.: 45 gms.; C.: 1266 + vegetables

Jackie Diachun
Lexington, Kentucky

ALTERNATIVES TO GREEN SALAD
(For Days When You're Too Busy To Wash Greens)

With one of those marvelous machines which reduce vegetables to small dimensions at the turn of a crank or the push of a button, you can serve:

finely grated **carrots**, with **vinaigrette dressing** (p. 46).

green pepper strips, dressed with half **yogurt**, half **mayonnaise.**

chopped **celery**, dressed with **vinaigrette** with 1 T. **Dijon mustard** stirred in.

coarsely grated **beets**, dressed with **yogurt-mayo**. This turns a warm pink color, and is delicious.

cole slaw (red or green cabbage) with **vinaigrette, yogurt-mayo** or **vinegar-mayo.**

sliced **cucumbers** with **vinaigrette** or **yogurt-mayo.**

Many of these salads improve with keeping, so they can be made early in the day and spend time in the refrigerator until dinner.

Chris Mulford
Swarthmore, Pennsylvania

SUMMERTIME SALAD

2 **cucumbers**
¼ to ¾ C. chopped **onion**
3 large **tomatoes**
½ t. **salt** (or less)

Peel half the skin from the cucumbers. Dice all the vegetables. Add salt to taste and mix.

This is great when the garden is in season. No need for any dressing!

PROTEIN: 9.4 grams; CALORIES: 180   *Barb Littlejohn*
Storm Lake, Iowa

DADDY'S FAVORITE SALAD

2 **cucumbers**, peeled,
   thinly sliced
3 or 4 **green onions**,
   finely chopped
½ t. **salt** (or less)
1 C. plain **yogurt**

Mix vegetables and salt lightly. Cover and refrigerate 1 to 2 hours to blend flavors. Stir in yogurt and serve.

This is an old German favorite.

PROTEIN: 14.5 grams; CALORIES: 202

Cheryl Brungardt
Denver, Colorado

BEAN SALAD

2 C. mixed cooked **beans** (pinto,
  garbanzo, red, soy, etc.)
2 C. sliced **wax, green** and/or
  broad beans
1 C. **bean sprouts**
1 C. chopped **green pepper**
2 stalks **celery**, chopped
1 mild **onion**, chopped

Optional:
2 C. chopped **broccoli** or
  cauliflower, blanched
2 **carrots**, sliced
2 hard-cooked **eggs**, sliced
  PROTEIN: 121.3 grams; CALORIES: 1836 + dressing

basic vinaigrette dressing (p. 46).

Steam wax, green and/or broad beans until tender-crisp. Mix with other salad ingredients. Pour dressing over salad. Refrigerate. Will keep for up to 2 weeks.

Dorell Miekle   *Rindalee M. Skimina*   *Holly Raymond*   *Elsie J. England*
Powell River, B.C., Canada *Highland, Indiana*   *Rotorua, New Zealand* *Oklahoma City, Oklahoma*

BUDGET BEAN SALAD

3 to 4 C. cooked **kidney beans**
2 C. **peas**, slightly cooked
2 stalks **celery**, sliced
1 large **dill pickle**, chopped
3 or 4 hard-cooked **eggs**, chopped
½ t. or less **salt**
dash of **pepper**

PROTEIN: 95.8 grams; CALORIES: 1569

Optional:
6½ oz. **tuna**
1 C. **cheese**, Cheddar or Swiss,
  cubed
wheat germ as topping

Dressing:
2 to 3 T. **mayonnaise**
2 to 3 T. plain **yogurt**
1 t. **dill weed** or dry mustard

Stir salad ingredients together. Mix in dressing. Chill.

Carolyn S. Graves   *Cindy Butler*   *Catherine Meany*
Rantoul, Illinois   *Ottawa, Ont., Canada*   *Downers Grove, Illinois*

PEAS AND CHEESE SALAD

2 hard-cooked **eggs**, chopped
2 C. cooked **peas**
1 C. diced Cheddar **cheese**
1 C. diced **celery**
2 T. diced **pickle**
1 T. chopped **onion**
¼ C. plain **yogurt**
¼ C. **mayonnaise** (p. 48).

Combine all ingredients. Serve chilled.
  Easy to make, this salad is high in in protein.

PROTEIN: 89.7 grams; CALORIES: 1732

Nancy Hart   *Chere Kane*   *Le Anne Fay*   *Linda Triplett*
Libertyville, Illinois *Valparaiso, Nebraska* *Birch Run, Michigan*   *Schenectady, New York*

SPROUT SALAD

3 C. **alfalfa sprouts**
2 **carrots**, thinly sliced
1 medium **onion**, chopped
1 stalk **celery**, sliced
basic vinaigrette dressing (p. 46)

Toss all ingredients with vinaigrette dressing. Serve immediately. Fast and delicious!

PROTEIN: 9.9 grams; CALORIES: 188 + dressing

Barbara Bahun
New Carlisle, Ohio

COLD SALAMI SALAD

½ head **lettuce**, torn
8 oz. mixed, cooked **vegetables**
1 **tomato**, cut in wedges
8 oz. cooked **garbanzo beans** (chick peas), drained
thinly sliced **salami**, cut up (p. 243)
black olives
marinated artichokes, cut up (optional)

basic vinaigrette dressing (p. 46)

Vary amounts of ingredients according to your taste. Combine all ingredients and toss with dressing.

For variety, try raw vegetables and other meats, such as cold **chicken, turkey, beef** or cooked **shrimp.**

Patti Fox
Greeley, Colorado

TACO SALAD

1 lb. ground **beef**
½ C. finely chopped **onion**
1 t. **chili powder**
¼ t. **salt**
½ t. **garlic powder**
¼ t. **basil**
½ C. **tomato paste**
1 C. **water**
2 C. cooked **kidney beans** (optional)
½ lb. **cheese**, grated
8 **taco shells**, crushed or corn chips

Salad Ingredients:
lettuce, cucumbers, tomatoes, green peppers, carrots, black olives, cauliflower, avocado

Brown meat and onion; drain. Add seasonings. Stir in tomato paste and water. Simmer until liquid has been absorbed. Add kidney beans, if desired. Chill.

Make salad with ingredients desired. At serving time, add chilled meat, grated cheese and crushed taco shells. Serve with your family's favorite dressing. A great picnic meal. Pack makings in individual plastic bags in refrigerated cooler and combine in a larger bag just before serving.

PROTEIN: 128.7 grams; CALORIES: 2695 + salad

Many LLL Contributors

HOT OR COLD SPINACH SALAD

6½ to 13 oz. **tuna** or salmon
1 lb. fresh **spinach**, shredded
  or frozen, thawed
½ C. **mayonnaise** (p.48)
½ C. **buttermilk**
4 **eggs**, beaten
¾ C. grated Parmesan **cheese**
½ C. whole wheat **bread crumbs**
½ t. **garlic powder**
½ T. **celery seeds** (optional)
¼ t. **pepper**
½ C. **sesame seeds**

Optional:
sliced **mushrooms; olives;
sunflower seeds; sprouts;**
other **spices**

Mix mayonnaise, buttermilk, eggs, ½ C. Parmesan cheese and bread crumbs. Add seasonings. Stir in tuna, spinach and sesame seeds. Pour into a greased 9 x 9" pan. Top with remaining Parmesan cheese. Bake at 350° for 35 minutes.

May be served hot for a custardy, aromatic main dish, or cold for a yummy salad. Be prepared for lots of recipe requests. I feel good about serving healthful foods that are quick to fix and make good leftovers or snacks.

PROTEIN: 143.2 grams; CALORIES: 2576

*Arla Ford
Creston, Iowa*

HERBIE
(A Green Salad with Marinated Vegetables and Seafood)

1 C. (6½ oz.) cooked **shrimp,**
  drained
1 lb. **green beans**
1 medium **zucchini,** sliced
2 stalks **celery,** chopped
2 **scallions,** chopped
2 hard-cooked **eggs,** chopped

Dressing:
⅓ C. white wine **vinegar**
⅔ C. olive **oil**
1 clove **garlic,** minced
½ t. **tarragon**

½ head *each* Romaine and
  Boston **lettuce**
½ C. **alfalfa sprouts**
chopped, fresh **parsley**

Cook green beans until just tender, 8 to 10 minutes. Drain, cool with cold water, pat dry. Cook zucchini 2 to 4 minutes. It should still be crunchy. Drain and dry. Mix vegetables with shrimp. Mix dressing ingredients in a jar; shake well. Toss vegetable mixture with ½ C. of the dressing. Add eggs; toss again. Chill 1 to 2 hours. Line a salad bowl with lettuce and sprouts. Add vegetable mixture, sprinkle with parsley. Add more dressing. Toss.

This is an example of creative salad-making which appeals to everyone in our family. We often build a meal around it. It makes a great dish to take to a buffet dinner.

PROTEIN: 74.3 grams; CALORIES: 1931

*Caroline Seligman
De Kalb, Illinois*

ANGELICA'S GERMAN RICE SALAD

6½ oz. **tuna** or bonita, drained
1 medium **onion**, chopped
3 hard-cooked **eggs**, chopped
1 large **dill pickle**, chopped
1 large **bell pepper**, chopped
1 to 3 T. **oil**
1 to 2 T. **vinegar**
2 C. cooked **brown rice**
3 large **tomatoes**, chopped

Have all ingredients cold. Mix tuna with onion, eggs, pickle and pepper. Add oil and vinegar; toss. Add rice. Add more oil and vinegar if desired. Add tomatoes. Chill well. If you wish, garnish with **tomato, lemon** wedges and **parsley.**

This makes a good hot weather supper with hard **rolls** or **breadsticks** and a light dessert. Recipe is courtesy of a lovely young woman from West Berlin.

P.: 92.2 gms.; C.: 1173

Sue La Leike
Cape Coral, Florida

CELESTIAL CHICKEN SALAD

4 C. cooked, diced **chicken**
1½ C. chopped **celery**
½ t. **salt** (or less)
1 T. **lemon juice**
1 C. **mayonnaise** (p. 48)
  or yogurt
½ C. unsweetened **pineapple** chunks, drained
1 C. **mandarin oranges**
½ lb. **grapes**
½ C. chopped **nuts**
1 C. **yogurt** or sour cream

Combine chicken, celery, salt, lemon juice and mayonnaise; chill overnight. The next day, combine fruit, nuts and sour cream. Add to chicken mixture and toss. Chill 4 hours before serving. Good with **turkey,** too.

PROTEIN: 53.2 grams; CALORIES: 3248

Terry Dollar
Gibson City, Illinois

CRUNCHY CHICKEN SALAD

2 C. cooked, diced **chicken**
2 C. cooked **brown rice,** cooled
½ C. chopped **green onion**
¼ C. **oil**
¼ C. wine **vinegar**
½ C. chopped **celery**
¾ C. **mayonnaise** (p. 48)
6 oz. unsweetened **pineapple,** diced or crushed, drained
½ t. **salt**
dash of **pepper**

The night before, mix rice, onion, oil and vinegar. Chill overnight. Prepare remaining ingredients and refrigerate. Next day, combine ingredients. For more crunch, try adding chopped **pecans** or **walnuts,** chopped **apple,** sliced **water chestnuts** or chopped **green pepper.** Add mayonnaise as needed. Chill at least 2 hours. You may chop, dice and measure while the children are asleep and combine when they are awake. A nice change of pace for leftovers. Try it with **turkey** or **ham.**

PROTEIN: 133.2 grams; CALORIES: 2217

Kris Berg
La Habra Heights, California

CREAM PUFF MINIATURES FOR CHICKEN SALAD

½ C. **butter**
1 C. **water**
1 C. whole wheat pastry **flour**
4 **eggs**

Combine butter and water in large saucepan; bring to boil. Reduce heat. Add flour; stir vigorously until mixture forms a ball. Remove from heat. Add eggs, one at a time, beating until smooth after each. Drop by level tablespoonfuls on ungreased cookie sheets. Bake at 400° for 20 minutes or until puffy and golden. Cool, away from drafts. Cut tops off. Fill with your favorite chicken, turkey or tuna salad. Also good for dessert filled with pudding or fruits. Replace tops. Good for snacks, lunch or company. Freeze unfilled.

PROTEIN: 41.6 grams; CALORIES: 1576

BASIC CHICKEN SALAD

2 C. finely chopped cooked
  chicken
½ C. finely chopped **celery**
½ t. **onion salt**
dash **garlic powder**
dash of **pepper**
⅓ C. **mayonnaise** (p. 48)
2 to 4 hard-cooked **eggs**, chopped
  (optional)

Combine all ingredients. Refrigerate until ready to use. Fill **cream puffs** just before serving.

PROTEIN:135.4 grams; CALORIES: 1465

Barbara H. Wenzel
Oklahoma City, Oklahoma

RICE SALAD

3 C. cooked **brown rice**
½ C. sliced **celery**
¼ C. chopped **onion**
¼ C. chopped, fresh **parsley**

Optional:
2 to 3 C. chopped **vegetables**
  (carrots, peppers, peas,
  zucchini, etc.)
½ to 1 C. cubed, cooked **poultry,**
  fish or meat
½ C. **nuts** and/or **seeds**

Dressing:
I. ½ to ¾ C. **basic vinaigrette
   dressing** (p. 46), *or*
II. ½ to ¾ C. **yogurt-mayo
   dressing** (p. 48)

Combine salad ingredients along with any optionals you wish. Mix Dressing I or II; pour over salad. Stir and chill. Garnish with **tomato** wedges and **parsley**, if desired. Use your imagination and create a new salad each time!

Dressing I.—PROTEIN: 14.3 grams, CALORIES: 939
Dressing II—PROTEIN: 19, CALORIES: 894

Michele Nicosia   Patricia Macchiarolo   Sue Bunting   Jenny Ryburn
Warrensburg, Missouri Bedford, Pennsylvania Lake Villa, Illinois Salisbury, North Carolina

TABOULI
(Middle Eastern Salad)

½ to 1 C. **bulgur**
2 to 4 C. **water** to cover
1 to 2 C. chopped fresh **parsley**
⅓ C. chopped **onion**
  or scallions
1 to 3 **tomatoes**, cut up
1 medium **cucumber**, chopped

Optional:
1 C. chopped fresh **mint**
1 C. sliced **mushrooms**
1 **green pepper**, diced
2 to 3 **radishes**, sliced
½ C. **bean sprouts**
2 hard-cooked **eggs**, sliced

Dressing:
½ C. fresh **lemon juice**
  or lime juice
¼ C. **olive oil**
½ t. **salt** or garlic salt,
  or less
dash of **pepper**
1 T. fresh **dill weed** (1 t. dried)
  or 1 T. oregano (optional)

lettuce
pita bread
Feta **cheese** chunks

Soak bulgur in water until soft. Drain. Chop vegetables finely; stir into bulgur. Combine dressing ingredients; stir into salad. Chill. Serve on lettuce or in pita bread. Garnish with Feta cheese, if desired.
  A Syrian friend shared this recipe.   *PROTEIN: 37.9 grams; CALORIES: 1347 + pita*

Maureen Curry   *Marilynn Berry*
Kutztown, Pennsylvania   *Lawrenceville, Georgia*

CURRIED RICE SALAD

3 C. cooked **brown rice**
1 C. chopped **apple**
½ C. **raisins**
¼ C. chopped **onion** (optional)
2 **bananas**, sliced
½ C. sliced **almonds**

Dressing:
½ C. **mayonnaise** (p. 48)
1 t. to 1 T. **curry powder**

Combine salad ingredients, reserving half a banana. Mix mayonnaise and curry. Stir into salad. Garnish with reserved banana slices. Chill.

PROTEIN: 34.1 grams; CALORIES: 2381

Beverly Rodgerson
Hyattsville, Maryland

Quiches & Pies

CLASSIC QUICHE

4 to 8 slices **bacon,** cooked and
   crumbled (optional)
2 or 3 T. chopped **onion** or chives
½ to 1 C. steamed **vegetables,**
   well drained (broccoli,
   cauliflower, spinach) or
   sliced sauteed mushrooms
1 C. grated **cheese** (Swiss,
   Cheddar or Monterey Jack)
4 **eggs**
1 C. **milk** or cream
dash of **salt**
dash of **pepper**
dash of ground **nutmeg** or mace
2 T. grated Parmesan **cheese**
9 or 10" **pie shell** (p. 266)

Lightly butter bottom of the crust.
Sprinkle bacon, onion, vegetables
and cheese into pie shell. Combine
eggs and milk until well blended.
Add seasonings. Pour egg mixture
over ingredients in pie shell. Sprinkle with Parmesan cheese. Bake at
350° for 35 minutes or until knife inserted in center comes out clean.
Cool 10 minutes before serving.

Variation: Substitute for bacon, ½
to 1 C. cooked **ham** or **chicken** cut
into small pieces.

PROTEIN: 94.1 grams; CALORIES: 2059

Dolly Brown
Fairfax, Virginia

Mary Jo Johnson
Shavertown, Pennsylvania

Anne Barnes
Toronto, Ont., Canada

Barb Searing
Spencer, Ohio

TOFU QUICHE

1 C. sliced **mushrooms**
2 **onions,** sliced
1 clove **garlic,** minced
¼ C. **oil**
1 lb. fresh **spinach,** steamed,
   chopped and drained (10 oz.
   frozen, thawed and drained)
1 t. **molasses** (optional)
¼ C. tamari **soy sauce**
1 lb. **tofu**
½ to 1 C. grated hard **cheese**
¼ C. **oil**
1 T. **sesame** seeds
2 T. grated Parmesan **cheese**
1 T. **wheat germ**

9" **pie shell** (p. 266)

Saute mushrooms, onions and garlic in ¼ C. oil. Stir in molasses, if
desired, and soy sauce. Simmer for
10 to 15 minutes. Whip tofu and ¼
C. oil in blender. Fold into mushroom mixture. Add hard cheese and
spinach. Pour into a partially baked
pie crust. Sprinkle on sesame seeds,
Parmesan cheese and wheat germ.
Bake at 350° for about 30 minutes,
until set. Let stand for 10 minutes
before serving.

PROTEIN: 107 grams; CALORIES: 2395

Lois Lake Raabe
Easton, Connecticut

TOFU-CHEESE-EGG QUICHE

1 lb. **tofu**
½ **onion,** thinly sliced
4 or 5 **mushrooms,** thinly sliced
1 T. **oil**
¼ C. **wheat germ** or 10" pie shell
2 T. **sesame seeds**
1 **tomato,** thinly sliced
1 C. **cottage cheese**
2 large **eggs**
2 T. whole wheat **flour**
¼ to ½ C. grated hard **cheese**

Saute onion and mushrooms in oil. Drain on paper towel. Lightly grease pie plate. Sprinkle with wheat germ to cover, or use pie shell. Sprinkle on sesame seeds. Spread onion-mushroom mixture over seeds; top with half the tomato slices. Blend tofu, cottage cheese, eggs and flour. Add hard cheese, reserving some for topping. Pour into pan and arrange remaining tomato slices on top. Sprinkle with reserved cheese. Bake at 350° for 30 to 40 minutes.

PROTEIN: 105.6 grams; CALORIES: 1322

Jane Friedland
Washingtonville, New York

QUICHE CRUSTS

Rice Crust:
1½ C. cooked **brown rice**
2 T. **butter,** softened
2 T. chopped **onion**
¼ t. **basil**
1 **egg,** slightly beaten

Combine ingredients. Press into bottom and sides of greased 9" pie plate. Use any quiche filling. Tuna tastes especially good in this crust.

PROTEIN: 12.5 grams CALORIES: 570

Kay Kunkel
Faribault, Minnesota

Fried Potato Nest:
3 C. grated, raw **potatoes**
3 T. **oil** or melted butter

Toss ingredients. Press into bottom and sides of 9" pie plate. Bake 15 minutes at 450° or until golden. Pour in any quiche filling. Ham is particularly tasty with this crust.

PROTEIN: 9.6 grams; CALORIES: 714

Claudia Kiko
Canton, Ohio

Whole Wheat Bread Crust:
2 or 3 slices of **bread,** in
    crumbs

Press crumbs into bottom and sides of 9" pie plate. Use with creamy filling, such as Classic Quiche.

PROTEIN: 5.2 grams; CALORIES: 134

Mary Jo Johnson
Shavertown, Pennsylvania

Whole Wheat Cheese Crust:
1 C. whole wheat **flour**
⅔ C. grated, sharp Cheddar
    cheese
¼ C. chopped **almonds** (optional)
½ t. **salt**
¼ t. **paprika**
6 T. **oil**

Combine dry ingredients. Stir in oil until dough begins to stick together. Set aside ½ C. of the dough. Press remaining crust into bottom and sides of 9" pan. Bake at 400° for 10 minutes. Remove from oven. Pour in quiche filling. Sprinkle reserved crust on top.

PROTEIN: 41.7 grams; CALORIES: 1661

Jean S. Toole
Anderson, South Carolina

EGGPLANT PIE

1½-lb. **eggplant**, peeled and
sliced ½" thick
2 **tomatoes**, sliced
1 **green pepper**, sliced into rings
1 **onion**, sliced
1 C. sliced **mushrooms** (optional)
1 medium **zucchini**, sliced
(optional)
2 T. **oil**
1 T. wine **vinegar**
1 clove **garlic**, minced
½ t. **salt** (or less)
dash of **pepper**
1 t. *each* **basil** and **oregano**
4 slices Provolone **cheese**
½ C. shredded Mozzarella **cheese**

Broil eggplant 8 minutes on one side
only. Arrange slices, broiled side
down, overlapping sides and bottom
of a 10" pie pan. Arrange tomato,
pepper and onion (also mushrooms
and zucchini, if used) in alternating
layers on top. Sprinkle with oil, vinegar, garlic, salt, pepper, basil and
oregano. Bake at 375° for 25 minutes. Top with cheeses and bake 15
minutes more.

PROTEIN: 61 grams; CALORIES: 1146

Lois Lake Raabe
Easton, Connecticut

TOMATO TOFU PIE

1 medium **onion**, chopped
2 T. **oil**
1 C. **spaghetti sauce** (p. 199)
½ t. **salt** (or less)
dash of **pepper**
1 lb. **tofu**, chopped in
small pieces
6 oz. grated Muenster **cheese**
2 T. chopped fresh **parsley**
9" **pie crust** (p. 266) (optional)

Saute onion in oil. Add sauce, salt
and pepper, and stir 5 minutes. Remove from heat and add tofu and
most of the cheese (save some for
top). Stir together and pour into a 9"
round baking dish or whole wheat
pie crust. Top with remaining
cheese. Sprinkle with parsley. Bake
at 350° for 20 to 30 minutes.

PROTEIN: 101.1 grams; CALORIES: 2257

Without the crust, this is good for
those with wheat allergies. We serve it with a salad for a light dinner.

PROTEIN: 85.1 grams; CALORIES: 1361

Linda Hyatt
Oakton, Virginia

MAGIC QUICHE

1 C. grated Swiss **cheese** or
other hard cheese
4 or 5 **eggs**
2 C. **milk** or cream
½ C. whole wheat flour or
LLL Baking Mix (p. 123)
dash of **salt**
dash of **pepper**
butter for greasing pie plate

Optional:
12 slices nitrite-free **bacon**,
diced, fried and drained
½ to 1 C. chopped **onions**,
green peppers or mushrooms,
sauteed

Layer bacon, cheese and vegetables
in buttered 10" pie plate. Blend eggs,
milk, flour and seasonings. Pour
over other ingredients. Let sit 5 minutes. Bake at 350° about 50 minutes,
or until golden brown and a knife inserted in center comes out clean.

PROTEIN: 73.2 grams; CALORIES: 1270

Rita Lare
Akron, Ohio

VEGETABLE PIE

Crust:
½ C. **butter**
1¼ C. whole wheat **flour**
2 t. **baking powder**
½ t. **salt**
½ C. plain **yogurt**

Filling:
2 C. finely chopped **broccoli**
⅓ C. diced **onion**
1 C. grated **cheese**
2 medium **tomatoes**, sliced
⅓ C. **mayonnaise** (p. 48)
1 t. **basil**

Cut butter into flour, baking powder and salt. Add yogurt to this crumbly mixture. Pat the dough into greased 9 or 10" pie pan. Layer filling over crust in order given. Bake at 450° for 10 minutes, then at 350° for ½ hour.

PROTEIN: 71.7 grams; CALORIES: 2625

Linda Rankin
Grand Rapids, Michigan

TAMALE PIE

2 C. cooked **beans**, kidney
or other
½ C. chopped **onion**
½ C. chopped **green pepper**
1 **tomato**, diced
¼ C. diced **black olives**
(optional)
1 C. **corn** (optional)
1 clove **garlic**, minced
1 t. **cumin**
1 to 3 t. **chili powder** (p. 286)
¼ t. **oregano**
½ t. **salt** (or less)
1 C. grated sharp **cheese**
½ lb. ground **beef**, browned
(optional)
1 recipe **cornbread** (p. 125)

Simmer beans in their cooking liquid with vegetables and spices for 10 minutes. Stir in half the cheese, and the beef, if desired. Prepare cornbread batter. Pour half the batter into oiled 10" pie plate or 9 x 13" pan. Add the hot bean mixture, then remaining batter. Bake at 425° for 15 minutes. Top with rest of the cheese. Bake 10 minutes longer.

PROTEIN: 160.3 grams; CALORIES: 3286

Sandy Naylor
Ft. Eustis, Virginia

Marsha Rullman
Flagstaff, Arizona

Debbie Byrd
Little Rock, Arkansas

COUNTRY POTATO PIE

2 large **potatoes**, grated
½ t. **salt**
2 T. **butter**
1 C. grated Swiss or Cheddar **cheese**
1 medium **onion**, diced
2 **eggs**
1 C. **milk**
2 T. chopped fresh **parsley**
½ t. **salt** or less
½ t. **pepper**
1 t. **paprika**
½ t. dry **mustard**

Using 1 T. butter, grease bottom and sides of a 9" pie pan. Press in prepared potatoes to form crust. Sprinkle with cheese. Saute onion in remaining 1 T. butter and spread over cheese. Beat the rest of the ingredients together, then carefully pour over crust. Bake at 375° for 45 minutes, until crust is golden and a knife inserted in pie comes out clean. The pie slices better if it is allowed to cool 10 minutes after leaving the oven.   *P.: 60.2 gms.; C.: 1321*

Anne Murphy
Glen Rock, New Jersey

CHEESE AND POTATO PUFF PIE

1 lb. **cottage cheese**
1 small **onion**, chopped
1 small clove **garlic**, minced
2 C. mashed **potatoes**
2 **eggs**, beaten
dash of **cayenne pepper**
½ t. **salt**
dash of **pepper**
½ t. **basil**
½ C. grated **cheese**
1 T. chopped, fresh **parsley**

9" **pie shell** (p. 266)

Combine ingredients, reserving grated cheese and parsley for topping. Spoon into crust. Sprinkle with cheese and parsley. Bake at 350° about 1 hour, or until browned and firm. Let stand 10 minutes before serving.

PROTEIN: 115 grams; CALORIES: 2186

Laurie Carroll
Suttons Bay, Michigan

PIZZA PIE

1 unbaked **pie shell** (p. 266).

Filling:
1 lb. fresh **pork sausage** (p. 282)
¾ C. chopped **onion**
4 **eggs**, slightly beaten
½ C. **milk**
1 C. grated Cheddar **cheese**
dash of **pepper**
½ t. **oregano**

Topping:
1 C. **tomato sauce**
3 oz. Cheddar **cheese**, thinly sliced

In skillet, brown sausage and onion; drain well. Combine filling ingredients in bowl, adding meat and onion, and pour into pie shell. Bake at 375° for 25 minutes, until knife inserted near center comes out clean. Spread with tomato sauce; arrange cheese slices in spokes on top. Return to oven for 5 to 8 minutes to melt cheese. Cut and serve.

PROTEIN: 161.4 grams; CALORIES: 3176

Carol Stohs
St. Louis, Missouri

EASY-CHEESY HAMBURGER QUICHE

1 lb. ground **beef**
½ C. **mayonnaise** (p. 48)
½ C. **milk** (optional)
3 **eggs**
½ t. **salt**
dash of **pepper**
2½ to 3 C. grated, sharp Cheddar
  cheese
½ C. chopped **onion**
10" **pie shell**(p. 266)

Brown meat and drain. Blend mayonnaise, milk, eggs and seasonings. Add meat, cheese and onion. Pour into pie shell. Bake at 350° for 35 to 45 minutes or until knife inserted in center comes out clean. Let stand 15 minutes before serving.

Easy on the budget, but filled with protein. Serve with a green or gelatin salad.   *PROTEIN: 195.2 grams; CALORIES: 4031*

Judy Torgus
River Grove, Illinois

Shirley Tuttle
Blowing Rock, N. Carolina

Edna Barnes
Jefferson City, Missouri

CHICKEN SALAD PIE

4 poached **chicken breasts**
  (2 C. cut-up meat)
1 T. unflavored **gelatin**
1½ C. chicken **broth**
1 C. **mayonnaise** (p. 48)
1 C. **yogurt** or sour cream
1 T. **lemon juice**
a few drops of **tabasco sauce**
¾ t. **dill weed**
dash of **pepper**
  (white, if possible)
¾ C. sliced, pimento-stuffed
  olives
¼ C. sliced **almonds**
3 T. minced **green onion**
1 C. minced **celery**
¼ t. **salt**
paprika to garnish

1 10" baked **pie shell** or
  15 tart shells (3" diameter)

In saucepan, soften gelatin in broth. Heat, stirring, to dissolve. Cool. Combine mayonnaise, yogurt, lemon juice, Tabasco sauce, dill weed and pepper in large bowl. Slowly stir in gelatin broth. Fold in chicken, olives, almonds, onions and celery. Mix well. Season to taste. Chill 1 to 2 hours, until mixture mounds slightly. Stir occasionally while in refrigerator. Watch carefully, as it begins to set around edges. You do not want it to set in bowl. Turn chicken mixture into pie shell; sprinkle with paprika. Chill several hours until firm.

This was the main dish at our daughter Laird's baptism brunch. I doubled the chicken mixture and filled 30 tart shells. This will also fill three 9" pie shells. I make a whole wheat pastry with some grated Parmesan **cheese** mixed in. To complete the menu, serve herb steamed zucchini, tomatoes stuffed with brown and wild rice, and baked spiced pears for dessert.   *PROTEIN: 165.7 grams; CALORIES: 3390*

Diana Reardon
Dallas, Texas

PORK PIES

pastry dough for a 2-crust,
9" pie (p. 266)

French Canadian Tourtiere

1½ lbs. very lean ground **pork** or
mixture of pork and beef
1 medium **onion**, chopped
1 clove **garlic**, minced
½ t. **salt** (or less)
dash of **pepper**
½ C. hot **water**
¼ t. crushed **celery seeds**
1 large **potato**, grated
ground **cloves** to taste
1 small **bay leaf**

Prepare pie crust. Combine remaining ingredients in a saucepan. Cook, uncovered for 20 minutes. Cool; pour into pie shell. Place top crust over meat. Seal; prick with fork. Bake at 450° for 30 minutes until crust is brown.

At home, this pie was a traditional Christmas dish. But I find it so handy, I make it any time of the year. It freezes beautifully. Just warm in the oven. It's ideal to prepare before baby is born for a quickly made meal during the first few hectic weeks.

P.: 142.4 gms.; C.: 1466 + pastry   *Louise Atfield*
                                           Deep River, Ontario, Canada

Mimi's French Meat Pie

2 lbs. lean ground **pork**
1 **onion**, chopped
1 **apple**, grated
1 **potato**, grated
1 t. *each* **sage** and
ground **cinnamon**
½ t. **salt** (or less)
¼ C. **water**

Prepare crust. Brown pork in covered frying pan for 10 minutes. Stir often. Drain fat. Add onion and simmer 5 to 10 minutes. Add remaining ingredients. Proceed as above.

Any "extras" may be made into small pies for the children. (See Piroshki, p. 216)

P.: 187 gms.; C.: 1942 + pastry   *Betty Monnett*
                                           Elgin, Illinois

Easter Meat Pie

1½ lbs. ground **pork**
7 to 8 **eggs**, well beaten
2 C. **bread crumbs**
½ t. **salt** (or less)
dash *each* **pepper** and **sage**

Prepare crust. Mix remaining ingredients. Pour into pie shell. Cover with crust; seal edges. Prick with fork. Bake 1 hour at 350°. **Note:** Mashed potatoes may be used instead of pastry for the top. Spread over meat during last 15 minutes of baking. Sprinkle with **paprika**.

P.: 202.4 gms.; C.: 2521 + pastry   *Deborah Herr*
                                           Kingston, Ontario, Canada

MEXICAN DINNER

Crust:
½ C. whole wheat **flour**
½ t. **salt**
½ t. **baking powder**
¼ C. **shortening**
½ C. **buttermilk**, yogurt or
   sour half-and-half
1 **egg**

Filling:
1 lb. ground **beef**
2 t. **chili powder**
½ t. (or less) **tabasco sauce**
½ t. (or less) **salt**
2 C. cooked **kidney beans**
½ C. chopped **onion**
¾ C. **tomato paste**
½ C. chopped **lettuce**
½ C. chopped **tomato**
½ to 1 C. grated Cheddar **cheese**

Combine crust ingredients in a medium bowl. Stir until blended. Batter will be lumpy. Pour into greased and floured 9 or 10" pie pan. Spread batter thinly to within ¼" of the rim.

Brown beef and drain. Combine with the remaining ingredients except lettuce, tomato and cheese. Spoon into crust. Bake at 425° for 20 to 30 minutes. Cool 5 minutes. Top with lettuce, tomato and cheese.

This is similar to tacos, but easier for kids to eat. I've used the crust for quiches and souffles. It's so much quicker and easier than a rolled crust.

PROTEIN: 160.5 grams; CALORIES: 2665

Mary Atkinson
Delavan, Wisconsin

MAGIC MEAT PIE

1 lb. ground **beef**
1 medium **onion**, chopped
2 T. whole wheat **flour**
2 C. **water**
1 C. sliced **carrots**, cooked
10 oz. **peas**
1 T. **worcestershire sauce**
¼ t. **salt** (or less)
dash of **pepper**
12 unbaked **biscuits** (p. 124)

Brown meat and onion. Add flour and water. Cook until thick. Add all remaining ingredients except biscuits. Put hot mixture in a 9 x 13" pan and top with biscuits. Bake at 425° for 20 minutes, until biscuits are done.

PROTEIN: 153.4 grams; CALORIES: 2679

Arla Crosier
Yakima, Washington

POPEYE'S SURPRISE PIE

2 lbs. fresh **spinach**, steamed
   and chopped or frozen,
   thawed and drained
2 **eggs**
¾ C. **wheat germ**
½ C. cubed **cheese** (Swiss or
   white Cheddar)
3 t. **worcestershire sauce**
pinch of **garlic powder**
dash of **salt**

9" unbaked **pie shell**

Combine ingredients. Pour into pie shell. Bake at 400° for 20 to 30 minutes. This is nice with a **tomato salad.** *PROTEIN: 113.2 grams; CALORIES: 2050*

Chris Bates
Toms River, New Jersey

SHEPHERDS' PIE

6 to 8 **potatoes**
1 **carrot**, cubed
½ C. **milk**
1 **egg**, beaten
1½ lbs. ground **beef** or
   ground turkey
½ C. chopped **onion**
½ C. **wheat germ**
2 T. **nutritional yeast**
2 C. **tomato sauce**
1 C. **green beans**
1 C. **corn**
½ t. **salt**
dash of **pepper**
1 to 2 C. grated **cheese**

Cook potatoes and carrot. Mash with milk; whip in egg. Brown and drain beef and onion. Add all ingredients except potato mixture and cheese. Pour into 3-qt. casserole. Spread mashed potatoes over meat. Top with cheese. Bake at 350° for 40 minutes. May also be baked in a 9" **pastry shell.**

PROTEIN: 222.3 grams; CALORIES: 3094

Patricia Y. Gobrecht	*Jean Lafferty*
Hanover, Pennsylvania	*Indianapolis, Indiana*
RoJean Loucks	*Maureen D. Nevins*
Assaria, Kansas	*Newcomb, Maryland*

TEXAS QUICHE

4 oz. **green chilies** or
   nacho peppers
12 large **eggs**
2 lb. grated Cheddar **cheese** or
   1½ lb. Cheddar and ½ lb.
   Jalapeno cheese

Chop green chilies in blender. Add eggs. Pour into bowl and combine with grated cheese. Pour into greased 10 x 15 x 2" baking dish. Bake at 350° for 30 to 35 minutes, or until knife inserted in center comes out clean. Cool. Cut into small squares. This is great for meetings. Toddlers love the bite-sized pieces. Freeze leftovers.

PROTEIN: 306.2 grams; CALORIES: 4648   *Janice Harris*
Wharton, Texas

Variation: Omit nacho peppers, or layer them in only half the baking dish.

CHICKEN POT PIE

4 C. cooked **chicken,** turkey or
   beef, cut in small pieces
4 C. chicken **stock** (p. 30)
   or broth
1 T. fresh, chopped **parsley**
   (1½ t. dry flakes)
1 C. chopped **onion**
1 C. chopped **celery**
2 C. sliced **carrots**
1 C. diced **potato**
1 C. **green beans**
1 C. **peas**
⅓ C. **flour** (whole wheat pastry
   flour works well)
½ C. **water**
biscuit dough (p. 124)

Put stock in large pot. Add parsley, onion, celery, potato, carrots and beans. Cook until tender. Add peas. Blend flour with water; add to pot, stirring until broth thickens, about 5 minutes. Add meat to pot; turn off heat. Meat will warm while you make biscuits.

Put chicken mixture in a 2 to 3-qt. casserole, or smaller pans. Top with biscuits. Bake at 450° for 15 minutes. Reduce heat to 350° and continue baking until biscuits are done.

This is a hearty, economical and nutritious meal. It may be made early in the day and refrigerated until ready to bake. Make it fancier by using a shaped biscuit cutter. Or try using a whole wheat **pie crust** (p. 266) on the top.

PROTEIN: 235.1 grams; CALORIES: 2914

Many LLL Contributors

CHEESE SOUFFLE

1 C. medium **white sauce**
3 **egg yolks**, beaten
1 C. grated cheddar **cheese**
3 **egg whites**, stiffly beaten

Optional: any of the following
2 C. cooked **spinach**, chopped
and drained
2 C. cooked **broccoli**, chopped
and drained
1½ C. cooked **corn** with
½ C. chopped **onion**
and/or **green pepper**

Prepare white sauce. Stir in egg yolks slowly. Add cheese (and vegetable, if you wish). Mix thoroughly. Gently fold in egg whites half at a time. Scoop lightly into 1½ qt. souffle dish or casserole. Set in pan with water 1" deep. Bake at 350° for 35 to 45 minutes or until golden brown and puffed.

If you do not have a classic souffle dish, a straight-sided casserole dish will do. A souffle rises better if it can adhere to the sides of the dish. If you do butter the dish, be sure to sprinkle the inside with Parmesan cheese so the eggs can stick. Refrigeration for several hours will also help produce a puffier souffle.

No need to tiptoe around the house while the souffle bakes, but please do not open the oven door until the 35 minutes have elapsed or your souffle may collapse. Serve immediately. *PROTEIN: 58 grams; CALORIES: 1119*

Ellyn Wadyka
Somerville, New Jersey

Beth Adcock
Watervliet, New York

Cynthia Hyatt
Farmington, New Mexico

Wendy Lampert
Columbus, Ohio

EASY BROCCOLI SOUFFLE

6 **eggs**, beaten
12 oz. Cheddar **cheese**, grated
6 T. whole wheat **flour**
¼ lb. **butter**
2 C. **cottage cheese**
1 lb. **broccoli**, steamed and
chopped

Combine all ingredients in well-buttered casserole. Bake at 350° for 1 hour, or until knife inserted in center comes out clean. Cool 10 minutes before serving.

PROTEIN: 203.1 grams; CALORIES: 3051

Linda Rankin
Grand Rapids, Michigan

EASY GREEN CHILI SOUFFLE

½ lb. Cheddar **cheese**, grated
½ lb. Jack **cheese**, grated
4 oz. **green chilies**, diced
8 large **eggs**, well beaten
1 pt. (or less) **yogurt**
guacamole (p. 75) and **chili
salsa** (p. 252)

Place grated cheeses and chopped chilies in buttered 9 x 12" pan. Combine eggs with yogurt. Pour over the cheese. Bake at 350° for about 45 minutes. Allow to set for 10 minutes before serving. Top with guacamole and chili salsa, or serve them as condiments.

*PROTEIN: 140.1 grams; CALORIES: 2721 +
guacamole*

Stacy Laputz
Long Beach, California

STRATA

6 to 10 slices whole wheat **bread**
1 to 2 C. grated Cheddar **cheese**
2 to 3 C. **milk**
3 to 6 **eggs**
1 to 2 t. dry **mustard**
1 t. **paprika**
½ t. **salt**
1 t. **thyme** (optional)
2 t. **worcestershire sauce**, (optional)

Optional:
Any of the following to total 2 C.:
Cooked **chicken**, turkey, or ham, sliced or chopped
sausage or bacon, browned and drained
chopped **spinach** or broccoli, steamed and drained
sliced **mushrooms** and **onions**, sauteed

Arrange half the bread, in slices or cubes, on bottom of a greased 9 x 9" or 9 x 13" baking dish. Layer thus: half the cheese, all the meat and/or vegetables, remaining bread and remaining cheese. Beat milk, eggs, and seasonings; pour over casserole. Let stand for 1 hour (or refrigerate, covered, for up to 24 hours). Bake at 350° for 45 to 60 minutes, until a knife inserted in the center comes out clean. For a change, substitute ¼ to ½ C. dry white **wine** for an equal amount of milk.

Using more eggs and milk will yield a custardy texture, while using the smaller amount results in a "bread quiche."

Bread, cheese and egg souffles (stratas) have many virtues. They benefit from long soaking, especially whole grain or stale bread, so you can prepare them a day ahead. They use less expensive egg and milk protein with little or no meat. With the addition of vegetables, they are a complete meal. They are attractive, taste good cold or reheated and even use up stale bread.

PROTEIN: 80.7 grams; CALORIES: 1439

Mary Lord
Stone Mountain, Georgia   *Jackie Diachun*
Lexington, Kentucky   *Susan Marquess*
Dallas, Texas

CHEESE FONDUE

1 lb. Swiss **cheese**, cubed or grated
2 T. **flour**
1½ C. **apple juice**, or cider or buttermilk
dash of **salt** and **pepper**

Toss cheese with flour. Heat apple juice in large skillet or fondue pot over low heat. Gradually add cheese cubes. Stir continually until it is all melted. Serve with cubes of French bread, dipped into the melted cheese. This is terrific with apple cider in season.   *Janice Knight Hartman*
Millsboro, Delaware

PROTEIN: 125.2 GRAMS; CALORIES: 1926

CHEESE ROULADE

Roulade:
3 T. fine whole wheat **bread crumbs**
2 T. **butter**
2 T. whole wheat **flour**
1 C. **milk**
½ t. **salt**
¼ t. dry **mustard**
¼ t. **pepper**
10 medium (8 large) **eggs**, separated
½ C. grated Cheddar **cheese**
1 T. **parsley** for garnish

Filling:
8 or 10 slices nitrite-free **bacon**, chopped
½ C. chopped **green onions**
½ lb. **mushrooms**, chopped
1 T. **lemon juice**

Sauce:
6 T. **butter**
4 T. whole wheat **flour**
2½ C. **milk**
1 t. **salt**
¼ t. dry **mustard**
¼ t. **white pepper**
2½ C. grated Cheddar **cheese**

Roulade: Grease a 10 x 15" jellyroll pan (cookie sheet with edge) and line with waxed paper. Butter the paper and sprinkle with bread crumbs. In a saucepan, melt butter; stir in flour. Blend in milk with wire whisk. Bring to a boil, stirring until smooth and thick. Add seasonings. Remove from heat. Beat egg yolks and whisk into hot mixture. Return to low heat, stirring constantly. Add ¼ C. Cheddar cheese. Beat egg whites until stiff and fold into this mixture. Spread on paper in pan and bake at 350° for 15 to 20 minutes, or until firm but not tough. While this bakes, prepare filling and sauce.

Filling: Fry bacon until crisp; add and saute onions and mushrooms until just tender. Add lemon juice. Keep warm.

Sauce: Melt butter in saucepan. Stir in flour; add milk and bring to a boil, stirring until smooth and thick. Add seasonings and grated cheese. Plan to reheat before serving.

When roulade is done, invert pan on a surface sprinkled with the remaining ¼ C. cheese. Remove waxed paper. Add ½ C. of the cheese sauce to filling and spread over surface. Roll up the roulade and place on serving platter. If made ahead, wrap in aluminum foil. Allow 15 to 20 minutes for reheating. To serve, pour part of the hot cheese sauce on top; garnish with parsley. Slice and pass around the remaining sauce.

PROTEIN: 217.1 grams; CALORIES: 5343

Deborah Herr
Kingston, Ont., Canada

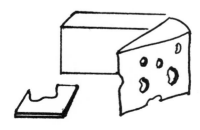

CHEESE RAREBIT

1 to 4 T. **butter**
1 T. whole wheat **flour** or
  cornstarch
¼ t. **salt**
¼ t. dry **mustard**
dash of **cayenne pepper**
pinch of **garlic powder** or ¼ t.
  ground **nutmeg**
1 C. **milk**, white wine, cider
  or beer
3 to 4 C. grated **cheese** (Swiss
  is traditional, Cheddar
  and Jack are fine)
1 loaf **sourdough** or **French
  bread**, cut in cubes
fruits and **vegetables**, cut up

Optional:
6 **English muffin** halves
6 slices of **bacon**, cooked
  and crumbled
3 to 6 hard-cooked **eggs**, cubed

*PROTEIN: 102 grams; CALORIES: 1570
+ bread, fruits & vegetables*

*Nadine Bowlus
Jackson, Mississippi*

Melt butter in saucepan. Mix flour or cornstarch and seasonings. Stir into butter. Cook until thickened, stirring constantly. Stir liquid in slowly. (The alcohol will evaporate from the wine.) Add cheese to white sauce a little at a time, stirring in a figure-eight motion. Taste frequently. When the taste suits you, transfer to fondue pot or warming tray, to keep hot while serving. Dip bread, fruit and vegetables. Try dipping in the figure-eight pattern to reduce stringiness of cheese.

Or serve by placing bread cubes and vegetables into bowls and topping with rarebit. Or pour rarebit over English muffins.

Broiled Cheese. Put any white grated cheese into individual oven-proof serving bowls. Broil until bubbly. Serve with fruits and vegetables as above.

*Carol Kriz
Boise, Idaho*

*Marilu Richins
Othello, Washington*

FLAT SALMON SOUFFLE

1 lb. **salmon**, drained and boned
1½ C. thin **white sauce** (p. 251)
4 **eggs**, beaten

Prepare white sauce in a 3-qt. baking dish. Add salmon; stir in eggs. Set dish in pan of water 1" deep. Bake, uncovered, at 375° for 45 minutes, or until center is set. This is my mom's souffle recipe. I don't seem to have time to separate eggs and beat the whites. It tastes as good this way, even if it isn't as fancy.

PROTEIN: 137.4 grams; CALORIES: 1674

*Sue Smith
Newport News, Virginia*

CREAMED EGGS

2 C. medium **white sauce** (p. 251)
1 **onion**, chopped and sauteed
6 hard-cooked **eggs**, peeled and
  halved or diced
6 slices toasted **bread**
2 T. chopped **parsley**, chives or
  green pepper (optional)
½ C. grated **cheese** (optional)

Add white sauce and cheese to sauteed onion. Add eggs and heat. Serve on toast, or English Muffins.

PROTEIN: 90.7 grams; CALORIES: 1999

*Anne Lewis-Volk
Crimora, Virginia*

Snacks

INVENT-A-DIP

1 C. **yogurt**
½ to 1 C. **cottage cheese**
½ to 1 C. **mayonnaise**
salt and **pepper** to taste
seasonings (below)

Mix basic ingredients. Add seasonings of your choice. (For a change, try using only yogurt or only cottage cheese with the seasonings.) Experiment with flavors—invent your own dip!

Seasonings:

#1: 1 t. to 1 T. **dillweed**, 1 to 2 T. minced **onion**, 1 t. **garlic powder**, dash of tamari **soy sauce** or **Worcestershire sauce**

#2: ½ C. minced **cucumber**, 2 T. minced **parsley**, 1 t. **garlic powder**, ¼ C. minced **green onion**.

#3: ½ C. grated **Cheddar cheese** or other sharp cheese, 2 T. **Parmesan cheese**, ¼ C. minced **green onion**.

#4: 1 t. to 1 T. prepared **horseradish**, 2 T. minced **onion**.

#5: 1 t. to 1 T. **curry powder**, 2 to 4 T. **sesame seeds**.

#6: 1 to 2 T. crushed **anchovy fillets**, ¼ C. **Parmesan cheese**, ¼ C. minced **green onion**, 1 t. **garlic powder**.

#7: 1 lb. fresh **spinach**, steamed, drained, and chopped (or frozen, thawed, drained, chopped), and ¼ to ½ C. minced **green onion**.

Many LLL Contributors

DRY DIP MIX

½ C. grated Parmesan **cheese**
2 T. toasted **sesame seeds**
salt and **pepper** to taste
1 t. **paprika**
1 t. **celery seed**
½ t. **garlic powder**

Combine the ingredients. Store in refrigerator. To use add 1 or 2 T. of mix to 1 cup of **yogurt** or sour cream and chill. Serve as a dip with raw **vegetables.** This keeps indefinitely and is very nice to have on hand. The children love it and will eat an amazing amount of vegetables this way! The dip mix itself makes a very good gift.   *PROTEIN: 20.1 grams; CALORIES: 288*

Maralyn Feige
Westfield, New Jersey

GUACAMOLE
(Avocado Dip)

1 ripe **avocado**
1 T. **white vinegar** or lemon juice
1 to 3 T. minced **onion**
1 small **tomato**, chopped and seeded
dash of **salt**

Avocado is ripe when it gives to light thumb pressure. Mash the avocado with the vinegar and onion. Stir in the tomato and salt. Serve with raw vegetables or tortilla chips. This is authentic Mexican dip.

PROTEIN: 6.1 grams; CALORIES: 398   *Helen Palmer*
Edgewater Park, New Jersey

BEAN DIP
("Something's Wrong with This")

4 C. cooked **beans** (pinto, red, pink or kidney)
½ C. minced **onion** (about 2 small onions)
4 oz. **green chilies** (optional)
1 to 4 T. cider **vinegar** (use larger amount if chilies are omitted)
½ t. **salt**
¼ t. **pepper**
dash of **tabasco sauce** (optional)
1 t. ground **cumin**
1 t. ground **oregano**
1 t. **garlic powder**
1 t. **chili powder** (optional)
2 C. grated **cheese** (Cheddar, Colby or Monterey Jack)

Drain freshly cooked, hot beans and toss into food processor with remaining ingredients. Process until cheese is melted and mixture is smooth. Taste, adding additional vinegar and/or seasonings, if needed. Serve hot, with **tortilla chips** .

This works well in a bean pot, heated in a 350° oven for 30 minutes. The heavy earthenware pot helps keep the dip hot longer. Also good hot or cold as sandwich or burrito filling.

Our family calls this the "Something's Wrong with This" Dip, because the first time I made it, I invited their critical comments (well developed during the testing for **Mother's In The Kitchen**). They kept dipping and tasting, saying, "Yes, something's wrong with it. It needs something, but I don't know what it is." Then suddenly they realized they had eaten *all* of it, so they decided that the only thing wrong with it was that it was all gone. It's now a family favorite.

PROTEIN: 149.3 grams; CALORIES: 2322

Roberta Bishop Johnson
Champaign, Illinois

HUMMUS
(Garbanzo Spread)

2 C. cooked **garbanzos,** drained, reserving liquid
1 clove **garlic,** minced
2 to 4 T. **tahini** (sesame butter) or peanut butter
juice of ½ **lemon,** or 1 lime (or more to taste)
paprika to taste
1 T. **oil**
tamari **soy sauce** to taste
2 T. fresh **horseradish** (optional)
⅓ C. plain **yogurt** (optional)
parsley as garnish

Mash or puree all ingredients, thinning with bean cooking liquid (or plain yogurt) as necessary. Serve with raw vegetables, whole grain crackers, or pita bread; as thick dip or sandwich-type spread.

PROTEIN: 47.4 grams; CALORIES: 942

Barbara Dick
Seattle, Washington

Mary Paget
Fairfield, Connecticut

Linda Weber Collins
Tallahassee, Florida

Alice Ziring
Mercer Island, Washington

CREAM CHEESE BALLS WITH RAISINS

8 oz. **cream cheese**
½ C. chopped **raisins**
¼ C. chopped **nuts**
¼ C. **sunflower seeds**
¼ C. toasted **wheat germ**
¼ C. dry **milk powder**
¼ C. **nutritional yeast**
(optional)

Mix ingredients together with your hands. Form into small balls. Try using wheat germ as coating instead of mixing it in, or use any of the Cheese Ball variations (p. 78).

PROTEIN: 67.8 grams; CALORIES: 1711

Carrot Granola Cheese Balls. Use grated Cheddar **cheese** in place of the cream cheese. Add 1 C. finely grated **carrot** and 1 t. **honey.** Roll in fine **granola** and chopped, fresh **parsley.** (For a very fine coating, crush granola in a plastic bag with a rolling pin or whiz in food processor.)

Rebecca Langford   Carole Miller
Old Town, Maine   Cumberland, Maryland

CANTERBURY CHEESE

10 oz. **cheese** (Cheddar or
Longhorn)
10 oz. **cheese** (Swiss or Jack)
10 to 12 stalks **celery,** chopped
⅓ C. chopped **onion** (2 T.
dried flakes)
½ lb. **butter,** at room
temperature
¼ t. **paprika**
pinch of **garlic powder**
3 T. **mayonnaise** (p. 48)

Grate or process cheeses, celery and onion. Blend in butter, paprika and garlic powder. Stir in mayonnaise, a tablespoon at a time, stirring until mixture is of a spreading consistency. Use as a sandwich filling or on crackers; or give it as a gift. Use dry onion flakes when longer storage is desired. Makes about 4 C. *P.: 153.5 gms.; C.: 3448*

Linda Miller
McPherson, Kansas

SAUSAGE BALLS

10 oz. grated Cheddar **cheese**
1 lb. bulk **sausage**
2 C. **LLL Baking Mix** (p. 123)

Melt cheese in top of double boiler. Combine all ingredients in mixing bowl. Knead with fingers until thoroughly mixed. Form into small balls about 1" in diameter. Bake on cookie sheets at 350° for 15 to 20 minutes.

You may make balls ahead of time and store in refrigerator or freezer. Also good reheated. Great for breakfast, snacks and as appetizers.

PROTEIN: 161.7 grams; CALORIES: 3929

Carol Smith
Oklahoma City, Oklahoma

CHEESE LEATHER

Cheddar is best for this, but any firm cheese will be tasty. Put a layer of small chunks or grated cheese in a non-stick pan and heat in a 300° oven until melted into a thin sheet. Remove with a fork. Pieces of this are delicious in a warm breakfast biscuit or to eat right out of your hand.

Judy Beckert
Greenville, North Carolina

CHEESE BALL

1 C. grated sharp Cheddar **cheese**
1 C. grated mild Colby **cheese**
½ C. (1½ oz.) grated Parmesan **cheese**
8 oz. **cream cheese**
1 T. **milk**
1 small clove **garlic**, crushed or ½ t. garlic powder
dash of **salt**
dash of **worcestershire sauce**
½ C. chopped **nuts** (walnuts, pecans or slivered almonds) or sesame seeds

Have all ingredients at 60° for easy mixing. Combine all ingredients except nuts. Form into ball or log and roll in nuts. (You may need to chill before forming into ball or log.) Refrigerate until used. Serve with crackers, raw vegetables or fresh fruit. These also make lovely holiday gifts. You can color the coating by adding mild paprika or chopped parsley with nuts.

PROTEIN: 98.9 grams; CALORIES: 2278

Butter-Lemon: For extra creaminess, add ¼ lb. **butter.** Add 1 T. chopped **parsley** or chives and 1 t. **lemon juice.**

PROTEIN: 99.7 grams; CALORIES: 2715

Bleu Cheese Ball. Substitute **blue cheese** for Parmesan and omit Colby cheese. Add ⅔ C. chopped ripe **olives** to mixture.   *P.: 92.2 gms.; C.: 2445*

Pineapple Crunch. Increase **cream cheese** to 1 lb. Omit other cheeses. Add 8½ oz. unsweetened, crushed **pineapple**, well drained. If you like add ¼ C. chopped **green pepper** and 2 T. chopped **onion.**   *P.: 45.4 gms.; C.: 2156*

Yogurt-Wheat Germ. Try moistening ingredients with **yogurt** or sour cream or substituting toasted **wheat germ** for half of the nuts.

P.: 105.9 gms.; C.: 2236
Many LLL Contributors

CRACKER SNACKS

whole grain crackers
cheese, grated or sliced
crumbled bacon (or leftover **sausage bits, ground beef, ham**, or **peanut butter**)

Top crackers with cheese, and sprinkle on leftover meat *or* spread crackers with peanut butter, then top with cheese.
    Broil either variation until cheese is melted.

These are great for appetizers or for helping little ones hang on until dinner's ready!

Donna Marris   *Lois Lake Raabe*
Sumter, South Carolina   *Easton, Connecticut*

JELLY SQUARES

1 C. **water**
3 T. unflavored **gelatin**
6 oz. can frozen **juice concentrate**, thawed

Measure water into 1 qt. saucepan and sprinkle gelatin on top. When it softens and swells, turn on heat to low; stir as gelatin dissolves (or heat in microwave oven for 30 seconds). Add juice concentrate, blend well. Pour into flat dish (8" square or 7" x 12") and chill until set. Cut into 1" squares and serve as finger food. These stay firm at room temperature, but store extras in refrigerator.

Apple, grape, and orange juice are good flavor choices. Fresh or bottled juice may be used in place of concentrate and water; 2 C. is the proper amount to use in that case. *PROTEIN: 53.6 grams; CALORIES: 2631*

For Easter treats, use a deviled egg tray to mold jellies.

Karen Myers
Butler, Pennsylvania

Jacki Glover
Calgary, Alberta, Canada

Linda Alico
Bothell, Washington

Donna Gleeson
Corning, New York

SUNSHINE SANDWICHES

1 C. **peanut butter**
3 oz. **cream cheese**, softened
¼ C. **orange juice concentrate**
2 T. grated **carrot**
2 T. chopped **raisins**

8 slices whole wheat **bread**

Mix ingredients together. Spread on the bread, making 4 large sandwiches. Serve with a sunshiny smile!

PROTEIN: 94.6 grams; CALORIES: 2392

Toni Schwer
Muncie, Indiana

WALDORF SANDWICHES

8 oz. **cream cheese**
1 T. **milk**
2 t. **lemon juice**
1 C. diced **apple** (1 large)
½ C. snipped **dates**
¼ C. chopped **walnuts**
buttered **alfalfa sprouts** (optional)

PROTEIN: 26.2 grams; CALORIES: 1396

Blend softened cream cheese with milk and lemon juice. Add apple, dates and nuts. This is great filling for raisin bread. Stuff celery with what's left, for an after-school treat!

Ronnie Barhite
Medina, New York

GORP
(Good Old-Fashioned Raisins and Peanuts)

1 C. of each:
  dry roasted **peanuts**
  raw **sunflower seeds**
  raisins
  chopped **dates** or other
    dried fruit
  unsweetened **coconut chips**
  carob chips
  roasted **soy nuts**
  pumpkin seeds

Mix the nuts, seeds, and fruit. Vary the ingredients according to supply and tastes.

A great trail snack—a nutritious alternative to "empty calorie" snacks. Keeps well.

PROTEIN: 151.8 grams; CALORIES: 4262

Barbara Faust   Debra Sexton
Springfield, Ohio   Bloomington, Illinois

MATTHEW'S MUNCHIES

1 C. roasted unsalted **peanuts**
1 C. **raisins**
½ C. dried **apples**, chopped
½ C. dried **apricots**, chopped

Optional:
¾ C. **carob chips**
½ C. **coconut**, flaked
½ C. roasted **soybeans**
½ C. **sunflower seeds**

Combine peanuts and dried fruits with any or all the delicious extras. Store tightly covered in cool place. Serve this to pre-schoolers who can chew thoroughly and well, in small cups—naturally sweet, nutritious, and filling. Makes a nice gift too, in a festive jar. PROTEIN: 36 grams; CALORIES: 1262

Linda Worzer
Garland, Texas

TANGY NUTS

1 to 2 C. raw **nuts** or **seeds**,
  any combination
2 T. tamari **soy sauce**
1 t. **kelp powder** (optional)

PROTEIN: 20.6 grams; CALORIES: 803

Combine sauce with kelp—if used. Pour over nuts/seeds, and stir well to coat. Let mixture stand 5 minutes, then roast at 300° for 10 minutes, stirring twice during cooking time. This makes a nutritious anytime snack.   Christina Pinkerton
Loveland, Colorado

CELERY BOATS

2 large stalks **celery**
1 medium **banana**, mashed
3 T. **peanut butter**
¾ t. **seeds** (sesame or
  sunflower)
1 to 2 t. **honey** (optional)
1 T. **raisins** and/or **almonds**

Cut celery stalks to desired lengths. Mix together banana, peanut butter, seeds and honey. Fill up "boats" (stalks) and top with raisins or almonds, or both.

PROTEIN: 14.4 grams; CALORIES: 492

Twila Jones
Rolla, Missouri

CREATIVE EATING FOR TODDLERS

Toddlers love to help—include them in your meal preparation:

- they can tear lettuce, put sliced vegetables into the salad bowl or pot
- they love to stir so when you are stirring at the stove give them a pot and spoon and let them stir at the table or on the opened dishwasher door;
- they like to pour. Measure your ingredients and have your toddler pour them into the bowl.

Give your toddler a small piece of bread dough to play with while you knead the rest.

Toddlers can put eating utensils onto the table.

Try being creative at meal times—how about a picnic under the kitchen table on a rainy day—invite a favorite stuffed animal or doll to dinner.

Toddlers do better with small frequent meals several times a day.

Use your toddler's toy dishes—little cups have less to spill and are easier to manage—it is fun to pour your own from a toy tea pot.

Keep nutritious snacks on toy plates covered with clear wrap in the fridge so your toddler can help himself.

Chicken liver cut into small pieces and put onto toy plates became chicky-treats at our house.

As your toddler becomes older, cocktail forks can be fun to eat with.

Finger foods are the mainstay of many toddlers' diets.

Celery stuffed with cream cheese or peanut butter becomes a creative experience when the toddler is given raisins for decorating.

Have a shaker with wheat germ so that your toddler can "salt" his food with that rather than salt.

Jelly squares don't have to be squares—use cookie cutters.

Cut sandwiches with cookie cutters.

Cheese on the end of a pretzel becomes a Cheese Pop.

Popsicles made with fruit juice, fruit juice mixed with yogurt, fruit juice mixed with pieces of fruit and even some vegetables are a wholesome treat.

Have fun with food. Make eating a happy, relaxed experience.

Jacki Glover
Calgary, Alberta, Canada

Food On The Move

(Or "I'm hungry and I can't wait")

For errands, trips, hiking, camping and whenever there's no time to sit down and eat. Giving a child one of these tasty and nourishing foods can help stave off hunger pangs and avoid hungry grouchiness.

Recipes in this cookbook:

Yogurt Shakes (in a thermos
    while traveling)
Cheese Leather
Crispy Cheese
Cracker Snacks
Toasty Tofu
* **Ants on a Log**
* **Celery Boats**
* **Matthew's Munchies**
* **GORP**
* **Fruit Leather**
* **Beef Jerky**
  Stuffed Vegetable Take-Along
  Frozen Banana Bites
* **Chunky Granola Bars**
  Grandma's Half-Moons
  Dandy Candy
  Goodie Balls

Also:
  Milkshakes and Slushes
* Fruit Slices with Cheese
* Raw Vegetables with Dip
  Small Pieces of Quiche
  Broiled or Grilled Cheese
    Sandwiches
  Other Sandwiches
  "Pocket Bread" filled with
    Eggs, Spreads, or Salads
  Crackers and Cheese
  Peanut Butter and Apple
  Breadsticks and Whole Wheat
    Pretzels
  Muffins, Rolls and Bagels

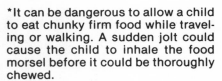

*It can be dangerous to allow a child to eat chunky firm food while traveling or walking. A sudden jolt could cause the child to inhale the food morsel before it could be thoroughly chewed.

P.S. Why not always carry a plastic bottle of water as kids can get thirsty anytime?

Drinks

MILK SHAKES

1 C. **milk**
1 C. **berries**, and/or 1 whole
  fruit, such as banana
1 **egg** (optional)
¼ C. dry **milk powder**
1 t. **vanilla**
¼ to 1 t. nutritional **yeast**
  (optional)

Blend all the ingredients together.

PROTEIN: 26.9 grams; CALORIES: 421
Many LLL Contributors

YOGURT SHAKES

1 C. **yogurt**
½ C. **milk**
½ C. **tofu** (optional)
1 **egg**
1 t. **vanilla** or almond extract
fresh or frozen **fruits** or
  juices, such as:
  1 banana
  1 C. berries
For extra protein add:
  1 to 2 t. **nutritional yeast**
  or powdered   milk

Mix all ingredients together. Be inventive, and enjoy!

PROTEIN: 35.6 grams; CALORIES: 543
Many LLL Contributors

GREEN DRINK

2 C. **pineapple juice**
½ to 1 C. fresh **mint** leaves
¼ to ½ C. fresh **parsley**
¾ to 1 C. assorted **greens**
  (sprouts, lettuce, cabbage,
  etc.; not too much of any
  strong tasting one)

Whirl ingredients in blender until finely chopped. Let stand a few minutes. Strain if you like. Serve over ice, garnished with sprig of mint.

PROTEIN: 3.4 grams; CALORIES: 292

Lois Lake Raabe
Easton, Connecticut

REGAN'S TEA

6 to 12 2" **cinnamon** sticks
1 to 2 t. whole **cloves**
1 whole **nutmeg**
8 **allspice berries**
2 C. **tea leaves**, regular or herb
4 T. grated **orange peel**, dried
4 T. grated **lemon peel**, dried

Wrap cinnamon sticks and spices in cloth and crush with a hammer (or grate in blender). Combine this blend with tea leaves and dried citrus peel. Store in airtight container. Use 1 heaping teaspoon per cup of boiling water to make tea. Sweeten with honey, as desired.

Kathy Kilduff
Randolph Center, Vermont

HOT CUP O' CAROB

3 T. **carob powder**
½ C. **milk**
1 T. **honey**
⅔ C. dry **milk powder**
1 t. **vanilla**
dash **cinnamon**
2 C. very hot **water** or **milk**

Whirl carob and ¼ cup milk in blender. Add remaining milk, honey, dry milk, vanilla, and cinnamon; blend again. Pour in the hot water, blend and serve. Fills two mugs generously. *PROTEIN: 27 grams; CALORIES: 494*

Cold Carob (Mix). Mix dry **milk powder** and **carob powder** for an even quicker drink. Use 1 part carob with 4 parts powdered milk. Place 2 T. of this mixture in a mug, add 1 T. cold milk to make a smooth paste. Fill cup with cold water and stir in honey to taste. *PROTEIN: 4.7 grams; CALORIES: 59*

Becky Shaw	*Carol Luck*	*Crisanne Forsythe*	*Janice Holz*
Victoria, B.C., Canada	*Ottawa, Ontario, Canada*	*Sandwich, Illinois*	*Bad Axe, Michigan*

WINTER MEETING CIDER

8 C. **apple juice**
3 C. **water**
½ C. **honey**
3 **cinnamon** sticks
6 whole **allspice** berries,
   or ½ t. ground allspice
12 **cloves**
½ t. ground **nutmeg**
1 C. **lemon juice**
1 **orange**, sliced

Combine apple juice, water, honey and spices; bring to boil; simmer 30 minutes. Let stand overnight; strain. Add citrus to spiced apple drink; reheat, but don't boil. Makes about 1 gallon.

PROTEIN: 3.1 grams; CALORIES: 1609

Pineapple Cider. Omit lemon juice and reduce honey to ¼ to ⅓ C. Add 2 C. **pineapple juice.** Proceed as for cider.

Cranberry-Apple Wassail. Omit orange and lemon juice, replacing it with 3 C. **cranberry juice.** In slow cooker, heat all ingredients at low setting for 5 to 6 hours. Remove the cooled fruit. Serve drink garnished with fresh slices of **orange.**

Deb Dewey	*Ann Calandro*	*Elaine Force*	*Debbie Guy*
Rochester, New York	*Longwood, Florida*	*Visalia, California*	*Hattiesburg, Mississippi*

EASY HOMEMADE APPLE JUICE CONCENTRATE

Put as many apples as you like in large pot with enough water so that they float and will not scorch. Simmer over medium heat about 25 minutes, or until fruit is tender and skins have split. Strain juice through jelly bag or an old pillowcase. Pour into plastic freezer containers, remembering to leave ½" headroom. Freeze or can. When ready for juice, dilute the concentrate at the rate of 1 part concentrate to 4 to 6 parts water (to taste). Unless the fruit is extremely tart, no sweetening is needed. The opened container of concentrate will keep several days in the fridge if you do not want to dilute the entire amount at once.

Variation: Try using **plums, crabapples, cherries, berries** or even **rhubarb** —whatever is on hand or in season. Use each fruit individually or combine two or more for a new taste treat. A great use for windfalls.

Brenda Santer
Estevan, Saskatchewan, Canada

Kids' Cookbook

A NOTE TO PARENTS

PARENTS: These recipes are designed for your children. The very simple ones can be done by pre-schoolers and even some toddlers with your guidance. The list of skills at the beginning of each recipe will help you or your reading child select those recipes appropriate for his or her age and abilities.

Cooking and working in the kitchen provide an excellent atmosphere for learning for your child. He will learn how to follow directions and read, work out simple math and science problems, and develop better coordination. Most of all, he will learn about good nutrition. You may be surprised what your child will eat if he makes it himself.

At first it may take some time and patience on your part, to be sure that your child can handle a given set of skills. Working with your child this way will also provide an opportunity for you to spend some special time with her. Once you feel confident in her capabilities, give her a chance to work on her own. Do stay nearby whenever your child uses sharp knives, the stove or oven or any electrical appliances.

—Helen Palmer

HINTS AND SAFETY TIPS

1. **Wash** your hands before working with food.
2. **Get** everything you need. If you have any questions ask an adult.
3. **Wash** fruits and vegetables before using them.
4. **Use** a cutting board for slicing and chopping.
5. **Turn** pot handles away from the front of the stove while cooking.
6. **Use** a wooden spoon when stirring in a pot on top of the stove.
7. **Ask** for your parent's permission before you use sharp knives, the stove or oven or any electrical appliance such as the blender, food processor, mixer, toaster, electric fry pan or griddle.
8. **Set** the timer or watch the clock so things do not overcook.
9. **Turn** off the stove or oven when you are finished.
10. **Clean** up as you go along, or when you are finished.

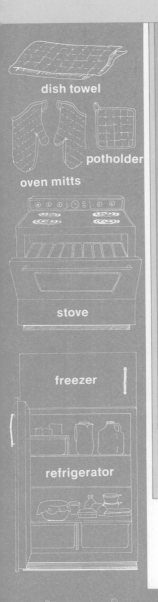

dish towel

potholder

oven mitts

stove

freezer

refrigerator

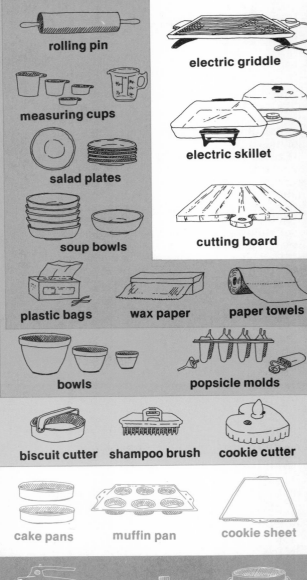

rolling pin

measuring cups

salad plates

soup bowls

electric griddle

electric skillet

cutting board

plastic bags

wax paper

paper towels

bowls

popsicle molds

biscuit cutter

shampoo brush

cookie cutter

cake pans

muffin pan

cookie sheet

hands

electric mixer

blender

large pot

kids' cookbook

straws

toothpicks

popsicle sticks

airtight container   **colander**   **gelatin mold**

pot   **frying pan**   **small pot**

doughnut cutter   **grater**   **plastic cups**

pan   **loaf pan**   **pie plate**

wooden spoon

slotted spoon

spatula

melon baller

apple corer

sharp knife

vegetable peeler

knife

pastry brush

pastry wheel

pancake turner

can opener

pizza cutter

knife
fork
spoon

potato masher   **measuring spoons**

egg beater   **strainer**

Summer

FROZEN BANANAS

You will need
Tray or baking pan
Ice cream sticks,
   plastic spoons or
   popsicle handles
   (optional)
Plastic bag
Small paper cups
Knife

bananas, peeled

Toppings (use
   any or all)
yogurt
peanut butter
wheat germ
nuts or **seeds**,
   chopped fine
pureed **fruits**
applesauce
coconut

Can you
Cut bananas in half?
Put stick in thicker end?
   (optional)
Freeze bananas on tray?
Put frozen bananas in bag?
Chop nuts or seeds?
Put toppings in small cups?
Roll or dip bananas in
   toppings?

1. Cut bananas in half.
2. Insert stick in thicker end.
3. Place bananas on tray or
   small pan; put in freezer.
4. When frozen, store in sealed
   plastic bag in freezer until
   ready to use.
5. Put toppings into small cups.
   Dip banana before each bite.
6. Allow bananas to thaw
   slightly so you can bite into
   them. Eat plain or roll or dip
   into any of the toppings (use
   wet toppings first so others
   will stick).
   Bananas can also be used
unfrozen without the sticks.

Pam Norton
Auburn, California

YOGURT SUNDAES OR PARFAITS
(try this for a birthday party)

You will need
2 medium bowls
Measuring cups and spoons
Spoon or ice cream scoop
Knife
Electric mixer or egg beater
6 dishes, plates, or glasses

Can you
Use measuring cups and
*   spoons?*
Mix ingredients in bowl?
Scoop yogurt into dish?
Slice fruits?
Chop nuts?
Decorate yogurt with toppings
*   for sundaes?*
Layer fruit and yogurt in glasses
*   for parfaits?*

4 C. plain **yogurt**
1 t. **vanilla**
2 T. **honey**

Toppings: choose any or all
bananas, sliced
fruit in season: strawberries,
   cherries, blueberries,
   peaches, apples, melons,
   sliced or cut up
raisins or other dried fruit
nuts, chopped
seeds, sunflower, sesame,
   pumpkin
coconut, shredded,
   unsweetened
fruit juice concentrate

1. Mix yogurt, vanilla and honey
   in bowl or use flavored
   yogurt.
2. Chop, cut up or slice any
   fruits or nuts you choose.
3. For sundaes, put scoop of
   yogurt in dish. Add toppings
   of your choice.
4. For parfaits, layer fruit and
   yogurt in pretty glasses.
   Add toppings, if you like.
5. Enough for 4 to 6 servings.

PROTEIN: 47.7 grams; CALORIES: 589 + toppings

Pam Norton   *Linda McCollough*
Auburn, California   *Abilene, Texas*

Kathie Oselka (age 9)
Union Pier, Michigan

CINNAMON 'SICLES

You will need
Medium size bowl
Measuring cup and spoons
Fork or spoon
6 Popsicle molds
Freezer

1 C. plain **yogurt**
1 C. **applesauce**
1 T. **honey**
½ t. ground **cinnamon**

Can you
Mix ingredients with fork?
Use measuring cups and
    spoons?
Pour mixture into molds?
Put filled molds in freezer?

1. Blend ingredients in bowl
   with a fork or spoon
2. Pour into popsicle molds.
3. Put filled popsicle molds in
   freezer .
4. When frozen take out of
   freezer. Enjoy!

PROTEIN: 12.4 grams; CALORIES: 288

Rose Hufnagel
Rochester, Pennsylvania

INSTANT ICE CREAM

You will need
Blender
Measuring cups and spoons
Spatula or wooden spoon
Plastic cups

2 C. frozen **fruit** (blueberries,
    strawberries, peaches or
    bananas)
1 C. **milk** or cream
2 to 4 T. **honey** (optional)

Can you
Use a blender?
Use measuring cups and
    spoons?
Stop blender and rearrange
    ingredients with spoon?

1. Put fruit, milk and honey in
   blender.
2. Blend on high speed until
   smooth. You may have to
   stop the blender, scrape
   down the sides, replace cover
   and blend some more.
3. Serve immediately as soft ice
   cream or pour into plastic
   cups and freeze for an hour or
   so.   PROTEIN: 10.5 grams; CALORIES: 457

Kay Hoover   Joann Grohman
Media, Pennsylvania   Dixfield, Maine

UNBELIEVABLE JAM
(even a pre-schooler can make this)

You will need
Potato masher or blender
Large bowl for mashing in
Large spoon
Strainer or colander, lined with
cheesecloth or nylon net
set in bowl
Knife for spreading

Can you
Mash, crush or blend fruit?
Spoon or pour mashed fruit into
strainer set in bowl?
Put bowl with strainer in
refrigerator overnight?
Spread jam on bread?

fruit in season (strawberries, peaches, apricots, raspberries, blackberries, blueberries, or nectarines)
small amount of **honey**, if you like it sweeter
bread or crackers

1. Mash or crush fruit in bowl with potato masher or use blender on medium speed.
2. Set strainer over another bowl large enough to collect juice from mashed fruit; spoon or pour fruit into strainer.
3. Put in refrigerator overnight to allow juice to drain into bowl.
4. The next day, add honey to "jam" if you like.
5. Spread on bread or toast.
6. Refrigerate any that is left.
7. You may drink the juice.

Karen Wedman
Blueberry Mt., Alberta, Canada

JUDY KRUGER'S PEANUT BUTTER DIP

You will need
Spoon or fork
Bowl
Knife

Can you
Mix ingredients in bowl?
Cut up vegetables for dipping?

1 C. **peanut butter**
1 C. plain **yogurt**
¼ C. unsweetened **coconut** (optional)
vegetables (carrots, celery, cucumbers, cauliflower)

1. Mix peanut butter, yogurt and coconut together in bowl.
2. Cut up vegetables; use to scoop up the dip.

PROTEIN: 79.8 grams; CALORIES: 1715 + vegetables

Nancy Johnson
Greeley, Colorado

PICTURE SALADS
(try this at your next birthday party)

You will need
Knife
Vegetable peeler
Grater
Corer
Spoon
Paper or salad plates
Forks and spoons

lettuce leaves
carrots, cut in sticks,
    circles or grated
celery, cut in sticks, thin
    strips or sliced
tomatoes, cut in half,
    wedges or sliced
green or **red peppers**, cut in
    strips
cucumbers, sliced
zucchini, sliced or grated
pimento, sliced
olives, whole or sliced
pickles, whole or sliced
pears, cut in half or sliced
peaches, cut in half or sliced
apples, cut in half or sliced
bananas, sliced or quartered
strawberries, whole
pineapple, rings or chunks
raisins, apricots, prunes
oranges, cut in smiles or sliced
grapes, seedless or seeded
coconut, grated, unsweetened
cottage cheese
eggs, hard-cooked, sliced or
    cut in half
cheese, sliced, cubed or grated
nuts (peanuts, walnuts, pecans,
    almonds, cashews)

Can you
Make hardcooked eggs?
Peel, slice or cut-up fruits,
    vegetables and eggs?
Use a grater?
Put pieces of fruits, vegetables,
    eggs, cheese, meats, nuts and
    seeds together to create your
    own salad?

1. Select the ingredients you
   plan to use.
2. Cut, slice or grate as needed.
3. Use the fruits and vegetables
   to make a person, an animal
   or a picture. Here are a few
   ideas to get you started.

Carole Miller   *Margaret MacPherson*
Cumberland, Maryland   *Hudson, Mass.*

Perry the Mouse

SUNSHINE SALAD
(a summer treat)

You will need
Small saucepan
Blender or grater
Measuring cups and spoons
6 C. bowl or mold
Potholders

Can you
Turn on the stove?
Heat juice to dissolve gelatin?
Use measuring cups and spoons?
Use blender?
Slice and peel carrots?

2 T. unflavored **gelatin** or
  2 envelopes
½ C. **orange juice**
1½ C. **orange juice**
2 T. **lemon juice** (optional)
½ t. **almond extract** (optional)
1 C. raw **carrots,** sliced
2½ C. **crushed pineapple** with
  juice (20 oz. can)

1. Sprinkle gelatin over ½ C. orange juice in saucepan; stir over low heat until gelatin dissolves.
2. Remove from heat using potholders and pour into blender with remaining orange juice, lemon juice, almond extract, and carrots.
3. Blend at medium-high speed for a few seconds or until carrots are finely chopped. If you do not use a blender, grate the carrots and mix ingredients in bowl.
4. Pour into bowl or mold and stir in pineapple with juice. Do not use fresh or frozen pineapple as the mixture will not gel.
5. Chill in refrigerator until set, about 2 to 3 hours.

Gayle Brunner   Jean Brinkman   PROTEIN: 19.3 grams; CALORIES: 664
New Holstein, Wisconsin Erie, Pennsylvania

Clown

Raggedy Ann

AMBER'S TUNA ROLLS

You will need
Can opener
Small bowl
Fork, teaspoon, tablespoon
Knife (optional)
Grater (optional)
Toothpicks (optional)

Can you
Use a can opener?
Drain liquid from a can?
Use a grater? (optional)
Use a knife for chopping?
  (optional)
Mix ingredients in bowl?
Put tuna salad on lettuce
  leaves and wrap like a
  package?
Spread mixture on bread or stuff
  into pita bread?
  (optional)

6½ oz. **tuna**
1 to 2 T. **mayonnaise**
large **lettuce** leaves, pita
  bread or sliced bread

Optional additions:
1 T. chopped **apple**
1 T. chopped **celery**
1 T. grated **carrot**
1 t. **sunflower seeds**
1 T. **raisins**
1 t. fresh, chopped **parsley**

PROTEIN: 38.1 grams; CALORIES: 584

Amber Palmer, age 6   Barbara Kerr
Edgewater Park, New Jersey Brussels, Ont., Canada

1. Open can of tuna and drain oil or water.
2. Chop or grate apples, celery and carrot.
3. Mix tuna, mayonnaise and optional additions you like in a bowl.
4. Place a heaping tablespoonful of mixture in center of lettuce leaf. Wrap like a package, folding one corner over another for three sides, then roll to close. Secure with a toothpick. Or stuff into pita bread or spread on bread. Serves 4 to 6, depending on appetites.

SUMMER ICE
(slurpy alternative)

You will need
Blender
Wooden spoon
Small paper cups
Spoon or straw
Can opener, if needed

Can you
Use the blender?
Use the can opener, if needed?
Add juice and ice to blender?
Stir mixture in blender?
Pour slush into cups?

6 oz. can frozen **juice concentrate** (apple, orange, grape)

ice cubes to fill blender ⅔ full

6 oz. **water** (use juice can)

1. Fill blender ⅔ full of ice cubes; add frozen juice and water.
2. Blend at medium-high speed until ice is of slurpy consistency; you may need to turn off blender and stir

mixture with wooden spoon; replace cover and resume blending.
3. Add more ice if you like it thicker.
4. Pour into small paper cups; serve with spoon or straw.
5. Makes enough to share with several friends.

Carol Fick
Dayton, Ohio

PROTEIN: 4.2 grams; CALORIES: 270

OVEN FRIED CHICKEN

You will need
Medium size bowl
Dinner plate
Measuring cups
Fork
9 x 13" baking pan
Potholders or oven mitts

Can you
Turn on oven?
Crack an egg?
Combine ingredients in bowl?
Dip chicken in egg mixture, then in breadcrumbs?
Put chicken in baking pan, then into oven?
Set timer?
Remove pan using potholders?

1 cut-up **chicken**
1 **egg**
¼ C. **milk**
½ to 1 C. **breadcrumbs** or wheat germ

Seasonings
¼ t. **garlic powder**
dash of **salt**
dash of **pepper**

1. Turn on oven to 400°.
2. Remove skin from chicken, if you like.
3. Mix egg and milk in bowl; mix breadcrumbs and seasonings on plate.
4. Dip chicken in egg, then in crumbs.
5. Place chicken in baking pan. Set timer. Bake for 1 hour, turning once with fork, if you like.
6. When chicken is done, remove pan from oven, using potholders.

PROTEIN: 186.1 grams; CALORIES: 1437

Helen Palmer
Edgewater Park, New Jersey

TUNABURGERS

You will need

Can opener
Medium size strainer
Medium size bowl
Measuring cups and spoons
Grater
Knife
Fork
Electric skillet or fry pan
Pancake turner
Paper towels

Can you

Use a can opener?
Crack an egg?
Use measuring cups and
 spoons?
Use a grater?
Cut lemon in half and squeeze
 out the juice?
Mix ingredients in bowl with
 fork?
Shape mixture into patties?
Use electric skillet or turn on
 stove?
Fry patties in hot oil?
Turn and remove patties with
 pancake turner?

12 oz. **tuna**, drained
1 **egg**
¼ C. **onion**, grated
1 T. **lemon juice**
¼ t. **pepper**
¼ C. **bread crumbs**
1½ T. **oil** for frying

1. Open can of tuna; dump into strainer and drain. Put tuna and egg into bowl.
2. Grate onion; squeeze lemon juice. Add to bowl along with pepper and bread crumbs.
3. Mix well. Shape into 6 or more patties.
4. Heat electric skillet to 300° or turn on burner to medium-high heat. Put enough oil in pan to cover bottom.
5. When pan is hot, put in patties. Fry until golden brown. Turn over to other side. Brown.
6. Remove with turner to paper towels to absorb some of the grease.

P.: 92.3 gms.; C.: 1190

Paula Glazer Vornbrock
Yakima, Washington

fall

ANTS ON A LOG

You will need
Knife

Can you
Break celery stalks in half?
Spread peanut butter on celery?
Decorate with raisins?

celery stalks
peanut butter
raisins

1. Break celery stalks in half.
2. Spread peanut butter on celery.
3. Decorate with raisins.

Jane Fox
Ottawa, Ontario, Canada

BANANA BOATS
(a pre-schooler can make this)

You will need
Knife
Spoon (optional)
Tablespoon

Can you
Peel a banana and slice it in half lengthwise?
Spread peanut butter on it?
Sprinkle coconut and granola?

1 banana
2. T. peanut butter
2 T. coconut
1 T. granola

1. Peel banana and slice in half lengthwise.
2. Spread peanut butter on each half.
3. Sprinkle with coconut and granola.
4. Share it with your sister or brother.

P.: 10.7 gms.; C.: 374

Carla Till
Rome, New York

PUMPKIN BREAD OR CUPCAKES
(great for a class party)

You will need
2 medium size bowls
Fork or spoon
Measuring cups and spoons
Knife for chopping
Large loaf pan (9 x 5 x 3)
   or muffin pans with
   cupcake liners
Potholders
Cooling rack
Knife for spreading
   icing (optional)

Can you
Turn on oven?
Set a timer?
Use measuring cups and
   spoons?
Mix ingredients in bowl?
Crack eggs?
Chop nuts?
Spoon batter into loaf pan or
   cupcake liners?
Remove cake from oven with
   potholders?
Invert loaf pan when cake is
   cooled to remove it?
Spread icing? (optional)

1 C. cooked mashed **pumpkin**
½ C. **oil** or soft butter
½ C. **honey**
2 **eggs**
1¾ C. wholewheat **flour**
   or 1 C. wholewheat and
   ¾ C. unbleached **flour**
1 t. **baking soda**
1 t. **baking powder**
½ t. **salt**
½ to 1 t. **cinnamon**
¼ to ½ t. **nutmeg**
⅓ C. **water**
½ C. chopped **nuts**
   (optional)
oil or **butter** for greasing
cream cheese (optional)
honey (optional)

Variation: Omit pumpkin.
Use yams, winter squash,
   or persimmon pulp.

1. Beat oil and honey together
   in bowl; add eggs; mix well.
2. Combine dry ingredients in
   another bowl.
3. Add dry ingredients and
   water to honey mixture.
4. Mix in pumpkin and nuts.
5. Preheat oven to 350°.
6. Grease loaf pan with oil or
   butter or put cupcake liners
   into muffin pans.
7. Spoon in batter.
8. Bake for 1 hour for loaf, or 20
   to 25 minutes for cupcakes.
9. Remove pumpkin bread from
   oven using potholders; put on
   cooling rack; cool loaf 15
   minutes before inverting to
   take it out of the pan.
10. If you like, ice with cream
    cheese thinned with honey or
    try **peanut butter frosting**.

PROTEIN: 52.3 grams; CALORIES: 2862 + icing

Susan McGowan
Calumet City, Illinois

Julie Clingan
Liberal, Kansas

Jennifer McKinney
Vienna, Virginia

PEANUT BUTTER FROSTING

You will need
Fork or electric mixer
Medium size bowl
Measuring cups and spoons
Knife for spreading icing

½ C. **peanut butter**
5 T. **butter**, softened
2 T. **honey**
1 to 3 T. **milk** (optional)

Can you
Beat with fork or use electric mixer?
Use measuring cups and spoons?
Mix ingredients in bowl?
Spread icing with knife?

1. Beat butters and honey in bowl with fork or electric mixer.
2. Add milk gradually, only if needed, until easy to spread.
3. Spread on cake or cupcakes with knife.

PROTEIN: 34.8 grams; CALORIES: 1415

Doris Franz Poling
Baltimore, Maryland

APPLE GOODIE
(a simple treat a preschooler can make)

You will need
Plastic bag with twist tie
4 small paper cups
Child's hands
Tablespoon

6 **graham crackers**
1 C. **applesauce**

Can you
Crush graham crackers in plastic bag?
Layer crumbs and applesauce in small cups?

1. Put graham crackers in plastic bag.
2. Seal with twist tie.
3. Crush crackers with hands.
4. Put tablespoon of applesauce in each cup, sprinkle with crumbs.
5. Continue layering applesauce and crumbs until cups are full.

PROTEIN: 5.8 grams; CALORIES: 358

Janice Knight Hartman
Millsboro, Delaware

GRAHAM CRACKERS

You will need

Large bowl for mixing
Medium size bowl
Measuring cups and spoons
Wooden spoon
2 cookie sheets
Rolling pin
Fork, Knife
Pastry wheel or pizza
    cutter (optional)
Potholders
Spatula
Airtight container
Shampoo brush (optional)

Can you

Mix ingredients in bowl?
Mix a stiff dough?
Use measuring cups and
    spoons?
Turn on oven?
Set timer?
Grease cookie sheets?
Roll out dough on cookie sheet?
Cut rolled out dough with knife?
Prick surface of crackers with
    fork?
Put cookie sheets in oven?
Remove cookie sheets from
    oven using potholders?
Cool crackers on cookie sheets?
Remove crackers with pancake
    turner when cool?

⅓ C. **oil**
⅓ C. **honey**
2 T. **molasses**
1 t. **vanilla**
2½ to 3 C. wholewheat **flour**
1 t. **baking powder**
½ t. **baking soda**
¼ t. **salt**
1 t. **cinnamon**
¼ to ½ C. **milk**
oil or butter for greasing

1. Mix oil, honey, molasses and vanilla in large bowl.
2. Combine 2½ C. flour with baking powder, baking soda, salt and cinnamon in medium bowl.
3. Add dry mixture to liquids, alternating with milk; mix well. When dough gets too stiff to mix with spoon, use hands.
4. If dough is too sticky, then add up to ½ C. more flour; form dough into ball.
5. Preheat oven to 300°.
6. Grease cookie sheets with a little oil or butter.
7. Divide dough in half.
8. Roll dough directly onto cookie sheets, to cover entire sheet.
9. Use knife to cut dough into 2½ inch squares, but do not separate.

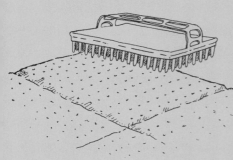

10. Prick surface of each cracker with fork or shampoo brush.
11. Bake for 15 to 25 minutes or until outer edges are slightly browned.
12. Remove cookie sheets from oven using potholders.
13. Let cool on cookie sheets.
14. When cool separate and remove with turner.
15. Store in air tight container.

PROTEIN: 42.4 grams; CALORIES: 2228

Janet Glover
Russiaville, Indiana

Jean Hall
Malden, Illinois

APPLE-CARROT-RAISIN SALAD
(with pineapple and nuts)

You will need
Large bowl
Knife
Grater
Measuring cups
Can opener
Small bowls or cups
Spoon or fork

Can you
Dice apples?
Grate carrots?
Use a can opener?
Chop nuts?
Use measuring cups?
Mix ingredients in bowl?
Put salad in refrigerator?
Add dressing to salad?
(optional)

2 or 3 **apples**, diced
2 or 3 **carrots**, grated
2 C. **pineapple**, chunks or crushed with juice
½ to 1 C. **raisins**
½ C. **nuts** or sunflower seeds (optional)

1. Prepare fruit and vegetables.
2. Mix all ingredients in bowl.
3. Chill in refrigerator for 2 hours.
4. Serves 6 to 8, as fruit cup or salad for light snack or dessert.

PROTEIN: 15.8 grams; CALORIES: 1133

Dressing (optional)
¼ C. **mayonnaise**
¼ C. **yogurt**
pinch of **cinnamon** and/or **nutmeg**
a drip of **honey**, if you like

1. Combine all ingredients in small bowl or cup.
2. Add to salad and mix well to coat fruit and vegetables.

PROTEIN: 3.4 grams; CALORIES: 432

Vickie L. Pavone
Bradenton, Florida

Lois Lake Raabe
Easton, Connecticut

PUMPKIN PAN ROLLS

You will need
2 large bowls
Measuring cups and spoons
Small saucepot
Large wooden spoon
Flat surface to knead on
Dish or hand towel
2 9'' round cake pans
Potholders or oven mitts
Cooling rack

Can you
Use measuring cups and
  spoons?
Melt butter over low flame?
Turn on burner?
Mix ingredients in bowl?
Knead bread dough?
Find warm, draft-free place to
  let bread rise?
Punch dough down when risen?
Roll dough into small balls?
Turn on oven?
Set timer? Put pans in oven?
Remove pans from oven with
  potholders?
Remove bread from pans and
  put on a cooling rack?

1 T. **yeast**
1 C. warm **potato water**
  (water leftover from
  cooking potatoes) or
  plain water
⅓ C. **honey**
3 T. **butter**
1 t. **salt** (or less)
½ C. dry **milk powder**
1 C. **pumpkin**, cooked,
  mashed or 1 C. canned
  pumpkin
1½ t. ground **cinnamon**
¾ t. ground **cloves**
¾ t. ground **nutmeg**
¾ t. ground **ginger**
4 to 5 C. whole wheat
  flour
1 to 2 t. **oil**

1. Dissolve yeast in water in
   large bowl.
2. Melt butter in small saucepot
   over low flame.
3. Add honey, butter, salt, milk
   powder, pumpkin and spices
   to yeast.
4. Gradually beat in 4 C. flour.
5. When dough is stiff, transfer
   to flat surface. Knead about
   15 minutes or until dough is
   a smooth ball, adding flour
   if necessary to keep dough
   from sticking.
6. Rub another bowl with oil.
7. Place dough in bowl, turning
   once so top is oiled.
8. Cover with towel and let rise
   in warm, draft-free place until
   doubled, about 1½ to 2
   hours.
9. Punch down and knead a few
   minutes more. Set aside.

10. Grease cake pans with remaining oil, using more if necessary.
11. Pull off pieces of dough and roll into 32 balls. Place balls, in a single layer, in cake pans.
12. Let rise, covered, about 1 hour.
13. Pre-heat oven to 375°.
14. When doubled, set timer, then put in oven to bake for about 25 to 35 minutes.
15. Remove from oven using potholders and put on cooling rack. Serve hot or cooled.   *PROTEIN: 95.3 grams; CALORIES: 2769*

Bryanna Clark
Union Bay, Canada

PITA BREAD SANDWICHES
(create your own nutritious quick lunch)

You will need
Knife
Grater
Cookie sheet
Potholders

pita bread (p. 145)

Filling (pick your own)
shredded **lettuce** or cabbage
grated **carrots** and **cheese**
chopped **cucumbers, peppers,**
   and **tomatoes**
sliced **avocados**
tuna, chicken, or turkey salad

Can you
Chop or slice vegetables?
Grate cheese and carrots?
Turn on oven to warm pita?
Remove pita from oven?

1. Pre-heat oven to 300°.
2. Cut pita bread in half; place on cookie sheet and warm for 5 to 10 minutes.
3. While bread is warming, prepare the filling you desire. There are no limits to the kinds of fillings you can use.
4. Fill pocket of pita bread and eat.   *Mary Jo Johnson*
Shavertown, Pennsylvania

APPLESAUCE CAKE OR CUPCAKES

You will need
Small pot
Measuring cups and spoons
Large bowl
Fork or spoon
9 x 5" loaf pan or muffin tin
Knife (optional)
Cupcake liners
Potholders or oven mitts
Cooling rack

Can you
Use stove?
Turn on oven?
Use measuring cups and
   spoons?
Chop nuts or apples?
Mix ingredients in bowl?
Grease pan?
Spoon batter into pan?
Set timer?
When done, remove pan from
   oven using potholders?
Remove cake or cupcakes from
   pan when cool?

1 C. **applesauce**
½ C. **honey**
½ C. **butter**, softened
1 ¾ C. wholewheat **flour**
1 t. **baking soda**
1 t. **salt** (or less)
1 t. ground **cinnamon**
½ t. ground **cloves**
½ t. ground **ginger**
½ C. **raisins**
½ C. **walnuts**, chopped
1 **apple**, chopped

1. Preheat oven to 350°.
2. Put honey and butter in small pot on stove. Melt over low heat. Or cream butter and honey together with fork in bowl.
3. Remove pot from heat. Add applesauce. Mix well.
4. Put flour, soda, salt and spices in large bowl. Add applesauce mixture. Blend well.
5. Chop nuts or apples, if you are using them.
6. Add with raisins and mix.
7. Grease pan or line muffin tins with cupcake liners.
8. Spoon in batter. Set timer. Bake 40 to 60 minutes for loaf pan, or 25 to 30 minutes for cupcakes. Both are done when toothpick inserted in center comes out clean.
9. Remove pans from oven using potholders.
10. When cool enough to handle, remove cakes from pan onto a cooling rack.

PROTEIN: 40.9 grams; CALORIES: 2855

Helen Palmer
Edgewater Park, New Jersey

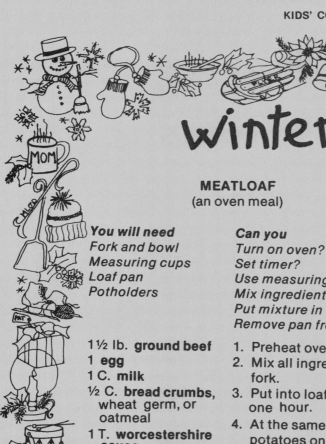

winter

MEATLOAF
(an oven meal)

You will need
Fork and bowl
Measuring cups
Loaf pan
Potholders

Can you
Turn on oven?
Set timer?
Use measuring cups?
Mix ingredients in bowl?
Put mixture in loaf pan?
Remove pan from oven?

1½ lb. **ground beef**
1 **egg**
1 C. **milk**
½ C. **bread crumbs,** wheat germ, or oatmeal
1 T. **worcestershire sauce**
¼ C. **chili sauce,** catsup or tomato sauce
½ t. **salt,** or less

4 to 6 medium **potatoes,** washed, dried and oiled (optional)

1. Preheat oven to 350°.
2. Mix all ingredients well with fork.
3. Put into loaf pan; bake for one hour.
4. At the same time put some potatoes on the oven rack to bake while the meatloaf cooks, if you like. They will also take about one hour.
5. Remove potatoes and pan of meatloaf with potholders.
6. Serve to 4 to 6 people, depending on how hungry they are.

Carol Hoefler
Zanesville, Ohio

Meatloaf—PROTEIN: 144.3 grams; CALORIES: 2315

Potatoes— PROTEIN: 10.4 grams; CALORIES: 380

"QUICK AND EASY" SPAGHETTI WITH MEAT SAUCE
(Parents' night off! The children cook dinner)

You will need
Large fry pan or skillet
Knife
Measuring cups and spoons
Spoon for stirring
Pot for noodles
Potholders
Colander set in large bowl.

1 to 2 lbs. **ground beef**
½ C. **onions**, chopped
¼ C. **green pepper**,
   chopped (optional)
1 C. **tomato paste**
1 C. **tomato puree**
1 t. **oregano**
2 cloves **garlic**, crushed
   or ½ t. garlic powder
½ t. **salt** (or less)
1 C. **mushrooms** (optional)

½ to 1 lb. **spaghetti** or
   noodles
boiling **water**
½ C. **Parmesan cheese**

Variation: Omit tomato
puree; add 1½ C. tomato
paste (instead of 1 C.) and
½ C. water.

Can you
Turn on stove and brown meat?
Chop vegetables?
Use measuring cups and
   spoons?
Add ingredients to pot; stir?
Boil water and cook spaghetti?

1. Pull off ground meat in small
   pieces; put in pan or skillet.
2. Turn on low heat under pan
   Brown meat; stir a few times.
3. When light brown, add onions
   and peppers; cook about 5
   minutes or until onion is soft.
4. Add tomato paste and puree.
5. Season with oregano and
   garlic; stir well. Add about
   ¾ C. water, if you like.
6. Add mushrooms if you like.
7. Let simmer on stove while
   you cook the spaghetti.
8. Bring large pot of water to
   boil; add spaghetti and stir.
9. Cook until tender, not mushy.
10. Using slotted spoon or tongs,
    lift spaghetti from water and
    place in colander set in large
    bowl to drain.
11. Serve with sauce and grated
    cheese.

PROTEIN: 158.3 grams; CALORIES: 2600

Janice Knight Hartman
Millsboro, Delaware

MEATBALLS

You will need
Medium size bowl
Measuring cups and spoons
Grater
Fork and knife
Baking sheet or shallow pan
Spoon
Paper towels

Can you
Chop onion and parsley?
Crack an egg?
Use grater?
Mix ingredients in bowl?
Shape meat mixture into balls?
Turn on oven?
Put meatballs on baking sheet?
Use measuring cups and
   spoons?
Put baking sheet into oven?
Set timer?
Remove baking sheet from oven
   using potholders?

1 lb. **ground beef**
2 T. **onion**, chopped fine
1 T. **parsley**, chopped fine
   or 1½ t. dried parsley
   flakes
1 C. grated **cheese**
1 **egg**, beaten
½ C. **wheat germ** or
   bread crumbs
½ t. **salt** (or less)

1. Mix all ingredients in bowl
   with fork.
2. Shape meat into 30 to 40
   meatballs about 1" in
   diameter.
3. Preheat oven to 350°.
4. Arrange on baking sheet an
   inch apart.
5. Put baking sheet in oven; set
   timer for 25 minutes.

6. When evenly browned, remove from oven using potholders.
7. Take meatballs off with spoon , placing on paper towels
   to absorb some of the   grease.
8. Eat as is, in a sandwich or add to spaghetti sauce.

PROTEIN: 138.6 grams; CALORIES: 2052

PEANUT BUTTER APPLES

You will need
Knife
Melon baller (optional)

Can you
Cut apple into pieces?
Fill center of apple with
   peanut butter?

apples
peanut butter

1. Halve or quarter apples.
2. Remove core with knife or
   melon baller.
3. Fill center with peanut butter.

Joann Grohman
Dixfield, Maine

GINGERBREAD PEOPLE
(even little ones can help with these)

You will need
Large bowl and spoon
Measuring cups and spoons
Cookie sheets
Cookie cutters
Table knife
Smaller bowl
Rolling pin (optional)
Potholders or oven mitts
Cooling rack or brown paper
Pastry bag or cake decorator
(optional)

Can you
Turn on oven?
Set timer?
Use measuring cups and
spoons?
Mix ingredients in bowl?
Press or roll out dough?
Press or roll out dough?
Use cookie cutters or knife?
Use pastry bag for decorating
(optional)?

¼ C. **honey**
1 C. **molasses**
1 large **egg**
½ C. **oil**
1¼ t. **cinnamon**
1¼ t. **ginger**
4 C. wholewheat **flour**
4 t. **baking powder**
½ t. **oil** or butter for greasing

For decorating (optional)
raisins, currants
carob chips
coconut
nuts and **seeds**
other **dried fruits**, cut-up
cream cheese thinned with
honey (can be colored with
natural fruit juices)

These cookies are very sturdy and make great Christmas tree decorations as well as great Christmas goodies. Remember to refrigerate them if you use the icing. Makes 6 to 8 dozen cookies.

1. Mix honey, molasses, egg, oil, ginger and cinnamon in large bowl.
2. Into small bowl measure out flour. Add baking powder.
3. Add flour to wet mixture. Mix well until dough is stiff.
4. Use hands to form dough into ball. Chill in refrigerator for 1 to 2 hours (the colder the dough, the easier it is to work with).
5. When ready to use dough, preheat oven to 325°.
6. Grease cookie sheets with oil or butter.
7. Press out pieces of dough by hand or roll to 1/8" thick right on cookie sheet, using a little flour on rolling pin or hands to prevent sticking.
8. Use cookie cutters or knife to cut out any number of shapes.
9. Decorate as you like before baking. Or use cream cheese and honey icing after cookies

are cool. Use a pastry bag or just ice. Decorations will stick to icing.
10. Bake for 10 minutes; bottom of cookie will be light brown.
11. Remove from oven with potholders. Transfer with pancake turner to cooling rack or brown paper.

PROTEIN: 71 grams; CALORIES: 3788 + decorations

Christina Pinkerton
Loveland, Colorado

FANTASTIC CAROB FUDGE

You will need
Medium size saucepot
Measuring cups and spoons
Knife for chopping
Wooden spoon
Potholders
8 x 8" pan

½ C. to 1 C. **honey**
1 C. **peanut butter**
1 C. **carob powder**
1 C. **nuts**, chopped or seeds
½ to 1 t. **vanilla**

Optional:
1 C. **coconut**
½ C. **wheat germ**

Can you
Turn on stove?
Use measuring cups and spoons?
Heat honey and peanut butter over low heat?
Chop nuts?
Add other ingredients to pot?
Mix ingredients in pot?
Spoon and spread mixture into pan?
Chill fudge in refrigerator?
Cut fudge into bite-sized squares when hardened?

1. Put honey and peanut butter in pot. Cook over low heat. Stir with wooden spoon.
2. When this is liquid, remove pot from burner. Add carob powder, nuts, vanilla, and coconut or wheat germ; mix well.
3. Spoon and spread mixture into pan.
4. Put in refrigerator to harden for an hour or more. If you cannot wait that long, put pan in freezer for 30 minutes.
5. When ready, cut in bite-size pieces and enjoy.

PROTEIN: 92 grams; CALORIES: 3043

Elizabeth Slawson
Lochport, Illinois

Brenda Jinkins
Nesbit, Mississippi

BETTER-LETTER SOUP
(with tiny meatballs)

You will need
Large pot
Knife
Vegetable peeler
Large spoon
Measuring cups
Frying pan
Soup bowls
Ladle

Can you
Peel and cut up vegetables?
Turn on stove?
Use measuring cups?
Add ingredients to pot on stove?
Make tiny meatballs?
Ladle soup into bowls?

1 T. **butter**
1 **onion**, peeled and cut up
2 small or 1 large **carrot**, peeled and sliced
1 whole **bell pepper**, cut-up
2 C. **water**
¼ to ½ C. **alphabet noodles** or small macaroni
½ to 1 lb. **ground beef**
1 C. (8 oz.) **tomato sauce**

Seasonings, to taste:
salt and **pepper**
paprika
bay leaves
basil
clove of **garlic**, peeled and cut in half

1. Turn on heat under large pot.
2. Melt butter in pot.
3. Add vegetables. Cook until onion is soft.
4. Take ground beef and pull off little pieces. Roll into meatballs.
5. Put meatballs into frying pan. Cook until brown on all sides.
6. Add water and alphabet noodles to large pot. Cook on low heat, stirring occasionally.
7. Add meatballs to large pot and stir in seasonings and garlic.
8. Add tomato sauce to soup; stir, adding water, if needed.
9. Cook on low heat for 45 to 60 minutes or until it's time for lunch or supper.
10. Ladle out soup into bowls.

PROTEIN: 34.2 grams; CALORIES: 733

Paul Richardson age 7
Black Hawk, Colorado

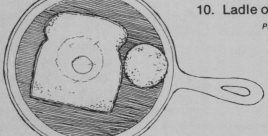

U F O

spring

UFO'S
(UNIDENTIFIED FRYING OBJECTS)

You will need
Skillet or frying pan
Biscuit or cookie
    cutter
Pancake turner
Plate
Butter spreader

For each serving:
1 **egg**
1 slice whole grain
    bread
1 T. **butter**
dash of **salt** and
    pepper

Can you
Turn on stove?
Fry an egg?
Butter bread?
Use a biscuit cutter?
Turn egg over with pancake
    turner?

1. Turn burner on to medium.
2. Melt half of the butter in
    skillet.
3. Spread the rest on one side
    of the bread.
4. Cut a hole in center of bread
    with biscuit or cookie cutter.
5. Fry both pieces of bread,
    buttered side up in skillet
    till bottom is brown.
6. Turn bread over with pancake
    turner and break egg into the
    hole.
7. Add dash of salt and pepper;
    continue cooking slowly until
    egg starts to set (cover pan
    briefly, if you want).
8. Turn bread again just to cook
    other side of egg.
9. Use turner to place UFO and
    cut out circle onto plate.

PROTEIN: 8.9 grams; CALORIES: 253

Diana Reardon   Rita Lare
Dallas, Texas   Akron, Ohio

FRENCH TOAST

You will need
Electric griddle or
*   fry pan*
Shallow bowl
Measuring cup
Forks
Pancake turner
Plates

Can you
Use electric griddle or turn on
*   on stove?*
Crack eggs?
Use measuring cups?
Mix ingredients in bowl?
Dip bread in egg mixture?
Melt butter?
Put dipped bread on hot griddle?
Turn French Toast with turner?
Remove bread from griddle with
*   turner to serving plate?*

2 T. **butter**
1 to 2 **eggs**
¼ to ½ C. **milk** or apple juice
½ to 1 t. **cinnamon**
4 slices whole grain **bread**
mashed **fruit**, jam, maple
    syrup or honey or
    Unbelievable Jam (p. 91)

1. Preheat griddle to 325° or fry pan over medium heat.
2. Melt butter on griddle or fry pan. Crack egg in bowl.
3. Mix egg, milk and cinnamon in bowl.
4. Dip each slice of bread into egg and milk mixture, coating both sides.
5. Put each piece on hot griddle, turning with turner when bottom is brown and somewhat crisp. Continue cooking until other side is done.
6. Remove from pan with turner. Put on serving plates.
7. Top with pureed fruit, jam, maple syrup or honey. Makes 4 pieces.
8. Put cooled leftovers in plastic bag. Seal and freeze. Pop into toaster for a quick breakfast. PROTEIN: 18.9 grams; CALORIES: 604 + topping

Helen Palmer
Edgewater Park, New Jersey

PERFECT HARD-COOKED
EGGS

Put 'em in cold water
Cook 'em 'til they bump.
Simmer for twelve minutes,
Peel 'em with a thump.

Lisa Johnson

PANCAKE MIX
(keep on hand for a surprise weekend breakfast)

You will need
Large bowl
Measuring cups and spoons
Spoon for mixing
Airtight container

6 C. whole wheat **flour**
½ C. **soy flour** or
   wheat germ
3 T. **baking powder**
1 T. **salt**
2 C. **dry milk powder**

Can you
Mix ingredients in bowl?
Use measuring cups and
   spoons?
Pour mix into container?
Store in dry place?

1. Mix all ingredients in bowl.
2. Pour mix into an airtight container.
3. Store in dry place for future use.

PROTEIN: 200 grams; CALORIES: 3484
1 C: PROTEIN: 22.9 GRAMS; CALORIES: 398

PANCAKES

You will need
Medium bowl
Measuring cups
Spoon
Skillet or griddle
Pancake turner

2 C. basic **pancake mix**
   (above)
4 **eggs**, beaten
1 to 2 C. **water**
1 t. **oil**, if needed

Makes 12 to 16 5'' pancakes

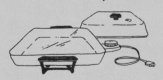

Can you
Mix ingredients in bowl?
Use measuring cups?
Crack eggs?
Turn on stove or cook on
   electric griddle?
Turn pancakes?

1. Preheat skillet or griddle, oil if necessary.
2. Put mix into bowl.
3. Add beaten eggs and water.
4. Mix well.
5. Pour or spoon onto heated, greased skillet or griddle.
6. Turn when surface is bubbly.
7. Cook a few more minutes till golden brown.
8. Remove from griddle to plates and serve with maple syrup, crushed fruit or applesauce.

PROTEIN: 70.6 grams; CALORIES: 1149

Susan Smith
Carlyle, Sask., Canada

APPLESAUCE CRAZY CAKE

You will need
8" square pan
Measuring cups and spoons
Fork
Knife
Toothpick
Cooling rack
Potholders or oven mitts

Can you
Turn on oven?
Use measuring cups and
 spoons?
Chop nuts?
Mix ingredients in pan with fork
 or spoon?
Set timer?
Put cake in oven?
Remove from oven using
 potholders or oven mitts?
Put cake pan on cooling rack?
Cut cake in pieces when cool?

1½ C. **flour** (whole wheat or
 unbleached)
⅓ C. **sugar** or honey
1 t. **baking soda**
½ t. **salt**
¾ to 1 t. **cinnamon**
¼ t. **cloves**
¼ t. **nutmeg**
1 t. **vanilla**
⅓ C. **oil** or melted butter
½ C. **water**
¾ C. **applesauce**
½ C. **nuts**, chopped
½ C. **raisins**
1 **apple**, chopped (optional
 in place of raisins and nuts)

1. Pre-heat oven to 350°.
2. Combine dry ingredients in
   pan.
3. Add vanilla, oil, water, honey
   (if used) and applesauce and
   mix well with fork, scraping
   sides to be sure that all the
   flour is mixed in.
4. Stir in raisins and nuts or
   chopped apple if you like.
5. Put in oven and bake for 25
   to 30 minutes or until
   toothpick comes out clean.
6. Remove pan from oven using
   potholders or oven mitts.
   Place on cooling rack.
7. Let cool before you cut it.

PROTEIN: 35.2 grams; CALORIES: 2193
Deidre Eiler
Renton, Washington

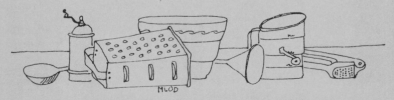

WACKY CAROB CAKE
(mix and bake in same pan)

You will need
8 inch square pan
Measuring cups and spoons

Spoon or fork
Knife
Toothpick
Cooling rack
Potholders or oven mitts

1½ C. whole wheat **flour**
(pastry flour preferred)
⅓ C. **honey** or
½ C. brown sugar
1 t. **baking soda**
½ t. **salt**
⅓ C. **carob powder**
1 t. **vanilla**
1 t. **vinegar**
⅓ C. **oil**
1 C. **water**
½ C. **raisins** (optional)
½ C. **nuts**, chopped
(optional)

Can you
Turn on oven?
Use measuring cups and
spoons?
Chop nuts?
Mix ingredients in pan with
fork or spoon?
Set timer?
Put cake in oven?
Remove from oven using pot-
holders or oven mitts?
Put cake pan on cooling rack?
Cut cake in pieces when cool?

1. Pre-heat oven to 350°.
2. Combine dry ingredients in
   ungreased pan.
3. Add vanilla, vinegar, oil,
   honey and water.
4. Blend well with fork, scraping
   sides to be sure that all the
   flour is mixed in.
5. Stir in raisins and nuts, if you
   like.
6. Put in oven and bake for 25 to
   30 minutes or until toothpick
   inserted in center comes out
   clean.
7. Remove pan from oven using
   potholders or oven mitts, to
   cooling rack.
8. Let it cool before you cut it.

PROTEIN: 140.3 grams; CALORIES: 2340

Ellen Kreckel   Lucy Herman
Bloomsbury, New Jersey Milford, New Jersey

Donna More   June Friesen
Haddenfield, New Jersey Altona, Manitoba, Canada

DANDY CANDY

You will need
Medium bowl or plastic bag
   (gallon size) with twist tie
   or seal
Fork and spoon
Measuring cups and spoons
Knife (optional)
8 x 8" baking pan (optional)
Baking sheet or plate
Plastic wrap or wax paper

1 C. **peanut butter**
1 C. dry **milk powder**
½ to ¾ C. **honey**
1 t. **vanilla**

Optional additions:
½ C. **carob powder** *or* 1 C.
   granola, rolled oats or
   puffed cereal
¼ C. **nuts**, chopped or seeds
coconut
wheat germ
wheat germ
sesame seeds
1 to 2 T. **water** (if mixture
   is too crumbly)

Can you
Use measuring cups and
   spoons?
Mix ingredients in bowl or
   plastic bag?
Chop nuts? (optional)
Roll mixture into balls or a log?
Pat mixture in baking pan?
Cover candy with plastic wrap?
Put candy in refrigerator to
   chill?
Cut or slice log or patted
   mixture into bite-size pieces?

1. Combine peanut butter, milk
   powder, honey and vanilla in
   bowl or plastic bag.
2. Mix with fork or spoon or
   squeeze plastic bag until
   ingredients are well blended.
3. For *fudgy* candy, add carob
   powder.
4. For *chewy* candy, add granola
   or oats.
5. For *crunchy* candy, add
   puffed cereal. These are a
   little harder to roll, so you
   may prefer to pat this mixture
   in a pan.
6. Chop nuts, if you like.

7. Shape into balls (about 1 rounded teaspoon each) or a log.
   Roll in coconut, wheat germ or sesame seeds or a combination of all three. Place on cookie sheet or plate.
8. Or pat mixture into pan.
9. Cover or wrap with plastic wrap and put in refrigerator to chill
   for about an hour or in freezer for 15 to 20 minutes.
10. Slice log or cut candy in pan into bite-sized squares.

PROTEIN: 110.7 grams; CALORIES: 2453

Maureen Curry   *Nancy Johnson*
Kutztown, Pennsylvania   *Greeley, Colorado*

Breads

BAKING WITH WHOLEGRAINS

With very few exceptions, all of the baked goods recipes in this book call for whole grain (usually whole wheat) flours. La Leche League recommends the consumption of foods "in as close to their natural state as possible" and the use of whole grain flour meets this requirement. The only processing that takes place is the grinding of the grain kernel, leaving the bran covering (which provides fiber) and the germ (which contains valuable protein, B vitamins, vitamin E and minerals), as well as the starchy endosperm intact. White flour contains only the endosperm and "enrichment" only replaces three to five of the 25 nutrients discarded with the bran and germ. Unbleached white flour is not nutritionally superior to ordinary bleached all-purpose flour, but it does not contain chemicals from the bleaching process. Try not to use it except for special occasions.

A nutritionally superior white flour can be made by adding powdered milk, soy flour and wheat germ to unbleached white flour. Devised at Cornell University, it is called **Cornell Mix** and has the nutritional content similar to whole wheat, but without the very important fiber. To make it, place in the bottom of your 1 C. measure 1 T. *each* **wheat germ, soy flour** and **powdered milk,** then fill the cup with unbleached white flour. To save time, mix in your cannister 5 lbs. unbleached flour and 1 C. *each* wheat germ, powdered milk and soy flour. Cornell Mix can be used in any special recipe calling for white flour, even noodles and pastries. It makes a good transition from all-purpose white flour to whole wheat, but is not meant to replace whole wheat as a staple.

If your family absolutely refuses to eat even half-whole wheat baked goods, substitute Cornell Mix for the whole wheat flour called for and replace it with whole wheat flour, a very little bit at a time, each time you bake. Have patience—in time you will find that they actually *prefer* whole wheat in many recipes! Most cookies, muffins, pancakes and those cakes sweetened with dried fruit and molasses are excellent made with 100% whole wheat flour—those of us who made the change from white to whole grain several years ago cannot imagine how we ever ate them made with white flour!

Whole wheat flour can be successfully substituted for white flour in your favorite recipes, cup for cup. It does not need to be sifted unless you wish to remove some of the coarser bran for a more delicate product. This can be done if you cannot find whole wheat pastry flour, which makes lighter cakes and breads leavened with baking powder or soda. (All-purpose whole wheat flour or hard bread flour is better for yeast breads.) Whole wheat pastry flour is not available in many communities, or it may be prohibitively expensive, in which case sifted ordinary whole wheat flour works very well.

Because it contains the germ, which houses natural oils, whole grain flours may become rancid if not stored properly. Buy flour from a store with a rapid turnover of stock to insure that your flour is fresh (or grind it in a home flour-mill), then store in a cool place in a tight container. Some families invest in a second-hand refrigerator to store bulk flour, wheat germ, oils, etc. Whole grains and flours should not be frozen because extreme cold destroys vitamin E.

Other wholegrain flours you may wish to try are soy flour (whole or defatted), which is very high in protein and may be substituted for powdered milk in baking for those allergic to dairy products; oat flour, which can be made by whirling rolled oats in your blender; brown rice flour; whole rye flour or meal (also called pumpernickel flour); millet flour; barley flour; buckwheat flour; and undegerminated cornmeal, yellow or white. If someone has an allergy to wheat, experiment with non-yeast breads using these flours. (Yeast bread needs about ⅔ wheat flour because no other flour contains the gluten necessary for light yeast bread. Breads and desserts leavened with baking powder and soda do not need gluten for leavening.)

Not all wholegrain flours are alike. They vary in quality and texture from place to place and brand to brand. Whole wheat flour should be light tan, powdery with just a little coarseness from the bran. The bran should not be in large flakes. Stoneground whole wheat flour is a little grittier in texture, with no discernible bran flakes. Wholegrain flours should be free of preservatives and bleaching agents—check the label because some brands do contain them. Cornmeal should be similar in texture to that found on supermarket shelves, if not finer. All other wholegrain flours should be powdery and sweet-smelling. If they are gritty, they should be labelled "meal." If your community supplies only inferior wholegrains, complain to your supplier and demand a good product. If you have had baking failures, they may be due to very coarse or old flour. Coarse flours need an experienced hand for success. They could be whirled in the blender and/or sifted if there is no other brand available, and they need more liquid than a fine flour. Only experiment will tell you how much more.

If you are new to whole grain baking, be patient with yourself and your family. Experiment with the tested recipes in this book and search out the best ingredients available. Make gradual changes, confident that you are improving your family's nutrition while they discover new eating pleasures.

—Bryanna Clark

CRACKERS—FINALLY!

2 C. whole wheat **flour**
    (preferably pastry flour)
1 t. **salt**
½ t. **baking soda**
¼ C. **butter**
½ C. **buttermilk** or
    ½ C. milk mixed with
    2 t. lemon juice
1 large **egg**
coarse **salt** (for topping)

Combine flour (pastry flour makes crisper crackers), salt and soda. Cut in butter until mixture has texture like oatmeal. Add milk and egg; blend to make stiff dough. You may need to add more flour, as whole wheat varies a lot. Knead thoroughly. Roll 1/8" thick on floured board, cut into squares and place on lightly greased cookie sheet. Prick with fork, sprinkle with salt. Bake at 400° until lightly browned (about 10 minutes).

When I first began to "do-it-myself" I found recipes for everything we wanted except soda crackers. I couldn't imagine that they were something only a factory could produce. Much experimentation led to this formula; now this is one more item we don't buy in a store.

PROTEIN: 43 grams; CALORIES: 1354

J. J. Fallick
Appleton, Wisconsin

DIGESTIVE BISCUITS

1½ C. whole wheat **flour**
½ C. rolled **oats**
¼ C. **wheat germ**
¼ C. **sesame seeds**
¼ t. **baking soda**
¼ t. **salt**
2 T. dry **milk powder**
¼ C. **sugar** or 3 T. honey
½ C. **butter**
⅓ C. cold **water**
1 t. **vanilla**

Combine dry ingredients in large bowl. Cut in butter to make coarse, even crumbs. Combine water and vanilla and drizzle over flour mixture. Blend until dough can be packed into a ball. Roll onto floured board or between 2 sheets of waxed paper 1/8" thick. Cut into 3" circles. Bake on greased cookie sheets at 325° for 20 to 25 minutes. They should not brown at all. Cool and store in airtight containers. Makes about 3 dozen biscuits.

We like to make these for special occasions with various cookie cutters: hearts for Valentine's Day, shamrocks for St. Patrick's Day, ducks for Easter. They keep very well. *PROTEIN: 49.3 grams; CALORIES: 2151*

Carolyn Thomas
Victoria, B.C., Canada

CROUTONS

6 slices whole wheat **bread**,
    cubed
½ C. **soy sauce** or melted butter
Seasonings: garlic powder,
    pepper, oregano or any other
    herbs

Spread cubed bread on cookie sheet. Sprinkle generously with soy sauce or butter and desired seasonings. Bake at 325° until crisp, turning often. May be stored in an airtight container in refrigerator for several weeks. *P.: 25 gms.; C.: 429*

Barbara Bahun   *Paula Harper-Christensen*
New Carlisle, Ohio   *Woodinville, Washington*

HOW TO SUBDUE THE COOKIE MONSTER AT HOLIDAY TIME
(and the rest of the year, too)

In order to enjoy the fun of baking with my children (now ages 3 and 5), while avoiding the sugar-related problems, I invented "cracker cookies." They look a lot like cookies, but taste a lot like crackers, which they are. Who wants to miss the fun and delicious aromas of baking, especially during the holidays? Using any cracker recipe, my kids and I have all the fun of mixing, rolling, cutting with cookie cutters, decorating with sesame seeds, unsweetened coconut, sunflower seeds, raisins, other dried fruits, baking and, best of all, eating. I have accumulated a large collection of cookie cutters (open ones work best with cracker dough) which spend most of their time in the sack of toys used with playdough, but which can also produce bells at Christmas, hearts at Valentine's Day, chickens for Easter and so forth. We also like to cut out biscuits using fancy cutters. Sunday breakfast is a lot more fun with a moon, or a mushroom, or a whale-shaped biscuit on your plate.   *Mary Margaret Coates*
Wheat Ridge, Colorado

CRISPY CRACKERS, BREADSTICKS OR TEETHING BISCUITS

whole wheat **bread dough**   Save a few handfuls of dough after the first rising when you make bread. Knead in a little more flour. *For Breadsticks:* roll the dough into ropes about 6" long. *For Crackers or Teething Biscuits:* roll the dough out about 1/8th inch thick on a floured surface. Cut into squares, sticks or rectangles (or whatever shape your young helper suggests) and arrange close together, but not touching, on a greased cookie sheet. Prick with a fork. If desired, sprinkle with coarse **salt**, herb-flavored **salt**, sesame or poppy **seeds**. Bake at 325° about 10 minutes, or until lightly browned. Cool on racks. Store in airtight containers.   *Eleanor Bohlken*   *Barbara Wilmes*
Springville, Iowa   *Le Sueur, Minnesota*

TODDLER-ON-THE-RUN BREADSTICKS

1 C. whole wheat **flour**
1 t. **cinnamon**
1 t. **baking soda**
¼ C. **butter**
¾ C. grated Cheddar **cheese**
1 **egg**, beaten
1 T. cold **milk**

Mix flour with cinnamon and soda. With pastry blender, cut in butter and cheese until mixture becomes coarse crumbs. Blend in egg beaten with milk. Stir with fork until dough clings together.

Take teaspoonfuls of dough and roll into little sticks. Place 1" apart on ungreased cookie sheet. Bake 8 to 10 minutes at 375°.

Having a "toddler-on-the-run," I often find it hard to find something good for him to eat while he's busy at his day-long job of exploring. Good take-along for League meetings too!   *PROTEIN: 44.3 grams; CALORIES: 1269*

Kathy Quinones
West Amherst, New York

BREAD STIX SNACK MIX

9 slices whole wheat **bread**
½ C. **butter**
½ t. **salt** or 1 T. soy sauce
½ t. **onion** or **garlic salt**
2 T. **honey** (optional)
2 T. **sesame seeds**
½ c. **raisins** or chopped dates
½ C. **pumpkin seeds**
½ C. chopped, dried **apricots**
   or other dried fruit (optional)
½ C. roasted **nuts**, sunflower
   seeds or peanuts

Use day-old bread, and cut slices into sticks 1 x ¼". Melt butter with salt, onion salt, honey and sesame seeds. Pour over bread sticks in a large bowl, tossing to coat. Spread on a cookie sheet and bake 15 minutes at 325°, stir with spatula and bake 15 minutes more.

When cool, add dried fruits and nuts. Store in airtight container. To re-crisp, place in 275° oven for 5 to 7 minutes. *PROTEIN: 53.6 grams; CALORIES: 2631*

Mary Lardinois
Green Bay, Wisconsin

DOUGHNUT GLAZE

6 T. unbleached or whole wheat
   flour
6 T. melted **butter**
4 T. **brown sugar** or honey
½ C. **honey**
2 t. **vanilla**

Beat the flour into the hot butter until mixture is smooth. Stir in sugar, honey and vanilla; return to heat and simmer 1 minute, stirring all the time. Use *immediately*.

PROTEIN: 6.4 GRAMS; CALORIES: 1577

Jean Baker White
Van Buren, Maine

YORKSHIRE PUDDING

1 C. sifted whole wheat or
   unbleached **flour**
½ t. **salt**
2 **eggs**, beaten
1 C. **milk**
¼ C. hot **beef drippings** or
   melted butter

Stir flour and salt together in medium mixing bowl. Beat eggs and milk together in another bowl. Slowly add liquids to flour, beating until batter is perfectly smooth. Cover and chill 2 hours. Heat drippings or butter in a shallow 8 x 8" pan. Pour in cold batter, and bake at 425° for 25 to 30 minutes. Cut into squares and serve immediately. For variety, divide the drippings among 12 muffin-tin cups; heat well. Half-fill each cup with cold batter and bake at 400° for 25 to 30 minutes.

Eaten with a salad and onion soup on chilly nights, there are never any leftovers! *PROTEIN: 36.8 grams; CALORIES:* 1581

Denny Mead   *Geni Wixson*   *Jeanette Marshall*
Midwest City, Oklahoma *Germantown, Maryland* *Melbourne, Florida*

Quick Breads

Nothing rounds out a meal like fresh, hot bread and the recipes in this section lend themselves to last-minute menu decisions. Take 10 minutes to whip up a batch of wholesome biscuits or muffins and pop them into the oven beside your bubbling casserole. Or surprise the family on a week-day morning with hot cornbread or muffins. These breads provide plenty of opportunity to use healthful ingredients which might be new to your family and to use seasonal fruits and vegetables. They are the ideal replacement for low-nutrition snacks and can even pinch-hit for dessert.

Unlike yeast breads, which need vigorous kneading to develop the gluten necessary for a high-rising bread, quick breads are leavened with baking powder or baking soda and acid (like buttermilk). You need a light hand to produce light quick breads—mix lightly and briefly or you will have a tough bread. Muffins and quick loaf breads should be mixed only until the dry ingredients are moistened; they should never be beaten. Biscuit dough should be kneaded very lightly and briefly before rolling out. Get the bread into the hot oven as soon as it is mixed.

Ordinary all-purpose whole wheat flour will do very nicely in these recipes (sift if the bran particles are large), but buy whole wheat pastry flour if it is available and reasonably-priced, because it contains less gluten and is ideal for non-yeast baking. Please read **Baking with Whole Grains** on p. 120 for a detailed discussion of wholegrain flours and ideas for families who are new to wholegrain baking.

The quick loaf recipes in this section are designed for a standard 9 x 5 x 3" loaf pan, but you can experiment with coffee cans, bundt pans and smaller loaf pans, adjusting the time accordingly. An **oven thermometer** is a valuable aid to home baking, because it has been found that American ovens can vary within a range of *250º*! To test for doneness, insert a toothpick, straw or cake tester in the center of the loaf. If it comes out clean, the bread is done. If not, bake a little longer and test again. If the outside seems to be cooking faster than the inside, lower the temperature.

If the bread is not eaten immediately (and many of the fruit and vegetable breads improve if left for a day or two) it should be cooled completely, wrapped in foil or plastic and refrigerated or frozen.   *BCC*

WHOLE WHEAT QUICK BREAD

2 C. whole wheat **flour**
½ C. soy **flour**
1 t. **baking soda**
1 t. **baking powder**
½ t. **salt**
¼ C. **wheat germ**
¼ C. dry **milk powder**
1½ C. **milk**
½ C. **honey** or molasses

Combine dry ingredients. Add milk and honey, stirring until moistened. Let stand 20 minutes in a greased 9 x 5" loaf pan. Bake at 350° for 35 to 50 minutes or until a toothpick comes out clean. A lovely bread for breakfast with lots of protein.

PROTEIN: 69.2 grams; CALORIES: 1938
Kay L. Dake
Kimberly, Wisconsin

LLL BAKING MIX

8 C. **flour** (whole wheat, whole
  wheat pastry, or Cornell Mix,
5 T. **baking powder**
1 T. **salt**
1 to 2 C. dry **milk powder**
1½ C. **oil**, butter or fat

Combine dry ingredients well in a
large bowl. Cut in oil or butter with
fingers to make fine crumbs. Store
in a tightly covered container in the
refrigerator. Recipe may be doubled.

Note: milk powder may be omitted
in case of milk allergy.
Makes 11 C.

Optional:
½ C. **nutritional yeast**

PROTEIN: 185.4 grams; CALORIES: 5630
1 C. = P.: 16.8 gms.; C.: 512

High-Protein Mix. In place of 8 C. flour, use 5½ C. whole wheat flour, 1 C.
soy flour and 1½ C. **wheat germ.**   *P.: 232 gms.; C.: 5836*   *1 C. = P.: 21.1 gms.; C. 531*

Whole Grain Mix. In place of 8 C. flour, use 5 C. whole wheat flour, 1 C.
bran, 1 C. **wheat germ** and 1 C. **cornmeal**, oatmeal (or oat flour, made by
whirling rolled oats in blender), rye flour, brown rice flour, or other whole
grain flour.   *PROTEIN: 185.4 grams; CALORIES: 5630*   *1 C. = P.: 16.8 gms.; C.: 512*

Janet Roy   Karen Morgan   Anne Harvey   Doris Falconer
Manitouwadge, Ont., Can. Dublin, Ohio   Topeka, Kansas   Bismarck, North Dakota

TO USE THE LLL BAKING MIX:

BISCUITS

3 C. **LLL Baking Mix**
⅔ C. **milk** or water

Optional:
grated **cheese**
herbs or spices

Stir milk into Mix just until moistened. Knead briefly on floured surface; roll or pat out to ½" thick and
cut into biscuits. Bake at 450° for 10
minutes.   *P.: 52.1 gms.; C.: 1646*

Drop Biscuits. Use 1 C. milk and drop by spoonfuls onto greased cookie
sheet. Bake as above. Makes 18   2" biscuits.   *PROTEIN: 54.9 grams; CALORIES: 1700*

Gladine McCall
Uniontown, Pennsylvania

COFFEE CAKE

2 C. **LLL Baking Mix**
¼ C. **brown sugar** or honey
1 **egg**
⅔ C. **milk** or water
2 to 3 T. melted **butter** or oil

Topping:
2 T. **brown sugar**
¼ C. **LLL Baking Mix**
1 t. **cinnamon**
1 T. **butter**
¼ to ½ C. chopped **nuts** (optional)

Beat together sugar, egg, milk and
melted butter and stir into Mix just
until moistened. Fold in nuts, if
used. Spread batter into greased 9"
layer cake pan or 8" square pan. In a
small bowl mix topping ingredients
until crumbly. Sprinkle over batter.
Bake at 400° 20 to 25 minutes.

PROTEIN: 53.3 grams; CALORIES: 2180

QUICK BISCUITS

2 C. **flour:** any combination of whole wheat, unbleached, oat flour or Cornell Mix (p. 120); bran, wheat germ or rolled oats

½ t. **salt**

2 t. **baking powder**

¼ to ½ C. **butter** or oil

⅔ C. **milk**

Optional:

½ C. **sesame seeds**

½ to 1 C. grated **cheese**

2 T. **sugar** or molasses

Stir together dry ingredients. Cut in butter until crumbly. Add milk until dough forms into a ball. Knead gently 5 to 10 times—do not overwork or biscuits will be tough. Roll or pat out on a floured surface about ½ inch thick. (For flakier biscuits, fold dough into thirds toward the center and roll out again, gently. Repeat 2 or 3 times.) Cut into squares or rounds with a floured glass or small can with both ends removed. Bake on an ungreased cookie sheet at 400 to 450° for about 15 minutes. Serve hot. These are so easy to make and taste so good! *P.: : 38 gms.; C.: 1349*

Variations:

Food Processor Method. Process dry ingredients and butter until crumbly, 10 to 15 seconds. Add milk all at once. Process until it clumps a little, about 7 seconds. Proceed as above.

Unrolled Biscuits. Pat small balls of dough into biscuit shapes, or press dough into a lightly greased 8" square pan and cut into squares.

Drop Biscuits. Use ¾ C. milk, stir dough just until blended, then drop by teaspoonfuls onto greased cookie sheet

Buttermilk or Yogurt Biscuits. Omit milk and 1 t. baking powder. Add ⅔ C. **buttermilk,** sour milk or yogurt and ¾ t. **baking soda.**

Scottish Tea Scones. Increase butter to 6 T. and add 1 **egg.** *P.: 35.1 gms.; C.: 1620*

Many LLL Contributors

MUFFINS

3 C. **LLL Baking Mix**

3 to 4 T. brown **sugar** or melted **honey**

1 C. **milk** or water

1 **egg**

3 to 4 T. melted **butter** or oil

Optional:

1 C. **fruit**

½ C. chopped **nuts** or seeds

1 T. **cinnamon**

Beat sugar, milk, melted butter and egg together and stir into Mix just until moistened. Fold in fruit and/or nuts, if used. Fill 12 greased muffin cups and bake at 425° for 20 minutes. *P.: 61.4 gms.; C.: 2258*

CORNBREAD

1½ C. **LLL Baking Mix**
¾ C. yellow **cornmeal**
1 T. **honey** or sugar (optional)
1 **egg**
1 C. **milk** or water

Combine Mix, cornmeal and honey. Add milk and egg, beaten together. Stir just until moistened and pour into an 8" square pan or hot greased cast iron skillet. Bake at 400° 25 to 30 minutes.

PROTEIN: 46.2 grams; CALORIES: 1611

The LLL Baking Mix can be used just like any commercial biscuit mix (with tastier and more nutritious results!). Experiment with it to make dumplings, soda bread, nut breads, cookies, cakes and breadsticks.

Bryanna Clark
Union Bay, B.C., Canada

PUMPKIN CORN BREAD

2 t. **oil** or melted butter
⅓ C. **honey** or sugar
2 **eggs**
2 t. **vanilla**
1 C. cooked, mashed **pumpkin**
¼ C. **cornmeal**
2 t. **baking powder**
½ t. **salt**
⅔ C. dry **milk powder**

Mix together oil, honey, eggs and vanilla. Stir in pumpkin. Combine cornmeal, baking powder, salt and dry milk powder. Mix into liquids. Bake in greased 9 x 5 x 3" loaf pan at 350° for 40 minutes. Cool in pan 15 minutes. Invert onto wire rack to cool thoroughly.

PROTEIN: 34.5 grams; CALORIES: 1144

Judy Caldwell
Ventura, California

CORNBREAD

1 C. undegerminated yellow
   cornmeal
1 C. whole wheat **flour**;
   Cornell Mix (p. 120);
   or part or all rye, oat, brown
   rice or soy flour, or cornmeal
   or wheat germ
½ t. **salt**
2 t. **baking powder**
2 to 4 T. melted **butter**
   lard or oil
1 to 4 T. melted **honey**, maple
   syrup, molasses or brown
   sugar (optional)
1 to 2 **eggs**
1 C. **milk**

Optionals:
1 T. **nutritional yeast**
¼ C. chopped **nuts**
¼ C. **raisins** or dried apricots,
   chopped
½ C. sauteed **onions**
crumbled **bacon** or chopped **ham**
up to ½ C. **sesame seeds**
¼ t. **oregano** and ½ t. **thyme**
up to 1 C. grated **cheese**

Combine dry ingredients in a medium bowl. In another bowl (or blender), combine liquid ingredients. Pour into dry ingredients and stir just until combined; do not overbeat. Pour into a greased 8" square pan and bake at 400° about 20 minutes. Serve warm with butter. Batter may be used for muffins or corn sticks. Great with baked beans, or with syrup for dessert! Try it split and covered with chili, too. For a crispy crust, pour batter into a *hot* 10" cast iron skillet.

P.: 42.2 gms.; C.: 1353

Variation: Omit milk. Add 1 C. **buttermilk, yogurt** or sour milk and ½ t. **baking soda.**   *Many LLL Contributors*   *PROTEIN: 41.8 grams; CALORIES: 1426*

WHOLE WHEAT BATTER BREAD

1 to 3 T. **yeast**
2½ to 3 C. warm **water**
  and/or **milk**
2 T. to ½ C. **honey**, sugar,
  molasses or sorghum
up to ½ C. **butter** or oil
1½ t. **salt**
6 C. whole wheat **flour**

Optionals:
Substitute ½ to 1 C. **millet**,
  rolled oats, cracked wheat,
  or other grain for same
  amount of flour
Add ½ to 1 C. cooked, mashed
  squash or sweet potatoes
Add any or all of these:
  up to ⅓ C. **nutritional yeast**
  up to ½ C. **soy flour**
  up to ½ C. **wheat germ**
  up to 2 C. dry **milk powder**
  up to 1 C. **sunflower seeds**
  up to 1½ C. **bran**
  1 to 3 C. **raisins**
  2 t. dried **herbs**
  2 T. ground **cinnamon**
  handful of **nuts**
Add 1 t. crushed **oregano**, ½ t.
  garlic powder or 1 t. fresh
  minced garlic and ½ C.
  finely chopped **pepperoni**
Substitute 2 C. rye **flour** for
  same amount of wheat flour
  and add 2 T. **caraway seeds**

Dissolve yeast in liquid with honey. Add butter, salt and 3 C. flour. Mix or beat well (beating improves texture). Stir in remaining flour and optionals, if desired. Let rise until doubled (time will vary according to how much yeast is used). Batter may rise in the refrigerator overnight. Divide in half and place in greased loaf pans. If dough is stiff enough, it may be kneaded briefly and shaped into loaves. Let rise until it peaks over top of pan. Bake at 350° for 30 to 60 minutes. Brush tops with butter, if you like, and cool on rack before slicing (very soft bread may slice more easily after refrigeration). Recipe may be halved or doubled. This bread is flat on top, not rounded like other yeast breads.

Try making one plain loaf and one variation, or 2 variations from one batch. Made with no fat and a little molasses, this is a traditional Irish bread.

This bread is great for moms with new babies (and older babies too) or those who think they don't have time to make bread. Once you are familiar with the recipe, it takes no longer to make than a batch of brownies! It's delicious, nutritious, and easy!

PROTEIN: 99.1 grams; CALORIES: 2545

Many LLL Contributors

SUPERLOAF

2½ C. whole wheat **flour**
1 t. **baking soda**
1 t. **baking powder**
1 t. **salt**
¼ t. ground **cinnamon**
½ C. **honey** (or part molasses)
¼ C. **oil**
1½ C. **buttermilk**
½ C. chopped **nuts**
1 T. grated **orange rind**
  (optional)

Sift together dry ingredients. Add to honey, oil, buttermilk, nuts and orange rind. Mix well. Let stand 20 minutes in a greased 9 x 5" loaf pan. Bake at 375° for 45 minutes to 1 hour.

This bread is great for a last minute company dessert. Takes just a few minutes for a busy mom to stir up and tastes like she went all out!

PROTEIN: 61.8 grams; CALORIES: 2543

Michelle Faszio
Loveland, Colorado

WHEAT-OAT SNACK BREAD

1 C. whole wheat **flour**
1 C. oat **flour** (grind rolled oats in blender)
2 t. **baking powder**
½ t. **salt**
1 C. **milk**
2 T. **oil**
1 T. **molasses** (optional)

Combine dry ingredients. Combine liquids separately, then add to dry ingredients, stirring to moisten. Place on a greased and floured cookie sheet. With floured hands, pat into a circle about ½" thick. Prick all over with a fork. Bake at 450° for about 10 minutes. Cut into wedges, and serve hot with cheese or butter.

The oat flour gives a different, slightly sweet taste to this snack bread.

PROTEIN: 48.4 grams; CALORIES: 1535

Buttermilk Oat Bread. Omit 1 t. baking powder and the milk. Add ½ t. **baking soda** and 1 C. **buttermilk**, sour milk or yogurt. *Brenda Wilson*
Carlyle, Saskatchewan, Canada

WALNUT BRAN QUICK LOAF

1½ C. warm **milk**
⅓ C. **molasses**
1 C. **bran**
2 C. whole wheat **flour**
1½ t. **baking powder**
½ t. **baking soda**
½ t. **salt**
1 **egg,** beaten
¼ C. **oil**
½ C. coarsely chopped **nuts**

Mix milk, molasses and bran. Let stand to soften bran. Meanwhile separately mix flour, baking powder, baking soda and salt. Set aside. Stir egg and oil into bran mixture, then add to dry ingredients, stirring just to moisten. Stir in nuts. Bake in a greased 9 x 5" loaf pan at 350° for 50 to 55 minutes. Cool in pan for 10 minutes. Invert onto rack.

This loaf is great when even bran muffins seem to require too much fussing. It is very popular at our morning LLL meetings. Not too sweet, and tastes so good with cheese.

PROTEIN: 59.6 grams; CALORIES: 2281   *Polly Forgan*
Winnipeg, Manitoba, Canada

BASIC NUT BREAD

¼ C. **butter**
¾ C. **brown sugar** or honey
2 **eggs**
2½ C. whole wheat **flour**
¾ t. **baking powder**
1½ t. **baking soda**
1½ t. ground **cinnamon**
1½ C. plain **yogurt**
1 C. chopped **nuts**

Cream butter, sugar and eggs. Separately combine flour, baking powder, baking soda and cinnamon. Add to butter mixture, along with yogurt and nuts, and mix well. Bake in a greased and floured 9 x 5" loaf pan at 350° for 55 to 60 minutes.

PROTEIN: 85.8 grams; CALORIES: 3079
Joanne Patton
Evansville, Indiana

Variation: Omit ¾ C. yogurt. Add ¾ C. mashed or pureed **fruit**.

QUICK SOURDOUGH BISCUITS

1 C. **sourdough starter** (p. 164)
1 C. whole wheat **flour**
2 t. **baking powder**
½ t. **sugar** (optional)
½ t. **baking soda**
½ t. **salt**
2 to 4 T. **butter** or oil

Mix together flour, baking powder, sugar, soda and salt. Cut in butter or oil until crumbly. Add starter, stir and knead gently until all flour is absorbed. Roll dough out on a floured surface ½" thick and cut into biscuits. Place on greased cookie sheet. Brush with melted **fat** or cream for a golden crust. Let rest in a warm place for 15 minutes. Bake at 425° for 12 to 15 minutes. Recipe may be doubled. This dough makes great cinnamon rolls, too.

PROTEIN: 21.8 GRAMS; CALORIES: 838

Drop Biscuits. Increase oil to ⅓ C. Mix into dry ingredients along with starter. Drop by tablespoons onto ungreased cookie sheet. Bake immediately.

Bryanna Clark
Union Bay, B.C., Canada

Brenda Strand
Fessenden, North Dakota

QUICK SOURDOUGH BREAD

3 C. whole wheat **sourdough starter** (p. 164)
2 C. whole wheat **flour**
1 t. **baking soda**
1 t. **salt**
2 T. **honey**
2 **eggs**
5 T. **oil**
⅓ C. **water**

Mix all ingredients together; beat well and pour into two 8 x 4" greased loaf pans. Bake at 350° for 70 to 90 minutes.

This recipe is a super time saver for a new mother. It mixes up as quickly as a batter bread and is moist and easily sliced. No kneading or waiting—just mix up and bake.

PROTEIN: 61.9 grams; CALORIES: 2109

Wanda Rezac
Marlboro, Massachusetts

EMILY'S HEALTH LOAF
(Unsteamed Boston Brown Bread)

2½ C. whole wheat **flour** or
  2 C. whole wheat flour and
  ½ C. cornmeal
2 t. **baking soda**
1 t. **salt**
2 C. **buttermilk**
½ C. dark **molasses**

Optional:
1 C. **raisins**
½ C. chopped **nuts**

Mix dry ingredients. Add raisins and nuts, if used. Add combined buttermilk and molasses and stir just until moistened. Spoon into 2 greased 1-lb. cans, 1 9 x 5 x 3" loaf pan, or 4 1½-cup loaf pans or cans. Bake at 350° for 40 to 50 minutes, or until knife comes out clean. Remove from pan and cool on rack or serve hot.

Bake small loaves when you have guests and serve on a wooden board —adds a very nice touch.

PROTEIN: 56.8 GRAMS; CALORIES: 1576

Renny Northrop
Summit, New Jersey

Pat, Mary Ann and John Haws
Avon, Minnesota

SOURDOUGH CORNBREAD

1 C. **sourdough starter** (p. 164)
2 T. melted **butter**
1½ C. **cornmeal**
½ C. plain **yogurt**
2 **eggs**
1 t. **baking powder**
1 t. **salt**

Mix all ingredients together and let rise for an hour or so. Bake in a greased pan (preferably a preheated cast iron skillet) at 375° for 20 minutes. *PROTEIN: 40.7 grams; CALORIES: 2748*

Carma J. Kimball
Elgin, Illinois

OATMEAL BREAD

2 C. whole wheat **flour**
2 C. rolled **oats**
¼ C. **wheat germ**
1 t. **baking powder**
1 t. **baking soda**
1 t. **salt**
½ C. **molasses**
2 T. melted **butter**
1 C. **raisins**
1⅔ C. **buttermilk**

Mix dry ingredients. Add remaining ingredients. Mix well. Let stand in a greased 9 x 5" loaf pan for 20 minutes. Bake at 350° for about 1 hour. Remove from pan immediately.

I serve this bread for snacks and desserts, often doubling the recipe with one loaf for the freezer. My 3-year-old loves it with fresh fruit and milk as a light breakfast or lunch—a switch from a regular meal, but hearty and nutritious. *P: 84.6 g; C: 2788*

Linda Jackson
Baltimore, Ohio

IRISH SODA BREAD

4 C. whole wheat **flour**
3 t. **baking powder**
1 t. **baking soda**
1 t. **salt**
¼ C. **butter**
1¼ C. **raisins** or currants
1 **egg**, beaten
1¾ C. **buttermilk** or
  1½ C. plain **yogurt** and
  ¼ C. milk
1 T. **honey** or molasses

Combine flour, baking powder, soda and salt. Cut in butter until it reaches a coarse meal consistency. Add raisins. Combine liquids separately. Add to dry ingredients. Mix until soft dough forms. Knead gently until smooth (about 3 minutes). Shape into two balls. Flatten each slightly and cut an X ¼" deep in their tops with sharp knife or scissors. Place on a greased cookie sheet, or 2 round pans, and bake at 375° for 35 minutes. This easy, nutritious bread replaces cookies and other sweets. Good for breakfast, too! *PROTEIN: 90.4 grams; CALORIES: 2852*   *Anne Murphy*
Glen Rock, New Jersey

ZUCCHINI OR CARROT BREAD

1½ C. grated **zucchini** or
  carrots, or ½ of each
½ C. **oil** or melted butter
½ C. **honey,** brown sugar or
  molasses
2 **eggs,** beaten
1 t. **vanilla**
1½ C. whole wheat **flour**
½ t. **baking soda**
½ t. **baking powder**
½ t. **salt**
1½ t. **cinnamon**
½ C. chopped **nuts**

Optional:
½ C. **raisins**
½ t. **nutmeg**

Beat together oil and honey. Add eggs, vanilla and zucchini; mix well. Sift dry ingredients and add to liquid mixture. Stir in nuts.

Bake in greased 9 x 5 x 3" loaf pan at 350° for 45 to 60 minutes, or until tests done. Cool in pan 10 minutes. Invert onto wire rack and cool. Wrap and refrigerate or freeze.

PROTEIN: 47.6 grams; CALORIES: 2675

Carrot-Walnut Bread. Use 1½ C. *ground* **walnuts** in place of ½ C. chopped walnuts.

Many LLL Contributors

APPLE BREAD

2 C. grated **apples**
¼ C. **oil** or butter, softened
½ C. **honey** or brown sugar
2 T. **buttermilk** or sour milk
1 to 2 **eggs**
2 C. whole wheat **flour**
1 t. **baking soda**
1 t. **baking powder**
½ t. **salt**

Optional:
1 to 2 t. **vanilla**
1 T. **cinnamon**
½ C. **raisins**
½ C. chopped **nuts**

Topping: (optional)
2 T. **butter**
2 T. *each* **flour** and **sugar**
1 t. **cinnamon**

Cream oil and honey together. Add vanilla, if desired, and buttermilk and egg. Sift dry ingredients; add to liquid mixture. Fold in apples and optional nuts and raisins. Pour into greased 9 x 5 x 3" loaf pan. Sprinkle mixed topping ingredients on top, if used. Bake at 350° for 45 minutes. Cool before removing from pan. *PROTEIN: 40.4 grams; CALORIES: 2066*

Apple Carrot Bread. Omit ½ C. grated apples. Add ½ C. grated **carrots.**

Georgine Christensen   *Peggy Wiedmeyer*   *Sharon Harmon*   *Charlene Erikson*
Peshastin, Washington   *Richfield, Wisconsin*   *Shawnee, Kansas*   *Lindenwold, New Jersey*

Pear Bread. Omit grated apples. Add 1½ C. diced, unpeeled **pears.** Omit buttermilk. Add ¾ C. **sour cream** or yogurt. Use only 1 t. **cinnamon.** Add ½ t. **nutmeg** and 1 t. grated **lemon rind.** Use 1 C. chopped **nuts.** Bake 1 hour; turn out onto rack to cool. *Marie Kraus*
Pleasant Hope, Missouri

ALLEGHENY APPLESAUCE BREAD

1 C. unsweetened **applesauce**
½ C. melted **butter** or oil
½ C. **honey** or brown sugar
2 **eggs**
1½ C. whole wheat **flour**
½ C. **wheat germ**
1 t. **baking soda**
1 t. **baking powder**
½ to 1 t. ground **cinnamon**
¼ to ½ t. ground **nutmeg**
½ to 1 C. **raisins**
½ C. **sunflower seeds** or
  chopped nuts

Optional:
1 t. **vanilla**
½ t. **salt**

Beat together butter and honey. Add eggs, mixing well. Add vanilla, if desired, and applesauce. Combine dry ingredients, raisins and seeds, and add to liquid ingredients.

Bake in greased 9 x 5 x 3" loaf pan at 350° for 55 to 60 minutes. Allow to cool in pan 30 to 45 minutes; turn out. Wrap and store overnight before slicing. Freezes well.

PROTEIN: 73.4 grams; CALORIES: 3017

Joyce G. Bliss
Lawrenceville, Georgia

Louella Ericksen
Succasunna, New Jersey

Denise Cavaliere
Cherry Hill, New Jersey

Oatmeal Applesauce Bread. Omit wheat germ. Add 1½ C. rolled **oats.**

PROTEIN: 69.8 grams; CALORIES: 3229

Alice McCawley
Fortville, Indiana

Mary Knapp
Kaukauna, Wisconsin

APPLE DATE BREAD

1 C. finely chopped **apples**
1 C. chopped **dates**
½ C. **honey** or brown sugar
1½ C. **milk**
1 **egg**, lightly beaten
1 t. **vanilla**
3 C. whole wheat **flour**
1 T. **baking powder**
1 t. **salt**
1 C. unsweetened, shredded
  coconut
1 t. ground **cinnamon** or nutmeg
  (optional)

Combine honey, milk, egg and vanilla. Mix dry ingredients and add; blend well. Stir in apples and dates.

Bake in greased and floured 9 x 5 x 3" loaf pan at 350° for 50 minutes, or until tests done. Cool on wire rack. Wrap and refrigerate overnight.

PROTEIN: 74.9 grams; CALORIES: 3032

Karen Elkins
Minot AFB, North Dakota

WHOLE WHEAT BANANA NUT BREAD

1 C. mashed **bananas**
   (3 medium)
⅓ C. **oil** or melted butter
½ C. **honey** or brown sugar
2 **eggs**, beaten
1¾ C. whole wheat **flour**
½ t. **salt**
1 t. **baking soda**
¼ C. hot **water**
½ C. chopped **nuts**

Beat oil and honey together. Add eggs, mix well. Stir in bananas. Add sifted dry ingredients alternately with hot water; mix until smooth.

Bake in greased 9 x 5 x 3" loaf pan at 325° for 55 to 60 minutes. Cool on wire rack for ½ hour before slicing. Freezes well.

PROTEIN: 52.5 grams; CALORIES: 2733

Many LLL Contributors

Frozen Bananas: Peel and freeze unused ripe bananas for later use.

CORNY BANANA OAT BREAD

1 C. mashed ripe **bananas**
   (2 to 3 medium)
½ C. **oil** or melted butter
½ C. **honey** or brown sugar
2 **eggs**
1 C. whole wheat **flour**
½ C. **cornmeal**
½ C. rolled **oats**
¼ C. **wheat germ**
1 t. **baking soda**
¼ t. **salt**

Cream oil and honey. Add eggs one at a time. Combine dry ingredients; add to honey mixture alternately with bananas. Bake in greased 9 x 5 x 3" loaf pan at 350° for 1 hour, or until center tests done.

PROTEIN: 54.8 grams;CALORIES: 2961

Sharon Matuszek
Chatham, New York

SOURDOUGH BANANA BREAD

1 C. **sourdough starter** (p. 164)
1 C. mashed ripe **banana**
½ C. **butter**
¼ to ½ C. white or **brown sugar**
   or honey
2 **eggs**
2 C. whole wheat **flour**
1¼ t. **baking soda**
1 t. **salt**
¼ C. **raisins** (optional)

Mix together butter, sugar, eggs, banana and sourdough starter. Sift together flour, baking soda and salt; add to sourdough mixture. Mix well. Stir in raisins, if desired. Let mixture sit for 10 minutes to bubble, then stir. Pour into greased 9 x 5 x 3" loaf pan. Put into cold oven. Set heat at 350° and bake for 45 to 65 minutes. Cool on wire rack.

PROTEIN: 55.4 grams; CALORIES: 2624

Variations: Substitute 1 C. cooked **squash** or pumpkin, or grated zucchini for bananas. Add ground **cinnamon, cloves** and **allspice** for extra flavor.

Marie Lundstrom
Cambridge, Wisconsin

CRANBERRY BREAD

1 C. **cranberries**, coarsely
  chopped
1 fresh **orange**
2 T. **oil**
hot **water**
2 C. whole wheat **flour**
½ t. **baking soda**
1½ t. **baking powder**
½ t. **salt**
½ C. **honey** or sugar
1 **egg**
½ C. chopped **nuts**

To the juice (about ½ C.) and 1 T. grated rind of the orange, add oil and enough hot water to make ¾ C. liquid. Add this to sifted dry ingredients. Blend in honey and egg; fold in cranberries and nuts.

Bake in greased 9 x 5 x 3" loaf pan at 325° for 1 hour. Cool in pan 15 minutes; invert onto wire rack. Freezes well.

PROTEIN: 47.9 grams; CALORIES: 2097

Jeanie Donaldson
Ridgecrest, California

Peggy Cato
Great Falls, Montana

Patty Ellul
Danbury, Connecticut

Connie Kaiser
Pocatello, Indiana

WHEAT GERM BREAD

2 C. whole wheat **flour**
1 t. ground **cinnamon**
½ t. ground **nutmeg**
½ t. ground **ginger**
3 T. **nutritional yeast**
2 **eggs**
1 C. **milk**
⅓ C. **oil**
¼ C. **molasses**
¾ C. **wheat germ**
½ to 1 C. **raisins** or other
  dried fruit

Mix flour, spices and nutritional yeast. Beat eggs, milk and oil. Add to dry ingredients. Add molasses, wheat germ and raisins. Mix well. Pour into a greased 9 x 5" loaf pan. Bake at 350° for 45 to 55 minutes.

This makes a nice dessert loaf. I also fix it without fruit when I need a quick loaf of sandwich bread and don't have time to make yeast bread.

PROTEIN: 99 grams; CALORIES: 2708

Sandi Roberts
APO, New York

RHUBARB BREAD

2 C. finely diced **rhubarb**,
  raw or frozen
⅔ C. **oil**
1½ C. **brown sugar**, packed
1 **egg**
1 t. **vanilla**
1 C. **buttermilk**
2½ C. whole wheat **flour**
1 t. **baking soda**
1 t. **salt**
½ C. chopped **nuts**

Mix together oil, brown sugar, egg, vanilla and buttermilk. Add sifted dry ingredients. Fold in rhubarb and nuts. Pour into 2 greased 9 x 5 x 3" loaf pans. Bake at 350° for 60 minutes. Store in refrigerator.

PROTEIN: 39.2 grams; CALORIES: 4075

Beth Ann Carroll
Hurricane, W. Virginia

AN INTRODUCTION TO YEAST BREADS

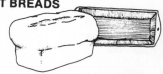

Why bake your own bread? Here are seven good reasons: (1) **thrift**; (2) **nutrition** (if you use 100% wholegrain flour and add things like wheat germ, soy flour, etc.); (3) **purity** (if you use pure, unbleached flours your bread will contain none of the 25 different chemicals used to bleach flour, retard spoilage and simplify manufacture); (4) **quality** (what could be fresher than homemade bread?); (5) **variety** (you can experiment with hundreds of breads); (6) **satiation** (one slice of homemade bread is more satisfying than several slices of store-bought); and, last but not least, (7) **pleasure**—from the physical act of breadmaking, the creativity, the satisfaction of a job well done, the appreciation of family and friends, and the joy of sharing.

You don't need a lot of fancy equipment to bake bread. Any 3 or 4 quart bowl will do for a 2-loaf batch. For anything larger, a big wooden salad bowl, an enamel dishpan or a canning kettle will work fine. Even loaf pans are unnecessary—you can use any baking pan, placing the loaves side by side, or making round or long loaves. Large coffee or juice cans (the kind with the label painted on), well-greased, make excellent bread pans. If you prefer conventional loaf pans, use 8 x 4" ones for loaves containing 3 to 4 cups of flour, 9 x 5" pans for loaves containing 4 or more cups. 8 x 4" pans make a higher, rounder loaf if your dough is a heavy, grainy type.

Your **oven** is your most important piece of equipment and no oven is exactly the same as another. You will have to become acquainted with "hot spots" and "cold spots" in yours, and turn your pans around during baking to compensate, if necessary. Most ovens are hotter towards the back. If you use glass pans, turn your oven down 25°. Baked goods with large amounts of honey and/or soy flour should also be baked at slightly lower than normal temperatures. We urge you strongly to spend a little on an **oven thermometer**. A survey of ovens showed that they can vary as much as 100° F. (or 55° C.). Even if your oven thermostat is adjusted regularly, it can lose its accuracy over a period of several months. An oven thermometer will prevent many disappointments.

Just as oven temperatures can vary, so can room and water temperatures, and humidity in the air. All of these variations in environment, as well as differences in ingredients, make bread-making a very inexact art. Recipes are guides only. Rising and baking times (if given at all) are approximate at best. Your house may be warmer and drier than your next-door neighbor's, so you may need to add slightly less flour than she does to your dough, and your dough may rise a half an hour faster than hers. The dough itself is very flexible. It will, unlike a touchy cake batter, accommodate emergencies and interruptions. It can be made to fit into any life-style. At any step along the way, the dough can be oiled, wrapped loosely with plastic and refrigerated until you have time to deal with it again. Bread is a wonderful outlet for the creative baker, too, because you can add things to it, substitute ingredients, change flavorings and come up with a whole new recipe! That is why many of our recipes have ranges of ingredients.

When it comes to basic ingredients, buy the best you can afford. **Flour** should be fresh, local if possible, and 100% whole wheat, nothing added, nothing removed. Unbleached white flour contains no bleaching agents, but it is no more nutritious than bleached white flour. Try to use it only for special occasions, or, if your family is not used to wholegrains, keep adding more whole wheat to your unbleached until they are used to 100% whole wheat. **Cornell Mix** is a nutritionally superior white flour which you can mix yourself. See **Baking with Whole Grains** on p. 120 for directions for making it, and more information on whole grain flours, storage, purchasing, nutritional content, and transition from white to whole grain baking.

If possible, buy flour made from hard wheat, sometimes called bread flour. It contains more gluten, the protein substance which helps the bread rise with the action of the yeast. Strong kneading or beating strengthens the gluten and results in a higher-rising bread. Stoneground flour is said to retain more nutrients than ordinary flour because it is ground at lower temperatures. It is a little grittier than ordinary flour, but makes excellent bread. Buy it if you can (or get a home flour mill), but don't pay exorbitant prices for it. All-purpose whole wheat flour, usually a mixture of hard and soft wheats, makes very good bread, but do not make yeast bread with whole wheat pastry flour—it does not have sufficient gluten for good bread.

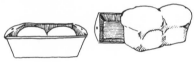

Yeast referred to in this chapter means **Dry Active Baking Yeast**. Don't confuse it with brewer's yeast or nutritional yeast, which is nutritious food, but will not make bread rise! Dry active yeast is much more readily available than old-fashioned cake, or compressed, yeast, has a longer life and is easier to store. To save money, buy dry active yeast in bulk from a natural foods store and keep it in a tightly covered jar in the refrigerator or freezer. 1 T. bulk yeast equals 1 package dry active yeast or one package (⅔oz.) cake yeast.

Salt, in small quantities, is needed to check the action of the yeast and to produce an even textured bread. Without salt, your bread might rise too quickly and then fall flat. It might taste flat, too. Salt brings out the flavor of the grain and makes sweetening virtually unnecessary. Our recipes contain minimal amounts of salt.

Sugar, honey, molasses and other sweeteners are added to bread doughs to hasten the action of the yeast, but they are not really necessary. Most French bread contains no sugar at all. The dough may rise a little more slowly, but the yeast can feed off the starch in the flour and many people believe that a slow rising develops the flavor. Honey adds to the keeping qualities of bread but over-use of liquid sweeteners may make bread heavy. Large quantities of molasses may be overpowering. Don't over-sweeten—let the taste of the grain come through. Try natural sweeteners like sprouts and fruit juices, or **Diastatic Malt** .

Fats are optional, but they improve the keeping qualities of bread. Butter and oil are most common (try Super Butter, p. 282), but you can use any pure fat without BHT and BHA. Solid fat makes a higher-rising bread and is definitely preferable for greasing pans (oil causes bread to stick to the pan). Solid fat should be softened or melted before mixing into the dough. If you are using honey too, melt them together. Lecithin, a soy product, may be used in place of fat in breads and to grease pans.

The **liquid** in bread dough can be milk (which makes a smooth, more cake-like bread), water, vegetable-cooking water, juice or stock. **Milk does not need to be scalded unless it is raw!** Pasteurization kills the enzyme in raw milk which interferes with the action of the yeast. If you want to add eggs for a more tender, airy bread, omit ¼ C. of liquid for each large egg that you use. Grated or mashed fruits or vegetables also provide liquid. Omit about ½ C. liquid for each C. of fruit or vegetable you use.

One of the secrets of light, high-rising 100% whole wheat bread is **potato cooking water**. (The other secrets are excellent flour, vigorous kneading, a small amount of solid fat in the dough, a light hand with the sweetener, sufficient rising time and, if desired, eggs in the dough.) Potato starch seems to be the ideal yeast food. Save the water in the refrigerator each time you boil potatoes (it doesn't matter if you leave the skins on, as long as they are clean). You don't have to use all potato water—just a little will do the trick if that's all you have. Add powdered milk if you prefer milk in your bread. If you never boil potatoes, keep a chunk of cooked potato (baked is fine) in the freezer at all times and simply whirl it in the blender with hot water when you bake bread. Potato water can be used in any bread recipe, except French-type breads, where a firm, chewy texture is desired.

If you have a **milk allergy** in your family and a bread recipe calls for milk, simply substitute soy milk, water or potato cooking water for the milk. It will not harm the bread.

Our **Key Bread Recipe** (100% Whole Wheat Bread) contains detailed directions for bread-making, including mixing, kneading, rising, baking and many alternative methods. The rest of the bread recipes in this book are given in shortened form in order to include as many as possible. Refer to the Key Bread recipe if any step is unclear.

Once you have mixed your dough you may be looking for a **warm spot to rise the dough.** Try a car seat on a sunny day (open a window); on top of the stove while baking something else (make sure it's not *too* hot, though); a shelf over stove, heater or radiator; in the oven which has been slightly heated and turned off, with the oven light or pilot light on, or a large pan of hot water on the oven floor; on a rack above a sinkful of hot water; in a basin of warm water; in a styrofoam cooler with a jug of hot water; or out on the kitchen counter on a hot day. The temperature should be 70 to 80° F.

To **shape an ordinary loaf** of bread, divide your dough evenly, knead each piece briefly and press it into a small rectangle. Roll or fold it into a loaf shape and pinch the "seam" and ends. Place seam-side down in the greased pan. See the illustrations for different shapes of loaves and rolls that you can make. After rising in the pan you can **decorate** the loaves by slashing the tops with a sharp knife or razor blade. See illustrations for some designs you can make. You can glaze your bread before and during baking for a professional-looking shiny crust with Egg Wash, Egg White Glaze or Cornstarch Glaze (p. 144). Brushing with milk or fat aids browning, too. For interest, sprinkle the loaves with poppy, sesame or caraway seeds or rolled oats.

Store your bread in a paper bag if it will be eaten within a few days. Plastic bags promote mold. You can freeze bread in plastic or foil, which is handy for quick oven-thawing. If you slice bread before freezing (a good use for an electric knife) you can easily separate slices for last minute sandwiches (they will be thawed out by lunch-time and keep the filling cold). Save leftover bread in a paper bag and use for stuffings, puddings, breading mixes, pie crust crumbs, croutons, meat-stretching, even emergency pet food (soak in milk)! Feed it to your animals, if necessary, but please don't throw it away!   *—Bryanna Clark*

KEY BREAD RECIPE
Basic 100% Whole Wheat Bread
2 Loaves

This recipe is the "daily bread" of many families. It can be the basis for an infinite variety of breads—just look at all the optional ingredients! The directions are more detailed than the other recipes in this section and are meant to be **general directions** for the entire section. Please refer to them (and to the Introduction) to clarify unfamiliar terms and techniques.

There are four steps to breadmaking: Mixing; Kneading; Rising and Shaping; and Baking. Each step has alternate methods. Try them all to see which suits you best, or which might be useful to you in different situations. (For instance, the Refrigerator Rise method is handy for busy mothers or for holiday breakfasts when you want hot rolls or bread for breakfast, but don't want to get up at 4 a.m.!)

This recipe may be halved, doubled or tripled.

1 to 2 T. **yeast**
2¼ to 2¾ C. warm **liquid** (p. 136)
1 to 4 T. **honey**, molasses or
    other sweetener *or*
    1 T. **diastatic malt**
2 t. **salt**
¼ C. **butter** or oil (optional)
6 to 8 C. whole wheat **flour**

PROTEIN: 103.2 grams; CALORIES: 3019

Mixing:
Conventional Method: In a large bowl, dissolve yeast in warm liquid (about 85° or like baby's bathwater) with 1 t. honey. When it bubbles up (5 to 10 minutes), add remaining honey, salt, butter and 3 C. flour. Beat by hand 200 strokes (use a wooden spoon if possible—it's light and strong), or 2 minutes at medium speed with an electric mixer. This strengthens the gluten and makes the bread rise more easily. Add 1 more cup flour and beat briefly.

Sponge Method: Now, with either method, you have what is called a "sponge." Some cooks prefer to let this sponge rise once before adding the rest of the flour and kneading the dough. They feel that this softens the bran and makes a lighter bread. It is entirely a matter of preference. To raise the sponge, cover it loosely and set in a warm spot (p. 136) until it has doubled in size, about 1 hour *or* place it in the refrigerator or other cool spot and let it rise overnight.

Rapid-Mix Method: In a saucepan, mix liquid, honey, salt and butter to about 120° (as hot as you can stick your finger in it without burning). Mix yeast with 2 C. flour in a large bowl and pour in hot liquid. Beat 300 strokes by hand or 2 or 3 minutes with electric mixer. Make sure you can see no undissolved yeast granules. Add 2 more C. flour and beat briefly.

Optional:
up to 3 **eggs** (omit ¼ C. liquid
    for each egg)
Omit equal amount of flour for
each ½ C. or more dry
ingredient used:
    ¼ to ⅔ C. **wheat germ**
    ½ t. to 1 C. dry **milk powder**
    ½ C. **bran**
    ¼ to ¾ C. gluten **flour**
    1 to 2 T. **kelp powder**
        (instead of salt)
    ½ C. rolled **oats** or other grain
    ½ C. cooked **cereal**

up to 1½ C. rye **flour** (with
    1 to 2 T. caraway seeds,
    if desired)
up to 2 C. soy **flour**
2 to 3 T. **nutritional yeast**
¼ C. **sesame** and/or **sunflower**
    seeds (ground or whole)
¼ C. **cornmeal**
½ C. chopped **nuts**
1 C. **raisins**
½ C. **rice bran**
2 T. **bone meal powder**
2 T. **lecithin**

Kneading:
Add remaining flour (and optionals) until a soft dough results. If you use the larger amount of liquid or liquid sweetener, you will need the larger amount of flour, but the amount is never exact because the age of the flour and the humidity in the air can affect the amount of flour you need to use from day to day.

Turn dough out onto a firm surface. It should be low enough so that you can straighten your arms out comfortably. The kneading surface and the dough should be lightly floured. Knead the dough by pushing the palms of your hands firmly into the dough, folding the dough over towards you, giving it a quarter-turn and repeating—push, fold, turn—for 5 to 15 minutes. You can even slam the dough down hard every so often! Add more flour as you knead, but don't allow the dough to become too dry, or your finished bread will be crumbly. Only experience can tell you, but soon you will know when you have added enough flour. Sometimes the dough kneads well but still sticks to your hands—in that case it is preferable to oil the surface and your hands rather than flour them.

For some, kneading is a satisfying experience, but for those to whom it is a chore, or a physical impossibility, a dough hook on a heavy duty electric mixer or a food processor gives excellent results. Follow the directions given with your machine. Directions for making bread in a food processor are given below.

The dough is kneaded sufficiently when it is firm, springy ("elastic") and smooth ("satiny"). The more you knead, the more height and finer texture your bread will have.

Rising and Shaping:

Conventional Method: Place the kneaded dough in a greased bowl large enough for the dough to double in size. (Just wash your mixing bowl in warm water, if it's large enough, dry it, and oil or grease it—it will be nice and warm.) Turn the dough over so that the top is greased too. Cover loosely with a towel (or a clean diaper), foil, waxed paper or plastic wrap. Place in a warm spot, about 85° (p. 136) until it has doubled in size. (You can let it rise in the refrigerator for several hours or overnight if you prefer.) The length of time it takes depends on the temperature and the amount of yeast used. 1½ hours is average. It's okay to over-rise at this point. Punch down the dough (literally!). You can let it rise one or several more times, if you wish (each successive rise will take less time), but this is *not* necessary.

Shape into 2 loaves and place in 2 greased loaf pans (or other pans). If you used 6 to 7 C. flour, use 8 x 4" pans; 8 C. flour should fill two 9 x 5" pans. Use a solid fat for greasing—oil is absorbed and makes the bread stick to the pan. Grease the tops of the loaves, to prevent drying and to give a golden crust. Cover *loosely* and let rise in a warm place until doubled in size. Poke a corner of a loaf with your little finger. If it fills in immediately, it needs more rising. If the dent remains, it has risen enough. If the dough appears puffy and blistered, it has risen too far and will fall when baked. Punch down, shape and rise again.

If you like, you can raise the loaves in the refrigerator for several hours. (This is good insurance for mothers of small children, who seem to have more than their share of interruptions and emergencies!)

If you are in a hurry, you can omit the first rising and simply place the dough in pans after kneading, but the bread will have a coarser texture.

After the bread has risen in the pans, you may glaze, slash or decorate it. (See "An Introduction to Yeast Breads.")

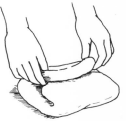

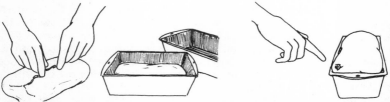

Rapid Rise: Omit first rising in bowl. Shape kneaded bread and place in loaf pans as above. Place in a **cold** oven and turn oven to 200° for about 20 minutes. When bread has doubled, turn oven to 350° and bake for 45 minutes. (If you have an electric oven with top element, cover loaves loosely with foil while oven heats up and remove for the remaining baking time.)

Refrigerator Rise: Use 2 T. yeast and do not omit butter or oil (this method requires some fat in the dough). Let kneaded dough rest with the bowl turned upside down over it for 20 minutes. Shape into 2 loaves and place in greased pans as above. Oil tops of loaves and cover loosely with plastic wrap. Let rise in refrigerator from 2 to 24 hours. Take bread out of refrigerator and let stand at room temperature for about 10 minutes while oven heats up.

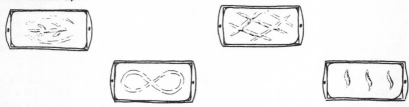

Baking:
Conventional Method: Preheat oven to 350 to 375°. Place loaves on center rack and bake for about 35 minutes, or until golden brown. To test for doneness, take one loaf out of pan and tap the bottom. If it sounds hollow, it's done. Or stick a cake tester through the bottom—if it comes out clean, it's done. Cool bread on racks, or place it crosswise on pans so that air can circulate around it while it cools. This keeps the crust from getting soggy. If you like a soft crust brush it with melted butter or milk after you remove it from oven and/or cover it with a clean cloth while it cools.

Cold Oven Method: Let loaves rise until just above tops of pans and place in a **cold** oven. Set oven to 325 to 375° and bake loaves for about 45 minutes. (If you have an electric oven, cover the bread loosely with foil while the oven heats up, then remove it.) Some cooks feel that this method saves rising time and prevents bread from falling. It does save energy.

Many LLL Contributors

PROCESSOR BREAD

If you have a food processor, you might like to try making bread in it, one loaf at a time. Dissolve ½ to 1 T. **yeast** and ½ to 2 T. **honey** in ¼ C. warm **liquid**. Position metal knife blade in processor bowl. Add 3 to 4 C. **flour**, 1 t. **salt** and 2 T. **butter** and process 5 seconds. With processor running, add **yeast** mixture through chute, then add 1 to 1¼ C. **liquid** in a slow, steady stream to make the dough form a loose ball. Stop processor immediately. Knead dough by hand a few times and proceed as for Basic Bread.

Marti Miller
Raleigh, North Carolina

MICROWAVE BREAD

Use Rapid-Mix method, heating liquids in microwave oven to 120 to 130°, using temperature probe or thermometer to check temperature. For rising, place dough in a non-metal bowl, cover with plastic wrap and heat in microwave oven for 15 seconds. Let stand 5 minutes. Timing is important! Too much heat will kill the yeast. Repeat 3 to 5 times, until dough has doubled in size. Knead 5 minutes. Rise again in microwave oven as before. Knead briefly and shape into rolls or loaves. Place in greased glass pans. Brush tops with oil and cover with plastic wrap. Rise again in microwave oven as before. I cannot get all my bread and rolls in my microwave at once, so I raise some not quite double. They finish rising while I raise the rest in the microwave. Bake in a conventional oven.

Claudia Michalec
Wharton, Texas

GRANOLA BREAD

Use part **milk**, part water, for liquid in Basic Bread. Use molasses for sweetener. Add ½ C. **granola**, ½ C. **raisins**, ½ C. **sunflower seeds** and 2 T. grated **orange rind**. Serve warm with homemade soup.

Marie Bloom
Hamilton, Montana

"SOURDOUGH" BREAD

Use Sponge Method, but let it set 2 or 3 days, until it smells nice and sour. Then proceed with recipe.

APPLE CIDER WHEAT BREAD

Use **apple cider** as the liquid, 4 T. **honey**, 1½ t. **salt** and ½ C. **oil**. Proceed with Basic Bread recipe.

Cindy Karl
Arden, North Carolina

DATE-NUT BREAD

To Basic Bread add ½ to 1 C. **wheat germ**, 1 C. snipped **dates** and ½ C. (or more) chopped **nuts**.

Ellen J. Blacketer   *June Benson*
Plainfield, Indiana   *Ovid, New York*

SUGARLESS CINNAMON ROLLS

Roll 1 loaf bread dough into a 9 x 13" rectangle. Spread with softened butter, sprinkle with **cinnamon**. Core and finely chop 1 small **apple** (no need to peel). Sprinkle apple and ½ to 1 C. **raisins** over dough. Press with rolling pin. Roll up lengthwise like a jellyroll and cut in 1" slices. Place in greased baking pan, let rise until doubled and bake at 350° for 25 to 35 minutes. Brush with butter when done. Makes about 12 rolls.

Deirdre Eiler
Renton, Washington

HAMBURGER BUNS

When dough is ready for shaping, divide it into 16 equal parts and roll each into a ball. Flatten each ball into a 4" circle. Place on greased cookie sheets. (Dough will shrink a little.) Brush tops with oil or melted butter. Let rise until doubled. Brush tops with **Egg White Wash** (p. 144). Sprinkle with poppy or sesame seeds, if you wish. Bake at 400° for 15 minutes, changing position of baking sheets once during baking.

Carol Tag
Springfield, Missouri

FLOWER POT BREAD

For a beautiful bread which accentuates the "earthy" quality of whole grain bread, bake your favorite bread recipe in a clean unglazed clay flower pot! The best size is 4½" deep by 5½" across. The pots need "seasoning," like cast iron, before using, or the bread will glue itself to the pot! Rub it inside and out with any kind of fat and bake it at high heat (at least 400°) two or three times, about 30 minutes each time. You can do this while you're baking something else. Use loaves with about 2 C. flour per loaf, or enough dough to fill the greased pot just over half full before rising. Let the dough rise to within 1½" of the top of the pot. Bake in a hot oven (425 to 450°) for about 30 minutes. For an extra crispy crust, spray the loaves with cold water after 15 minutes. When almost baked, slip the loaves out of the pots and finish the loaves on a cookie sheet for a crusty outside. Cool on racks, then serve in the flower pot for effect!

Bryanna Clark
Union Bay, B.C., Canada

Knead until the dough is silky like a baby's bottom.

Sherron Collins   *Adrienne Collins*
Grand Rapids, Michigan   *St. Louis, Missouri*

DIASTATIC MALT
(An Alternative to Sugar)

1 C. wheat berries
tepid **water**

In a wide-mouth quart canning jar, with the ring fitted with a plastic strainer, fine cheesecloth or rust-proof mesh screening, soak wheat berries overnight in water to cover. Drain well and place the jar in a shallow pan, tilted so that excess water can drain out and air can circulate. Cover loosely with a cloth. Keep in a warm, dark place, rinsing and draining twice a day. When the sprouts are about the same length as the grain, rinse and drain well and spread the sprouts on 2 ungreased cookie sheets. Dry in a 150° oven, no hotter, for about 8 hours, or until sprouts are crunchy. Grind them in a food mill, seed grinder or blender. Store in a dry, airtight container in the refrigerator. Will keep indefinitely. Use in yeast breads at the rate of about 1 T. malt in place of about ¼ C. honey or other sweetener. Use to flavor milkshakes and cereal, too.

Linda Sue Siebert
Ann Arbor, Michigan

Barbara Atkisson
Onalaska, Washington

When we "entertain" in winter I make individual-sized loaves and serve with hamburger stew. The guests "ooh" and "aah" over freshly baked bread and never notice the lack of steak! *Roberta S. Rogers*
Newport News, Virginia

MULTI-GRAIN BREAD

3 C. warm **water**, or 1 C. warm water to dissolve yeast and water and eggs to equal 2 C.
1 to 2 T. **yeast**
1 T. to ½ C. **honey**, sugar or molasses
6 C. whole wheat **flour**
¼ to ½ C. **oil** or butter
2 t. **salt**
3 C. mixed **grains**, your choice: rolled oats; soy flour or grits; bran; wheat germ; rye flour or flakes; cracked wheat or bulgur; barley flakes

Optional:
½ to 1 C. dry **milk powder**
½ to 1 C. chopped **nuts** and/or whole or ground **seeds** (sesame, flax or sunflower)
¼ C. **nutritional yeast**

Dissolve yeast in water with honey. When bubbly, stir in mixed grains, 1½ C. flour and eggs, if used. Beat well and let rise 1 hour. (You may omit this rising, but it softens the grains.) Add oil, salt, optionals and remaining flour. Knead at least 10 minutes. Do not allow dough to become too dry. Knead with oil if necessary. Let rise until doubled. Punch down and shape into 2 loaves. Place in greased 8 x 4" loaf pans. Let rise until doubled and bake at 350° for 45 to 50 minutes, or until golden brown. Cool on racks. Brush with melted **butter**, if desired.

Irresistible when hot and scrumptious cool! Even confirmed white-bread-eaters enjoy its hearty flavor. For a change, bake in *well*-greased 46-oz. juice cans. *Many LLL Contributors*

PROTEIN: *171.4 grams; CALORIES: 3981*

CORNSTARCH GLAZE

1 t. **cornstarch**
½ C. cold **water**

Mix in a small saucepan and cook, stirring, over high heat, until thickened. Brush on bread before and during baking for a shiny, crisp crust. Good on French bread.

PROTEIN: 0 grams; CALORIES: 12

EGG WASH

1 whole **egg**
1 T. **water**

Beat together with a fork and brush on bread before baking. Makes a shiny, brown crust, good for sweet breads.   *PROTEIN: 6.2 grams; CALORIES: 78°*

EGG WHITE GLAZE

1 **egg white**
1 T. **water**

Beat together with a fork and brush on bread before baking. Also suitable for French breads.

PROTEIN: 3.4 grams; CALORIES: 16

ITALIAN OR FRENCH BREAD

1 to 1½ T. **yeast**
2 C. very warm **water**
1 to 2 T. **sugar**, honey or
    date sugar (optional)
1½ t. **salt** or 1 t. kelp powder
6 C. **flour** (2 C. unbleached and
    and 4 C. whole wheat, or your
    own combination)

Optional:
2 t. **cornmeal**
2½ T. **oil**

Dissolve yeast in water with salt and sugar (if used). Beat in enough flour (about 3 C.) to make a batter. Beat until smooth. Allow to rise until doubled, if you wish. Beat in enough flour to make a pliable dough. Knead 5 to 10 minutes, using as little extra flour as possible. Let rise until doubled one or two times. Knead again briefly and shape into 2 oblong loaves. Place on greased cookie sheet sprinkled with cornmeal. Let rise until doubled. Make 3 or 4 diagonal slits on loaf tops with a sharp knife or razor blade. Bake at 400° for 20 to 25 minutes (or place in a cold oven and turn to 400° and bake 45 minutes—cover loosely with foil while oven heats up if you have an electric oven). Cool on racks.

For a crisp crust, bake the bread on unglazed ceramic tiles; place a pan of boiling water in the bottom of the oven; brush or spray the loaves with water (using a plant mister, if you have one) before and during baking; and/or glaze with Egg White Wash (p. 144) or Cornstarch Glaze (p. 144). Sprinkle the loaves with poppy or sesame **seeds**, if you like, or make them into braids or sub rolls.   *PROTEIN: 93.8; CALORIES: 2469*

Barbara Moher   *Gerry and Geni Wixson*   *Sylvia Fink*   *Esther Rosen*
Plymouth, Connecticut   *Germantown, Maryland*   *Miami Beach, Florida*   *Breckenridge, Michigan*

PITA OR POCKET BREAD
(Bible Bread)

1 T. **yeast**
1 T. **honey** or sugar
2½ C. warm **water**
1½ t. **salt**
1 T. **oil**
6 to 7 C. whole wheat **flour**

Dissolve yeast and honey in water. When bubbly, add salt, oil and 6 C. flour. Knead 5 to 10 minutes, adding more flour if necessary. Let rise until doubled, about 1 hour. Punch down and divide into 12 to 20 equal pieces, depending on how large you want the pitas. Roll each into a ball and roll out on a floured surface about ¼" thick. Place circles on greased cookie sheets and let rest 30 to 45 minutes. Heat oven to 450°. Just before baking, turn the pitas over. Bake 8 to 10 minutes, switching position of pans halfway through. The pitas should be puffed in the middle and only slightly browned. To keep them soft place them inside of a paper bag to cool, or eat them warm. Recipe may be halved or doubled.

These freeze well and are great to have on hand for quick meals or bag lunches. Freeze wrapped in foil and thaw, still wrapped, at 350° for about 15 minutes.

A plain old sandwich quickly becomes special when the bread has its own magic pocket! To serve, slice in half and fill with traditional meatballs, kabob meat or felafel (fried chickpea balls,(p. 209), marinated vegetables and yogurt, or your favorite sandwich filling. Or use as taco shells or to scoop up chili or stew. Also great for individual pizzas.

If you want to be assured of each bread forming a pocket, try baking them on hot ceramic tiles (extra unglazed floor tiles, for instance—place in oven before preheating) PROTEIN: 99.3 GRAMS; CALORIES: 2608   *Many LLL Contributors*

QUICK POCKET BREAD
(Pita)

1 T. **yeast**
½ to 1 T. **honey**
½ C. warm **water**
½ t. **salt**
1 to 2 C. whole wheat **flour**
sesame seeds (optional)

Dissolve yeast and honey in water and let it stand until bubbly. Add salt and enough flour to make a sticky dough. Knead until smooth. Pinch off 6 equal portions of dough and roll them into balls. Pat between your palms to make flat circles. If desired, sprinkle kneading surface with sesame seeds and press each circle down to pick up some of the seeds. Place circles on greased cookie sheet and set oven to broil. Place sheet in middle of oven under heated broiler. (In a gas oven, place on lowest rack of broiler.) When first side is slightly browned, flip breads over and brown other side. They bake quickly, so watch carefully. Serve hot as you would ordinary pita.

These are really quick and can be a nice addition to a meal when you want bread, but don't have a lot of time. Great with spaghetti and chili, and they reheat well. *PROTEIN: 19 grams; CALORIES: 453 Suzanne Parker   Jackie Diachun*
Griffin, Georgia   Lexington, Kentucky

TWO-WAY OATMEAL BREAD

2 C. hot scalded **milk** or boiling
   water (1 C. may be buttermilk)
1 to 2 C. rolled **oats**
¼ to ½ C. **brown sugar**, honey
   or molasses
¼ to ½ C. **butter** or oil
2 t. **salt**
2 T. **yeast**
5 to 7 C. whole wheat **flour**

Optional Ingredients:
1 small grated **potato**
up to ½ C. **wheat germ**
up to ½ C. **bran**
1 T. **nutritional yeast**
1 C. cooked **oatmeal**
1 T. **lecithin**
¼ t. **ginger**
up to 1 C. dry **milk powder**
1 C. **raisins** with
   1 T. **cinnamon**

Conventional Method:
½ C. warm **water**

Rapid-Mix Method:
2 **eggs**

Conventional Method:
Pour boiling liquid over oats, sugar, butter and salt in a large bowl. Cool to lukewarm. Dissolve yeast in warm water. Add to oat mixture, along with any optional ingredients desired. Beat in flour to make a soft dough.

Rapid-Mix Method:
In a large bowl, mix 2 C. flour, oats, yeast and salt. Add hot liquid with butter and sugar. Beat 2 minutes with electric mixer or 200 strokes by hand. Add eggs and any optional ingredients desired. Beat in flour to make a soft dough.

Knead dough 5 to 15 minutes, adding more flour if necessary. Let rise until doubled, at least 1 hour. Punch down and divide into 2 loaves. Place in greased 8 x 4" loaf pans and let rise until slightly over edge of pan. (Or let rise in refrigerator overnight.) Bake at 350° to 375° about 45 minutes, or until golden brown. Brush tops with butter if desired and cool on racks. Recipe may be halved or doubled (but do not double yeast).

This recipe can be made chock-full of good things and makes a nice breakfast bread (children love it with peanut butter, cream or cottage cheese), a hearty accompaniment to a mostly-vegetable stew or any meal a little short on protein, or a pinch-hitter for dessert. The smell of it baking will tempt the fussiest eater—it's better than any commercial air deodorizer!   *Conventional Method—PROTEIN: 115.2 grams; CALORIES: 3333*
Rapid-Mix Method—PROTEIN: 127.6 grams; CALORIES: 3489   Many LLL Contributors

I really recommend getting into the habit of starting the sponge the night before and rising it in the refrigerator. Psychological benefits are great—with only 10 minutes effort, the bread is started and you don't have to knead until the next day. When the next day comes, you have to do *something* with it, so you have tricked yourself into it and, presto! (or almost), you are eating slices of fresh, warm bread! I spend about 10 minutes in the evening after I wash the dishes and about 20 minutes in the morning, not counting rising and baking.
                                                        Barbara Atkisson
                                                        Onalaska, Washington

CHALLAH OR EGG BREAD
(Jewish Sabbath Loaves)

The tradition of serving twisted loaves on the Sabbath has its origin in the manna the Israelites received in the desert. They would collect a double portion of manna on Friday for the Sabbath, as manna did not fall on the Sabbath—therefore the use of two loaves. The manna fell on a cover of dew and was covered with dew. We duplicate these two covers with the tablecloth below the loaves and a special cover which is removed only after the Kiddush (blessing over the wine) is made and the appropriate blessing for the loaves. The twisted shape of the loaves duplicates that of the loaves in the Temple.   *Bonnie Z. Kupinsky*

2 T. **yeast**
2 C. warm **water**
2 to 3 **eggs**
¼ to ½ C. **honey** or sugar
2 t. **salt**
2 T. to ⅓ C. **butter** or oil
7 to 8 C. whole wheat **flour**
    or Cornell Mix
egg wash
Optional:
sesame or **poppy seeds**
Add ½ C. *each* soy **flour** and
    wheat germ for high protein
    Challah

Dissolve yeast in water. Add eggs, honey, salt, butter and about 3½ C. flour. Beat well by hand or with electric mixer. Add remaining flour to make a soft dough. Knead 5 to 10 minutes, adding more flour if necessary. Use as little flour as possible for a delicate Challah. It should be velvety soft. Let rise until doubled, 1½ to 2 hours. Punch down and let rise again, if desired. Shape into 2 twisted or braided loaves; place on greased cookie sheets and let rise until doubled. Brush with egg wash and sprinkle with seeds, if desired. Bake at 350 to 375° for 30 to 45 minutes, until golden brown. Serve warm or cool. Dough can also be made into regular loaves or rolls. *Biteavon—* Hearty appetite!

PROTEIN: 134.3 grams; CALORIES: 3492

Bonnie Kupinsky
Oak Park, Michigan

Karen Myers
Butler, Pennsylvania

Sarah Barnett
Spring Valley, New York

Variations: Use scalded **milk** instead of water OR add ½ C. dry **milk powder**. Use ½ to 1 C. butter and up to ⅔ C. honey or sugar. Salt may be reduced to 1 t. or less. 4 **egg yolks** may be used in place of 2 whole eggs for a richer bread. 1 t. **vanilla** or **rum** may be added. Crust may be brushed with melted **butter** after baking for a soft crust. (With these additions and variations, the recipe is simply Egg Bread and no longer authentic Challah, or Sabbath Bread.) This dough can also be used for cinnamon bread or rolls.

Leora Gerber
Dalton, Ohio

Sheila Terrill
Kinsman, Ohio

HIGH PROTEIN WHEAT BREAD

1½ C. **water**
1 C. **cottage cheese**
⅓ to ½ C. **honey**, molasses
  'or brown sugar
1 T. to ¼ C. **butter** or oil
6 to 7 C. whole wheat **flour**
2 T. **yeast**
2 t. **salt**

Optional:
1 to 2 **eggs**
⅓ C. dry **milk powder**
⅓ C. soy **flour**
⅓ C. **wheat germ**
½ to ⅔ C. rolled **oats**
1 C. chopped **nuts**
⅔ C. **bran**
⅔ C. **raisins**

Heat water, cottage cheese, honey and butter to 120°. Combine in a large bowl with 3 C. flour, yeast, salt, sugar and eggs (if used). Beat 2 minutes with electric mixer or 200 strokes by hand. Stir in optionals and remaining flour to make a stiff dough. Knead until smooth and elastic. Let rise until doubled, about 1 hour. Shape into 2 loaves; place in greased 8 x 4" loaf pans and let rise until doubled, 45 to 60 minutes. Bake at 350 to 375° for 35 to 50 minutes. Cover loosely with foil if tops brown too fast.

A real treat! This has good texture and the cottage cheese gives it extra protein. Even if the kids want only toast for breakfast, they have a good start with this bread.

Without options—P.: 132.8 gms.; C.: 3216
With all options: PROTEIN: 197.1 grams; CALORIES: 4865
Many LLL Contributors

SPROUTED WHEAT BREAD

2 T. **yeast**
2 C. warm **water** or milk
¼ to ⅓ C. **molasses** or honey
6 to 7 C. whole wheat **flour**
  (may be part triticale)
2 t. **salt**
¼ C. **oil**
1½ to 2 C. **sprouted wheat**
  (about ¼" long)

Optional:

2 **eggs** and 2 C. rolled **oats**

Dissolve yeast in water with molasses. Stir in 3 to 3½ C. flour to make a sponge. Let sponge rise until doubled, if desired. Add salt, oil, sprouted wheat and optionals and mix well. Add enough remaining flour to make a kneadable dough. Knead 7 to 8 minutes, adding more flour if necessary. If you did not rise the sponge, let dough rise once until doubled. If you did rise sponge, omit this rising. Divide dough in half and shape into loaves. Place in greased loaf pans and let rise until doubled.

Bake at 400° for 10 minutes, then at 375° for 25 to 30 minutes. Cool on rack. Recipe may be halved or doubled.

Wheat berries (or kernels) may be sprouted like any other seed. They are quite sweet and also good in tuna salad or soup. Sprouted wheat helps whole wheat bread rise. See index for sprouting information.

Gerry Chamberlin   *Bonnie Bushart*
Cedar Falls, Iowa   *Webster, New York*

HARVEST HEALTH BREAD

½ C. **wheat kernels** (wheat berries) and water to cover, or 1½ C. any cooked grain
1 T. **yeast**
2¼ C. warm **water**
¼ C. **brown sugar** or honey
½ C. **cornmeal**
1 C. rolled **oats**
4¼ C. whole wheat **flour**
2 T. **butter**
1½ t. **salt**

Soak wheat kernels overnight. Cook in soaking water until kernels swell and soften (in a slow-cooker overnight, for instance). Leave any remaining water and cool to lukewarm.

Dissolve yeast in ¼ C. water with a pinch of the sugar. Add to wheat in a large bowl with remaining water, sugar, cornmeal, oats, ½ C. flour, butter and salt. Stir in remaining flour. Knead 10 minutes. Let rise until doubled. Punch down and let rise again. Shape into 2 loaves and place in greased 8 x 4" loaf pans. Let rise until doubled. Bake at 350° for 35 to 40 minutes. Cool on racks. Brush with melted **butter**.

My mother-in-law and I developed this recipe in order to use the wheat that my husband combined out of the fields on our farm. Whenever he harvests the wheat, I save a large canful in order to have a good supply to use in this bread. It freezes very well.   *PROTEIN: 115.2 grams; CALORIES: 3356*

June Beeler
Sutter, Illinois

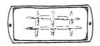

SESAME-COTTAGE CHEESE BREAD

2 T. **yeast**
¾ C. warm **water**
2 C. **cottage cheese** (at room temperature)
¼ C. **honey** or sugar
1½ t. **salt**
½ C. raw **sesame seeds**
2 T. **butter**
2 **eggs**, beaten
4 to 5 C. whole wheat **flour**
1 **egg white**

Dissolve yeast in water and mix with cottage cheese, honey, salt, sesame seeds, butter and eggs. Gradually add flour and knead until no longer sticky. Let rise until doubled. Shape into 2 loaves and place in 2 small, greased loaf pans. Let rise until just above the tops of pans. Mix egg white with 1 T. water and brush tops of loaves. Sprinkle with sesame seeds. Bake at 350° for 25 to 30 minutes. Best stored in refrigerator after a day. Makes a yummy toast!   *PROTEIN: 156.1 grams; CALORIES: 3062*

Debbie Brown
Guatemala

Cottage Cheese Rolls. Omit sesame seeds and add ½ t. **baking soda.** Form into 32 balls and place in 2 greased 9" square baking pans. Bake as above. High protein and delicious! Freezes well.

Pat Zee
Glassboro, New Jersey

Carla Till
Rome, New York

Warm water is the temperature of baby's bath water; hot water is the temperature of Mom's bath in winter.

Barbara Pfeifle
Lexington, Kentucky

"KNOCK YOUR SOCKS OFF" RAISIN BREAD

1½ T. yeast
1½ T. honey
¼ C. lukewarm water
½ C. hot milk
½ C. butter
2 T. honey
2 T. molasses
1 T. nutritional yeast
1 t. salt
½ C. plain yogurt
½ C. unsweetened applesauce
½ C. rolled oats
8 C. whole wheat flour
4 eggs
1 heaping T. ground cinnamon
1 C. dark raisins
½ C. sunflower seeds
¼ C. sesame seeds
½ C. chopped walnuts
1 C. packed grated carrots

Dissolve yeast and 1½ t. honey in water. Heat milk with butter and pour into a large bowl. Stir in honey, molasses, nutritional yeast, salt, yogurt, applesauce and oats. Beat in 1 C. flour, eggs and foamy yeast. Add 1 more C. flour, cinnamon, raisins, sunflower seeds, sesame seeds, walnuts and carrots. Add remaining flour, 1 C. at a time, mixing well. Knead 10 minutes and let rise until doubled, about 1 hour. Punch down and let rise again ½ hour. Shape into 3 loaves. Place in greased loaf pans. Let rise until almost doubled, 30 to 40 minutes. Bake at 350° for 40 minutes. Brush tops with melted butter and sprinkle with cinnamon. Bake 10 minutes longer. Cool on racks. A good gift bread.

A raisin bread so good it will, as my husband Angelo says, "knock your socks off"! *PROTEIN: 217 grams; CALORIES: 6320*

Mary Anne Gross-Ferraro
Highland Mills, New York

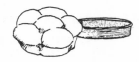

BONANZA BREAD

2 C. whole wheat flour or
  1 C. whole wheat flour
  and 1 C. brown rice flour
⅓ C. wheat germ
⅓ C. dry milk powder or
  soy milk flour
2 t. baking powder
½ t. salt
¼ C. carob powder (optional)
1 t. ground coriander (optional)
¾ C. dried fruits
¾ C. chopped nuts or seeds or
  ¼ C. nuts and ¼ C. peanut
  butter
3 eggs
½ C. oil
¼ C. molasses
¾ C. prune or orange juice
1 C. mashed banana

Combine dry ingredients, including dried fruit and nuts. Separately mix liquids, banana and peanut butter, if used. Add to dry ingredients. Stir until just combined. Pour into a greased 9 x 5" loaf pan, and bake at 325° for 1¼ to 1½ hours, or bake in muffin tins at 350° for 20 minutes. Makes 36 muffins.

A bonanza is something rich or valuable, and you will find this bread lives up to its name in both flavor and nutrition.

PROTEIN: 82.9 grams; CALORIES: 3984

Jean Ann Merrill   *Barbara Dick*
Southgate, Kentucky   *Seattle, Washington*

SAN FRANCISCO FIREHOUSE BREAD

2 T. **yeast**
¼ C. warm **water**
½ C. chopped **onion**
3 T. **oil**
1⅔ C. **milk**
⅔ C. dry **milk powder**
3 T. **honey**
1 t. **salt**
½ C. snipped fresh **parsley** or
8 t. dried
½ t. **dill weed**
¼ t. **sage**
¾ C. **cornmeal**
4 C. whole wheat **flour**

Dissolve yeast in water. Cook onion in oil until tender. Add to milk with yeast, honey, salt and herbs. Mix in cornmeal and 2 C. flour, beating well. Add remaining flour and knead 3 to 5 minutes. Let rise until doubled, about 1 hour. Divide in half and shape into oval loaves. Place in 2 *well*-greased 1-lb. coffee cans. Let rise until doubled, 30 to 45 minutes. Bake at 350° for 45 minutes, covering loosely with foil during the last 15 minutes.

This is really yummy served with peanut butter. This recipe was given to me by my mother. It is a favorite in our house, and when I serve it to guests, they usually request the recipe.   *PROTEIN: 129.7 grams; CALORIES: 3147*

Eve Dufault
Waukegan, Illinois

My children love to help with making bread. I bought some tiny bread pans for them and they each make their own little loaf.   *Linda McCullough*
Abilene, Texas

COULDN'T BE EASIER SLOW-COOKER BREAD

1 T. **yeast**
¼ C. warm **water**
1 C. warm **milk** or buttermilk
½ C. rolled **oats**
1½ t. **salt**
2 T. **oil**
2 T. **honey**
1 **egg**
¼ C. **wheat germ**
2¾ C. whole wheat **flour**

Grease a deep metal or glass bowl or 1-lb. coffee can. Turn slow-cooker on high to preheat.

Dissolve yeast in water. Combine with milk, oats, salt, oil, honey, egg and wheat germ. Add flour and knead until smooth and elastic, about 5 minutes. Turn dough immediately into bowl or can and cover *loosely* with foil. In bottom of slow-cooker place ½ C. water and a trivet or some crumpled foil. Place can or bowl on this, cover and bake on high for 3 hours.   Top of bread will not necessarily brown.

Just 15 minutes work time! A great way to have nutritious, fresh bread with a minimum of fuss, especially for small families. You don't waste oven energy for just one loaf of bread. Nice for a hot summer day.

PROTEIN: 78.5 grams; CALORIES: 2043

Wanda D. Rezac
Marlboro, Massachusetts

. . . for those considering making all of their family's bread—I heartily recommend it. Do get your husband and children involved. My husband can bake bread as well as I can, and now we collaborate—that is, one starts it, and the other takes over if necessary.   *Geni Wixson*
Germantown, Maryland

FILLED YEAST LOAF

After first rising, roll each loaf into a 15 x 18" rectangle. Fill with suggested fillings (or your own) and roll up carefully lengthwise. Pinch ends so filling does not fall out. Place on greased cookie sheet, cover and let rise about 1 hour. Bake at 350° for about 30 minutes. One loaf feeds 4 people. Freezes well. Be creative and enjoy!

Suggested Fillings:
Italian: ½ lb. bulk **sausage**, cooked (for 1 loaf)
shredded Mozzarella **cheese**
sauteed sliced **onions** and **green peppers**
tomato sauce spread over above items
Swiss: cubed leftover **ham**
grated Swiss **cheese**
All Vegetable: cut-up, cooked **broccoli, carrots, onions,** or **beans**
alfalfa or mung **bean sprouts**
grated **cheese**, if desired

Susan Hickman
Mastic, New York

BOHEMIAN RYE BREAD

4 C. warm **water** or potato water (p. 136)
1½ T. **honey**
1 T. **salt**
1½ t. **yeast**
1½ t. **caraway seeds**
1½ C. whole wheat **flour** combined with 2½ C. rye **flour**
2 **potatoes**
2 T. **butter**
2 T. **oil**
3¼ C. whole wheat **flour**
3¼ C. rye **flour**

To make sponge, mix water, honey, salt and yeast in a large bowl. Beat in seeds and combined flours. Beat well with a wooden spoon. Let rise 1 hour.

While sponge is rising, cook potatoes until soft. Drain and mash them, whipping in butter and oil. Stir potatoes into sponge and add remaining flours. Beat well with a heavy wooden spoon or paddle 10 to 15 minutes. (This takes the place of kneading and is hard work! For weaker arms, use a dough hook on a heavy-duty mixer or knead as in variation below.) Dough should be stretchy. Let rise 1 hour. Stir down and let rise ½ hour more. Divide into 2 or 3 parts. Knead each part briefly, adding flour as needed to form a loaf (dough will be stickier than most bread doughs). Place in greased bread pans and let rise 45 minutes. Do *not* allow to over-rise. Bake at 350° for 1¼ hours, or until well browned. Remove from pans and let sit in turned-off oven for 20 minutes to form a hard crust. A moist "peasanty" bread.

This recipe is a little more involved than other breads, but it is such a part of my husband's heritage. His great-aunt, who came from Czechoslovakia as a young girl, baked 8 to 10 loaves for the family every week until she was 91 years old. (I remind myself of that when I am beating that heavy dough!) It is unlike any bread that can be purchased, making it well worth the time and effort which go into it!

Pam Oselka
Union Pier, Michigan

PROTEIN: 206.3 grams; CALORIES: 5000

Polish Rye Bread. Use ½ t. **sugar** and 1 T. **molasses** instead of honey. Omit oil and butter. Knead dough rather than beating it. Dough can be shaped into balls and baked on cookie sheets. Bake at 400° for 10 minutes, then 350° for 50 minutes. Cool on racks.

Pat and MaryAnn Haws
Avon, Minnesota

KAROL'S RAISIN-RYE BREAD

1 C. **water**
⅓ C. **bulgur wheat**, cracked
wheat or 1 C. cooked wheat
cereal
1 T. **yeast**
¼ C. lukewarm **water**
1 T. **honey**
½ C. scalded **milk**
⅓ C. **honey**
2 T. **butter**
½ t. **salt**
3 T. **nutritional yeast**
3 T. soy **flour**
3 C. whole wheat **flour**
1 t. **cinnamon** or more
2 T. **wheat germ**
1 C. rye **flour**
1 C. seedless **raisins**

Bring 1 C. water to boil; add wheat and simmer 10 minutes. Dissolve yeast in ¼ C. water with 1 T. honey. Pour milk over remaining honey, butter and salt and mix with wheat. Cool to lukewarm and add yeast. Add nutritional yeast, soy flour and about 1⅔ C. wheat flour. Beat in cinnamon, wheat germ, rye flour and raisins. Add remaining wheat flour to form a stiff, sticky dough. Knead 10 to 15 minutes, adding more flour as needed. Let rise until doubled, about 1 hour. Punch down and shape into 1 round loaf. Place in a greased 9" round cake pan and let rise until doubled. Bake at 350° for 45 to 60 minutes until nicely browned. Brush with butter for a soft crust, if desired. Recipe may be doubled. *PROTEIN: 118 grams; CALORIES: 3247*

I got this, my favorite bread recipe, years ago from the woman who is my daughter's fairy godmother. Great toast!

Sue LaLeike
Cape Coral, Florida

HEIDELBERG RYE BREAD

2¼ C. whole wheat **flour**
¼ C. **carob powder**
2 T. **yeast**
1 T. **caraway seeds**
2 C. **water**
½ C. **molasses**
2 T. **butter**
1 t. **salt**
2½ C. rye **flour**

Combine whole wheat flour, carob powder, yeast and caraway. Heat water, molasses, butter and salt in a saucepan until very warm. Beat into flour mixture until smooth. Add enough rye flour to make a slightly stiff dough. Knead about 10 minutes, adding more rye flour if needed. Cover and let rest 20 minutes. Divide in half and shape into 2 round loaves about 6" across. Place on greased cookie sheet and slash tops with sharp knife or razor blade. Brush with **oil** and let rise until doubled, about 1 hour. Bake at 350° for 45 to 50 minutes or until loaves sound hollow when tapped. Cool on racks and refrigerate. *PROTEIN: 97.2 grams; CALORIES: 2693*

Dagmar Harper
Elmhurst, Illinois

Anise Rye Bread. Omit carob powder, reduce caraway seeds to 1 t. and add 1 T. **anise seed**. Let dough rise until doubled before shaping.

Pat and MaryAnn Haws
Avon, Minnesota

BASIC DOUGH FOR ROLLS AND SWEET BREADS

1½ to 3 t. **yeast**
1 C. warm **water,** milk or
buttermilk (add ½ T. baking
soda with buttermilk)
1 to 4 T. **honey,** sugar or
molasses
2 T. to ½ C. **butter** or oil
¾ t. **salt**
up to 2 **eggs**
3 C. whole wheat **flour**

Optional:
sesame, poppy or sunflower
seeds
herbs
spices
chopped, sauteed **onion**
raisins, or other dried fruit
chopped **nuts**

Dissolve yeast in liquid with honey. When bubbly, add butter, salt, eggs and half the flour. Beat well for several minutes by hand or with electric mixer. Add remaining flour (may need slightly more if you add eggs) to make a soft dough and knead 5 to 10 minutes. Let rise until doubled. If you use the larger amount of yeast and put dough in a very warm place, it will rise in less than half an hour. You may also let it rise several hours or overnight in the refrigerator. Punch down dough and shape into rolls. Place on greased cake pans, cookie sheets or muffin tins. Let rise until doubled. Bake at 375° about 20 minutes.

The recipe may be doubled or tripled. The shaped rolls may rise in the refrigerator, if you like (hot cinnamon buns for breakfast!), or keep the dough in an airtight container in the refrigerator for about a week to make rolls as needed.

Braid the dough into a loaf (p. 147) for a festive supper bread. Rolls or bread may be sprinkled with seeds. For variety, add your favorite herbs or spices. Dill weed and garlic powder and/or onions make delicious herb rolls. Dried fruits and nuts make wonderful holiday breads. Use your imagination!
PROTEIN: 52.8 grams; CALORIES: 1411

Many LLL Contributors

Caramel Pecan Rolls. Combine ¾ C. honey and 1 T. blackstrap molasses and spread in bottom of a buttered 13 x 9" baking pan. Sprinkle 1 C. whole or chopped **pecans** over this. On a floured surface, roll dough out into an 18 x 12" rectangle. Brush with 2 T. melted butter and spread with ¼ C. honey mixed with 1 t. **cinnamon.** Sprinkle with ½ C. chopped **pecans.** Roll up lengthwise, pinch to seal and cut into 1" slices. Place, cut side down, in prepared pan. Let rise until doubled, then bake at 375° for 25 to 30 minutes. Cool 1 minute, then invert onto wire rack. Let stand 1 minute before removing from pan.   *PROTEIN: 68 grams; CALORIES: 3713*

Cathy Storlie
McHenry, Illinois

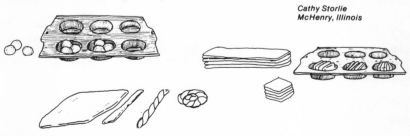

Cinnamon Rolls or Bread. Use basic dough, with or without eggs, or add ½ a **lemon**, grated rind and juice; ¼ t. **nutmeg**, mace or cardamom, 1 T. **orange juice**; and/or ½ C. **raisins**. Roll dough out as above and spread with 2 T. to ¼ C. honey, or white or brown sugar and 1 t. **cinnamon**. If you have not added raisins to dough, you can sprinkle them on now, if you wish. Roll up lengthwise, seal and cut into 1" slices for cinnamon rolls. Place in greased 13 x 9" pan. For cinnamon bread, roll dough up starting from the short end, pinch ends and place in greased loaf pan. Let rise until doubled and bake at 375° until golden brown. Brush top of bread with melted butter and cool on rack. Warm rolls may be iced with Powdered Milk Icing (p. 279), if desired.

Jan Cooper   *Geni Wixson*   *Brenda Kent*
Vicksburg, Mississippi   *Germantown, Maryland*   *AnKeny, Iowa*

Orange Raisin Nut Bread. Use **orange juice** as liquid, and use only 1 T. butter or oil and 1 T. honey. Add ½ T. grated **orange rind**, ½ C. **raisins** and ¼ C. chopped **walnuts**. Shape into loaf and place in greased loaf pan. Let rise until doubled and bake at 375° for 45 minutes. Brush with melted butter while cooling. *PROTEIN: 58.2 grams; CALORIES: 1895*

Pulla (Finnish Coffee Bread). Use **milk** as liquid and add a heaping ¼ t. **cardamom**. Shape dough into a braided loaf (p. 147) and brush with Egg Wash (p. 144) before baking. Sprinkle with crushed **sugar** or chopped **almonds**, if you wish. Bake at 375° for 25 to 30 minutes, or until golden brown.

Leslye Korvola
Fairbanks, Alaska

SUMMER SQUASH ROLLS

3¾ C. whole wheat **flour**
1 T. **yeast**
3 T. **honey**
1 t. **garlic salt**
¼ C. **oil**
1 C. grated **yellow squash**
¾ C. **milk**
1 **egg**
½ t. **dill weed**

In a large bowl, combine 1½ C. flour, yeast, honey and garlic salt. In a saucepan, heat oil, squash and milk to 120°. Pour into flour mixture, add egg and dill weed and stir in enough flour to make a soft dough. Knead about 5 minutes. Let rise 1½ hours, or until doubled. Punch down and divide into 24 balls. Place in 2 greased 8" round cake pans. Let rise 45 minutes, or until nearly doubled. Bake at 375° for 20 to 30 minutes, or until golden brown. Cool on racks or serve warm.

My daughters like helping to make these and none of the 24 pieces of dough is ever the same size—makes for fun dinner conversation! My children aren't fond of cooked squash, and this is a good way to introduce the taste of it. *PROTEIN: 77.5 grams; CALORIES: 2351*   *Linda Helminiak*
West Chicago, Illinois

BEAN BREAD

2 T. **yeast**
1 C. warm **water** or stock
4 T. **honey**
2 C. cooked dried **beans,** such as pinto, red, kidney, navy, soy, etc.
1½ T. **oil**
8 C. whole wheat **flour**
2 t. **salt**
dash of **pepper**

Dissolve yeast in water with honey. Mash beans well with a little stock. Add oil and 4 C. of flour. Beat until smooth. Add salt, pepper and 3 to 4 more cups flour to make a stiff dough. Knead 5 to 10 minutes. Let rise 1½ to 2 hours. Punch down and let rise 30 minutes longer, if desired. Divide into 2 or 3 loaves and place in greased loaf pans. Let rise until doubled. Bake at 450° for 15 minutes, then at 375° 45 minutes longer. Brush loaves with butter or oil after baking for a soft crust; with water for a hard crust. A good way to introduce soybeans to the diet.   *PROTEIN: 173 grams; CALORIES: 4206*   *Marjorie Stone*
Mastic Beach, New York

ONE HOUR DINNER BREAD

4 T. **yeast**
3 C. warm **water**
¼ C. **honey**
2 **eggs**
½ C. **butter**
1¾ t. **salt**
1 C. dry **milk powder**
8 C. whole wheat **flour**

Optional:
Use ½ C. *each* soy **flour** and **wheat germ** instead of 1 C. flour

PROTEIN: 178.3 grams; CALORIES: 4756

Dissolve yeast in water with honey. Add eggs, butter, salt, milk powder and flour. Moisten well and let rest 5 minutes. Knead 5 minutes, adding more flour if necessary, and divide into 3 loaves. Place in greased 8 x 4" loaf pans. Let rise in warm oven 20 minutes. Without removing bread, turn oven to 350° and bake 30 minutes (if you have an electric oven, cover loaves loosely with foil while oven heats). You now have 3 loaves of delicious, nutritious bread. This is a good basic recipe for a beginner and can be varied in many ways to make hot rolls, cinnamon rolls, raisin bread, etc.—just use your imagination. It is also very economical—you get 3 loaves of bread from 8 C. of flour. This recipe has your bread mixed, kneaded and baked in one hour. My family loves it. Happy baking!
Connie Lehman
Ada, Ohio

ANGEL BISCUITS

1 T. **yeast**
5 T. lukewarm **water**
2 C. **buttermilk,** warmed
5 C. whole wheat **flour**
5 t. **baking powder**
1 t. **salt**
½ t. **baking soda**
3 T. **sugar** or honey
¾ C. **butter**

Dissolve yeast in water and buttermilk. In another bowl, sift together flour, baking powder, salt, soda and sugar. Cut in butter and add yeast. Knead slightly and roll the dough out ½" thick on a floured surface. Cut with a biscuit cutter and bake on a greased cookie sheet at 450° for 10 minutes.

These do not have to rise before baking. The dough can be kept covered in refrigerator for 1 to 2 weeks. Great for small and large families alike because it keeps so well in the refrigerator and you just bake what you need.   *Joanne Wilheim*
PROTEIN: 101.8 grams; CALORIES: 3658   *Brookfield, Wisconsin*

POTATO ROLLS OR BREAD

1 T. **yeast**
1½ C. lukewarm **water** or
   potato water (p. 136)
¼ to ½ C. **sugar** or honey
1½ t. **salt**
2 **eggs**
¼ to ½ C. soft **butter** or oil
1 C. lukewarm mashed **potatoes**
7 to 7½ C. whole wheat **flour**

Optional:
½ to ⅔ C. dry **milk powder**
mixture of:
   ½ C. *each* **wheat germ** and **bran**
   ½ C. mixed **bulgur wheat** and
   cooked **soy grits**
or mixture of:
   ¾ t. ground **cinnamon**
   1¼ C. **raisins**

Dissolve yeast in water. Add sugar, salt, eggs, butter, potatoes, and any optional ingredients. Stir in flour to make a pliable dough. Knead 5 to 10 minutes. Let rise until doubled in a warm place, or cover and let rise in refrigerator for at least 2 hours. Form dough into about 48 balls and place in greased baking pans or muffin tins; or make into 2 loaves. Let rise until doubled. Bake rolls at 400° for 15 minutes; loaves at 350° for 30 to 40 minutes. Recipe may be halved or doubled.

PROTEIN: 129 grams; CALORIES: 3791

Linda Tibbs	*Kathy Eikmann*	*Kathy Dombrowski*	*Sara Reuning*
Pekin, Illinois	*Stow, Ohio*	*Greendale, Wisconsin*	*Bristol, Tennessee*

Papa's Holiday Bread. Use ½ C. honey and ¼ C. butter. Use 1 C. **milk** and 4 eggs for liquid. Add ¼ t. crushed **cardamom** and 1/8 t. ground **ginger.** Form into loaves.   *PROTEIN: 153.2 grams; CALORIES: 4434*   *Bonnie Yaeger*
Yonkers, New York

Apple Cinnamon Rolls. Replace ½ C. flour with ½ C. **soy flour.** Use only 2 T. oil and 2 T. honey. Divide dough in half and roll each half into a 12 x 9" rectangle. Mix 2½ C. chopped **apples,** ⅓ C. **sugar,** 2 t. ground **cinnamon** and ⅓ C. chopped **nuts** (optional). Spread over the 2 rectangles and roll them up lengthwise. Pinch to seal and cut in 1" slices. Bake as for rolls.

The aroma reminds me of the smell of homemade cinnamon bread baking in my grandmother's oven—delicious!

Suzanne Diachenko
Bowie, Maryland

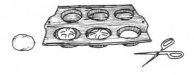

WHOLE WHEAT HAMBURGER OR SANDWICH BUNS

2 T. **yeast**
3 to 6 T. **honey**, sugar or
  molasses
2½ C. warm **water** or
  2 C. water and 2 eggs
¼ to ½ C. **oil** or butter
2 t. **salt**
7 to 8 C. whole wheat **flour**

Optional:
½ C. dry **milk powder**
substitute for equal amount
  of whole wheat flour:
  ½ to 1 C. soy **flour**
  ¼ to ½ C. **wheat germ**
  1 C. rye **flour**

Dissolve yeast and honey in water. When bubbly, add oil, salt (eggs and optionals, if used), and flour. Knead 5 to 10 minutes, then let rise until doubled, one or two times. To shape, roll out dough ½" thick on a floured surface and cut into rounds with wide-mouth canning jar rings, a large can with both ends removed, or a biscuit cutter (for little folks' hamburger buns). Or form pieces of dough into balls and flatten them to the proper size between the palms of your hands. You may also use the dough for submarine or hero rolls or hot dog buns. Place rolls on greased cookie sheets and let rise 20 to 30 minutes *or* let rise overnight in the refrigerator. If you wish, brush the tops with **egg wash** (p. 144) and sprinkle with **poppy** or **sesame seeds**. Bake at 350° to 400° until golden brown (approximately 15 minutes). Cool on racks.

Try using small pieces of dough to make faces on the buns. This is a nice workable dough and older children could use it for other shapes such as flowers, animals, etc.   *PROTEIN: 118.3 grams; CALORIES: 3525*

Sharon Falatovics   Geni Wixson   Linda Turcotte
Michigan City, Indiana   Germantown, Maryland   Holliston, Massachusetts

Variation: For my son's 5th birthday treat at nursery school, this recipe made 3 Teddy bears. Each portion of dough was divided in two. Then one piece was cut again to make two smaller pieces. The largest piece was the bear's belly. One of the other pieces was shaped for the head and the remaining piece was cut into 7 smaller pieces for ears, paws and nose. Just before baking, we added eyes and belly-button of raisins.

Judy Smith
Ventura, California

JIFFY HAMBURGER BUNS

4 to 4½ C. whole wheat **flour**
2 T. **yeast**
1 C. **milk**
¾ C. **water**
½ C. **oil**
3 to 4 T. **honey** or molasses
1 t. **salt**

Optional:
2 **eggs** in place of ½ C. water

Stir together 2 C. flour and yeast. Heat milk, water, oil, honey and salt until very warm (120 to 130°). Pour into yeast and flour mixture. Beat 3 minutes with electric mixer or by hand 300 strokes. Add enough additional flour to make a soft dough. Beat well or knead briefly. Let rest 10 minutes. Roll out ½" thick on well-floured surface. Cut into 3 or 4" rounds with canning jar ring or tuna can. Let rise on greased baking sheets for ½ hour. Bake at 400° until lightly browned, 12 to 15 minutes. Cool on racks. Makes 12 to 15 buns. Recipe may be doubled.

The dough can be risen in the refrigerator for one hour to overnight before shaping and can be used for dinner rolls, cinnamon buns, pizza dough, crescent rolls, or small loaves of bread. Rounds cut ¼" thick may be stacked before baking for an easily split hamburger bun. Or, to eliminate rolling out, you may scoop up a clump of dough with floured hands and press it flat between your palms. For hot dog buns, pull the round into an oblong shape, flatten and fold over once. They will split easily after baking.

These buns add to the flavor of the hamburger—they don't just hold the lettuce and pickles in! Homemade hamburger buns impress everyone at a summer barbecue.   *PROTEIN: 67.7 grams; CALORIES: 2982*   *Many LLL Contributors*

NO-KNEAD YEAST ROLLS

2 T. **yeast**
½ C. warm **water**
2 C. **milk** or water
½ C. **butter** or oil
¼ to ½ C. **honey** or sugar
1½ t. **salt**
6 C. whole wheat **flour**

Optional:
2 to 4 **eggs** (omit ¼ C. liquid
   for each egg used)

Dissolve yeast in warm water. Heat milk, butter, honey and salt in a saucepan until very warm. Add with yeast to flour in a large mixing bowl. (Note: if you use eggs, add at this point; do not heat with milk.) Beat well and let rise 15 to 50 minutes. Stir down. The dough may be shaped immediately or refrigerated for several hours or days before shaping. Pat dough out on a floured surface and cut with a biscuit cutter, or shape into crescents, rolls, pinwheels or other shapes (p. 155). Or simply spoon dough into greased muffin tins. Let rise until doubled, at least 15 minutes in a warm place, or several hours in refrigerator. Bake at 375 to 400° for 10 to 20 minutes, or until golden brown. Brush generously with melted butter before or after baking, if desired. Recipe may be halved or doubled.   *Many LLL Contributors*

These taste a lot like homemade whole wheat bread, but require lots less time and effort. Leftovers may be split and, with a little cheese, become an easy, nutritious cheese toast for breakfast. Make a large batch and keep the dough in an airtight container in the refrigerator for fresh rolls anytime. Dough may be used for sweet rolls, too.   *P.: 119.9 gms.; C.: 3890*

Quick Buttermilk Rolls. Use 2 T. yeast, ½ C. honey, ¾ C. butter, melted, 2 t. salt, 3 beaten eggs and 1 C. warm **buttermilk**, in place of the milk. Add ¼ t. **baking soda.** Use slightly less flour.   *PROTEIN: 122.9 grams; CALORIES: 4381*

Rindalee M. Skimina
Highland, Indiana

BRAN ROLLS

1 C. **bran**
½ C. **butter**
2 T. **honey**
1 t. **salt**
¼ C. dry **milk powder**
1½ C. hot **potato cooking water** (p. 136)
1 T. **yeast**
1 **egg**
3 to 4 C. whole wheat **flour** or 2½ C. unbleached flour combined with ½ C. soy flour and 2 T. wheat germ

Mix bran, butter, honey, salt, milk powder and potato water. Cool until lukewarm. Add yeast and egg. Add 2 C. flour to liquid. Beat 2 minutes. Beat in enough flour to make a soft dough. Knead until smooth and elastic, 5 to 10 minutes. Let rise until doubled, about 1 hour. Punch down and let rise again, about 30 minutes. Shape into 24 rolls (or cinnamon rolls or loaf). Let rise until doubled. Bake at 375°, 15 minutes for rolls, 30 minutes for loaf.

PROTEIN: 77.4 grams; CALORIES: 2507

It has become a tradition for me to bring these rolls to all League family meetings. The children eat them for snacks. Recipe may be doubled. Freezes well.

Pat Jensen
Everly, Iowa

HEARTY BROWN BREAD

2 large **potatoes**
¾ C. **cornmeal**
3 C. **water**
2 T. **yeast**
2½ t. **salt**
5 C. whole wheat **flour**
4 C. rye **flour**

Cook potatoes in a small amount of water. Mash with their cooking water and place in a large mixing bowl. In the pan used for cooking potatoes, mix cornmeal and water and bring to a boil, stirring constantly. Add to potatoes. Let cool to lukewarm. Mix in yeast and let stand 5 minutes. Add salt and 2 C. whole wheat flour. Beat 1 minute. Add rye flour, then whole wheat until mixture is too stiff to stir. Knead for at least 10 minutes, adding more whole wheat flour as needed (dough will be sticky at first). Shape into 2 loaves and place in greased loaf pans. Let rise until just over edge of pan—1 hour or more. Bake at 375° for 50 to 60 minutes, or until bottom sounds hollow when tapped. When cool, refrigerate. This bread is easier to slice after 2 or 3 days. Excellent toasted!

PROTEIN: 184.9 grams; CALORIES: 4307 *Helen Riley*
Lawton, Oklahoma

Use toast cut into animal shapes for children. *Many LLL Contributors*

WHOLE GRAIN SOFT PRETZELS

1 T. **yeast**
1½ C. warm **water**
1 T. **honey** or brown sugar
1 t. **salt**
3½ C. whole wheat **flour**
½ C. **wheat germ**

Optional:
3 T. **oil**
½ C. dry **milk powder**

Glaze:
1 **egg** beaten with 1 T. **water**

Toppings:
coarse salt
sesame seeds
poppy seeds

Dissolve yeast in water with honey. When bubbly, stir in salt, optionals if used, and 2 C. flour. Beat until smooth. Add wheat germ and remaining flour to make a soft dough. Knead until smooth and elastic, about 5 minutes. Let rise until doubled, 45 to 60 minutes. Punch down and divide into 16 equal parts. Roll each piece into a rope 16 inches long. This is where the family can help! Kids love making "snakes" and have unusual ideas about the pretzel's eventual shapes. The initials of everyone's names or numbers for their ages are possible ideas. See picture for traditional pretzel shape.

Transfer pretzels to greased baking sheets with a wide spatula and let rise 20 minutes. Your "artist" can brush glaze on the tops and sprinkle with desired topping. Bake at 400° for about 20 minutes, or until golden brown. Cool on racks.

Shaped dough freezes well. To bake, dip frozen pretzel in water, sprinkle with coarse salt and bake about 30 minutes. Frozen baked pretzels can be thawed in a 350° oven 5 to 6 minutes.

This is a great snack for your child to share with school friends, especially if he/she's had a hand in making them. It's a fun group activity, too.   *PROTEIN: 87.1 grams; CALORIES: 1850*

> *Millie Conway*
> *Canton, Michigan*
> *Lisa Newell*
> *Phoenix, Arizona*
> *Ellen Wadyka*
> *Somerville, New Jersey*

Variation: For that characteristic chewy texture, after the pretzels have risen 20 minutes, lower them gently one at a time with a slotted spoon into 2 qts. boiling **water** with 3 T. **salt**. Boil 1 minute, drain well and place back on baking sheet. Glaze and bake as above.

> *Linda Tibbs*
> *Pekin, Illinois*
> *Ruth Chaney*
> *Appleton, Wisconsin*

After baking I let my 4-year-old "paint" breads with a stick of butter.

> *Elaine W. Good*
> *Lititz, Pennsylvania*

WHOLE WHEAT ENGLISH MUFFINS

2 C. warm **water**
½ to 1 C. dry **milk powder**
1 to 2 T. **honey**
3 T. **butter** or oil
1 t. **salt**
1 T. **yeast**
5 to 6 C. whole wheat **flour**
cornmeal

Combine water, milk powder, honey, butter, salt and yeast. Let rest 5 minutes. Beat in flour slowly until you have a soft, kneadable dough. Knead 5 minutes and let rise 1 hour. Punch down and pat out on a floured surface ½ inch thick. Cut into 3 to 4 inch rounds, using a glass or empty tuna can. Place muffins on cookie sheets liberally sprinkled with cornmeal. Let rise half an hour, then bake on a medium-hot, lightly greased skillet, griddle or electric pan, 10 minutes per side. Split with a fork, toast and serve hot. Makes 12 4-inch muffins.   *PROTEIN: 98.2 grams; CALORIES: 2636*

Variations: Add ⅔ C. **raisins** and 1 t. **cinnamon** to liquid ingredients before adding flour. *Or* omit 1½ C. flour and add 1½ C. rolled **oats, bran** and/or **wheat germ.**   *Many LLL Contributors*

No-Knead Whole Wheat English Muffins: Add only 4 to 5 C. flour, until you can no longer stir. Do not knead dough before rising.   *Janice Hartman*
Millsboro, Delaware

Oven-Baked English Muffins: Omit ½ C. water. Add ⅔ C. **yogurt.** Sprinkle tops of muffins with cornmeal and place another cookie sheet on top of the muffins, so that it rests directly on them. Let rise ½ hour and bake at 375° for about 15 minutes.   *Jean Baker White*
Van Buren, Maine

GETTING STARTED WITH SOURDOUGH

During the Goldrush, when the prospectors set out, they carried with them a naturally fermenting dough—sourdough. To this they added flour and water to make their loaves of bread. Before each baking, though, some of the dough was saved and treasured to ensure tomorrow's bread. This American frontier tradition (carried from the Old Countries, where some rural women and even bakeries still follow it) has since become a creative outlet for today's home-baker. And starter can still be passed down from generation to generation as it was done in the past when children married and left home.

Some home-bakers grow very attached to their starter! Writes **Carma J. Kimball** of Elgin, Illinois: "The main thing is understanding your starter. Many people think of it as sort of a ready-mix, but it's not. It is a living thing. Do you talk to your plants? Maybe not, but I'm sure you realize that they are alive and require regular care. So does your sourdough. Mine has a name—Sidney the Sourdough—and is 10 years old. That's older than my eldest child. Sidney lives in a dormant stage in the refrigerator, in a crock with a lid. I don't use him every day, but if I did he would live out in the cupboard."

Sourdough has the nutritional advantage of being made of yeasts and bacteria, which have some protein value. Furthermore, if you are spooked by double-acting baking powder, sourdough gives you a most tasty alternative because baking soda reacts with it to create the gases which cause breads and cakes to rise. It can be used in almost any recipe for quick breads, cakes, cookies, etc. For recipes using about 2 C. of liquid, substitute 1 C. sourdough starter for about ¾ C. liquid and use about 1 t. baking soda for each cup of starter.

Yeast breads can be converted to sourdough, too. You can simply substitute 1 C. sourdough starter for ¾ C. liquid in any 2 loaf recipe, or, for more sourdough flavor, leave out the yeast and start your bread the night before. Make a "sponge" (see p. 138) with the starter, liquid (in same proportions as above) and about half the flour and let it sit in a warm place overnight. In the morning add all the other ingredients (except the yeast) to the bubbly mixture and proceed with the recipe, allowing a little more time for rising. (And remember that sourdough breads are stickier to knead than ordinary yeast breads, so don't add too much flour.)

If you find sourdough yeast-type breads made entirely with whole wheat flour too sour and heavy (this should not be a problem with non-yeast breads), try adding eggs, mashed potatoes or potato cooking water (p. 136) in place of all or some of the liquid; adding some yeast to help the rising; or ¼ t. baking soda per cup of starter to "sweeten" it a little. Or use part unbleached flour or Cornell Mix (p. 120) which is unbleached flour with added soy flour, wheat germ and powdered milk.

When your starter or the batter ("sponge") for bread or pancakes is fermenting, it should be kept at 85 to 100° F. Above 110° will kill it. See p. 136) for ideas on where to keep it warm. Take your starter out of the refrigerator several hours before using it *or* use it cold and use 110° liquid in the recipe. The liquid that collects at the top of the starter can be stirred back in, unless it turns pink in which case all the starter except ¼ C. should be discarded and you'll have to start another batch with the remainder. Don't worry about molds—just scrape the moldy encrustations off the inside of the crock with a spoon and throw them away (they are not harmful). Occasionally, you might want to clean out the crock. Pour the starter into a clean jar and wash the crock. Let it air-dry before replacing the starter.

Once you become accustomed to using your sourdough starter, you'll find yourself inventing new recipes all the time. Nothing can compare with the aromatic succulence of those crusty, sour loaves and the subtle tang of sourdough quick breads and desserts!

Karen Myers *Stella Belair* *Marie Lundstrom* *Bryanna Clark*
Butler, Pennsylvania *Blakeney, Ont., Canada* *Cambridge, Wisconsin* *Union Bay, B.C., Canada*

SOURDOUGH STARTER

1 T. **yeast**
2 C. warm **water**
2 C. **flour**, whole wheat
or unbleached

Dissolve yeast in water in a 1½ to 2-qt. glass jar or crock. Do not use metal. Let stand 10 minutes. Stir in flour. Cover with a lid or plastic wrap and let stand in a warm place overnight or at room temperature for about 2 days, until bubbly and slightly sour-smelling. Let stand longer if you like it more sour. Use immediately, leaving a little in the jar, or store, covered, in the refrigerator. When you use some, stir equal amounts of warm water and flour back into remaining starter and let stand until bubbly. Stir down before returning to refrigerator. If starter gets too sour, discard 1 C. and add 1 C. warm water and 1 C. flour and let stand as above. Starter will last indefinitely if used at least once a week.   *PROTEIN: 35 grams; CALORIES: 823*

Karen Myers   Wanda Rezac   Carma J. Kimball
Butler, Pennsylvania   Marlboro, Massachusetts   Elgin, Illinois

SOURDOUGH BREAD

2 C. **sourdough starter**
1 C. **milk**, scalded
¼ C. **butter**
¼ C. **sugar** or honey
2 t. **salt**
2 t. **baking soda**
5 to 7 C. **flour** (your choice)

Optional:
1 T. **yeast**
½ C. **wheat germ** (add with flour)

Stir butter, sugar and salt into milk and cool to lukewarm. Add sourdough starter. Dissolve soda (and yeast, if used) in a little warm water and stir in. Add flour until dough is kneadable and knead well. Let rise for 3 hours (about 1 hour if yeast is used). When doubled, punch down and shape into 2 loaves. Place in greased loaf pans and let rise until above edges of pans. Bake at 400° for 25 to 30 minutes. This dough can be used for rolls or cinnamon rolls, and dozens of variations with herbs, cheese, etc.   *PROTEIN: 100.4 grams; CALORIES: 3151*   Marie Lundstrom
Cambridge, Wisconsin

WHOLE WHEAT SOURDOUGH ENGLISH MUFFINS

½ C. **sourdough starter**
1 C. **milk**
2¾ C. whole wheat **flour**
1 T. **brown sugar** or honey
½ t. **salt**
½ t. **baking soda**
cornmeal

Combine starter, milk and 2 C. flour. Stir well, cover loosely and let sit at room temperature 8 hours or overnight. Then stir together ¾ C. flour, sugar, salt and soda. Add this to the sourdough mixture and beat thoroughly, adding more flour if necessary to make a soft, pliable dough. Knead for 3 minutes. Roll out ½" thick on a floured surface and cut into 3 to 4" rounds with a glass, cookie cutter or empty tuna can. Place on cookie sheet liberally sprinkled with cornmeal and let rise 45 minutes. Bake on a medium-hot, lightly greased griddle, skillet or electric pan, 8 to 10 minutes per side. Split with a fork, toast—and enjoy! These make a delightful, cheap and easy breakfast treat.   *PROTEIN: 60.7 grams; CALORIES: 1634*

Carolyn Callaghan   Laurie Owens
Leavenworth, Kansas   Cincinnati, Ohio

SOURDOUGH MIXED-GRAIN BREAD

1 ½ C. **sourdough starter**
1 ½ C. warm **water**
3 C. whole wheat **flour**
2 T. **yeast**
1 ½ C. warm **water**
2 T. **honey**
2 T. **molasses**
3 T. **oil**
1 T. **salt**
½ C. **sunflower seeds**
2 T. **sesame seeds**
1 T. **poppy seeds**
3 C. rye **flour**
1 C. soy **flour**
2 to 3 C. whole wheat **flour**

Make a sponge by mixing together in large bowl the starter, water and whole wheat flour. Let stand covered overnight. Dissolve yeast in 1 ½ C. water with honey and molasses. Let stand 10 minutes. Add to sponge with oil, salt, seeds, rye and soy flour. Beat 3 minutes with electric mixer or 300 strokes by hand. Add whole wheat flour to make a soft dough. Cover and let rest 10 minutes. Knead 10 minutes. Let rise 2 hours. Punch down, knead briefly and shape into 3 loaves. Place in greased loaf pans and let rise until doubled, about 1 hour. Bake at 350° for 45 to 50 minutes. Loosely cover with foil during last 15 minutes if tops are browning too fast.

PROTEIN: 209.5 grams; CALORIES: 4837

Karen Myers
Butler, Pennsylvania

SOURDOUGH RYE BREAD WITH SEEDS

1 C. **sourdough starter**
1 C. warm **water**
2 C. rye **flour**
1 T. **yeast**
1 C. warm **water**
2 t. **salt**
1 T. **caraway seeds**
1 T. **poppy seeds**
1 C. rye **flour**
3 C. whole wheat **flour**
3 T. **cornmeal**
1 **egg white**

In a large bowl, mix starter, 1 C. water and 2 C. rye flour. Cover and let stand overnight.

In morning, dissolve yeast in 1 C. water and add to sponge with salt, seeds and rye flour. Mix well, adding whole wheat flour. Cover and let rest 10 minutes. Knead about 10 to 12 minutes. Dough will be tacky. Let rise for 3 hours. Punch down and knead briefly. Divide in half and form into long loaves. Place on cookie sheet sprinkled with cornmeal. Let rise until doubled, about 1 hour.

Brush loaves with egg white beaten with 1 t. **water**. Bake loaves on bottom oven rack at 400° for 25 minutes, or until they sound hollow when bottoms are tapped.

For crustier loaves, place a pan of hot water in oven, or spray loaves with plant mister before and halfway through baking.

P.: 113.7 gms.; C.: 2702

Karen Myers
Butler, Pennsylvania

Finnish Sourdough Rye Bread. Omit 2 C. warm water. Use 2 C. warm **beer**. Shape into round loaves. *Note on use of beer:* For those that do not drink beer, remember that when alcohol is cooked, it evaporates. Using beer in this recipe gives it a unique taste and texture to which nothing can compare. Light beer works fine.

Rita Pisano
Holbrook, Arizona

BAKED DOUGHNUTS

1⅓ C. warm **water**
1½ T. **yeast**
¼ C. **honey** or brown sugar
5 T. **oil**
2 **eggs**, beaten
½ t. **salt**
1 t. **nutmeg**, cinnamon or
　allspice
⅓ C. non-instant dry **milk**
　powder or ⅔ C. instant
5 C. whole wheat pastry **flour**
　(approximately)
3 T. **cornmeal**
3 T. **oil**
doughnut glaze (p. 119)
　(optional)

Stir water, yeast, honey, oil and eggs together in a large bowl. Let stand 5 minutes to soften yeast before adding salt, spice, milk powder and 2½ C. flour. Beat 5 minutes, using an electric mixer. Add enough flour to make a soft, kneadable dough. Knead about 5 minutes adding as little flour as possible. A slightly sticky dough will ensure a lighter product than a dry dough will. Let dough rise 1 hour in oiled bowl. Punch down and let rise ½ hour. Roll dough out ½" thick; cut into doughnut shapes, placing cut-outs on cornmeal-sprinkled baking sheets. Brush tops lightly with oil.

Let rise 1 hour. Bake at 375° for 15 minutes. Glaze *immediately* if desired. Best eaten warm; or freeze and reheat. Makes about 2½ dozen doughnuts. 　　*PROTEIN: 103.5 grams; CALORIES: 3612 + glaze*

Carol Hoefler
Zanesville, Ohio

DOUGH DABS

bread dough: your favorite
　recipe, after first rise,
　about 1 loaf's worth
Oil: enough to fill a 9"
　skillet ½" deep, about 1½ C.

Divide dough in half. Roll each half out on floured surface 1/4 to 3/8" thick. Cut into strips 1" wide and no longer than 5". Make a lengthwise cut in the middle of each piece, about 3" long. Heat oil until a pea-sized piece of dough floats to the top when dropped in. Heat will have to be adjusted as you fry. Place one layer of pieces in skillet. When undersides are lightly browned, turn with a fork and brown other side. Drain on paper and serve warm with butter and homemade soup or chili. Continue frying until dough is used up. Oil may be strained, refrigerated and re-used.

This was my German grandma's recipe, which I think was never written down before. It's easy to do and delicious. Makes soup a meal. We do this every bread-baking day in the winter and we get to eat hot bread while the other loaves are still rising. Also tends to keep the other loaves from being "raided" while cooling off!

J. J. Fallick
Appleton, Wisconsin

Variation: Roll dough ½" thick and cut into squares, triangles or doughnuts. Dip fried bread into honey-butter or cinnamon-sugar, or split and fill with jam. Eat fresh!

Bryanna Clark
Union Bay, B.C., Canada

CREOLE DOUGHNUTS
(Beignets—pronounced Beng-yeah)

2 T. **oil** or butter
1 T. **honey**
½ t. **salt**
¾ C. hand hot **water** (110°)
½ C. evaporated **milk**
1½ t. **yeast**
1 **egg**, beaten
3 C. whole wheat **flour** (approximately)
oil for frying

In a large mixing bowl, stir together the oil, honey, salt, water, milk and yeast. Let mixture sit 5 minutes to soften yeast. Stir in egg, then slowly beat in flour until you have a soft dough that can be dropped from a spoon. Let rise in bowl 20 minutes. Meanwhile, heat oil to 365°. Drop spoonfuls of dough into the oil. *Do not crowd!* When beignets are golden brown on all sides, remove from oil and drain on paper towels. Roll in **cinnamon-sugar**, if desired, and serve while still warm.

The dough may be frozen and removed from the freezer the night before it is needed. Thaw in refrigerator and by morning it will have risen and be ready to cook.   *PROTEIN: 65.3 grams; CALORIES: 1759 + oil and sugar*

Jean Giesel
Melrose, Florida

MILKLESS, EGGLESS DOUGHNUTS
(Non-Yeast)

shortening or oil for frying
1 C. **water**
¼ C. **oil**
½ C. **honey** or brown sugar
6 oz. **tofu**
3 C. whole wheat **flour**
1 T. **baking powder**
½ t. **salt**
½ t. **nutmeg**
doughnut glaze (p. 119) (optional)

Begin heating enough shortening (to 375°) in deep, heavy saucepan to reach 2-inch depth. Meanwhile, as it heats, stir the water, oil and honey together in a large mixing bowl. Beat in the tofu, then add the flour, baking powder, salt and nutmeg all at once. Stir just enough to blend. Roll dough to ½" thickness on a floured surface, adding a little extra flour, if needed, to prevent sticking. Cut doughnuts out. Drop carefully into hot fat. Do not crowd! Turn frequently until doughnuts are golden all over, then drain on paper towels. Glaze immediately, if desired.

These doughnuts are very quick to make. By the time the fat is hot, I am ready to cook the first batch. These doughnuts are the old-fashioned kind. No one in my family feels deprived when I make them—especially my allergic child, who can eat them! The tofu helps make up for the protein that would be missing, since there are no eggs or milk in this recipe.

PROTEIN: 61.7 grams; CALORIES: 2355 + oil and glaze

Beverly Morgan
San Jose, California

FLOUR TORTILLAS OR CHAPATHIS

4 C. whole wheat **flour**
1 t. **salt**
¼ t. **baking powder** (optional)
¼ to ½ C. **butter** or oil (optional)
1 C. warm **water**

Mix dry ingredients together. Rub in butter or oil. Add water to make a soft, pliable dough. Knead briefly. Divide dough into 12 to 16 balls. Cover and let rest 15 to 20 minutes. Flour well and roll into a thin circle between sheets of waxed paper, flouring as needed to prevent sticking. Bake on an ungreased, heavy skillet or griddle until brown specks appear on cooking side. Flip over and cook other side. These store well in refrigerator or freezer.

Try cutting out triangles of cooked tortillas and frying in hot oil until golden. Drain on paper and sprinkle with salt. These make great "chips" for dipping in taco sauce or guacamole!   *PROTEIN: 64.4 grams; CALORIES: 2033*

Taco Shells. Use up to 1⅓ C. **cornmeal** or masa harina in place of an equal amount of flour. Fry the cooked tortilla in a little hot oil, folding it in half and holding it in shape with tongs while you fry both sides. Drain well. May be reheated in hot oven.

*Lore'e Clark
Mission, Kansas*   *Evie Miller
Potter, Nebraska*   *Marie Bloom
Hamilton, Montana*

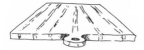

CORN TORTILLAS
(Tortillas de Maiz)

2 C. **masa harina** (Mexican cornmeal especially for tortillas)
1⅓ C. **water**

Add water to the masa all at once and mix quickly with your fingers. Cover with a clean wet cloth and set aside while you heat up a griddle or frying pan. Cast iron works well, or you may use an electric skillet or griddle. Let it get very hot and do *not* grease. If possible, have one person make the tortillas and another person cook them. Make the dough into 8 balls and roll them out into 7" rounds between sheets of waxed paper with a rolling pin *or* use a tortilla press (available in cookware shops), placing the dough between sheets of plastic wrap before pressing. Carefully peel off one sheet of waxed paper or plastic and flip the tortilla onto the hot pan; carefully, but quickly peel off the other sheet. (Or peel off both sheets before placing in the pan —experiment to see which way works best for you.) When the edge of the tortilla begins to look dry (about 1 minute), flip it over and cook for another minute. It's okay if it has a few scorched spots. Stack the cooked tortillas in a clean towel. Fresh tortillas should be soft and moist.

You can store cool tortillas in foil and refrigerate or freeze. Reheat in a 350° oven before serving, for about 15 minutes (thaw first). To keep the tortillas hot for as long as 2 hours, wrap the hot foil package in a towel, then in a dozen sheets of newspaper.

Tortillas may be toasted on a barbecue grill, under a broiler, or directly over a gas flame, turning often with tongs, until soft and blistered. Fry tortillas in ½" hot fat in a skillet one at a time, turning often with tongs, until crisp and slightly puffy (1 minute or less). Drain. Cut into strips for tortilla chips.

We usually make about 4 dozen tortillas at a time, with the family working on an assembly-line basis. Once you get the hang of it, it doesn't take very long.

Masa Harina is available in supermarkets, natural food stores and co-ops in most areas of North America. If you can't find it, you might like to try making your own. *PROTEIN: 10.2 grams; CALORIES: 808* *Bryanna Clark*
Union Bay, B.C., Canada

FRESH MASA
(Hominy)

9 C. shelled dry **corn** (3 lbs.
  field or dent corn)
3 qts. cold **water**
¾ C. **hydrated lime** (3 oz.)

Note: Dried corn may be purchased at a health food store or feed store. Do **not** use quick-lime or anhydrous lime—they are dangerous. Hydrated lime does not have the burning effect of quick-lime. It is oxide of calcium and Mexicans who cannot afford dairy products traditionally get their dietary calcium from eating tortillas.

Cover the corn with the water in a large enameled or stainless steel pot, like a canner (don't use aluminum). Add the lime and bring to a boil. Boil, covered, for about 1 hour, until the skins peel off. Remove from heat and pour some cold water into the pot to hasten cooling. When cool enough to handle, swish the corn around and rub with fingers. The skins will come off in the water. Rinse the corn under running cold water until the water runs almost clear. Now you have hominy or nixtamal. It can be ground fresh in a hand or electric meat grinder or food mill with the finest plate, or a *steel*-burr hand mill. The meat grinder or food mill makes a slightly coarse masa, which our family didn't mind, but you might want to run it through twice. A food processor might work too. The masa seems drier than dough made from masa flour, but tortillas are easily made following the same directions as for Corn Tortillas (p. 168). They are delicious—with an indescribable fresh corn flavor! 4½ C. of nixtamal makes about 20 tortillas. Fresh nixtamal can be frozen.

If you like, you can dry the nixtamal and then crack it for grits or grind it into masa flour. *PROTEIN: 115.7 grams; CALORIES: 4654* *Bryanna Clark*
Union Bay, B.C., Canada

KATIE'S NOODLES
(Homemade Pasta)

3 **egg yolks**
1 whole **egg**
1 t. **salt**
1 T. **water**
about 2 C. whole wheat **flour**

Beat eggs until light. Add salt and water, and beat again until light. Add flour, 2 T. at a time, mixing lightly with a fork until a ball forms. Without kneading, roll out ½ at a time, turning often and adding flour as needed. When it is 1/16th" thick, transfer dough to a towel-covered surface until it is dry enough to be rolled up loosely without sticking to itself (½ hour or more, depending on temperature and humidity). Roll up, jellyroll fashion and cut to desired width. Cook in boiling, salted water or broth until tender, 3 to 8 minutes, depending on thickness, or freeze for later use.

I learned from my old German Grandma that well-beaten eggs make light noodles. She made me beat them by hand; and I never earned a better comment than, "Well, maybe that'll do." However, these noodles are easy after a little practice and tasty even when you're a beginner. Whole wheat flour not only adds nutrition but makes noodles easier to roll out than the white flour ones Grandma Katie made.   *J. J. Fallick*
PROTEIN: 46.6 grams; CALORIES: 1055   Appleton, Wisconsin

Variations:

#1 Omit egg yolks. Add 1 more whole **egg**.   *PROTEIN: 44.4 grams; CALORIES: 956*

#2 Omit 1 C. whole wheat flour. Add 1 C. unbleached **flour** or Cornell Mix (p. 120).

#3 For colored noodles, omit the water and replace it with one of the following: **Red Noodles:** 1 T. **tomato paste. Green Noodles:** 1½ T. strained **spinach. Light Green Noodles:** 1½ T. puree of **green peppers. Yellow Noodles:** 1 T. **milk** or water. Use only unbleached flour or Cornell Mix. **Brown Noodles:** 1 T. milk and use only whole wheat flour. **Orange Noodles:** 1½ T. pureed **carrots**. Proceed with general instructions.

EGGLESS WHOLE WHEAT NOODLES

3 C. whole wheat **flour**
   (approximately)
¼ C. unprocessed **miller's bran**
   (optional)
½ t. **salt**
1 C. plain **yogurt**

In a large bowl, stir bran, 2 C. flour and salt together. Stir in the yogurt; mix well. Continue adding flour until dough is stiff enough to roll out. Knead briefly. Let dough rest 5 minutes. Divide in half, and roll each half out, as thinly as you can (for better taste and faster cooking!), on a floured surface. Transfer dough to a towel-covered surface and dry about ½ hour. Dust with flour and roll each sheet of dough up, jelly-roll fashion. Slice at ¼" intervals. Separate the noodles and let dry 2 hours before adding to simmering water or soup. Cook, uncovered, about 10 minutes, or until tender.

If you or anyone in your family has an allergy to eggs, these noodles can be a life-saver, adding a unique flavor everyone will like. They can be used in casseroles or any other dish where noodles are required.
*PROTEIN: 59.9 grams; CALORIES: 1343   Tamara Lee Mitchell
Cabot, Arkansas*

GALLOPING GALUSKA
(Quick drop noodles)

Large pot of boiling **water** or
   soup
½ C. **milk**
1 **egg**
¾ C. whole wheat **flour**
¼ t. **salt**
dash **pepper**

Variation:
2 T. melted **butter**

Beat egg and milk together, stir into flour and salt and pepper. Place batter on a plate with a small rim and tip over the boiling liquid. When the batter begins to run over the edge, cut it off with a sharp knife or metal spatula edge as you would cut off extra crust from the edge of a pie. Dip the knife into the hot liquid after each stroke and repeat. After the noodles float, let them cook about ½ a minute. If the noodles are to be served with soup, just reduce the heat to low until serving time. **To serve the noodles separately**, remove from liquid with slotted spoon and drain. Place in heavy skillet or baking dish with melted butter. Turn noodles to coat with butter and keep them from sticking to each other. Keep warm until serving time. The slowest part of this recipe is waiting for the water to boil so if you have a pot of soup ready to serve, you can have noodles in less than 10 minutes. Helps "sturdy up" or stretch a meal. Makes about 2 cups of noodles. *PROTEIN: 22.4 grams; CALORIES: 458*

With butter—P.: 22.6 gms.; C.: 674
Roberta Bishop Johnson
Champaign, Illinois

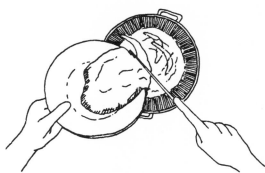

CHEWY NOODLES

2 **eggs**
¼ t. **salt** or onion or garlic salt
½ t. **sage** (optional)
2 T. **water**
1 to 1¼ C. **flour** of choice

Beat eggs, salt, sage and water until thoroughly blended. Add flour, a little at a time, until a dough forms. Knead until smooth, then roll to about 1/8" thick. Cut into strips of desired width and length, and cook 10 minutes in boiling water or soup stock. Professional noodle makers, don't look! This recipe is for people who really like to sink their teeth into something when eating noodles and for moms who don't have time for rolling the dough so thin and drying it to get those prize-winning skinny noodles. *PROTEIN: 28.4 grams; CALORIES: 558*

Ronaele Berry
Johnstown, Nebraska

SOURDOUGH HERB ROLLS

1 C. **sourdough starter** (p. 164)
1½ C. warm **water**
2 T. **honey**
2 T. **oil**
1 t. **salt**
¼ t. **oregano**
¼ t. **basil**
1/8 t. **thyme**
2 C. whole wheat **flour**
1½ to 2 C. unbleached **flour**

Optional:
1 t. **yeast**
½ C. dry **milk powder**
1 **egg**, beaten
½ C. **wheat germ**

Add water (with dissolved yeast, if used) to starter in a large bowl. Add honey, oil, salt and herbs along with optional milk powder, egg and wheat germ. Mix well. Add flour, ½ C. at a time until a thick but beatable batter forms. Beat 100 strokes. Add remaining flour and knead about 10 minutes. Let rise until doubled, 1 to 1½ hours (longer if optional yeast is not used). Punch down and form into rolls. Let rise in a greased 9 x 13" pan until doubled. Brush with water and bake at 375° for 30 minutes. Makes 12 huge rolls.

My family loves these with spaghetti or lasagne. Combining sourdough with herbs produces an interesting flavor. The addition of milk and eggs makes for a softer roll, but detracts somewhat from the tartness of the sourdough. Try it both ways, and vary the herbs to find your favorites.

Beth Elmore
Elkhart, Indiana

PROTEIN: 57.8 grams; CALORIES: 2110

SOURDOUGH CRACKED WHEAT BREAD

½ C. boiling **water**
1 C. **milk**
¼ C. **maple syrup**
½ C. **sourdough starter** (p. 164)
1½ t. **salt**
1 T. **yeast**
½ C. warm **water**
1 C. **cracked wheat**
1 C. whole wheat **flour**
4 C. unbleached or whole wheat **flour**

In exactly this order, mix boiling water, milk, syrup, starter and salt in a large bowl. Dissolve yeast in warm water; when foamy, add to large bowl. Beat in cracked wheat, whole wheat flour and 1 C. unbleached flour. Add remaining flour and knead until smooth. Let rise until doubled. Form into 2 loaves and place in buttered pan of your choice. Let rise until doubled. Bake at 375° for 45 to 50 minutes. *PROTEIN: 110.1 grams; CALORIES: 3129*

Constance Harris
Warsaw, Illinois

BETTER-THAN-CRACKERS

flour or **corn tortillas** (p. 168)
melted **butter**

Lay tortillas, round or cut in wedges, on large flat pans. Brush top side with melted butter, turn, repeat for the other side. Place pans in cold oven. Turn heat to 375°. Watch carefully; when oven temperature reaches 375°, turn oven **off**. Don't open door; let tortillas remain in oven until cool.

These make an excellent "go with" for soups, guacamole, or cheese spreads. No one can guess what they are!

Diana Reardon
Dallas, Texas

Vegetables

BAKED FRESH ASPARAGUS

3 T. melted **butter**
12 spears fresh **asparagus**
2 T. chopped **onion**
2 T. chopped **celery**
2 T. grated **cheese** (Cheddar
   or Mozzarella)
¼ C. **bread crumbs**
pinch of **oregano**
½ t. **salt** (or less)
dash of **pepper**

Put butter in shallow 8 x 8" baking dish. Arrange spears in dish. Combine other ingredients and pour over spears. Cover and bake at 375° for ½ hour. *PROTEIN: 12.2 grams; CALORIES: 529*

CHINESE-STYLE BROCCOLI OR SPINACH

4 C. **broccoli** (florets 1" long,
   stems cut thinly) or 1 lb.
   fresh spinach
2 T. **oil**
½ C. chicken or beef **broth**
1 T. tamari **soy sauce**
2 T. slivered **almonds** or
   sesame seeds

Heat oil in heavy skillet or wok. Add broccoli and stir-fry 2 to 3 minutes, until vegetable is bright green. Add broth and soy sauce; simmer, covered, 3 minutes. Garnish with almonds or sesame seeds. (Almonds or seeds may be roasted in oil 2 minutes before adding broccoli, if desired.) This technique works equally well using other fresh green vegetables, such as **green beans, celery,** or **peppers,** and is sure to please. *PROTEIN: 23.8 grams; CALORIES: 516*

Dorothy MacDonald   Anne Weidenhammer
Fonthill, Ont., Canada   Saskatoon, Sask., Canada

POTATO PANCAKES

3 large **potatoes**, grated
1 medium **onion**, minced
2 **eggs**
¼ C. dry **milk powder**
¼ C. **wheat germ**
1 T. tamari **soy sauce**
1 T. **oil** for frying

Alice Gilgoff
Douglaston, New York

Beat all ingredients together. Drop about 2 T. batter per pancake onto a hot, well-greased pan, and fry over medium heat, turning once, until both sides are crisp and golden. Serve with dollops of sour cream and/or applesauce, though they are just as good with a generous sprinkling of cheese melted on top.

PROTEIN: 44 grams; CALORIES: 953

STUFFED MUSHROOMS

8 oz. fresh **mushrooms**
lemon juice
2 T. finely chopped **onion**
1 to 2 T. **butter**
¼ t. chopped fresh **parsley**
1 clove **garlic**, minced
½ t. **salt** (or less)
dash of **pepper**
¼ C. white **wine** (optional)
½ C. shredded Mozzarella **cheese**
½ C. **bread crumbs**

Wash mushrooms. Remove and save stems. Put caps in shallow baking dish. Fill each cap ¼ full of lemon juice. Chop stems and saute with onion in butter until soft. Add parsley, garlic and seasonings, and cook 1 minute. Add wine, cheese and enough bread crumbs for a stiff mixture. Stuff each cap and bake at 350° for 10 to 15 minutes.

PROTEIN: 23.5 grams; CALORIES: 568

Patty Holtz
Geneva, Illinois

MUSHROOMS AND CHEESE

1 lb. fresh **mushrooms**
2 T. whole wheat **flour**
½ t. **salt**
¼ t. **pepper**
⅓ C. chopped **onion**
1 clove **garlic**, minced
3 T. **butter**
¼ C. **milk**
6 T. grated Cheddar **cheese**
1 C. plain **yogurt** or sour cream
whole wheat **toast**, cooked brown rice, or whole wheat pasta

Clean mushrooms, separating caps from stems. Slice stems, leave caps whole. Combine flour, salt and pepper in small paper bag; add mushrooms and shake bag to coat. Set aside. Saute onion and garlic in butter. Add mushrooms and cook gently for 10 minutes. Stir in milk, cheese and yogurt, cooking over low heat until cheese melts. Serve over prepared toast, rice or pasta.

PROTEIN: 40.7 grams; CALORIES: 894 + toast

Phyllis K. Collins
Medina, Ohio

STUFFED POTATOES

5 baked **potatoes**, hot from oven
1 C. plain **yogurt**
1 C. grated Cheddar **cheese**
3 T. **butter**
2 T. **milk**
2 T. finely minced **onion**
½ t. **salt** (or less)
dash of **pepper**
½ C. cooked and diced **bacon** (optional)
paprika and/or parsley for garnish

Carefully cut potatoes in half lengthwise and scoop out pulp. Reserve skin shells. Beat potatoes together with yogurt, cheese, butter, milk, onion, seasonings and optional bacon (an electric beater does the best job here). Stuff the skin shells with the new potato mixture, and reheat in a 400° oven for 15 minutes.

PROTEIN: 76.3 grams; CALORIES: 2032

Debi Musick
Weatherford, Oklahoma

Janine Leach
Lodi, California

Jennifer McKinney
Vienna, Virginia

DILLY CARROTS

1 lb. **carrots**, thinly sliced
1 t. fresh **dill** (½ t. dried)
2 T. **butter**

In 1-quart saucepan, steam carrots until tender, about 8 to 12 minutes. Drain. Add butter and dill; mix well.

PROTEIN: 4.4 grams; CALORIES: 374

Ginger Carrots. Omit dill. With butter, stir in 2 T. **orange juice**, ¼ t. ground **ginger** and ¼ t. ground **cinnamon.**   *PROTEIN: 4.5 grams; CALORIES: 389*

Linda Wierzer
Garland, Texas

SESAME VEGETABLES

1 T. **oil**
6 **carrots**, sliced ½" diagonally
6 **onions**, sliced ½"
⅓ C. **water**
3 T. **sesame seeds**

Heat oil in heavy skillet. Add vegetables and saute over medium heat about 5 minutes, stirring frequently. Add water and cover. Simmer until tender, about 5 to 10 minutes longer. Stir in seeds and serve. The carrots and onions complement the sweetness of each other.   *P.: 21.2 gms.; C.: 756*

Marion Haymann
France

YUMMY YAMS

6 medium **yams**
¼ t. ground **nutmeg**
¼ t. ground **cloves**
1 T. **vanilla** extract
1 T. **almond** extract
2 T. **honey**
1 C. plain **yogurt**
1 T. **butter**
1 **egg**

Scrub yams. Make a 2" slit in center of each and bake at 400° for 1¼ hours. Carefully halve yams lengthwise, scooping pulp into large bowl. Reserve skins. Add nutmeg, cloves, vanilla and almond extracts, honey, yogurt, butter and egg to pulp. Beat until fluffy. Mound this mixture into the skin shells or baking dish; bake at 350° for 15 minutes.

PROTEIN: 35.7 grams; CALORIES: 1490

Stephanie Merritt
Los Altos, California

PARSNIPS IN SAVORY SAUCE

4 **parsnips**, halved and cooked
2 T. **butter**
3 T. **flour**
1 C. parsnip cooking **liquid**
¼ t. **worcestershire sauce**
few drops of **onion juice**
¼ t. prepared **mustard**
½ C. grated **cheese**

Melt butter in 1-qt. saucepan; add flour, stirring constantly. Add liquid, stir until thickened and add seasonings. Arrange parsnips in 8" baking pan. Cover with sauce, top with cheese and bake at 350° for 20 to 30 minutes.

PROTEIN: 31.2 grams; CALORIES: 1130

Linda Church
West Lafayette, Indiana

SIDESHOW POTATOES

3 C. grated **potatoes**
2 T. melted **butter**
½ t. **salt** or less
dash of **pepper**
1 t. **paprika** (optional)

Toss potatoes, butter, salt and pepper together before patting into greased 11 x 13" pan. Sprinkle with paprika. Bake at 425° for 20 minutes. To double, use 2 large pans, as the potatoes must be spread out thinly.

PROTEIN: 6.5 grams; CALORIES: 444　　Barbara Rozek
Houston, Texas

PICKETT
(Potato Kugel)

3 C. coarsely grated
　baking potatoes
3 **eggs**
2 to 4 T. **minced onion** (optional)
dash **salt**
dash **pepper**
2 T. melted **butter**

Mix eggs, onion, butter and seasonings in large bowl. Grate potatoes into the mixture, or mix grated potatoes into it very quickly to avoid the potatoes' turning brown. Pour into greased 8 x 8" baking dish. Bake at 350° for 1½ hours or until crisp and brown on the top. Freezes well. Makes good finger food.

PROTEIN: 37 GRAMS; CALORIES: 743　　Roberta Bishop Johnson
Champaign, Illinois

OVEN FRIED POTATOES

6 large **potatoes**
¼ C. **oil**
2 T. grated Parmesan **cheese**
　(optional)
1 t. **salt**
½ t. **garlic powder**
1 t. **paprika**
½ t. **pepper**

Scrub potatoes well and cut into strips. Combine oil, cheese, salt, garlic powder, paprika and pepper in a plastic bag. Add potatoes and shake to coat. Spread strips on 2 cookie sheets in single layer. Bake at 400° for 20 to 30 minutes, or until golden brown and tender, stirring once. PROTEIN: 27.9 grams; CALORIES: 1381

Lois Lake Raabe　　Gail Kajiura　　　　Kitty Penrod
Easton, Connecticut　L'Orignal, Ont., Canada　Columbus, Ohio

O'BRIEN POTATOES

1½ C. **milk**
½ C. **butter**
6 medium **potatoes**, grated
½ **green pepper**, diced
½ sweet **red pepper**, diced, or
　¼ C. diced pimento
5 **scallions**, sliced, including
　green tops
½ t. **salt**

Heat milk and butter together until butter melts. Meanwhile, place potatoes, peppers, scallions and salt in a greased 2-quart casserole. Cover with warm milk mixture. Bake at 275° for 2 hours. The long, slow cooking enhances the potato flavor. Leftovers, if any, are wonderful fried for breakfast! P.: 28.3 gms.; C.: 1629

Sandy Williams
N. Little Rock, Arkansas

"PICKY-EATERS" BAKED CABBAGE
(Fussy Children's Favorite)

1½ lb. **cabbage**, shredded
1 C. medium **white sauce** (p. 251)
dash of ground **nutmeg**
½ t. **salt** (or less)
dash of **pepper**
1 C. chopped **peanuts**
1 C. grated Cheddar **cheese**

Steam cabbage just until tender-crisp. Season white sauce with dash of nutmeg, salt and pepper. In greased 4-qt. casserole, arrange layers of cabbage, sauce, nuts and cheese, ending with cheese. Bake at 425° for 15 minutes. *P.: 73.8 gms.; C.: 1604*

Kathi Ambrose
Kingston, New York

CORN AND CABBAGE SKILLET

1½ C. fresh **corn**
  (10 oz. frozen)
2 C. shredded **cabbage**
2 T. chopped **onion**
2 T. **butter**
½ C. cream-style **cottage cheese**
¼ C. **yogurt** or sour cream
2 T. grated Parmesan **cheese**
½ t. **salt** (or less)
dash of **pepper**

Cook corn; drain. Steam cabbage until tender, about 7 minutes; drain. In saucepan, saute onion in butter until soft. Add remaining ingredients and heat, stirring until cheese begins to melt. Combine half the cheese mixture with corn and half with cabbage. Arrange cabbage around sides of skillet, corn in center. Heat through. Easy dress-up for two common vegetables.

PROTEIN: 32.4 grams; CALORIES: 655

Eugenia Spady
Hays, Kansas

STUFFED VEGGIE TAKE-ALONG

I. Stuffed Peppers
  2 medium **green peppers**, cored
  6½ oz. **tuna**, drained
  ¼ to ½ C. **mayonnaise** (p. 48).
    and/or plain **yogurt**
  1 stalk **celery**, chopped
  1 small **onion**, chopped
    (optional)
  ½ t. **dill weed** (optional)
  ¼ t. *each* **salt** and **pepper**

II. Stuffed Tomatoes
  2 medium **tomatoes**
  1 C. **cottage cheese**
  ½ small **onion**, diced
    (optional)
  1 t. **dill weed** or basil

I. Reserve peppers. Mix other ingredients. Stuff into peppers.

PROTEIN: 50.5 grams; CALORIES: 806

II. Cut off stem end of tomatoes. Scoop out seeds and pulp. Mix cottage cheese, onion and herbs. Stuff into tomatoes.

PROTEIN: 34.6 grams; CALORIES: 327

These are favorites for school lunches, camping or hiking. They are easy for a young child to put together. Just add a piece of fruit to make a balanced meal.

Susan Henriquez
New Paltz, New York

PARTY PEAS

4 C. shelled **peas**
(20 oz. frozen)
½ C. **mushroom** pieces
¼ C. finely chopped **onion**
½ t. **salt** (or less)
dash of **pepper**
2 T. **butter**

Combine ingredients in steamer basket over 1" water, or in pot. Cover and steam until peas are tender.

PROTEIN: 37.3 grams; CALORIES: 704

Mary Ann Haws
Avon, Minnesota

STRING BEANS CREOLE

¼ C. chopped **onion**
¼ C. chopped **green pepper**
1 T. **oil** or bacon drippings
2 C. **green beans**
1 C. chopped **tomatoes**
½ t. **salt** (or less)
dash of **pepper**
¼ t. **marjoram** (optional)
¼ t. **oregano** (optional)
½ C. grated **cheese**
½ C. **bread crumbs**

Saute onion and pepper in oil. Combine with vegetables and seasonings in 2-quart greased casserole. Top with cheese and bread crumbs. Bake at 350° for 20 minutes.

PROTEIN: 27 grams; CALORIES: 657

Sue Bunting
Lake Villa, Illinois

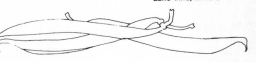

INDIAN STYLE GREEN BEANS

1 lb. **green beans**
2 to 4 T. **oil**
1 t. **mustard seeds**
½ C. chopped **onion**
¾ C. thinly sliced **carrots**
1 t. ground **coriander**
1/8 t. ground **ginger**
½ t. **salt** or less
1 to 2 T. **lemon juice**

Cut beans into 1" diagonal slices. Heat oil in large skillet or wok. Saute mustard seeds until they begin to "pop." Add vegetables; cook, stirring constantly, 5 minutes. Mix in seasonings, reduce heat, cover and simmer 8 to 10 minutes. Stir in lemon juice and serve.

PROTEIN: 10.7 grams; CALORIES: 457

Judith Manchester
Morrison, Illinois

SAUCY CAULIFLOWER

1 head **cauliflower**,
steamed whole
1 C. grated sharp Cheddar **cheese**
1 C. medium **white sauce** (p. 251)
1 T. melted **butter**
½ C. dry **bread crumbs**

Place cauliflower head in greased 1½-qt. casserole. Blend cheese into white sauce and pour over cauliflower. Top with buttered crumbs and bake at 350° for 30 minutes.
Good for potluck dinners.

PROTEIN: 57 grams; CALORIES: 1285

Mary Ann Terry
Lexington, Kentucky

GARDEN CASSEROLE

½ C. **broth**
4 C. **green beans,** sliced
4 C. **tomatoes,** chopped
½ C. **sunflower seeds**
¼ C. **sesame seeds**
½ t. **salt** (or less)
dash of **pepper**
1½ C. cubed **cheese** (Swiss
   or Mozzarella)
½ C. grated Cheddar **cheese**

Place all ingredients except cheeses in greased 3-quart baking dish. Cover and bake at 350° for 40 minutes. Stir in cubed cheese. Sprinkle grated Cheddar cheese on top and bake, uncovered, another 5 to 10 minutes.

PROTEIN: 140.5 grams; CALORIES: 2237

Luann Lee
Wapakoneta, Ohio

SPAGHETTI SQUASH

1 **spaghetti squash,** 1½ to 2 lb.
1 C. grated Cheddar **cheese**
1 C. grated Mozzarella **cheese**
1½ C. grated **zucchini** or diced
   green pepper
2 C. **tomato sauce**
½ t. **oregano**
½ t. **garlic powder**
½ t. **salt** (or less)
dash of **pepper**
½ C. grated Parmesan **cheese**

Cut squash in half lengthwise. Scoop out seeds. Place squash, cut side down, in 2" of simmering water; cover and cook 15 minutes. (Now call the kids to watch!) Holding the hot squash in a potholder, run the tines of a fork across its pulp—and like magic, there is your spaghetti! Mix the strands with the cheeses, zucchini or peppers, sauce, oregano, garlic, salt and pepper in a large bowl. Scoop back into squash shells. Sprinkle tops with Parmesan and bake at 350° for 20 minutes.

This is a "fun" vegetable—kids love the spaghetti strands, and it even tastes a little like pizza prepared this way! *PROTEIN: 66.3 CALORIES: 1302*

Shari Beckett
Bolingbrook, Illinois

ACORN SQUASH PLUS

2 **acorn squash,** halved and
   cleaned

Filling #1:
2 C. unsweetened, crushed
   pineapple, lightly drained,
   or unsweetened applesauce
¼ to ½ C. chopped **nuts**
¼ C. **raisins**
¼ lb. Cheddar **cheese,** grated
   (optional)
1/8 t. *each* ground **cinnamon** and
   nutmeg (optional)
PROTEIN: 48.7 grams; CALORIES: 1392

Filling #2:
½ C. **orange juice**
¼ C. **raisins** or 2 to 4 T. honey
¼ C. chopped **nuts**
2 T. **butter**
1/8 t. *each* ground **cinnamon**
   and **nutmeg**
PROTEIN: 19 grams; CALORIES: 926

Place squash, cut side down, in a shallow pan of water. Bake at 350° for 30 to 45 minutes until tender. (Or bake ahead and refrigerate.) Combine ingredients of filling #1 or #2. Fill squash cavities and place, cut side up, in a baking dish. Bake at 350° for 15 to 20 minutes, until hot.

Linda Weiner   *Sandy Eckstein*   *Linda Wierzer*
Edmonton, Alberta, Can. *Galloway, Ohio*   *Garland, Texas*

AUGUST GARDEN CASSEROLE

2 to 3 C. cooked **brown rice** or millet	Steam vegetables just until tender. In a greased casserole, layer grain
2 **carrots**, sliced	and vegetables. Top with cheese.
1 **zucchini**, sliced	Broil until cheese melts.
1 C. **broccoli** florets	To vary, try different vegetables.
1 C. **cauliflower** florets	Or use leftover vegetables and omit
¾ to 1 C. grated **cheese** (Jack, Cheddar or Muenster)	steaming step.

PROTEIN: 41.7 grams; CALORIES: 897

Ronaele Berry
Johnstown, Nebraska

VARIABLE ZUCCHINI CASSEROLE

4 C. thinly sliced **zucchini**	1 C. **cottage cheese** (optional)
⅔ C. thinly sliced **onion**	2 t. **oregano** or basil
2 C. **tomato** wedges	1 t. **garlic powder**
4 oz. diced **green chilies**	½ t. **salt** (or less)
1 C. **tomato sauce**	dash of **pepper**
4 strips **bacon**, fried and crumbled (optional)	*Optional Topping:*
1½ C. grated Provolone or Cheddar **cheese**	¼ C. grated Parmesan **cheese** ¼ C. **bread crumbs**

Butter a 3-qt. casserole. In order given, layer half of each: zucchini, onion, tomatoes, chilies, tomato sauce, bacon, mixed cheese and spices. Repeat. Top with crumbs and Parmesan, if desired. Bake, covered, at 350° for 25 minutes. Uncover and bake 10 minutes longer.

Without topping—P.: 100.4 gms.; C.: 135
With both toppings—P.: 111.6 gms.; C.: 153

LLL of *Mercerville, New Jersey*	*Diane Simcik* *St. Louis, Missouri*	*Beth Adcock* *Watervliet, New York*	*Trudi Tucker* *Grass Valley, California*

ZUCCHINI BOATS

6 small **zucchini**	Cut zucchini in half lengthwise;
2 T. **oil**	scoop out pulp, being careful to
½ t. *each* **rosemary** and **basil**	leave a sturdy shell intact. Heat oil
1 t. **oregano**	in heavy skillet and add rosemary,
½ t. **salt** (or less)	basil, oregano, salt, parsley, garlic,
1 T. chopped fresh **parsley**	onion, peppers, celery and mush-
3 cloves **garlic**, minced	rooms. Saute 2 minutes. Add zucchi-
1 C. chopped **onion**	ni pulp and tomatoes, and continue
½ C. diced **green pepper**	cooking until pulp is tender. Remove
½ C. sliced **celery**	from heat. Stir in cottage cheese,
¼ to ½ lb. fresh **mushrooms**, chopped	mixing until it melts. Arrange zuc- chini shells in oiled baking dish.
4 to 5 chopped **tomatoes**	Line each one with a layer of 1½ T.
½ lb. **cottage cheese**	Cheddar, then fill with vegetable/
2 C. grated Cheddar **cheese**	cheese mixture. Top with bread
1 C. **bread crumbs**	crumbs and remaining Cheddar.
	Bake at 350° for 45 minutes.

These are invariably popular with children, perhaps because of their shape and pizza-like flavor! *PROTEIN: 125.4 grams; CALORIES: 2221* *Marion Bueche* *Gray, Sask., Canada*

SQUASH BOATS I

1 **acorn squash,**
  halved lengthwise
½ lb. **sausage** (p.282), crumbled
½ C. chopped **onion**
½ C. chopped **celery**
½ t. **thyme**
½ t. **salt** (or less)
dash of **pepper**
1 C. diced **banana**
1 T. **lemon juice**
3 T. **bread crumbs**
2 T. chopped **walnuts**
1 T. melted **butter**
2 T. grated Parmesan **cheese**
  (optional)

Remove seeds and place squash in baking dish cut sides down. Add ½" water. Cover. Bake at 400° for 30 minutes. Brown sausage in a skillet; drain. Add vegetables and seasonings. Cook until vegetables are tender. Mix in banana, lemon juice and bread crumbs. Fill squash centers with mixture. Toss walnuts with butter and sprinkle over top. Bake uncovered 15 minutes. Top with cheese.

PROTEIN: 53.9 grams; CALORIES: 1469
Louise Cox
Fredericksburg, Virginia

BEAUTIFUL WINTER VEGETABLES

2 C. shredded **carrots**
2 C. shredded **beets**
2 C. shredded **rutabagas**
¼ C. **butter**

Melt butter in a skillet. Toss in the vegetables and cover to steam for a few minutes. Uncover and stir briefly until tender, several minutes only.

PROTEIN: 9.8 grams; CALORIES: 764
Joann S. Grohman
Dixfield, Maine

ANY-VEGETABLE CASSEROLE

12 slices **bacon,** chopped
1½ C. **garlic croutons**
1 lb. fresh or frozen **vegetables:**
  asparagus, carrots,
  potatoes, green beans,
  parsnips or cabbage,
  steamed until tender
4 hard-cooked **eggs,** sliced
1 C. thin **white sauce** (p. 251)
½ C. Parmesan **cheese**

Fry bacon and drain. In 9 x 9" shallow baking dish, arrange croutons, sliced vegetables and eggs in layers. Top with sauce. Sprinkle with cheese and bacon. Bake at 375° until bubbly, about 45 minutes.

PROTEIN: 89.9 grams; CALORIES: 1444

Mary Knapp
Kaukauna, Wisconsin

TOMATOES OREGANO
(Children's "Pizza Tomatoes")

6 medium **tomatoes**
oregano
garlic powder
½ t. **salt** or less
dash of **pepper**
1 C. soft **bread crumbs**
1 T. **oil**
½ C. Parmesan **cheese**

Cut tomatoes into 1" thick slices and place in shallow serving dish. Sprinkle each slice liberally with seasonings. Combine bread crumbs with oil and distribute evenly on each slice. Sprinkle with cheese. Serve as is, or broil 3 to 4 minutes to heat through. *P.: 37.8 gms.; C.: 859*

Kathy Nestlerode
York, Pennsylvania

STEAMED VEGETABLES

broccoli	**green peppers**	**peas**
cabbage	**greens**	**potatoes**
carrots	**Jerusalem artichokes**	**rutabaga**
cauliflower	**mushrooms**	**turnips**
celery	small **onions**	**winter squash**
eggplant	**parsnips**	**zucchini** or summer
green beans		squash

Choose any or all of the above. Use a steamer and a 6-quart or larger pot. Cut vegetables into 1" pieces and steam until tender, starting with longer cooking vegetables (carrots, broccoli, etc.), then adding quick cookers (like zucchini). Season to taste, dot with **butter** and serve.

STEAMED VEGETABLES MAIN DISH

5 C. steamed **vegetables**
2 C. medium **white sauce** (p. 251)
6 C. cooked **brown rice**
1 C. grated **cheese** of choice
soy sauce to taste

Combine vegetables and sauce. Serve over rice, adding cheese and soy sauce to taste. *Or:* Combine vegetables, sauce and favorite seasonings in greased 3-quart casserole. Top with cheese and bake at 350° until bubbly, about 20 minutes.

Marie Lundstrom
Cambridge, Wisconsin

Ellen Utley
Haubstadt, Indiana

Shannon Stieglitz
Norcross, Georgia

DANDY DANDELIONS

½ C. **milk**
1 **egg**
½ C. **flour** (approximately)
12 young, opened **dandelion
flowers**, removed from stems
oil for frying
salt

Heat 1 inch oil to 375° in heavy skillet. Meanwhile, beat milk and egg together. Have flour ready in a shallow bowl. Dip dandelions in egg mixture, then in flour to coat. Drop into hot oil, and cook until batter is golden. Remove with a slotted spoon, and drain on paper towels.

Served lightly sprinkled with salt, these taste like French fried vegetables; *or*, tossed with a mixture of ¼ C. sugar and 1 t. cinnamon, they taste like doughnut holes—a snack or dessert!

How many dandelion love bouquets have I been brought as a mother! What a neat way to use this humble flower and share that love back with all the members of my family!

Leslye A. Korvola
Fairbanks, Alaska

VEGETABLE GARDEN STEW

½ C. chopped **onion** (1 small)
2 T. **butter**
¼ C. chopped **green pepper**
1 small clove **garlic**, minced
1 large head **cauliflower**,
  broken into small
  pieces
3 large **tomatoes**, quartered
2 small **zucchini**, cubed
¼ C. hot **water**
¼ to ½ t. **salt** (or less)
dash of **pepper**
pinch of ground **sage**
¼ t. ground **thyme**
3 strips crisp, nitrite-free
  bacon as garnish (optional)

In large skillet, saute onion in butter until tender. Add remaining ingredients; cover and simmer 10 to 15 minutes until tender. Serve immediately, garnished with crumbled bacon, if desired.

I love this in summer because it's light and easy. If you grow your own vegetables, it will cost you next to nothing, and may be put together in a twinkling.

PROTEIN: 39.4; CALORIES: 792

Terrie Sewall
Fond du Lac, Wisconsin

FANCY VEGETABLE MEDLEY

1 C. thinly sliced **onion**
2 T. **butter**
2 C. diagonally sliced **carrots**
4 C. **broccoli** (stems thinly
  sliced, florets 1" long)
1 t. **basil**
¼ t. **garlic powder**
½ t. **salt** (or less)
dash of **pepper**

Saute onion in butter until transparent. Add carrots, and saute 5 minutes before adding broccoli stem pieces. Saute 2 minutes more, then add the florets, basil, garlic powder, salt and pepper. Cover and let simmer in its own juices 3 to 5 minutes.

This is really elegant! I often carry it to covered-dish dinners, and it is always a hit. I got the idea from expensive frozen vegetable combinations—check them out for other ideas. It's also a good way to use up small amounts of different vegetables.   *PROTEIN: 25.7 grams; CALORIES: 535*

Lavita Shelton
Farmland, Indiana

SQUASH BOATS II

2 medium **acorn squash**
¾ lb. **sausage** (p. 282)
  crumbled
2 C. **applesauce** or
  chopped apples
ground **cinnamon**

Prepare squash as in Squash Boats I on p. 181. Brown sausage and drain. Pour applesauce into squash halves. Top with sausage. Sprinkle with cinnamon. Bake 15 minutes.

PROTEIN: 65.3 grams; CALORIES: 1726

Karen White
Bloomington, Indiana

Skillet Dinners

GRAIN PILAF

1 **onion,** chopped
1 clove **garlic,** minced
2 T. **oil**
1 C. **bulgur,** cracked wheat
or brown rice
2 C. **liquid** (stock, tomato juice
or water with 1 T. tamari
soy sauce
½ t. **salt** or less
dash of **pepper**

Optional:
½ to 2 C. chopped **vegetables**
(celery, mushrooms, peppers,
zucchini, etc.)
½ t. **oregano** and/or basil
½ t. **chili powder**
¼ to ½ C. **nuts** or seeds
1 C. leftover **meat** or poultry

Saute onion, garlic and optional vegetables in oil. Add grain, stirring to brown lightly. Add liquid and spices. Bring to a boil. Cover, simmer until grain is tender and liquid is absorbed. Stir in nuts or meat at the end, if desired.   *PROTEIN: 32.1 grams; CALORIES: 1150*

Alice Ziring   *Sally Jo Bongle*   *Joan D'Alessandro*   *Jody Currier*
Mercer Island, Washington   *Kewaunee, Wisconsin*   *Kent, Washington*   *Wells, Maine*

RICE PILAF

½ C. chopped **onion**
1 clove **garlic,** minced
1 C. raw **brown rice**
2 to 4 T. **oil** or 4 strips
nitrite-free bacon
2½ to 3 C. **liquid** (stock; broth;
water with 1 T. tamari soy
sauce; or a combination of
water with orange juice,
tomato juice or wine)
1 t. ground **cumin** and/or **curry
powder**

Optional:
½ to 2 C. sliced **vegetables**
(mushrooms, celery, sprouts, etc.)
1 C. cubed, cooked **meat** or poultry
3 hard-cooked **eggs,** chopped or
3 eggs scrambled
½ C. grated Cheddar **cheese**
2 C. cooked **garbanzo beans**
3 T. **seeds** (sunflower and/or
sesame)
¼ C. **almonds**
¼ C. sliced **olives**
½ C. **raisins**

Brown onion, garlic, rice and optional vegetables in oil or bacon. Add liquid and spices. Bring to a boil. Simmer, covered, until liquid is absorbed, 40 to 60 minutes. Fold in meat, eggs, cheese, beans and any other options desired. Heat through.

This recipe can make a side dish or provide a high-protein meal, depending on the amount and number of optional ingredients you use. It can have a different flavor each time you make it.

PROTEIN: 25 grams; CALORIES: 1071

Ellyce Warns   *Linda Higginson*
San Antonio, Texas   *Thomaston, Connecticut*

Andrea Sutherland Skall
Costa Mesa, California

BASIC STIR-FRY

½ to 1 lb. any **meat**, thinly
sliced; pieces of **seafood**; or
cubed **tofu** (optional)
2 to 4 C. fresh **vegetables**,
sliced thin diagonally
(celery, broccoli, cauliflower,
peppers, green onions, beans,
mushrooms, water chestnuts,
bamboo shoots, Chinese celery,
zucchini, summer squash,
julienned carrots)
snow pea pods
bean sprouts
4 to 6 T. **oil**
2 to 4 C. cooked **brown rice**

Marinade:
2 T. **soy sauce**
1½ t. **cornstarch**
2 t. **oil**
1 t. **honey** (optional)
dash of **pepper**
1 T. **sherry** (optional)

Marinate meat and/or seafood 10 to
20 minutes; several hours for tofu.
Or just use vegetables, if you wish.
Arrange vegetables on tray in order
of cooking times. Heat skillet or
wok. Add 1 to 2 T. oil. Add pieces of
meat, seafood or tofu, tossing with
spatula until done, about 3 or 4 minutes. Add longest-cooking vegetable
(such as carrots or celery); toss
about 1 minute. Add next vegetable.
Continue cooking vegetables, sav-
ing snow peas and sprouts for last.
Vegetables should be crisp but tender. If more oil is needed while cooking, drizzle some around sides of
pan. Add another recipe of marinade
if you want more sauce. Serve immediately over rice.

You may cut up vegetables early
in the day and cook when ready to
eat. This method ensures quick
cooking and maximum tenderness
with minimal nutritional losses.

Variation: Instead of marinating, cook meat, seafood or tofu with 2 cloves
crushed **garlic** and a small piece of **ginger root** (about the size of a teaspoon). Before serving, add about 2 T. **soy sauce**. You might even use
leftover meat, thinly sliced. Add it after the vegetables are cooked to just
heat through. For even greater variety, try adding **nuts** (walnuts, cashews,
almonds or peanuts), **sunflower seeds** or unsweetened **pineapple**
chunks.   *Many LLL Contributors*

FRIED RICE

1 to 2 C. any leftover **meat**,
seafood or tofu, cut into
small pieces
2 C. finely chopped **onions**
1 clove **garlic**, minced
1 to 2 T. **oil**
3 to 6 **eggs**, slightly beaten
2 to 4 C. cooked **brown rice**
4 **green onions**, finely chopped
1 C. **bean sprouts**
2 to 4 T. **soy sauce**

Saute onion and garlic in hot oil for
3 minutes. Push onions to the side;
add eggs and stir until firm, about 1
or 2 minutes. Add rice, green onions
and meat. Mix well to heat through.
Add sprouts and soy sauce. Stir
well. Making this earlier in the day
improves the flavor. Then just reheat
for dinner.

PROTEIN: 78.9 grams; CALORIES: 1153

For greater variety, add sliced **mushrooms**, chopped **green pepper**,
sliced **celery**, finely shredded **cabbage, peas** or slivered **almonds** when
you add meat. Nice change of pace for leftovers.   *Many LLL Contributors*

MARINATED TOFU

1 lb. **tofu**, thinly sliced
½ C. sliced **mushrooms**
(optional)

Marinade:
¼ C. tamari **soy sauce**
¼ C. **water**
¼ C. **sherry** or wine (optional)
1 clove **garlic**
1 t. ground **ginger**

Marinate tofu for at least 4 hours. To cook, broil tofu on both sides until golden, *or* brown in hot oil, *or* simmer in marinade (with sliced mushrooms, optional). Serve on a sandwich with cheese, over brown rice, in pita bread, or chopped into a stir-fry.

Save unused marinade to use again, or marinate poultry or meat in it. *PROTEIN: 38.1 grams; CALORIES: 356*

With marinade— PROTEIN: 49.3 grams; CALORIES: 494

Marianne Smisko   Bryanna Clark
Powell River, B.C., Can. Union Bay, B.C., Canada

EGGPLANT AND RICE

1 medium **eggplant**, cubed, or
4 to 5 zucchini, sliced
1 medium **onion**, chopped
4 to 6 T. **oil**
1 large **green pepper**, chopped
2 C. stewed or fresh **tomatoes**,
chopped
4 to 8 oz. Mozzarella **cheese**,
shredded
½ t. **basil** or rosemary
½ t. **oregano**
½ t. **salt** (or less)
dash of **pepper**
3 C. cooked **brown rice**

Saute eggplant and onion in oil until tender. Add green pepper and tomatoes. Simmer 5 minutes. Add cheese and spices. Simmer until cheese melts. Serve over hot brown rice.

Good with a tossed salad and homemade bread. *PROTEIN: 33.2 grams; CALORIES: 1595*

Renny Northrop   Rosemary Rivest
Summit, New Jersey Ft. Benning, Georgia

Variation: To hot cooked rice, stir in 1 T. **lemon juice** and 2 well-beaten **eggs**. Top with eggplant mixture. *PROTEIN: 45.7 grams; CALORIES: 1755*

Elena Hannah
St. John's, NFLD Canada

SLOPPY JOES

2 lbs. ground **beef**
1½ C. **tomato puree**
½ C. **cottage cheese**
½ C. grated **carrot** and
2 C. **corn** or 2½ C. mixed
vegetables

Brown and drain beef. Add tomato puree and simmer 30 minutes. Add the cottage cheese and vegetables. Simmer until corn is cooked. Serve on **buns** or **noodles**.

PROTEIN; 184.6; CALORIES: 1961

With buns— PROTEIN: 216.6; CALORIES: 2865

Sandi Roberts   Rea Standridge
APO New York   Sugarland, Texas

MEATLESS HASH FROM LEFTOVERS

1 small **onion**, chopped
2 T. **butter** or oil
1½ C. cooked **grains**
1½ C. cooked **legumes**
1 C. cooked **vegetables**
1 **tomato**, chopped
2 T. tamari **soy sauce**
dash of **pepper**
½ to 1 C. grated **cheese**

Saute onion in butter until tender. Add remaining ingredients except cheese. Heat through. Stir in cheese until it melts.

Use any grains (rice, bulgur, millet, wheat berries) and legumes (lentils, garbanzos, white beans, etc.) you have on hand. This is fast and delicious! I always cook twice as much grain and legumes as I need for another recipe, and use the extra later in the week for this hash, enchiladas, or other recipes.

Linda Rankin
Grand Rapids, Michigan

AUNT MARY'S BBQ

5 lbs. **roast beef**, stew beef
 or pork
BBQ Sauce:
1 medium **onion**, chopped
½ C. chopped **celery**
2 T. **butter**
1½ T. **worcestershire sauce**
½ C. **lemon juice**
2 T. **vinegar**
1 T. **honey** or
 2 T. brown sugar
1 C. **catsup** (p. 252)
½ C. **broth** from meat
1 t. **salt** (or less)
dash of **pepper**
4 to 8 whole **allspice** in a tea
 ball or cheesecloth (optional)

Simmer meat in large pot of water for 4 hours. Tear into small pieces. Saute onion and celery in butter in a Dutch oven. Add remaining ingredients; bring to a boil. Simmer 15 minutes. Add meat and heat through. Serve on 20 **hamburger buns.**

We serve this at all our family parties. It is best made a day ahead and reheated before serving. Try the sauce for basting steak.

PROTEIN: 320.25 grams; CALORIES: 5832

with buns: P.: 400; C.: 8092

Leslie Ostyn
Grant, Michigan

SKILLET DINNER

2 to 3 C. chopped, leftover **beef,**
 chicken, ham or turkey
2 C. **white sauce** (p. 251)
4 oz. **mushrooms**
1 small **onion**, finely diced
1 small **green pepper**, diced or
 in strips
½ C. **barley**
½ C. **cracked wheat**
2 to 3 C. **water**
½ t. **salt** (or less)
dash of **pepper**

Combine all ingredients and simmer for 30 minutes. Stir frequently, adding additional water as needed. Serve over **mashed potatoes** or potatoes boiled in jackets. Also good as "Sloppy Joes"-type filling for whole wheat **buns.**

PROTEIN: 142.1 grams; CALORIES: 1994

Linda Sue Siebert
Ann Arbor, Michigan

ARROZ CON FRIJOLES
(Tia's Cuban-Style Rice and Beans)

2 C. cooked **black turtle beans**
and their liquid
4 T. **oil**
1 medium **green pepper**, sliced
1 large **onion**, chopped
2 cloves **garlic**, minced
3 C. cooked **brown rice**

Mash beans and liquid slightly and heat until hot, stirring occasionally. Saute vegetables in oil until tender. Combine vegetables and beans. Serve over rice.

This can be served as a very thick soup before dinner, or as a whole meal with a salad. (The beans and rice make a complete protein.) This authentic recipe is from my husband's aunt, who lived in Cuba.

PROTEIN: 45.7 grams; CALORIES: 1570

Marcia Casais
Chatham, New Jersey

MOU-FAR-RAH-KAY

2 large **zucchini**, cubed
½ to 1 lb. ground **beef**
3 large **onions**, chopped
¼ t. **salt**
dash of **pepper**
dash of ground **allspice**
4 **eggs**

Steam zucchini. Brown beef and onion. Drain. Add seasonings. Mix with zucchini and simmer until it is nearly soft. Make 4 small wells in the mixture. Drop one egg into each well, cover pan to poach eggs. This is traditionally eaten by dipping it up with **pita bread**. Or you may use a fork and eat the bread on the side. My Syrian mother-in-law taught me to make this.

PROTEIN: 77.3 grams; CALORIES: 982

Janet Nazif
High Bridge, New Jersey

MOCK LOBSTER

1 lb. frozen **cod fillets**
2 **onions**, quartered
2 **lemons**, quartered
1 T. **dill seeds**
1 T. **celery seeds**
½ t. **salt** (or less)
water to cover fish
½ C. **butter**
2 T. **lemon juice**

Add onion, lemons and seasonings to water in a Dutch oven or large frying pan. Bring to a boil. Simmer 30 minutes. Add frozen cod. Cook until cod flakes easily, about 20 minutes. Drain in a colander. Serve with butter melted with lemon juice. This isn't lobster, but it tastes quite a bit like it and is so much cheaper.

PROTEIN: 88.3 grams; CALORIES: 1497

Elsie J. England
Oklahoma City, Oklahoma

Variation: Omit onion, lemon, dill and celery seeds. Add 1 T. **vinegar** and 1 T. **salt** to water. Boil. Add cod and cook as above.

Nancy Kimnach
Columbus, Ohio

Basic Poached Fish. Use **sole** or other fresh or thawed white fish fillets. Reduce onion to ¼ C. chopped onion and lemon juice to 1 T. Omit dill. celery seeds and butter. Add fish fillets. When water boils, cover and simmer 10 minutes, or until fish flakes easily with a fork. Drain liquid. Serve with **lemon** wedges and **paprika**.

Janet Harwell
Fort Worth, Texas

SALLY'S BEEF TERIYAKI FOR COMPANY

1½ lbs. **beef** (sirloin, round or chuck), cut in 1/8" strips
1½ T. **oil**
2 small bunches **green onions** (20 to 25), sliced with green ends
1 medium **onion**, thinly sliced
16 oz. **water chestnuts**, drained and sliced
1 C. thinly sliced **celery**
½ to 1 lb. **mushrooms**, sliced
1 lb. (2 C.) mung **bean sprouts**
¼ t. **salt** (or less)
dash of **pepper**
6 C. cooked **brown rice**
teriyaki sauce
cornstarch to thicken

Heat oil to medium-high in a large frying pan or Dutch oven. Add meat; stir-fry until lightly browned. Add onions, water chestnuts, celery and mushrooms. Cook 3 to 4 minutes, stirring occasionally. Pour teriyaki sauce over meat. Stir until thickened. Add sprouts, salt and pepper. Cook until sprouts are warm. Serve over brown rice.

Very fast, easy and fun dish to make—and delicious. Try adding other vegetables, such as **snow peas** or **green beans** along with the onions. Just add more sauce.

PROTEIN: 167.7 grams; CALORIES: 3895
+ cornstarch
Sally Jo Bongle
Kewaunee, Wisconsin

CHICKEN TERIYAKI

3 lb. frying **chicken**, cut up
1 to 2 T. **oil**

Teriyaki Sauce:
¼ C. tamari **soy sauce**
¼ C. **vinegar**
1 clove **garlic**, minced
dash of **pepper**
¼ t. ground **ginger**

Brown chicken in oil. Combine sauce ingredients; pour over chicken in skillet. Cover and simmer 30 minutes or until tender. This has all the traditional flavor of teriyaki without sugar. Good hot or cold. Try as a marinade or basting sauce for baking cut-up chicken or beef teriyaki.

PROTEIN: 177.6 grams; CALORIES: 1389   Ellyce Warns
San Antonio, Texas

LIVER TERIYAKI

1 lb. beef **liver**
¼ C. **flour**
¼ C. **soy sauce**
¼ C. **water**
1 **onion**, sliced
3 T. **oil**
2 C. hot, cooked **brown rice**

Slice liver into small strips. Remove membrane. Dust with flour. Mix soy sauce and water in a small bowl. Saute onion in oil over medium heat. Add liver. Brown quickly. Reduce heat; stir in soy sauce mixture. Cook until thickened. Add extra water if too thick. Serve over rice.

I used this recipe to introduce my husband to liver. He asked for seconds and now enjoys eating liver regularly, cooked a variety of ways. My toddler loves it too.

PROTEIN: 108.6 grams; CALORIES: 1545
Cathy Grant
Richmond, B.C., Canada

PAELLA

A traditional Spanish and Mexican dish, studded with chicken, sausage and whatever shellfish are locally available.

¼ C. **oil**
2 cloves **garlic**
2 C. **brown rice**
4 C. hot chicken **stock**
1 or 2 t. **saffron** (optional)
3 large **tomatoes**, cut into wedges
2 C. **peas** (fresh or frozen)
6 **artichoke hearts** (optional)
2 sweet **peppers** (red or green)
1 **chicken**, cooked and disjointed
¼ lb. **chorizo** or other hard dry sausage, sliced
8 **prawns**, large shrimp or crayfish, or 1-lb. lobster

A large, shallow 2-handled frying pan is used for paella, but you may substitute anything which is fairly heavy, has a cover and may be brought to the table. Paella may be cooked on top of the stove or in the oven. Heat oil in your pan. Add garlic; mash it in the oil and remove it when brown. Add and brown the rice. Add hot stock and correct the seasoning. Dissolve saffron in a little of the stock and add. Cover and steam until rice is almost done. Stir in the vegetables, stud surface of the rice with the chicken parts, sausage and shellfish. Replace cover and continue steaming until the shellfish is cooked, about 10 minutes more. Serve at once.

PROTEIN: 267.1 grams; CALORIES: 5626

Joann S. Grohman
Dixfield, Maine

TWO-WAY TOFU PARMESAN

1 lb. **tofu**, sliced crosswise into 8 slices

Marinade:
1 C. tamari **soy sauce**
¾ C. dry white **wine**
2 cloves **garlic**, minced
1 t. **oregano**

oil for sauteing
½ C. whole wheat **flour**
1 **egg** beaten with 2 T. **water**

Breading:
½ C. **wheat germ**
½ C. **bread crumbs**
½ t. **basil**
dash of **salt** and **pepper**

4 C. **spaghetti sauce** (p. 199)
½ t. **oregano**
½ lb. grated **cheese** (Cheddar, Monterey Jack, etc.)
¼ C. grated Parmesan **cheese**
2 T. chopped fresh **parsley**

Combine marinade ingredients. For tofu cutlets, marinate tofu for about 10 minutes. (This marinade may be refrigerated and used 3 or 4 times.) Dip tofu into flour, then egg mixture, then breading. Heat oil and saute cutlets until golden brown. Drain. If it's been a hard day, serve the cutlets this way with a vegetable or salad. *PROTEIN: 98.5 grams; CALORIES: 1466*

If you have lots of time, proceed as follows. In a 2-qt. casserole, layer: sauce, tofu, oregano, cheeses and parsley. Repeat, ending with the cheese and parsley.

Bake, covered, at 350° for 30 to 40 minutes. Let stand for 5 to 10 minutes before serving. *P.: 199.8 gms.; C.: 2987*

It is a recipe that both my husband and company thoroughly enjoy.

Barbara LeBouf
S. Lyndeboro, New Hampshire

STROGANOFF

1¾ to 2 lbs. **beef** (bottom
  round)
⅔ C. **butter** or oil
¾ C. chopped **onion**
1 clove **garlic**, minced
3 T. **flour**
½ C. **water**
1 C. dry **red wine**
2 **bouillon cubes**
¾ t. **salt**
3 T. **tomato paste**
1 t. **worcestershire sauce**

Sauce:
½ lb. **mushrooms**, sliced
¼ C. **butter**
¾ C. plain **yogurt**
¼ C. **milk**
2 C. **brown rice** or noodles,
  cooked

Cut meat into ¼ x 2" strips. Melt ½
of the butter in a large skillet. Add
onion and garlic and cook until golden. Remove; add remaining butter.
Dredge beef in flour and brown. Add
water, wine, bouillon, salt, cooked
onions and garlic. Simmer for 2
hours. Add tomato paste and Worcestershire sauce. Heat. May be
easily doubled. Freezes well.

Saute mushrooms in butter. Add to
meat along with yogurt and milk.
Heat through; do not boil, as yogurt
may curdle. Serve with rice or
noodles.

with Sauce & Rice—P.: 216.2 gms.; C.: 4538

Gloria Nicholson
Skowhegan, Maine

TOFU MUSHROOM STROGANOFF

1 small clove **garlic**, minced
½ small **onion**, chopped
½ lb. fresh **mushrooms**, sliced
1 to 2 T. **oil**
¼ t. **oregano**

Sauce:
1¼ to 2 lbs. **tofu**
2 to 3 T. **water**
1 T. tamari **soy sauce**
1 T. **vinegar**
1 small clove **garlic**, minced
½ t. grated **lemon rind**
¼ to ½ t. ground **ginger**

2 to 3 C. cooked **brown rice**
1 to 2 T. plain **yogurt** or
  sour cream
12 **almonds** (optional)
1 T. fresh **parsley** (optional)

Saute garlic, onion and mushrooms
in oil. Mix sauce ingredients in blender or food processor until smooth.
(The sauce may be made the day before and stored in the refrigerator, if
you wish.) Stir sauce and oregano into the mushroom mixture. Heat
through.
  Serve over brown rice, topped
with a teaspoon of yogurt. Garnish
with almonds and/or parsley, if desired.   *PROTEIN: 64.4 grams; CALORIES: 1176*

Marty Hardy
Park Ridge, Illinois

SCRAMBLED TOFU

5 strips nitrite-free **bacon**,
  crisply fried and crumbled
½ small **onion**, finely chopped
1 lb. firm **tofu**, cut into
  ½" cubes
2 T. tamari **soy sauce**

Drain all but 2 T. of the bacon drippings from a 10" skillet. Brown
onion in grease. Add tofu and simmer for 5 minutes. Add soy sauce
and stir gently until heated thoroughly.   *P.: 48.8 gms.; C.: 805*

BASIC CURRY SAUCE

2 small **onions**, finely chopped
¼ C. chopped **green onion**
3 cloves **garlic**, minced
2 T. **oil**
3 T. whole wheat **flour**
½ t. *each:* ground **cumin**,
  nutmeg, ginger, tumeric,
  allspice, cloves
1 t. ground **cinnamon**
¼ t. ground **chili pepper** or
  powder
1 C. chicken **broth** or bouillon
1 C. **milk**, yogurt or cream

Saute onions and garlic in oil. Add flour; stir well. Add spices and broth; cover and simmer while you prepare toppings and rice, about 30 to 60 minutes. Add milk just before serving, but do not boil after adding it.

PROTEIN: 14.9 grams; CALORIES: 543

CHICKEN OR TURKEY CURRY

2 C. (approximately) cooked,
  chopped **chicken** or turkey
1 large **apple**, chopped
1 C. unsweetened, crushed
  pineapple, drained
½ C. **raisins**
3 to 4 C. cooked **brown rice**

Toppings (use any or all):
  chutney; chopped **cucumbers**;
  chopped **onion**; unsweetened,
  shredded **coconut; peanuts;**
  chopped **tomatoes;** diced
  green pepper; chopped, hard-
  cooked **eggs; raisins;**
  sunflower seeds; chopped
  apple; unsweetened, crushed
  pineapple

Put toppings into small serving bowls. Add chicken, apple, pineapple and raisins to Basic Curry Sauce 5 minutes before serving. Heat through. Serve curry sauce over rice. Let everyone choose from the toppings. If you like, add just the chicken or turkey to the sauce; use the apple, pineapple and raisins as toppings.

Without toppings—P.·: 135.7; C.: 1710

Dawn Fitzgibbons
Vancouver, Washington

CURRIED COD

1 lb. **cod**, cut into pieces
3 T. **butter**
¾ to 1 C. minced **onion**
1 C. **milk**
½ t. **salt**
dash of **pepper**
1 T. **curry powder**
½ C. **soy nuts** or cashews
2 C. unsweetened **pineapple**
  chunks
2 C. cooked **brown rice**

Saute onion in butter. Add fish. Cover and cook 4 or 5 minutes, until it flakes easily. Mash cod. Add milk and seasonings. (The strength of curry varies. Start with 1 t., taste, add more if necessary.) Stir in nuts. Cover and simmer 5 minutes. Add pineapple; simmer 1 to 2 minutes longer. Serve over brown rice.

PROTEIN: 127.1 grams; CALORIES: 1120

Elena Hannah
St. John's, Newfoundland

CURRIED RICE

4 **onions,** finely chopped
1 clove **garlic,** minced
½ C. **sunflower seeds**
½ C. **raisins** or currants
1 t. **curry powder** *or*
  ¼ t. ground cumin and
  ¼ t. ground cloves and
  ¼ t. ground ginger *or*
  ½ t. ground cinnamon and
  ¼ t. ground cloves and
  ½ t. caraway seeds
dash of **pepper**
4 T. **butter** or oil
4 C. cooked **brown rice**

Optional:
3 stalks **celery,** sliced
½ to 1 C. sliced **mushrooms**
1 C. **peas**
1 C. cooked, diced **meat**
  or poultry
1 C. unsweetened, crushed
  pineapple, drained
¼ to ½ C. **cashews** or pistachio
  nuts
½ t. **salt** (or less)

Saute vegetables, optional meat, garlic, seeds, raisins and spices in butter. Toss in rice. Garnish with nuts and pineapple, if desired. This may be doubled, but still use 4 onions. Good as a side dish or stuffing.

PROTEIN: 35.9 grams; CALORIES: 1792

Helen Palmer
Edgewater Park, New Jersey

Louise Cox
Fredericksburg, Virginia

Martha Hartzell
Decatur, Georgia

Mandarin Rice Pilau. Cook brown rice in equal parts water and **orange juice.** Add 3 **oranges** in pieces, ¼ C. **almonds,** ½ C. **raisins.** Remove oranges before storing leftovers.

Stephanie Merritt
Los Altos, California

LENTIL CHILI

1 lb. ground **beef** or
  cubed tofu
1 medium **onion,** chopped
2 to 4 cloves **garlic,** minced
½ t. **salt**
dash of **pepper**
4 C. cooked **tomatoes**
6 oz. **tomato paste**
1 t. **chili powder**
1 t. ground **cumin**
½ t. ground **coriander**
  (optional)
1 C. **lentils**
1 C. **brown rice,** cooked or buns

Brown beef or tofu with onion and garlic. Add remaining ingredients. Simmer about 1 hour, or until lentils are done. Add seasoning as needed. Serve on rice or buns.

This recipe was created for those that like chili but don't care for kidney beans.

So . . . here it is, and it's simple.

PROTEIN: 163.7 grams; CALORIES: 2674

Linda Weiner
Edmonton, Alberta, Can.

Linda Ahlgren
Yigo, Guam

NOODLES AND CABBAGE

½ to ¾ lb. bulk **Italian
  sausage** (p. 282)
1 medium **cabbage,** shredded
½ C. **water**
½ lb. whole wheat **noodles,**
  cooked and drained

Brown sausage in large skillet or Dutch oven. Drain all but 2 T. fat. Add cabbage and water. Cover; simmer 7 to 10 minutes, until cabbage is crunchy but tender. Add noodles. Toss lightly until well mixed.

PROTEIN: 85.8 grams; CALORIES: 1630

Linda Church
West Lafayette, Indiana

FEIJOADA

2 C. dried **black beans**
8 C. **stock** or water
1 to 2 C. of several leftover
   meats (pork, sausage, ham,
   lamb, chicken or beef),
   cut in small pieces
1 t. **oregano**
½ to 1 t. **salt**
2 cloves **garlic**, minced
2 T. **oil** or butter
3 **tomatoes**, chopped
2 **onions**, chopped
Sprinkle of chopped, fresh
   parsley

Rice:
1 **onion**, chopped
2 **tomatoes**, chopped
2 cloves **garlic**, minced
3 T. **oil** or butter
2½ C. uncooked **brown rice**
5 C. boiling **water**

Soak beans overnight; drain. Add stock or water and simmer about 1 hour, or until half-cooked. Add meat, oregano, salt and 1 clove garlic. Continue cooking 1 to 2 hours, until flavors blend and beans are tender.

Heat oil in frying pan. Add remaining clove of garlic, tomatoes, onions and parsley. Saute until onion is soft. Add ⅓ of the bean mixture and mash together. Return mixture to bean pot. Keep it hot.

For rice, brown onion, tomatoes and garlic in oil. Add rice and boiling water. Cook over low heat for 45 minutes, or until rice is done. Put a mound of rice on each plate. Top with a generous portion of meat and beans, and a dash of **hot sauce** if you like.

This is traditionally served in Latin America with sliced **oranges** and cooked **greens**, such as spinach or chard. It is exotic, inexpensive, nutritious and tastes good when reheated the next day.

PROTEIN: 200.7 grams; CALORIES: 4844

Joann Grohman
Dixfield, Maine

CHICKEN AND BULGUR

1½ to 2 C. cooked, cubed
   chicken
½ C. chopped **celery**
½ C. chopped **carrots**
½ C. chopped **onions**
½ C. **mushroom** pieces
½ clove **garlic**, minced
10 oz. **broccoli**, cut in chunks
2 T. **oil**
¾ C. raw **bulgur**
2 T. **soy grits** (optional)
2 C. chicken broth

Saute vegetables in oil until onion softens. Stir in bulgur and soy grits. Coat bulgur well with oil. When sizzling, add crumbled bouillon cubes and water. Bring to a boil. Stir well; cover and simmer 20 minutes. Add chicken and more water if needed. Simmer 5 to 10 minutes longer, until chicken is hot.

This is simple, fast. Needs little else to make a meal. We are using more whole grains to stretch dollars and meat, as well as to improve our nutrition. The bulgur cooks faster than brown rice, provides a nice texture change. I sometimes add other vegetables that I have on hand.

PROTEIN: 82.9 grams; CALORIES: 1469

Judy Beckert
Greenville, North Carolina

CHICKEN NORMANDY

2 lbs. **chicken** pieces
2 T. **flour**
4 pieces nitrite-free **bacon**, diced
¼ C. **butter** or oil
1 **onion**, chopped
2 stalks **celery**, sliced
2 **apples**, cored and cut up
2 C. unsweetened **apple juice**
2 T. **cream** (optional)

Dust chicken with some flour. Brown with bacon in butter or oil. Remove. Saute onion, celery and apple until they begin to soften. Sprinkle in remaining flour. Stir and cook 5 minutes. Add juice. Bring to a boil. Return chicken to pan, cover and simmer gently 45 minutes. Remove chicken. Add cream to sauce, if desired. Good with **croutons**.

PROTEIN: 133.7 grams; CALORIES: 2532

Anne Barnes
Toronto, Ontario, Canada

SWEET AND SOUR SOYBEANS

1 clove **garlic**, minced
1 **onion** cut in thin wedges
2 C. diagonally sliced **vegetables** (carrots, celery, squash, green pepper, sprouts, broccoli, etc.)
2 T. **oil**
2 C. cooked **soybeans**
1 C. unsweetened **pineapple** chunks, drained

Sauce:
1 T. **cornstarch**
¼ t. ground **ginger**
2 T. tamari **soy sauce**
¼ C. **vinegar**
½ C. **pineapple juice**

2 to 3 C. cooked **brown rice**
1 chopped **tomato**
2 chopped **green onions** with tops
1 T. **sesame seeds, cashews, almonds** (optional)

Stir-fry garlic, onion and vegetables in oil until tender-crisp. Add soybeans and pineapple. Heat through. Mix sauce; pour over vegetable mixture. Cook until sauce boils and thickens. Serve over brown rice, garnished with tomatoes, green onions, nuts and seeds, if desired.

I serve this to friends as an introduction to soybeans. It is always well received, and is a big plus for the cook as all ingredients may be measured and chopped ahead of time, leaving only about 10 minutes of cooking at the last minute.

PROTEIN: 59.7 grams; CALORIES: 1522 + garnishes

Brenda Wilson
Carlyle, Sask., Canada

ORIENTAL OATS

1 to 2 C. chopped or sliced **vegetables:** onions, sprouts, mushrooms, broccoli, etc.
4 T. **oil** or butter
1½ C. rolled **oats**
2 **eggs**, beaten
¾ C. **liquid:** broth, stock or water with 1 T. soy sauce
1 C. diced **meat** (optional)

Saute vegetables in 2 T. oil. Coat oats with eggs and cook in remaining oil until dry and separate, 3 to 5 minutes. Add liquid and vegetables (and optional meat). Simmer until liquid is absorbed, stirring occasionally. *PROTEIN: 89.1 grams; CALORIES: 1649*

Mary Lederhos
Sterling, Colorado

Chris McNamara
West Chicago, Illinois

MEATBALLS STROGANOFF

meatballs
1 T. **butter** or oil
1 large **onion**, sliced or chopped
2 T. whole wheat **flour**
1¼ C. beef **stock** or bouillon
½ C. **yogurt** or sour cream
2 to 3 C. cooked **brown rice**
   or noodles

Brown meatballs in butter or oil. Remove them from pan. Saute onion about 5 minutes. Remove pan from burner. Stir in flour, then add beef stock. Return to stove, bring to a boil. Add meatballs. Simmer gently for 30 minutes. Add yogurt or sour cream. Gently warm through. Serve over rice or noodles.

PROTEIN: 158.1 grams; CALORIES: 2741

Jeri Bradshaw
Riverside, New Jersey

EASY BEEF STROGANOFF

1 lb. lean ground **beef**
1 **onion**, diced
¼ C. **catsup** (p. 252).
1 C. beef **broth**
½ t. **salt**
dash of **pepper**
¼ t. **garlic powder**
½ C. **yogurt** or sour cream
4 oz. **noodles** or rice, cooked

Brown ground beef and onion; drain. Add catsup, broth and spices. Simmer. Add yogurt just before serving. Serve over hot noodles or rice.

PROTEIN: 123.3 grams; CALORIES: 1390

June Beeler
Sutter, Illinois

SAUSAGE AND BEANS

1½ C. **beans** (white or kidney),
   soaked overnight and drained
1 lb. **Italian sausage** (p. 282)
1 T. **oil**
1 **onion**, chopped
½ t. **garlic powder**
1 **bell pepper**, chopped
1 lb. **tomatoes**, chunked (16 oz.)
⅓ C. **water** if fresh tomatoes
   are used
1 t. **sage**
¼ t. **salt**
dash of **pepper**
1 T. **tomato paste** or catsup
2 C. cooked **brown rice**

In a saucepan cover beans with water. Bring to a boil. Drain. Brown sausage in oil in skillet. Remove sausage and drain fat. Add onion, garlic and bell pepper. Cook until tender. Stir in tomatoes and ⅓ C. water. Bring to a boil. Cook 3 minutes. Add spices, paste and beans. Simmer, covered, 1 to 2 hours. Serve over rice. *PROTEIN: 151 grams; CALORIES: 2846*

Patricia Y. Gobrecht   *Ann Calandro*
Hanover, Pennsylvania   *Longwood, Florida*

BEEF 'N LIVER SLOPPY JOES

1½ lbs. ground **beef**
½ lb. ground **liver***
1 small **onion**, chopped
1 small **bell pepper**, finely
  chopped
2 T. **wheat germ**
1 C. **catsup** (p. 252).
1½ T. **worcestershire sauce**
1½ T. wine **vinegar**
1 T. **brown sugar**
¼ t. **celery seeds**
½ t. **salt** (or less)
dash of **pepper**
1 t. dry **mustard**

Brown beef in large skillet. Remove from pan with slotted spoon. Brown liver and vegetables in remaining grease. Drain. Add beef and rest of ingredients. Simmer 10 to 20 minutes. Serve on 8 **buns**.
This is my secret formula for getting my family to eat liver. It's a hit!
*Liver is easy to grind if frozen, cut into cubes and ground.

PROTEIN: 185.1 grams; CALORIES: 2021
With buns—P.: 217.1 gms.; C.: 2925

Karen G. Tornga
Muskegon, Michigan

BUBBLE AND SQUEAK

1 **onion**, diced
2 t. **oil** (unless sausage is
  to be included)
2 or 3 **potatoes**, chopped
  (more for a large family)
½ to 1 C. **meat** (ground
  meat, sausage, leftover
  roast or chicken, or meat
  substitute)
½ to 1 head **cabbage** (red
  or white)
¼ C. cider **vinegar**

Saute onion and any uncooked meat in oil. (An iron skillet works best.) Add potatoes and cook until half done. Wash and chop cabbage, drain slightly. Add to skillet and cook until cabbage is wilted and potatoes are done. Add leftover cooked meat. Stir in vinegar and cook a few minutes longer to blend flavors. Serve right from skillet.

PROTEIN: 43.8 grams; CALORIES: 913
Eleanor Bohlken
Springville, Iowa

ITALIAN BEEF AND VEGETABLE CASSEROLE

1 C. finely chopped **celery**
½ C. finely chopped **carrot**
½ C. finely chopped **onion**
2 cloves **garlic**, minced
⅓ C. **oil** (salad or olive)
1 lb. ground **beef**
¾ C. **tomato paste**
3 C. chopped **tomatoes**
1 t. **salt** (or less)
1½ t. **oregano**
1 t. **basil**
½ t. **thyme**
10 oz. frozen chopped **spinach**
4 oz. **noodles** (whole wheat or
  spinach), cooked
1 C. grated Cheddar **cheese**

Cook celery, carrot, onion and garlic in oil. Add beef and brown. Add tomato paste, tomatoes and seasonings. Simmer for 1 hour. Cook spinach and drain well; add with noodles to sauce. Turn into casserole. (May be frozen at this time.) Top with cheese before baking. Bake at 350° for 20 minutes if warm, or 45 minutes if cold. Great for a family with a new baby as it makes so much it is easily divided for more than one meal.

PROTEIN: 126.5 grams; CALORIES: 2747
Donna Cline
Champaign, Illinois

Pasta

GREEN SPAGHETTI

1 lb. **spaghetti**, cooked
and drained
10 oz. fresh or frozen **spinach**
or broccoli
¼ C. **broth**
½ C. grated Parmesan **cheese**
½ C. **milk**, cream or yogurt
4 T. **butter**

Steam the fresh spinach until just wilted, or the frozen until warm. Put spinach and its liquid into blender. Add warm broth and liquefy. Stir cheese and milk into the puree. Toss spaghetti with butter, then with green sauce.

PROTEIN: 101.2 grams; CALORIES: 2192

Many children who don't like spinach will eat Green Spaghetti. It is a bright, pretty green.

If you cook the spinach while the spaghetti is cooking, this is about as fast as the commercial brands of macaroni and cheese—and far better!

Nadine Bowlus
Jackson, Mississippi

Green Rice. Substitute 3 to 4 C. cooked **brown rice** for the spaghetti.

STUFFED JUMBO SHELLS

Sauce:
1 lb. ground **beef**
1 **onion**, minced
4 C. **tomato sauce**
¼ t. **chili powder**
pinch of crushed **red pepper**
¼ t. ground **cumin**
½ t. **oregano**
½ t. **basil**
2 cloves **garlic**, minced
½ C. sliced **mushrooms**

Filling:
3 C. mashed **cottage cheese**
8 oz. grated Mozzarella **cheese**
½ t. **salt** (or less)
dash of **pepper**
2 **eggs**
1 t. chopped fresh **parsley**
10 oz. **spinach** or broccoli,
cooked and drained (optional)

1 lb. **manicotti shells**, cooked
and drained

Brown beef and onion; drain. Add remaining sauce ingredients and simmer while preparing filling.

Stir filling ingredients together. To assemble, stuff each shell with about 1 T. of the filling. (A long-handled baby spoon works well.) Pour about ½ C. sauce in the bottom of a baking dish. Place stuffed shells in dish in a single layer. Pour remaining sauce over top. Bake at 350° for 30 minutes. (Stuffed shells freeze well. Bake at 350° for 45 to 60 minutes.)

PROTEIN: 319.8 grams; CALORIES: 4365

Cynthia L. Gray   *Karen Mytnick*
DeBary, Pennsylvania   *Sayreville, New Jersey*

Joan Hartley
Springfield, Illinois

VERY TASTY SPAGHETTI SAUCE
(Large Quantity for Feast or Freezer)

¼ C. olive **oil**
6 **onions**, chopped
2 **green peppers**, chopped
2 C. chopped **celery**
8 oz. fresh **mushrooms**
12 cloves **garlic**, chopped
2 lbs. ground **beef**
7 lbs. **tomatoes**, fresh or canned
26 oz. **tomato paste**
6 C. (48 oz.) **tomato juice**
2 to 3 T. **oregano**
4 t. **basil**
4 medium **bay leaves**
2 t. **salt**
dash of **pepper**
chopped **chilies** to taste
   (optional)
2 to 3 T. **flour**

Pour a thin layer of oil into an 8 to 10-qt. pot; add the onions, peppers, celery and mushrooms. Using medium heat, saute until tender. Add garlic and simmer a few moments more. Remove mixture to a bowl. Brown the meat in the pot. Add remaining ingredients except flour. Bring to a boil, reduce heat and simmer, uncovered, 1 hour. Remove tomato cores and bay leaves if possible. Mix the flour with a cup of sauce, then stir it into the pot. Continue cooking a few minutes more to thicken the liquid. Freeze in meal-sized quantities for fast defrosting.

When I taught high school, this spaghetti sauce was a hit with my fussy, 24-girl volleyball team. That was the supreme test! Serves about 20 to 30.   *PROTEIN: 256.5 grams; CALORIES: 3726*

Hilary McLeod
Mississauga, Ont., Canada

FRESH VEGETABLE SPAGHETTI

1 lb. **spaghetti**, cooked
4 C. chopped fresh **broccoli**
2 C. edible **pea pods**
2 C. fresh **string beans**
2 C. fresh **peas**
2 C. sliced **mushrooms**
4 medium **tomatoes**, chopped
1 T. **basil**
1 T. chopped fresh **parsley**
1 clove **garlic**, minced
½ t. **salt** or less
2 T. **olive oil**
½ C. **milk** or medium cream
⅔ C. grated Parmesan **cheese**

Blanch the broccoli, pea pods, beans and peas in boiling water for 3 minutes. Drain and set aside. Saute mushrooms, tomatoes, basil, parsley, garlic and salt in oil until mushrooms are soft. Stir in milk and and cheese. Warm over low heat. Add blanched vegetables, heat through. Serve over prepared spaghetti.

PROTEIN: 173.6 grams; CALORIES: 3020
Helene Scheff
North Kingstown, Rhode Island

BLENDER SPAGHETTI SAUCE

4 C. **tomatoes**
18 oz. **tomato paste**
2¼ C. **water**
2 **green peppers** (optional)
4 medium **onions**, chopped
3 cloves **garlic**
1 stalk **celery**, chopped
½ t. **salt** (or less)
dash of **pepper**

Process all ingredients or blend in batches. Simmer for 2 hours over medium-low heat. This is an easy way to use up those extra tomatoes at the end of the summer. It makes a really good-tasting, thick sauce and is a favorite in our neighborhood.

PROTEIN: 34.7 grams; CALORIES: 803
Jan Heller
New Holland, Pennsylvania

KATHY'S LASAGNE

Sauce:
½ lb. ground **beef**
¾ to 1 C. chopped **onion**
1 clove **garlic**, minced
3 C. chopped **tomatoes**
2 C. **tomato paste**
1 t. **salt**
dash of **pepper**
2 T. fresh, chopped **parsley**
　(1 T. dried flakes)
¼ t. **kelp powder** (optional)
½ to 1 t. **basil**
½ to 1 t. **oregano**
2 C. mashed **cottage cheese**,
　tofu or ricotta cheese
2 **eggs**
½ C. grated Parmesan **cheese**
4 T. fresh, chopped **parsley**
　or 2 T. dried flakes
8 oz. **lasagne noodles**, cooked
1 lb. shredded Mozzarella **cheese**

Brown meat and onion. Add remaining sauce ingredients. Simmer 30 minutes. Combine cottage cheese with eggs, Parmesan and 4 T. parsley. Refrigerate for ½ hour or more while sauce simmers.

Coat bottom of greased 9 x 13" pan with meat mixture. Layer half the noodles, half the Mozzarella, half the cottage cheese and half the sauce. Repeat. Sprinkle the top with 1 to 2 T. Parmesan **cheese** before baking, if you wish. Bake at 350° for 30 to 40 minutes. Let stand 10 to 15 minutes before cutting. Tofu variation is tops. Meat may be eliminated, but if so, let it stand overnight in the refrigerator before baking to blend flavors, as tofu needs time to absorb seasonings.

Kathy Siddons
Manchester, Connecticut

PROTEIN: 284.9 grams; CALORIES: 4072

Eggplant Lasagne. To sauce, add 1 medium **eggplant**, peeled, chopped, lightly steamed, then mashed.　　PROTEIN: 292.1 grams; CALORIES: 4222

Joan LeBlanc
Tulsa, Oklahoma

Spinach Lasagne. Steam 1 to 2 lbs. fresh **spinach**. Or thaw and drain 10 to 20 oz. frozen spinach. Layer half the spinach on top of the cheeses before adding sauce. Repeat.　　PROTEIN: 299.4 grams; CALORIES: 4190

Carol Smith　　　　　　　　　*Frances Bauer*
Oklahoma City, Oklahoma　*Pontiac, Michigan*

SPAGHETTI SAUCE WITH MEAT

1 lb. bulk **Italian sausage**
　(p. 282)
1½ lb. ground **beef**
2 medium **onions**, chopped
4 cloves **garlic**, minced
2 T. olive **oil**
4 C. chopped **tomatoes**
½ C. **water** or tomato liquid
1½ t. **salt**
dash of **pepper**
1 T. **basil**
½ t. **oregano**
3¾ C. **tomato sauce**
1½ C. **tomato paste**
2 T. **red wine** (optional)
1 T. chopped, fresh **parsley**
　(optional)

Saute onions and garlic in oil. Add meat and brown; drain. Add tomatoes, water and spices. Simmer ½ hour. Add tomato sauce. Simmer ½ hour. Add tomato paste. Simmer ½ hour. This sauce freezes well.

For **meatless sauce**, start with onions and garlic, and proceed from there. PROTEIN: 192.6 grams; CALORIES: 3660

Cindy Karl
Arden, North Carolina

JOE'S "SORTA LASAGNE"
(Baked Ziti)

1 lb. **ziti macaroni**, cooked
1½ C. **spaghetti sauce** with **meat**
1 **egg**
2 C. Ricotta **cheese** or
   cottage cheese
¾ lb. Mozzarella **cheese**, cubed
10 oz. **spinach**, cooked and
   drained

Mix egg into ricotta cheese. Mix all ingredients together in a 2½-quart casserole. Bake at 350° for 30 minutes.   *PROTEIN: 226.1 grams; CALORIES: 3708*

Fay and Joe King
Lodi, Wisconsin

MANICOTTI FILLING

2 C. **ricotta cheese** or
   cottage cheese
1 C. shredded Mozzarella **cheese**
¼ C. grated **cheese**
   (Romano or Parmesan)
1 **egg**, beaten
1 T. chopped, fresh **parsley**

Topping:
3½ C. **tomato puree**
¼ C. minced **onion**
1 clove **garlic**, minced

Combine cheeses, beaten egg and parsley. Spread a small amount of filling down the center of each **noodle** (p. 170) and roll up. Place, seam side down, in shallow 9 x 13" baking dish.

For topping, simmer tomato puree, onion, garlic and sugar together 45 minutes. Pour sauce over manicotti. Bake 30 minutes at 350°.

The filled noodles may be frozen on a tray, then stored in bags for an instant heat-up meal; frozen with sauce in a foil pan, it makes a great after-baby gift. It's delicious and special enough to serve company. It is especially economical if the ricotta is bought in a 3-lb. carton, and all other ingredients are tripled to make a big batch for freezing.

PROTEIN: 109.9 grams; CALORIES: 1760

Nancy W. Comstock
Mehoopany, Pennsylvania

CANNELONI

1 lb. **manicotti noodles**
1 C. cooked, chopped **chicken**
1 C. Ricotta **cheese**
2 C. grated Mozzarella **cheese**
¼ C. grated Parmesan **cheese**
1 lb. fresh or frozen **spinach**,
   cooked, drained and pressed
   dry
pinch of **thyme**
½ t. **salt**
dash of **pepper**
¼ C. **milk** or half-and-half
1 C. chicken **broth**
3 C. **tomato sauce** or **meatless
   spaghetti sauce** (p. 199)

Cook and drain noodles. Combine remaining ingredients, except broth and tomato sauce, in bowl. Fill noodles with mixture (a thin, long-handled baby spoon works well). Place in buttered baking dish. Pour broth and tomato sauce over noodles. Bake, covered, at 350° for 45 to 50 minutes. Freezes well.

PROTEIN: 194 grams; CALORIES: 2543

Terri Nash
Kirkwood, Missouri

MACARONI AND CHEESE

1½ C. **macaroni**, cooked
  (whole wheat or soy)
1 T. **butter**

Sauce:
1½ C. thin **white sauce** (p. 251)
1½ to 2 C. grated **cheese**
1 to 3 T. minced **onion**
1 t. dry **mustard**
1 to 2 **eggs**, beaten (optional)
½ C. dry **milk powder** (optional)
2 T. **nutritional yeast**
  (optional)

Topping (Optional):
¼ C. melted **butter**
1 C. **wheat germ** or bread crumbs

Variation:
2 C. cubed **ham** or
  1 C. cooked bacon pieces
1 to 2 C. sliced **tomatoes**

Stir and heat sauce ingredients until thick. Gently stir in cooked macaroni. Pour into greased 2-quart casserole. Dot with butter. Cover and bake at 350° for 20 minutes. If desired, sprinkle with topping ingredients and bake, uncovered, 10 minutes longer.

For a fancy dish, alternate layers of macaroni and sauce, **ham** or **bacon**, and **tomatoes**. Sprinkle with topping. Bake.

This recipe freezes well, so why not double or triple the batch?

PROTEIN: 217.6 grams; CALORIES: 4042
With topping: P.: 228.8 gms.; C.: 4618

Cathy Strahan   *Bobbie Jarvinen*
North Bend, Oregon   *Howell, Michigan*

Carol P. Constant
Chicopee, Massachusetts

SEASHORE CASSEROLE

12 to 16 oz. **salmon**, tuna or
  crab, drained and flaked
2 C. cooked shell **macaroni**
1½ C. medium **white sauce**
¼ C. chopped **bell pepper**
¼ C. chopped **onion**
1 C. grated Cheddar **cheese**
1 T. **lemon juice**

Optional:
sliced **mushrooms**
chopped, hard-cooked **eggs**
peanuts, cashews or almonds
peas

Prepare white sauce, sauteing vegetables before adding flour. Add ¾ C. grated cheese; stir over low heat until cheese melts. Add lemon juice. Fold in fish and cooked macaroni. Spoon into well-greased 2-quart casserole. Top with remaining cheese. Bake at 350° for 30 minutes. This may be made ahead and refrigerated; cook 10 minutes longer.

PROTEIN: 135.6; CALORIES: 2216

Emmy Eaton
Thurmont, Maryland

PASTINA

8 oz. very small **pasta**
2 C. **broth**
¼ C. **butter**
2 **eggs**, beaten
¼ to ½ C. grated **cheese** (Swiss,
  Cheddar or Parmesan)

Cook pasta in broth until tender. Stir in butter, eggs and cheese. Stir and heat through. If desired, sprinkle with a little more cheese.

This is a favorite of young and old!   *PROTEIN: 66.4 grams; CALORIES: 1562*
Marti Sears
Hilton Head Island, South Carolina

SURPRISE KUGEL
(Noodle Pudding)

¼ lb. whole grain **noodles**
2 T. **butter**
2 small **eggs**, beaten
1 C. **milk**
½ C. **yogurt**, sour cream or
cream cheese
¼ lb. **tofu**, crumbled (optional)
¼ to ½ C. **raisins**, chopped
apple or unsweetened, crushed
pineapple
¾ t. **vanilla**
2 t. ground **cinnamon** (optional)
1 T. **honey** (optional)

Topping (Optional):
3 T. melted **butter**
1 C. rolled **oats**
1 C. unsweetened, shredded
coconut
1 to 2 T. **honey**, molasses
or brown sugar
1 t. ground **cinnamon**

Myra Reese
Ventnor, New Jersey

Cook noodles until tender. In the oven, melt the butter in a 12 x 8" pan. Mix remaining ingredients; stir in cooked noodles. Mix half the melted butter into noodle mixture and keep the rest in the pan. Pour noodle mixture into the pan and bake at 350° for 40 to 50 minutes, until firm. If desired, mix topping ingredients and spread on kugel after 10 minutes of baking. Bake at 325° for 35 to 45 minutes more. You may double the recipe and freeze one pan.

The whole grains, eggs and dairy products combine to form a complete protein, with the tofu an extra bonus. That's the surprise—it's as healthful as it is good! Serve as a side dish or as a dessert.

PROTEIN: 53.9 grams; CALORIES: 1240
With topping— P.: 68.6 gms.; C.: 2307

Paula Glazer Vornbrock   *Linda Greengas*
Yakima, Washington   *Hamden, Connecticut*

CREAMY NOODLE-EGG BAKE

½ C. chopped **onion**
½ C. sliced **celery**
¼ C. **butter**
2 C. **cottage cheese** or ricotta
2 C. plain **yogurt**, mashed tofu,
milk or sour cream
2 to 3 **eggs**, beaten
½ t. **salt** (optional)
dash of **pepper**
10 oz. **pasta**, cooked and drained
1 to 2 C. **spaghetti sauce** (p. 199)

Optionals: Use any or all:
2 t. **seeds** (poppy or sesame)
1 to 2 t. tamari **soy sauce** or
Worcestershire sauce
¼ C. chopped, fresh **parsley**
¼ C. cooked **bacon** pieces
4 to 8 hard-cooked **eggs**, chopped
2 C. steamed **vegetables**

Saute onion and celery in butter. Combine cheese, yogurt, eggs and spices. Stir in pasta, sauteed vegetables and any optional ingredients you wish. Place in greased 9 x 13" baking dish. Spread spaghetti sauce over top, if desired. Bake at 350° for 25 to 30 minutes, until golden.

This versatile casserole may be made ahead, refrigerated or frozen and baked later. It is high in protein, delicious and easy on the budget.

PROTEIN: 158.1 grams; CALORIES: 2516

Veray Wickham   *Jan Goldenbogen*
Stockton, California   *Oshkosh, Wisconsin*
Nancy Meara
Sparta, New Jersey

Pizza

PIZZA SAUCE

½ C. chopped **onion**
1 clove **garlic**, minced
2 T. **oil**
3 C. chopped **tomatoes**
¾ C. **tomato paste**
¼ to ½ t. **salt**
dash of **pepper**
1 t. **oregano**
1 t. **basil**
1 **bay leaf**
¼ C. chopped, fresh **parsley**
(optional)

½ C. grated Parmesan **cheese**

Toppings:
½ lb. ground **beef**, browned
   and drained
½ C. chopped **green pepper**
1 C. sliced **zucchini**
1 C. sliced **mushrooms**
½ C. sliced **olives**
½ C. cubed **yellow squash**
½ C. cubed **eggplant**
2 **carrots**, grated
6 whole **spinach leaves**
¼ C. chopped **celery**
4 to 6 oz. **tofu**, in ¼" cubes

2 to 3 C. shredded Mozzarella
   cheese

Brown onion and garlic in oil until soft and golden. Add remaining sauce ingredients and heat to boiling over medium heat. Reduce heat and simmer for 2 hours, stirring occasionally, until sauce has thickened. Discard bay leaf. Makes enough sauce for 2 pizzas.

Spread sauce evenly over prepared Pizza Crust. Layer on your choice of toppings, ending with cheese. Bake at 425° for 15 to 20 minutes, until crust is golden.

Without toppings—P.: 19.9 gms.; C.: 677
With all toppings—P.: 164 gms.; C.: 2377

Freezer Pizza Sauce. Make basic sauce recipe in large quantities and cool completely in refrigerator. Then freeze in one-pint containers, leaving 1" of head room. Keeps frozen for 3 months. Thaw before using.

Pizza for the Milk-Allergic. Sprinkle ½ C. **nutritional yeast powder** over tomato sauce. Cover with 8 oz. thinly sliced **tofu**, then layer on toppings of your choice. Omit cheeses.   *Many LLL Contributors*

WHITE "PITZA"

whole wheat **pita** (p. 145)

Filling:
chopped, fresh **mushrooms**
sliced, pre-cooked nitrite-free
   sausage (p. 282)
chopped **onion**
shredded Mozzarella **cheese**

Cut pita in half and fill each pocket with some of each of the fillings. Place on greased cookie sheets. Bake at 350° for 5 to 10 minutes, depending on how full they are. Serve hot. Great for days when I'm just too busy. We keep the ingredients on hand most of the time, so my husband just throws it together when he gets home. These are delicious, non-messy pizzas similar to "white (no tomato sauce) pizza." Kids love to assemble them.   *Mary T. Gill*
Exeter, Pennsylvania

CRAZY CRUST PIZZA

Crust:
1 C. whole wheat **flour**
1 t. **salt**
1 t. **oregano**
2 **eggs**
⅔ C. **milk**

Topping:
1½ lb. ground **beef**
½ C. chopped **onion**
½ t. **salt**
dash of **pepper**
1 **green pepper**, chopped
(optional)
1 C. sliced **mushrooms** (optional)
1 C. **tomato sauce**
1 to 2 C. grated Mozzarella
cheese

Beat crust ingredients together until smooth and pour into a greased and floured 12" pizza pan. Brown beef with onion and season to taste. Drain. Arrange meat and vegetables over batter. Bake at 425° for 25 to 30 minutes, until crust is a deep golden color. Remove pizza from oven; drizzle with the sauce and sprinkle on the cheese. Return to oven for 10 to 15 minutes, to melt the cheese.

PROTEIN: 189.2 grams; CALORIES: 2439

Abby Simmons   Lore'e Clark
Terre Haute, Indiana   Mission, Kansas

PIZZA DOUGH

1 T. **yeast**
1 C. warm **water**
1 T. **honey** (optional)
2 T. **oil**
¼ to ½ t. **salt**
3 to 4 C. **flour** (all whole wheat
or part unbleached)

Dissolve yeast in water. Let yeast mixture stand for 10 minutes to start fermenting, then stir well. Stir in remaining ingredients, adding enough flour for a stiff dough. Turn out onto a floured surface and knead about 5 minutes, until smooth and elastic. Place in a greased bowl, turn dough to grease all sides. Cover with a towel and let rise in a warm place about 1½ hours, until doubled in bulk. Punch down and divide in half. Put each piece on a greased 12 to 14" pizza pan and push to the edges, forming a rim around the outside. Spread dough with Pizza Sauce and add toppings. Bake at 425° for 15 to 20 minutes, or until crust is brown.

PROTEIN: 51.1 grams; CALORIES: 1523

High Protein Pizza. Substitute 1 C. **soy flour** for 1 C. of the flour.

Cornmeal Crust. Substitute ½ C. **cornmeal** for ½ C. of the flour.

Freezer Pizza Dough. Substitute ¾ C. **milk** for ¾ C. of the water. Beat in one **egg** before adding the last of the flour. After kneading the dough, divide into 2 parts and wrap each piece well. Put in freezer. When ready to make pizza, remove dough from freezer, unwrap it and put in a greased bowl. Cover and let rise 4 to 5 hours. Use as directed above.

Many LLL Contributors

DEEP DISH (CHICAGO-STYLE) PIZZA

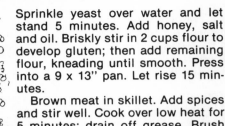

Crust:
1 T. **yeast**
1 C. warm **water**
1 t. **honey**
1 t. **salt**
1 T. olive **oil**
3 to 3½ C. whole wheat **flour**

Italian Sausage:
1½ lb. ground **pork**
1 clove **garlic**, minced
1 t. **fennel seeds**
½ t. **chili powder**

Topping:
2 to 3 C. grated Mozzarella **cheese**
2 C. sliced **tomatoes**
1 **green pepper**, chopped (optional)

Sprinkle yeast over water and let stand 5 minutes. Add honey, salt and oil. Briskly stir in 2 cups flour to develop gluten; then add remaining flour, kneading until smooth. Press into a 9 x 13" pan. Let rise 15 minutes.

Brown meat in skillet. Add spices and stir well. Cook over low heat for 5 minutes; drain off grease. Brush raised crust with oil. Sprinkle with *all* the cheese, cover with tomatoes and then spoon on meat mixture. Bake at 425° for 20 to 25 minutes.

We developed this by analyzing a pizza-joint pizza. Now it is a "house specialty." Some may call it weird pizza, but if you like Chicago-style pizza, you know the difference.

PROTEIN: 216.7 grams; CALORIES: 3472   Kathleen White
Logansport, Indiana

RICE CRUST FOR PIZZA

3 C. cooked **brown rice**
2 **eggs**, beaten
1 C. grated Mozzarella **cheese**

Mix the rice with eggs and cheese. Press into 10" pizza pan. Bake for 20 minutes at 450°. Put on sauce and toppings of your choice; bake 10 minutes longer.   *P.: 45.4 gms.; C.: 1006*

Lois Lake Raabe
Easton, Connecticut

ZUCCHINI PIZZA

8 4"-diameter **zucchini** or eggplant rounds, sliced ½" thick
2 large, ripe **tomatoes**, sliced
8 slices **cheese** (Cheddar, Mozzarella, or other)
½ C. finely diced **onion**
½ C. finely diced **green pepper**
1 to 2 t. **oregano**
2 T. Parmesan **cheese**

Simmer zucchini slices in 1" water for 3 minutes, turning once. Pat dry and arrange on broiler rack. Top each slice with tomato, cheese, a sprinkle each of onion and green pepper, then a shake of oregano and Parmesan. Broil until cheese melts and is bubbly—about 5 minutes.

This is a great lunchtime treat with the children.   *P.: 68.9 gms.; C.: 1115*

Variation: Omit tomatoes, onion, green pepper and oregano, and substitute that leftover cup of **tomato sauce** lurking in the fridge. Top with cheese; broil as above. I have even topped the zucchini rounds with refried **beans**, tomatoes and cheese. Broiled, the leftovers were super!

Linda Schutsky
Ronks, Pennsylvania

GROUND BEEF AND EGGPLANT SKILLET

1 lb. ground **beef**
1 clove **garlic**, crushed
1 **eggplant**, peeled and cubed
1 **green pepper**, chopped
1 **onion**, sliced
2 C. **tomatoes**
1 C. **tomato sauce**
½ t. **salt**
dash of **pepper**
1 t. **basil**
½ t. **oregano**
1 C. **brown rice**, cooked

Brown beef and garlic; discard garlic. Add eggplant; stir and cook 10 minutes. Add remaining ingredients. Cover and simmer 25 minutes, stirring occasionally. Serve over rice. May be made ahead and reheated.

PROTEIN: 109.1 grams; CALORIES: 1836

Sandra Long
Santa Ana, California

CALICO FISH

1 lb. **fish fillets**
1 T. **lemon juice**
½ t. **salt** (or less)
dash of **pepper**
2 C. **peas**
1 medium **carrot**, grated
1 small **onion**, sliced and
   separated into rings
3 T. **butter**

If fillets are large, cut into 5 or 6 pieces. Arrange in ungreased baking dish. Sprinkle with lemon juice and seasonings. Spoon vegetables over fish. Sprinkle with salt; dot with butter. Cover and bake at 350° for 20 to 30 minutes, until fish flakes easily.

This is not only a delicious way to stretch a pound of fish, but little eyes delight at the colors, shapes and textures as well.

PROTEIN: 99.7 grams; CALORIES: 986   *Sue Payne*
Cottage Grove, Wisconsin

QUICK CHEESE CHOWDER

2 C. medium **white sauce** (p. 251)
2 C. (½ lb.) grated Cheddar
   cheese
1½ C. **water**
2 medium **potatoes**, diced
½ C. chopped **celery**
½ C. chopped **carrots**
¼ C. chopped **onions**
1 C. cooked, cubed **ham**
   (optional)
½ t. **salt**
dash of **pepper**
dash of **hot pepper sauce**
   (optional)

Prepare white sauce. Add cheese. Stir until cheese melts. Bring water to a boil in a 3-qt. saucepan. Add vegetables; simmer until soft. Add cheese sauce and ham. Season to taste.   PROTEIN: 117.1 grams; CALORIES: 2289

Junie Hostetler
Tuscon, Arizona

VEGETABLE MORSELS

3 **eggs**
2 t. vegetable **salt** (or less)
1 t. **cumin**
¼ t. **pepper**
3 T. whole wheat **flour**
3 T. **sesame seeds**
3 T. **wheat germ**
2 **carrots**, grated
10 oz. leafy **greens**, cooked,
  chopped and well drained
1½ C. chopped **green beans**,
  cooked

Beat eggs with seasonings, flour, seeds and wheat germ. Stir in vegetables. Drop by spoonfuls onto greased cookie sheet. Bake at 450° for 10 minutes. Serve hot or cold with **pita** ("Pocket bread"), **yogurt** and **marinated vegetables** if desired. Experiment with other vegetables, flours and seeds in the morsels, adding cheese, nutritional yeast, etc. *PROTEIN: 47.7 grams; CALORIES: 740*

Bryanna Clark
Union Bay, B.C., Canada

SAUERKRAUT BALLS

3 C. **sauerkraut**
1 lb. ground **sausage** (p. 282)
¼ lb. ground **beef**
½ C. chopped **onion**
3 T. chopped, fresh **parsley**
½ t. dry **mustard**
½ t. **salt** (or less)
dash of **pepper**
1 t. **sugar** or honey
2 C. **bread crumbs**
3 **eggs**
2 T. **milk**

Drain and chop sauerkraut. Add sausage, beef, onion, parsley and seasonings. Brown. Turn off heat and add ½ C. crumbs and 1 beaten egg. Cool. Form into balls and coat with a mixture of 2 eggs and a small amount of milk beaten together. Roll in remaining crumbs and broil 2" from heat for 1 minute. Great finger food for kids, or a great party food.

PROTEIN: 142.7 grams; CALORIES: 2990

Diane Yale Peabody
Dayton, Ohio

FRIKADELLER
(Danish Meatballs)

1 lb. ground **pork**
1 small **onion**, chopped
1 **egg**
¾ to 1 C. **milk**
½ to 1 C. **wheat germ**
1 T. dried **parsley**
½ t. **garlic powder**
½ t. **salt** (or less)
dash of **pepper**
¼ t. **sage**
¼ t. **paprika**
dash of ground **nutmeg**

Combine all ingredients in a large bowl or food processor. Mix well. Mixture should be the consistency of drop cookies. Shape into 12 to 16 medium-sized meatballs. Place on a large cookie sheet. Bake at 350° for 30 minutes, turning once. May also be fried, 10 minutes on a side, over medium heat.

PROTEIN: 107.2 grams; CALORIES: 1925

Variation: Try with ground **beef**, or mix pork with **pork sausage** to equal 1 lb. Omit spices.

Barbara Kautz
York, Maine

MEAT BALLS ESPANOL

1 lb. ground **beef**
1 C. soft **bread crumbs**
¼ C. finely chopped **onion**
¼ C. finely chopped **celery**
1½ t. **worcestershire sauce**
1 **egg**
1 t. **garlic powder**
1 t. **salt**
¼ t. **pepper**
4 C. stewed **tomatoes**
2½ C. thinly sliced **zucchini**
½ t. **oregano**
½ t. **basil**
1 T. **cornstarch**
1 C. beef **broth**
1 C. raw **brown rice**

Combine beef, crumbs, onion, celery, Worcestershire sauce, egg, ½ t. garlic powder, salt and pepper. Form into 12 to 16 balls. Combine tomatoes, zucchini, ½ t. garlic powder, oregano and basil. Simmer 5 minutes. Blend cornstarch and broth. Stir into tomato mixture. Put rice in a shallow, greased pan. Pour tomato mixture over rice and add meatballs. Bake at 375° for 40 to 45 minutes, or until rice is done. A nice one-pan meal.

PROTEIN: 129.1 grams; CALORIES: 2285

Beverly Thomas
Leavenworth, Kansas

UN-MEATBALLS

1½ C. whole wheat **bread crumbs**
½ C. grated Cheddar **cheese**
½ C. chopped **nuts**
4 to 6 **eggs**, beaten
½ C. chopped **onion**
1 clove **garlic**, minced
½ t. **salt**
oil for browning
4 C. **spaghetti sauce** (p. 199)
½ C. grated Cheddar **cheese**

Combine crumbs, ½ C. cheese, nuts, eggs, onion, garlic and salt, kneading lightly with fingers. Shape balls using 1 T. for each, and brown lightly in oil. Place in 2-quart casserole, covering with sauce. Bake at 375° for ½ hour; then top with remaining cheese and bake 10 minutes more. These freeze and reheat well. *PROTEIN: 113.8 grams; CALORIES: 2277*

Margaret MacPherson
Hudson, Massachusetts

FELAFEL
(Garbanzo Balls or Patties)

4 C. cooked **garbanzo beans**, mashed
8 oz. **tofu**, mashed (optional)
⅓ C. whole wheat **bread crumbs**
3 T. **tahini** or oil
1 **hot red pepper**, chopped
pinch to ¼ t. *each:* **basil, thyme, marjoram, cumin, turmeric**
1 T. chopped **parsley**
1 to 3 cloves **garlic**, minced
½ t. **salt** (or less)
dash of **pepper**
1 to 3 **eggs**
½ C. whole wheat **flour**
4 T. **oil**

Combine mashed beans with crumbs, tahini, red pepper, optional tofu and seasonings. Add eggs, one at a time, to obtain a semi-soft consistency. Form 1" balls or small patties. Roll in flour. Deep fry or brown in oil. Drain on paper. Serve hot with **pita, yogurt,** sliced **tomatoes, lettuce** and **sprouts**.

This traditional Middle Eastern treat makes great picnic food—you can heat the felafel in foil over a campfire.

PROTEIN: 120.8 grams; CALORIES: 2533

Bryanna Clark   *Mary Trombley*
Union Bay, B.C., Canada   *Syracuse, New York*

MIGHTY MEATLOAF

2 lbs. ground **beef**
2 **eggs**
1 **onion,** chopped and sauteed
3 T. fresh, chopped **parsley**
  (1 T. dried parsley)
¼ C. **bread crumbs** or wheat germ
½ t. **salt** (or less)
¼ C. **milk** or water
3 to 4 large **carrots,** sliced
2 medium **zucchini,** sliced

Optional:
2 yellow **squash,** sliced
1 small **eggplant,** sliced
1 C. chopped **green beans**
1 C. sliced **celery**

Sauce:
2 **green peppers,** sliced in
  thin strips
8 oz. **mushrooms,** sliced
2 T. **oil**
3½ C. **tomato puree**

Mix all ingredients except vegetables. Put a thin layer of meat mixture into two loaf pans, or one 10 x 10" pan. Cover meat with one of the vegetables. Alternate layers of meat and vegetables, using one kind of vegetable at a time, ending with meat. *Or* chop or grate vegetables and mix into meat. Bake at 350° for 1 to 1½ hours, or until done.

For Sauce: Saute peppers and mushrooms in oil. Add tomato puree. Simmer 15 to 20 minutes. Serve over loaf.   PROTEIN: *214 grams; CALORIES: 2897*

Helen Palmer   *Paulette Young*
Edgewater Park, New Jersey   *Glen Ellyn, Illinois*

GREEN TURKEY AND CHEESE
(Leftover Thanksgiving Turkey Casserole)

1 lb. **spinach,** washed and
  chopped
1½ C. (or more) cooked, cubed
  turkey, chicken or ham
10 oz. Cheddar **cheese,** grated

Place spinach in buttered 10" casserole dish. Top with turkey, then cheese. Bake at 350° for 25 to 30 minutes. This is quick, easy and delicious.

PROTEIN: *181 grams; CALORIES: 1833*

Barbara Persensky
Canton, Michigan

EGG-FREE, WHEAT-FREE, MILK-FREE MEATLOAF

1½ lbs. ground **beef**
¼ to ½ C. raw, grated **potato**
¼ C. chopped **onion**
¼ C. grated **carrot**
¾ t. **salt** (or less)
dash of **pepper**
½ to 1 C. **liquid** (broth, gravy,
  tomato juice, etc.)
1 C. chopped **vegetables** (optional)
  (peas, carrots, green beans,
  celery, green peppers, etc.)

Mix all ingredients. Bake at 350° for 1 hour. You do not have to add the optional vegetables, but it is a good way for children to learn to enjoy them. Our favorite is peas. Even my fussy brother-in-law likes the vegetables in this meatloaf.

PROTEIN: *135.5 grams; CALORIES: 1466*

Beverly Morgan
San Jose, California

SALMON LOAF

1 lb. **salmon**, tuna or mackerel
½ C. **milk**
1 **egg**, beaten
½ C. rolled **oats**
½ C. **bran**
½ C. **wheat germ**
2 t. **lemon juice**
1 T. chopped **onion**
½ t. **salt** (or less)
¼ C. **sunflower seeds**
1 C. medium **white sauce** (p. 251) (optional)

Drain salmon, reserving liquid; mash bones. Add milk to liquid to measure 1 cup. Mix salmon, liquid and egg. Add remaining ingredients except white sauce. Mix. Spoon into an oiled loaf pan or 1-quart baking dish. Bake at 350° for 45 minutes, until firm. Top with white sauce if you like, before or after cooking.

The sunflower seeds make a delightful addition.

PROTEIN: 151.8; CALORIES: 2114
Mary Morse
Brighton, Colorado

TURKEY LOAF

1½ lbs. ground **turkey** or ground beef
1 C. rolled **oats**
½ C. **wheat germ**
2 **eggs**
1½ C. **tomato sauce**
1 **onion**, chopped
1 **green pepper**, chopped
1 T. **nutritional yeast** (optional)
¼ t. **garlic powder**
½ t. **onion powder**
½ t. **sage** or poultry seasoning
½ t. **salt**
dash of **pepper**

Combine all ingredients in a bowl. Mix well. Shape into a loaf. Bake in pan at 350° for 45 to 60 minutes. Serve with **mushroom sauce** .

PROTEIN: 219.9 grams; CALORIES: 2115
Debby Thielking
Syracuse, New York

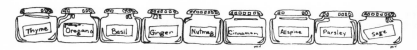

MUSHROOM SAUCE

½ C. (4 oz.) chopped **mushrooms**
¼ C. **oil** or butter
½ C. plus 2 T. whole wheat **flour**
2 C. **water** or vegetable stock
1½ C. **milk**
1 t. to 1 T. tamari **soy sauce**
pinch **garlic powder** (optional)

Saute mushrooms in oil until tender. Add flour and brown 1 minute. Add water and milk gradually, stirring to avoid lumps. Bring to slow simmer. Cook for 15 minutes, stirring occasionally. Add soy sauce and garlic powder. Serve over **turkey loaf** (above). This is a nice gravy without meat juices. Good on meat, meatloaf, vegetables, potatoes or whole wheat macaroni.

PROTEIN: 24.4 grams; CALORIES: 1004
Debby Thielking
Syracuse, New York

LENTIL BURGERS IN PITA
(Or Lentil Stew)

Burgers:
½ C. dry **lentils**
½ C. raw **brown rice**
1 **onion**, chopped
1 T. **oil**
2 C. **liquid** (water, stock)
½ C. **tomato juice**
1 T. tamari **soy sauce**
1 **potato**, diced
1 **tomato**, diced
1 **carrot**, sliced
1 stalk **celery**, sliced
wheat germ
dry **milk powder** (optional)
oil for frying

"Fixings":
pita bread
lettuce, shredded
onions, thinly sliced
tomatoes, sliced
cheese, sliced
catsup (p. 252)

Put lentils, rice, onion, oil and liquids into 2-quart pot. Bring to a boil, cover and simmer 30 minutes. Add vegetables. Bring to a boil, cover and simmer 30 minutes longer. Now if it's been that kind of day, call it quits at this point and serve Lentil Stew!   *PROTEIN: 41.2 grams; CALORIES: 1052*

On better days, mash stew. Shape into patties. Attain proper consistency by adding liquid, or wheat germ and dry milk. Coat patties with wheat germ. Brown in hot oil, 5 minutes per side. Tuck one patty in each pita, add "fixings" and pass the catsup!

Kids love this supper. It's nutritious, inexpensive and meatless.

Ingrid Berljawsky
Nepean, Ont., Canada

Sharon Falatovics
Michigan City, Indiana

Nancy Nay
Columbus, Ohio

Beth LeFever
Lancaster, Pennsylvania

COTTAGE CHEESE OR TOFU PATTIES

6 **eggs**, beaten
1 C. finely chopped **walnuts** or sunflower seeds
2 C. **cottage cheese** or crumbled tofu
1 **onion**, chopped (optional)
1 C. dry **bread crumbs** and/or toasted **wheat germ**
butter for frying

Optional:
herbs or curry powder
tomato sauce or gravy

Mix all ingredients together and shape into patties. Lightly brown in butter. Do not overcook! Vary by adding optional ingredients.

I tested these "burgers" on my teenage boys; they actually asked me for seconds!

PROTEIN: 126.6 grams; CALORIES: 2847

Joann S. Grohman
Dixfield, Maine

HEALTHBURGERS

1 lb. ground **beef**
¼ C. **wheat germ**
¼ C. **buttermilk**
2 T. minced **onion**
½ t. **salt** (or less)
dash of **pepper**

Combine all ingredients. Mix well. Shape into 6 patties. Grill, broil or fry as desired. Serve plain or on buns.

PROTEIN: 94.6 grams; CALORIES: 1010

Sandy Eckstein
Galloway, Ohio

SALMON PATTIES

1 lb. **salmon** with liquid
⅓ C. whole wheat **flour**
¼ C. **cornmeal**
¼ to ⅓ C. **wheat germ**
2 **eggs**, beaten
½ C. chopped **onion**
¼ C. chopped **bell pepper**
1 T. **lemon juice** or to taste
¼ to ½ C. **oil** for frying

Flake salmon, mashing the bones well. Mix all ingredients together. Form into 8 or 9 patties. Brown in ¼" oil over medium heat, about 15 minutes.

We like **cole slaw** and **applesauce** with this meal. Now I like serving my family a quick, nutritious meal without resorting to packaged foods.

PROTEIN: 132 grams; CALORIES: 2004

Pam De Los Santos
Keflavik, Iceland

SALMON CROQUETTES

12 to 16 oz. **salmon** or tuna,
  drained
2 medium **carrots**, grated
1 small **potato**, grated
1 **egg**, beaten
⅓ C. **wheat germ**
¼ C. **oil**

Mash salmon, breaking up bones. Mix in vegetables, egg and wheat germ. Form patties. Dip in additional **wheat germ**. Fry in oil on both sides. Drain on paper towels. Cool. Wrap individually in foil; freeze. When ready to use, bake at 400° for 10 to minutes.

My loving mother created this recipe and kept my freezer well stocked when my daughter arrived. This is a favorite of my daughter. I change the size of the patty to keep up with her appetite. It's good to carry along to restaurants and visiting.

PROTEIN: 109.4 grams; CALORIES: 1512

Diane Kussack
Yonkers, New York

CRAB OR FISHCAKES

2 C. **crab meat** or cooked,
  crumbled white fish
¾ t. **salt**
dash of **pepper**
1 t. dry **mustard**
2 t. **worcestershire sauce**
1 **egg yolk**
1 T. **mayonnaise** (p. 48)
1 t. chopped, fresh **parsley**
1 slice **bread**, crumbed
1 C. **wheat germ** or bread or
  cracker crumbs
¼ to ½ C. **oil** for frying

Mix all ingredients except crab and wheat germ. Stir in crab meat. Form into 8 small patties. Coat with wheat germ. Fry quickly in hot oil, about 3 minutes on each side.

PROTEIN: 108.7 grams; CALORIES: 1653

Sue Smith
Newport News, Virginia

KARNATZLACH

¼ C. **wheat germ**
2 T. **nutritional yeast**
¼ t. **paprika**
1½ lbs. ground **beef**
½ **onion,** grated
1 large **carrot,** grated
1 clove **garlic,** minced
2 t. **poultry seasoning** or
    thyme, marjoram and oregano
2 **eggs,** beaten
½ t. **salt** (or less)
dash of **pepper**

Mix wheat germ, yeast and paprika; set aside. Combine remaining ingredients. Form into rolls about the size of hot dogs. Roll in wheat germ mixture. Broil under moderate heat on a slightly oiled rack. Turn to brown on all sides. Serve with hot sauce or any way your family likes hot dogs!

PROTEIN: 155.3 grams; CALORIES: 1687

Mary Jo Johnson
Shavertown, Pennsylvania

VEGETABLE NUT LOAF

1 C. diced **carrots**
1 C. diced **celery**
⅓ C. chopped **onions**
⅓ C. **butter**
¼ C. whole wheat **flour**
½ t. **salt**
¼ t. **pepper**
1½ C. **milk**
¾ C. **wheat germ**
1 C. grated Cheddar **cheese**
1 C. chopped **walnuts** or pecans
3 **eggs,** beaten

Saute carrots, celery and onion in butter until the onions are soft. Stir in flour, salt and pepper, then the milk. Cook over medium heat until sauce thickens, stirring constantly. Remove from heat. Stir in the wheat germ, add cheese, stir until it melts. Finally, add the nuts and eggs. Mix thoroughly. Bake in a greased 9 x 5 x 3" loaf pan at 350° for 50 minutes. Cool 10 minutes before serving.

PROTEIN: 114.1 grams; CALORIES: 2772

Louise Thompson
Alexandria, Ont., Canada

SPINACH LOAF

10 oz. fresh **spinach,** chopped
    or frozen, thawed and drained
½ C. **cracker crumbs** or
    ⅓ C. bread crumbs
1 C. grated Cheddar **cheese**
1 **egg,** beaten
½ t. **salt** (or less)
dash of **pepper**
1 T. **lemon juice**
1 recipe **white sauce** (p. 251) or
    cheese sauce

Butter a loaf pan, and in it stir together the spinach, crumbs, cheese, egg, seasonings and lemon juice. Bake at 350° for 35 minutes. Serve with either white or cheese sauce. Even dedicated spinach-haters agree this is good.

PROTEIN: 60.8 grams; CALORIES: 1314

Alice Ziring   *Chris Schmelzer*   *Sandy Williams*
Mercer Island, Washington *Sidney, Ohio*   *N. Little Rock, Arkansas*

SOYBURGERS

2 T. **oil**
2 **onions**, finely chopped
2 to 4 cloves **garlic**, minced (optional)
4 to 6 stalks **celery**, chopped
4 C. cooked **soybeans**
2 C. cooked **millet** or brown rice
1 C. rolled **oats**
¼ C. tamari **soy sauce**
3 T. **catsup** (p. 252) or tomato paste
2 T. **nutritional yeast** (optional)
1 T. chopped, fresh **parsley**
2 t. *each* **rosemary** and **basil**
1 t. *each* **chili powder**, ground **cumin** and dry **mustard**

Saute vegetables in oil. Rinse soybeans several times. Drain. Mash thoroughly or puree in food processor. Combine with remaining ingredients. This makes 8 C. of soyburger mix. Freeze unused portion, or refrigerate for up to 5 days.

To cook, scoop out desired for each burger. Brown on both sides in oiled pan or bake in loaf pan at 350° for 40 minutes.

Excellent with cheese or gravy, or on rolls, pita bread or tortillas.

I got this recipe from a great co-op restaurant. I scaled down the beans, stepped up the spices, and voici!

PROTEIN: 131.9 grams; CALORIES: 2301

Sue La Leike
Cape Coral, Florida

CORNISH PASTIES
(pass-tees)

4 C. whole wheat **flour**
½ t. **celery seeds** (optional)
½ to 1 t. **salt** (or less)
⅓ C. **oil**
¾ C. ice **water**

Filling:
1 lb. **flank steak**, stew or ground beef or chicken
3 medium **potatoes**
1 medium **onion**
3 medium **carrots**
1 large **rutabaga** (optional)
½ t. **salt**
dash of **pepper**
1 T. **worcestershire sauce** (optional)

Mix dry ingredients and oil with fork. Add ice water gradually, blending until dough is soft. Roll 1/8" thick on floured board. Cut in circles about 4" to 6" in diameter (cut around a saucer or cut with large can). Set aside.

Run meat and vegetables through coarse blade of meat grinder, or dice them very finely. Mix meat, vegetables and seasonings. Spread on one half of dough. Lift side edges to center top and press together with fingers. Place pasties, seam side up, on lightly oiled baking sheet. Bake at 400° for 10 minutes; lower to 325°. Continue baking for 30 minutes. Serve hot or cold.

These are great for picnics or travelling. They freeze well after being baked. When travelling, let frozen pasties thaw en route.

PROTEIN: 177.2 grams; CALORIES: 3458
Linda Church   *Deanna Brekke*
West Lafayette, Indiana *Keewatin, Minnesota*

PIEROGI
(Polish Stuffed Dumpling)

3 to 3½ C. **sauerkraut**
(1 lb. 11 oz. can), save the
can to cut circles
4 T. **butter** or oil
1 medium or large **onion**,
chopped
½ t. **salt** (or less)
dash of **pepper**

Basic Dough:
4 C. whole wheat **flour**, sifted
½ t. **salt** (or less)
1 **egg**
1 C. lukewarm **water**

Cook sauerkraut 15 minutes or until liquid is absorbed. Push to sides of pan; melt butter and saute onion. Mix together; saute ½ hour, stirring occasionally. Season to taste.

While this is cooking, prepare dough. Mix ingredients together, adding water a little at a time. Dough should not be sticky. Roll out 1/8" thick on a lightly floured surface. Cut into circles using sauerkraut can. Fill each circle with a spoonful of kraut mixture. Fold in half; wet half the rim with water. Crimp with a fork. Drop into a large kettle of gently boiling water. Cook as you would homemade noodles, until they float to the top. Remove with slotted spoon. Let cool and dry on cake racks. Makes 25 pierogi.

When ready to serve, fry in **butter** or oil until golden on each side. For larger servings, dip in melted butter; bake at 350° in 9 x 13" pan until golden. They may be frozen and thawed before frying or baking. Try other fillings, such as **cottage cheese** and beaten **egg**, leftover mashed **potatoes** and grated **cheese**, or 2 **prunes** for each pierogi.

This Polish stuffed dumpling recipe has been in our family for years. I remember going to the Polish butcher shop with my dad on Sunday morning for hard rolls and pierogi. They are now very expensive and not always available, so I asked around until my dear aunt gave me this recipe.

PROTEIN: 59 grams; CALORIES: 2487

Kathleen White
Logansport, Indiana

PIROSHKI
(Beerocks)

yeast **dough** for 1 or 2 loaves
3 to 4 C. shredded **cabbage** or
2 C. **sauerkraut**
1 medium **onion**, chopped
1 lb. ground **beef**
¼ t. **salt**
dash of **pepper**
1 t. prepared **mustard**
(optional)

Let dough rise once. Steam cabbage for 10 minutes. Saute onion. Add meat and brown; drain grease. Add cabbage or sauerkraut and seasonings. Cool. Roll out dough to 1/8" thick. Cut out circles or squares about 6" across. Put meat and cabbage mixture in center of each circle or square, bring up the 4 sides and seal shut. Place on lightly greased cookie sheet, pinched side down, and let rise until almost double, about 45 minutes. Bake at 375° for 20 to 25 minutes. They freeze well. Serve hot or cold with potato salad, vegetable sticks, baked beans and fruit compote.

Try other meats, fish, deviled eggs, cottage cheese, potatoes or whatever is handy for a filling. Fruits, jams, jellies work well for a sweet filling.

Many LLL Contributors   *PROTEIN: 138.4 grams; CALORIES: 2460*

TEXAS RICE

1 C. chopped **onion**
2 T. **butter**
4 C. cooked **brown rice**
1 C. plain **yogurt** or sour cream
1 C. **cottage cheese**
1 t. **garlic powder** (optional)
1 t. **oregano** (optional)
½ t. **salt** (or less)
dash of **pepper**
¼ C. chopped **green chili peppers**
   or 1 C. chopped green peppers
1 large **tomato**, sliced
3 six-inch **zucchini**, sliced
2 C. grated Cheddar **cheese**

Saute onion in butter. Into hot rice, stir onion, yogurt, cottage cheese and spices. In oiled casserole, layer half the rice mixture, half the vegetables and half the cheese. Repeat, ending with cheese. Bake at 350° for 20 minutes. You may make this ahead, refrigerate it and bake it the next day. Or bake and freeze it for a busy day. *PROTEIN: 130.4 grams; CALORIES: 2450*

Janice Harris   *Stephanie Merritt*
Wharton, Texas   *Los Altos, California*

Marengo-Huntley LLL
Huntley, Illinois

WHITE SAUCE CASSEROLE

2½ stalks **celery**
1 small **onion**
2 large **carrots**
2 T. **oil**
1 to 2 C. cooked **soybeans**
1 C. **white sauce** (p. 251)
dash of **cayenne pepper**
½ to 1 t. **rosemary**
2 T. fresh or 1 T. dried **parsley**

Chop vegetables. Saute in oil. Grind soybeans. Combine all ingredients. Bake at 350° for 45 minutes.

This recipe is the result of several attempts to make a soy dish that my family enjoyed. We combined something from each, threw out other parts, and ended with this very tasty dish. *PROTEIN: 38.3 grams; CALORIES: 1087*

Linda Z. Gilbertson
Erhard, Minnesota

RICE-LENTIL CUSTARD

½ **onion**, chopped
1 stalk **celery**, chopped
2 T. chopped **green pepper**
1 **carrot**, grated
1 clove **garlic**, minced
1 C. cooked **lentils**
1 C. cooked **brown rice**
½ t. *each* **basil** and **thyme**

½ t. *each* **dill weed** and **celery seed**
2 T. **oil**
2 **eggs**, beaten
2 C. **milk**
2 T. tamari **soy sauce** or
   Worcestershire sauce
¼ to ½ C. grated or sliced **cheese**
   (Cheddar or Parmesan)

Saute vegetables, lentils, rice and seasonings in oil. Beat eggs with milk and tamari soy sauce. Combine the two mixtures in oiled casserole. Bake, uncovered, for 25 minutes at 350°. Top with cheese; bake 5 minutes longer. *PROTEIN: 58.3 grams; CALORIES: 1286*

Christine Ambrosone   *Brenda Wilson*
Buffalo, New York   *Carlyle, Sask., Canada*

LIVE LONGER CASSEROLE

3 small **zucchini**, sliced
1 C. sliced **mushrooms**
2 T. **butter**
3 large **tomatoes**, chopped
3 C. torn **spinach** leaves
½ t. **salt** (or less)
8 oz. whole wheat **pasta**, cooked and drained
6 oz. Swiss **cheese**, sliced
6 oz. Cheddar **cheese**, sliced

Saute zucchini and mushrooms in butter in a large skillet until softened. Add tomatoes, spinach and salt. Simmer for 15 minutes. Mix in pasta. Place in 9 x 13" casserole and arrange cheese slices on top. Heat under broiler for 5 minutes, or until cheese is bubbly.

PROTEIN: 151.8 grams; CALORIES: 2665

Susan Marquess
Dallas, Texas

BROCCOLI (OR SPINACH) CASSEROLE

4 to 6 C. bite-sized pieces of fresh **broccoli**, or 20 oz. frozen, thawed and drained broccoli or spinach
⅓ C. chopped **onion**
1½ C. grated Cheddar **cheese**
1 lb. cream-style **cottage cheese**
4 **eggs**, beaten
1 C. chopped **mushrooms** or corn kernels
½ t. **salt**
¼ t. **pepper**

In a buttered 2½-qt. casserole, stir together all the ingredients. Bake, uncovered, at 325° for 35 minutes or until lightly set. Let the casserole cool 10 minutes before cutting and enjoying it. This rest period helps ensure neater portions and reduces the chance of burning yourself on the hot cheese!

PROTEIN: 126.5 grams; CALORIES: 1507

Karen Nussbaum   *Julie Delaplane*
Peru, Illinois   *Anderson, Indiana*

SPINACH-RICE CASSEROLE

1 C. **milk**
4 **eggs**
1 T. **worcestershire sauce**
½ t. **tarragon**
4 C. cooked **brown rice**
10 oz. chopped **spinach**, steamed

¼ C. chopped **green pepper**
1 lb. grated **cheese**, Cheddar or Swiss
¼ to ½ C. **nutritional yeast** (optional)
½ t. **seasoned salt** (or less)
½ to 1 C. **seeds** and **nuts**

Blend liquids and tarragon. Stir in remaining ingredients except nuts and seeds. Pour into oiled casserole; top with nuts and seeds. Bake at 375° for 35 minutes.

PROTEIN: 199.7 CALORIES: 3480

Betsy Shafer   *Marti Koch*   *Ronaele Berry*
Cupertino, California *Gainesville, Georgia*   *Johnstown, Nebraska*

GARLIC CHEESE GRITS

1 C. **hominy grits**
4 c. **water**
1 t. **salt**
1½ C. grated Cheddar **cheese**
½ C. **butter**
½ C. **milk**
2 **eggs**, beaten
1 small clove **garlic**, minced

Cook grits in boiling salted water until water is absorbed. Add remaining ingredients. Bake in greased 2-qt. casserole at 350° for 1 hour.

PROTEIN: 66 grams; CALORIES: 1987

Jean Merrill
Southgate, Kentucky

EGGPLANT CUSTARD BAKE

1½-lb. **eggplant,** peeled and
 sliced ½" thick
2 **eggs**
1 C. **milk**
dash of **salt**
dash of **pepper**
⅓ C. minced **onion**
2 cloves **garlic,** minced
1 large **carrot,** grated
1 T. **oil**
1 t. **basil**
½ t. **oregano**
½ t. **salt**
2 C. **tomato sauce**
½ C. **sesame seeds**
½ C. grated Mozzarella **cheese**

Arrange eggplant in greased 9 x 13"
baking dish. Beat eggs, milk, salt
and pepper until smooth. Pour over
eggplant. Bake at 375° for 25 minutes, or until firm.

While custard bakes, saute onion,
garlic and carrot in oil for 5 minutes.
Add basil, oregano, salt and tomato
sauce. Simmer 10 minutes. Pour
sauce over eggplant custard. Sprinkle with seeds and cheese. Broil or
return to hot oven, until top is lightly
browned.

This recipe convinced our family
that a vegetable could be the basis
of a delicious, satisfying meatless
main dish. It is still one of our
favorites.   *P.: 71.2 gms.; C.: 1570*

Susan Kaseman
Alexandria, Virginia

LENTIL SAUSAGE CASSEROLE

2 C. dried **lentils,** cooked and
 drained (p. 290) (4½ to 5 C.
 cooked)
½ C. lentil cooking **liquid**
1 lb. **pork sausage,** crumbled
 (p. 282)
1 small **onion,** minced
½ t. **salt**
dash of **pepper**
1 T. **worcestershire sauce**
1 C. grated Cheddar **cheese**

Brown sausage in a skillet. Add remaining ingredients except cheese.
Pat into an oiled 9 x 13" baking dish.
Sprinkle with cheese. Bake at 400°
for 30 minutes.

This easy casserole is a favorite
of ours. Our toddler loves to eat it
with his fingers. It is also good reheated.   *P.: 197.9; CALORIES: 3433*

Marsha Wilson
Jefferson City, Missouri

KITCHENER SPECIAL

1 lb. **pork sausage** (p. 282)
½ C. chopped **onion**
½ C. sliced **celery**
½ t. **salt**
dash of **pepper**
1 t. **chili powder**
½ t. dry **mustard**
½ t. **celery seeds** (optional)
2 to 3 handfuls raw **noodles**
½ C. **water**
4 C. **tomatoes,** quartered
1 C. grated Cheddar **cheese**
¼ C. grated **cheese** for serving

Cut sausage into 1" lengths. Brown
in large pot or baking dish. Add
onion, celery and seasonings. Mix
well. Add remaining ingredients.
Simmer, or bake at 350°, for 30 minutes. Top with grated cheese and
serve hot, with **bread**.

This dish freezes well if fresh,
rather than frozen, sausage is used.

PROTEIN: 133 grams; CALORIES: 2733

Linda Mellway
Kitchener, Ont., Canada

CHEESE ENCHILADAS

Sauce:
3 T. oil
1 to 2 T. chili powder
2 T. flour
2 C. water
1 t. vinegar
½ t. garlic powder
½ t. oregano
½ t. salt (or less)

Tortillas:
8 tortillas (p. 168)
2 T. oil

Filling:
2 C. cooked pinto beans
4 T. chopped green onion
1 C. cottage cheese or
 grated sharp cheese
½ C. chopped green pepper
¼ C. chopped almonds or
 sunflower seeds
½ C. wheat germ (optional)
½ C. chopped black or green
 olives (optional)

Topping:
1 C. grated cheese
1 C. plain yogurt (optional)
2 T. chopped onion (optional)

Combine sauce ingredients. Bring to a boil; simmer 5 minutes. Fry tortillas in hot oil briefly. Mash beans and other filling ingredients. Divide filling among tortillas and roll up. Place seam side down in shallow baking dish. Pour sauce over all. Top with cheese. Bake at 350° for 20 minutes, basting occasionally with sauce. Serve with yogurt and onion mixture, if desired.

This is a quick and easy meal if you prepare the sauce and filling ahead of time.

PROTEIN: 152.2 grams; CALORIES: 3176

Christine Lebo　　*Laurie Carroll*
Hayfork, California　　*Suttons Bay, Michigan*

Dolly Brown
Fairfax, Virginia

ENCHILADAS

2 large chicken breasts, cooked
1 C. chopped onion
1 clove garlic, minced
2 T. butter
3 or 4 tomatoes, peeled and
 chopped, or 2 C. stewed
1 C. tomato sauce or
 4 C. tomatoes, boiled down
¼ C. chopped green chilies
1 t. ground cumin (optional)
½ t. salt
½ t. oregano
½ t. basil
12 corn tortillas (p. 168)
2½ C. grated cheese (Monterey
 Jack or any mild, firm cheese)
¾ C. yogurt or sour cream

Cut chicken into bite-sized pieces. Saute onion and garlic in butter. Add tomatoes, tomato sauce, chilies, cumin, salt, oregano and basil. Bring to a boil; reduce heat and simmer, covered, for 20 minutes. Remove from heat. Dip tortilla in sauce to coat and soften. Place some chicken and 2 T. cheese on each tortilla. Roll up, placing seam side down in a 9 x 12 x 2" pan. Blend yogurt into remaining sauce. Pour over tortillas. Sprinkle with remaining cheese. Cover and bake at 350° for 20 to 30 minutes. Do not overbake.

Try this with ground beef or refried beans instead of chicken.

PROTEIN: 198.2 grams; CALORIES: 2565

Kathleen Herndon
Topeka, Kansas

Variation: Omit yogurt. Use 1 more cup of tomato sauce.

BURROS

10 to 12 **tortillas**
½ recipe Bean Filling from
    cheese enchiladas
1 lb. ground **beef**, browned
    (optional)
2 C. grated Cheddar **cheese**
2 C. shredded **lettuce**
2 C. chopped **tomatoes**
hot sauce (optional)

In each tortilla, place 2 T. bean filling, 2 T. meat and 1 T. cheese. Roll up; wrap in foil. Fill all tortillas. Refrigerate or freeze, if desired. Bake at 350° for 30 minutes if freshly made, 45 minutes if cold, 1 hour if frozen. Serve with remaining cheese, lettuce and tomatoes.

On a particularly busy day, it's so easy to bake the frozen burros, and I have only the lettuce, tomatoes and cheese to prepare! Even the youngest toddler can handle a slice of burro himself. *P.: 204.8 gms.; C.: 3046*

Noelle Deinken
Thousand Oaks, California

HIGHLAND HOT POT

1 lb. **beef** (bottom round
    or chuck)
3 T. whole wheat **flour**
½ lb. link **sausages**, halved (p. 282)
4 medium **potatoes**, cut in
    ¼" slices
2 **apples**, peeled and cut in
    ¼" slices
1 **onion**, cut in ¼" slices
½ t. **salt** (or less)
dash of **pepper**
2 C. **tomato juice**
3 beef **bouillon cubes**
pinch of **sage**

Cube and flour beef. Put half the potatoes, apples and onion in 2½ to 3-qt. casserole. Add meats, then remaining fruit and vegetables. Season layers with salt and pepper. Heat tomato juice, dissolve bouillon, add sage. Pour over casserole. Bake, covered, at 350° for 1½ hours.

PROTEIN: 132.9 grams; CALORIES: 2535

Pan Usticke
Kingston, New York

BARBECUED SPARE RIBS

3 to 4 lbs. country-style
    spare ribs (or chicken
    parts)
1 large **onion**, sliced

Barbecue Sauce:
2 T. **vinegar**
2 T. **worcestershire sauce**
½ t. **salt**
dash of **pepper**
1 t. **paprika**
1 t. **chili powder**
¼ t. ground **nutmeg**
¾ C. **water**
¾ C. **catsup** (p. 252)
P.: 4.2 gms.; C. 223

Place onion slices on top of meat in 9 x 12" baking pan. Mix sauce ingredients. Pour over ribs. Cover and bake at 350° for 1½ hours. Uncover, baste, then continue baking for an additional 30 minutes.

Slow-Cooker: Layer ribs and onions in slow-cooker. Pour sauce over ribs. Cook on low for 8 to 10 hours. Save leftover sauce for marinating or basting chicken. *P.: 126 gms.; C: 2870*

Gayle Brunner   *Fran Vasi*
New Holstein, Wisconsin   *Barstow, California*

CABBAGE ROLLS

½ C. **millet**
1½ t. **oil**
dash of **cayenne pepper**
1½ C. **water**
½ C. grated **carrots**
½ C. chopped **onions**
½ C. grated Parmesan **cheese**
1 T. chopped, fresh **parsley**
6 to 8 large **cabbage leaves**,
   steamed, or more if small

Sauce:
1 C. **tomato sauce**
2 T. **lemon juice**
1 to 2 T. **honey**
½ t. ground **allspice**

Brown millet in hot oil in frying pan, stirring for 2 to 3 minutes. Add cayenne and water. Cover and simmer until water is absorbed, about 35 minutes. Mix in rest of ingredients except cabbage. Place 2 to 3 T. millet mixture into each cabbage leaf. Roll up. Lay, seam side down, in oiled baking dish. Cover with tomato sauce mixture. Bake at 325° for 30 minutes.

PROTEIN: 33.7 grams; CALORIES: 887

Delores Wilder
Boone, North Carolina

STUFFED GREEN PEPPERS

1 lb. ground **beef**
1 medium **onion**, chopped
½ lb. **mushrooms**, sliced
   (optional)
2 C. **tomato juice**
½ C. **brown rice**
4 oz. grated **cheese** (optional)
½ t. **salt**
dash of **pepper**
oregano, basil, rosemary,
   thyme, worcestershire
   sauce (optional)
6 **green peppers**

Brown meat; drain. Saute onion and mushrooms. Add tomato juice; bring to a boil. Add rice; cover and simmer until rice is tender (40 minutes). Add cheese and seasonings.

Cut tops from peppers; remove core and seeds. Steam for 5 minutes. Omit precooking if a crisper texture is desired. Stuff peppers. May be frozen at this time. Defrost before baking. Bake at 350° for 30 minutes.

PROTEIN: 107.6 grams; CALORIES: 1411

Marilynn Berry   *Christine Pando*   *Jan Gilpin*   *Cindy Garrison*
Lawrenceville, Georgia   *Roselle, Illinois*   *Taylorville, Illinois* *Canonsburg, Pennsylvania*

CABBAGE ROLLS

1 medium **cabbage**
2 lbs. ground **beef**
2 **eggs**
1 **onion**, chopped
1 T. **worcestershire sauce**
½ t. **salt** (or less)
dash of **pepper**
3 C. cooked **brown rice**
2 C. **tomato sauce**

Core and steam cabbage for 10 to 15 minutes. Separate leaves. Mix all other ingredients except tomato sauce. Place about ¼ C. meat mixture on each leaf.

Beginning at the thinner edge of the leaf, roll up around the meat. Line bottom of Dutch oven with leftover or torn leaves. Place cabbage rolls over these and cover with any

extra leaves. Pour tomato sauce over all. Cover and simmer for 2 hours. Rolls may be frozen and reheated in the oven. *PROTEIN: 215.5 grams; CALORIES: 3078*

Denise Parker   *Connie B. Comeaux*   *Karen Woodend*
Ridgecrest, California *New Iberia, Louisiana*   *Rockville, Maryland*

VEGGIE-RICE BAKE

6 medium **zucchini**, sliced
1½ to 2 C. cooked **brown rice**
  or whole wheat pasta
2 C. plain **yogurt** or tofu
½ to 1 C. diced **green pepper**
5 medium **tomatoes**, sliced
1 C. sliced **mushrooms**
3 **green onions** and tops, sliced
2 C. grated **cheese** (Cheddar,
  Jack or Muenster)

Steam zucchini until slightly tender. Layer in greased oblong pan in this order: rice, yogurt or tofu, vegetables, cheese. (Refrigerate at this point, if you are making this ahead.) Bake at 350° for 30 to 40 minutes.

PROTEIN: 114.9 grams; CALORIES: 1958

Dede Duly
Burbank, California

Janet Glover
Russiaville, Indiana

Variation: Saute vegetables (except tomatoes) in 2 T. oil. Add 4 C. tomatoes and their juice, ½ C. **tomato sauce**, ½ t. *each:* **basil, oregano, garlic powder, thyme, marjoram** and ground **cinnamon**. Stir in rice and tofu. Pour into greased casserole. Top with cheese. Bake at 350° for 20 minutes.

PROTEIN: 124.5 grams; CALORIES: 2270

Margaret MacPherson
Hudson, Massachusetts

SUPER SIX-LAYER CASSEROLE

1 C. raw **brown rice**
2 C. cooked **soybeans** or
  1 lb. ground beef, browned
1 C. sliced **onion**
1 **green pepper**, diced
2 C. grated **carrots**
½ t. **salt** (or less)
½ t. **basil**
2 C. **tomato juice**
2 T. **worcestershire sauce**
1 C. grated sharp **cheese**
¼ to ½ C. **wheat germ** (optional)

In oiled 3-qt. casserole, arrange ingredients: rice, beans or beef, onion, pepper, carrots. Salt lightly, if desired. Combine basil and liquids; pour over casserole. Top with cheese and wheat germ. Bake, tightly covered, for 1½ hours at 350°.

This dish is simple, nutritious, and appealing to all members of the family. *PROTEIN: 108.2 grams; CALORIES: 2087*

Barbara Faust
Springfield, Ohio

Janet Harwell
Fort Worth, Texas

DAVID'S FAVORITE CASSEROLE

1 lb. ground **beef**
1 **onion**, chopped
2 C. **tomato sauce**
½ t. **salt** (or less)
dash of **pepper**
8 oz. **noodles**, cooked
2 C. sliced **carrots**, cooked
1 C. **yogurt** or sour cream
1 C. **cottage cheese**
¼ C. fresh, chopped **parsley**
1 C. grated Cheddar **cheese**

Brown beef and onion; drain. Add tomato sauce and seasonings. Simmer 5 minutes. Blend noodles, carrots, yogurt, cottage cheese and parsley. In a 2½-qt. casserole, alternoodle mixture 4 times, beginning with meat and ending with noodles. Top with grated cheese. Bake at 350° for 30 minutes. Freezes well.

PROTEIN: 199.2 grams; CALORIES: 2758

Mary Pat Barney
Odell, Illinois

PORK CHOP 'N CABBAGE CASSEROLE

4 **pork chops**
¼ t. **salt**
dash of **pepper**
1 T. olive **oil**
½ medium head **cabbage**
2 **tomatoes**, quartered
½ C. **raisins**
garlic and **onion powder** to taste

Season chops; brown in oil. Remove from pan. Cut cabbage into 2" pieces. Mix with tomatoes and raisins in same pan. Saute 3 minutes. Sprinkle with garlic and onion powder. Lay chops on top of vegetables; cover. Simmer 45 minutes until cabbage is soft and raisins plump. This casserole goes well with **brown rice**.

PROTEIN: 108.1 grams; CALORIES: 1243

Linda C. Schutsky
Ronks, Pennsylvania

PORK CHOPS AND BROWN RICE

3 to 4 **pork chops**
1 C. **brown rice**
2½ C. boiling **water**
¼ t. **thyme**
½ C. chopped **green pepper**
¼ C. chopped **onion**
1 t. **garlic salt**
1 t. **worcestershire sauce**

Optional:
2 **tomatoes**
1 **onion**, sliced
½ **bell pepper**, sliced

Soak rice in water for at least 30 minutes. Brown pork chops. Set aside. In same frying pan, add remaining ingredients. Simmer 10 minutes. Pour rice mixture into a greased, 9 x 9" baking dish or leave in skillet, if ovenproof. Set chops (and vegetables, if you wish) on top. Cover. Bake at 350° for 1 hour.

PROTEIN: 94 grams; CALORIES: 1678

Susan Reed
Anderson, Indiana

Kathy Mead
Leland, Michigan

Glenda Caudle
Columbia, Tennessee

JOE'S GALICIAN CHICKEN AND RICE

1 **chicken**, cut up
3 **chicken backs** or backs and necks
2 slices nitrite-free **bacon**, cut up
pinch of **oregano**
3 **bay leaves**
dash of **saffron** (optional)
1 t. **salt**
dash of **pepper**
2 C. **brown rice**
4 C. **water**
1½ C. **peas** (10 oz. frozen)
2 C. (16 oz.) chopped **tomatoes** (optional)

Fry chicken pieces and bacon for 15 minutes. Remove to Dutch oven (one that can go from range to oven). Add seasonings, rice and water. Simmer, covered, for 30 to 45 minutes. Rice will be rich, golden color. Stir in peas and tomatoes. Bake, covered, at 400° for 20 minutes. Rice will be crispy on bottom of pot.

My father brought this recipe with him from Galicia, a province of Spain. It is a hearty, well-balanced meal. *PROTEIN: 271.9 grams; CALORIES: 3351*

Karen Vespignani
Lake Hiawatha, New Jersey

NANCY'S EASY CHICKEN AND RICE

3 lb. whole frying **chicken**
1 C. **brown rice**
2 C. **water**
½ t. **salt** (or less)
1½ T. **butter** or margarine
3 T. chopped, fresh **parsley**
   (1 T. flakes)
½ t. **salt** (or less)
dash of **pepper**

Optional:
½ C. chopped **onions**
½ C. chopped **celery**
¼ C. chopped **green pepper**
½ C. **raisins** (try golden)
½ C. chopped **nuts** (walnuts,
   pecans, almonds)
½ lb. **mushrooms,** sliced
1 C. unsweetened, crushed
   pineapple

Place rice, water, ½ t. salt, butter and parsley in 4-qt. casserole. Stir and bring to a boil. Salt and pepper chicken. Lay chicken on top of rice. Lower heat to simmer; cover tightly and cook 45 to 60 minutes, until water is absorbed and chicken is tender.

A good recipe to use when it is 4 o'clock and you don't know what to fix for dinner. It is easy, nutritious and delicious. For a fancier meal, saute any or all of the optional ingredients. Add to rice before serving.

PROTEIN: 188.3 grams; CALORIES: 2024
Nancy Porter
Fayetteville, Arkansas

CHICKEN AND RICE CASSEROLE

2 C. cooked, diced **chicken**
3 to 5 C. cooked **brown rice**
1 stalk **celery,** chopped
1 medium **onion,** chopped
2 medium **carrots,** chopped
1 medium **apple,** chopped
   (optional)
2 T. **oil**
2 t. **curry powder**
1 C. chicken **stock**
1 C. **milk,** yogurt or cream
½ t. **salt** (or less)
dash of **pepper**

Saute celery, onion, carrots and apple in oil. Cook 5 minutes. Mix all ingredients together. Put in lightly oiled 9 x 13" pan; sprinkle with additional curry powder. Bake at 350° for 40 minutes. Try other vegetables, more or less chicken or rice.

PROTEIN: 181.1 grams; CALORIES: 2128
Joanne Patton
Evansville, Indiana

CHICKEN ELVIRA
(Cuban-Style Chicken Fricassee)

3 lb. whole frying **chicken**
1 **green pepper,** cut up
1 **onion,** chopped
2 cloves **garlic,** minced
¼ C. **raisins**
¼ C. stuffed **olives,** cut in half
   or sliced
2 T. **tomato sauce**
½ t. ground **cumin**
1 C. dry **white wine**
1 C. **water**
½ t. **salt** (or less)
dash of **pepper**

Combine all ingredients in a large pot. Stir. Cover and simmer for 1 to 1½ hours, until sauce begins to thicken. Serve with steaming hot rice. Use sauce as gravy.

PROTEIN: 177.6 grams; CALORIES: 1473
Christie Hart de Rodriguez
Dumont, New Jersey

SEAFARERS' BAKE

1½ C. medium **white sauce**
  (p. 251)
8 oz. cooked, cleaned **shrimp,**
  cut into bite-sized pieces
1 lb. **fish fillets,** cubed
1 lb. fresh **spinach,** chopped and
  cooked or frozen, thawed
1 large **onion,** chopped
2 T. **oil**
3 oz. **cream cheese,** softened
1 C. cream-style **cottage cheese**
1 **egg,** beaten
1 t. **Italian seasoning** or
  ¼ t. *each* oregano, thyme and
  basil
¼ t. **salt** (or less)
dash of **pepper**
9 **lasagne noodles,** cooked
3 T. grated Parmesan **cheese**
2 T. seasoned **bread crumbs**
½ C. grated sharp Cheddar **cheese**
2 T. **butter**

Prepare white sauce. Add shrimp
and fish. Set aside. Squeeze excess
moisture from spinach. Saute onion
in oil until soft. Mix with spinach,
cream and cottage cheeses, egg and
seasonings. Arrange 3 noodles in
the bottom of a greased, oblong 9 x
13" baking dish. Spread with ⅓ of
the spinach, then ⅓ of the fish. Repeat layers, ending with fish. Mix
Parmesan with bread crumbs. Sprinkle on top. Bake at 350° for 45 minutes. Top with Cheddar cheese. Dot
with butter. Bake 5 minutes longer.
Let set 20 minutes before cutting into squares. Freezes well after baking. Takes 30 to 40 minutes to prepare.   *PROTEIN: 254 grams; CALORIES: 3568*

Rose Hufnagel
Rochester, Pennsylvania

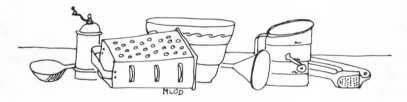

TUNA UNDER BISCUITS

6½ oz. **tuna,** drained
1½ C. medium **white sauce**
  (p. 251)
¼ lb. **mushrooms,** sliced
2 T. chopped or pearl **onions**
  (optional)
2 C. **peas**
⅓ C. **water**

Topping:
biscuit dough for **1**2 biscuits
  (p. 124)
1½ C. (6 oz.) grated **cheese**

Prepare white sauce, sauteing
mushrooms and onions before adding flour. Stir in tuna, peas and
water. Pour into a deep 2½-qt. baking dish. Place in oven and set at
425°. Prepare biscuit dough. Roll into a 10 x 12" rectangle. Sprinkle with
cheese. Roll jellyroll fashion, seal-
ing with your fingers as you roll.
Seal ends and slice into 12 1" biscuits. When tuna mixture is hot and
bubbly, remove from oven. Arrange
biscuits on top, crowding if necessary. Return to oven for 20 to 30 minutes until biscuits are brown.

PROTEIN: 177.5 grams; CALORIES: 3499

Carol Shively
Shreveport, Louisiana

SCALLOPED TUNA

12 oz. **tuna,** drained
2 C. medium **white sauce** (p. 251)
½ t. **salt**
dash of **pepper**
2 T. prepared **mustard**
3¼ C. cooked, sliced **potatoes**
1 C. chopped **onion**

Make white sauce. Add seasonings. Layer potatoes, tuna and onion in greased 1½-quart casserole. Add sauce. Bake at 375° for 45 minutes.

PROTEIN: 124.9 grams; CALORIES: 1941

Susan Renes
Moscow, Idaho

SPINACH-MUSHROOM CREPES

double recipe **Swedish pancakes** (p. 13)
1 C. chopped **onion**
1½ lb. fresh **mushrooms,** chopped
1 lb. chopped **spinach,** fresh or frozen
2 T. **butter**
1½ lb. grated **cheese** (Monterey Jack, Havarti, or Mozzarella)

Saute onions, mushrooms and spinach in butter for 10 minutes to make filling.

Assembly: Cover pale side of each crepe with a thin layer of cheese, then spoon 1 to 2 T. of filling down its middle. Roll up the crepe, and place it seam side down in an oiled, shallow baking dish, touching its "neighbors." Sprinkle remaining cheese on top of all the crepes. Bake at 350° for 15 minutes. This makes enough for 10 people, but leftovers freeze well.

PROTEIN: 279.5 grams; CALORIES: 4547

Marion Bueche
Gray, Sask., Canada

EASY BEANS

2 C. dried **beans**
4 to 5 C. hot **water**
1 to 2 **onions,** sliced (optional)
1 clove **garlic,** minced (optional)

Combine ingredients in a 3½-qt. slow-cooker. Put on high setting for 6 to 8 hours, or on low for 10 to 12 hours.

I freeze cooked beans in recipe-sized portions. I have found a slow-cooker a real time-saver. Dinner cooks itself while I play with my baby!

PROTEIN: 91.7 grams; CALORIES: 1414

Fran Vasi
Barstow, California

Variation #1: Add 3 T. **molasses,** 1 t. dry **mustard,** 1 t. ground **ginger** or chili powder, 1 C. **tomato sauce** or catsup, and 1 **green pepper,** chopped, to above recipe. Proceed as directed.   *PROTEIN: 91.7 grams; CALORIES: 1695*

Variation #2: Omit dried beans. Substitute 4 C. **sprouted soybeans.**

PROTEIN: 27.7 grams; CALORIES: 234

Gail Berke   Joan E. Branch   Susan Fortson Magee
Milford, Massachusetts Bremerton, Washington Brownsville, Texas

Stews

GRANDMA MARY'S AUTHENTIC HUNGARIAN BEEF PAPRIKASH

3 lb. **beef** chuck or round,
  cut into 1" cubes
3 T. **oil** to brown
2 large **onions**, chopped
1 to 3 t. **paprika**
1 t. **salt** (or less)
dash of **pepper**
4 T. fresh, chopped **parsley**
8 **potatoes**, cut up
8 **carrots**, sliced
water

Brown beef cubes in oil a few at a time. Return to pot; add onions, paprika, salt and pepper. Cook over low heat, adding water as needed. After 15 minutes, add parsley. Cook, covered, for 1½ hours or until tender. Add potatoes and carrots and enough water to almost cover. Cook over medium heat for 30 minutes. You may omit the potatoes and use **parsnips**; then serve with **rice, noodles** or **mashed potatoes**.

My husband's grandmother, an unparalleled cook, gave me this recipe in a treasure-chest-full when I married into the family. She taught this unskilled Irish-French-German bride to become an acceptable Hungarian cook.

PROTEIN: 249.7 grams; CALORIES: 6168

Gail Berke
Milford, Massachusetts

Slow-Cooker. Brown beef in oil. Transfer to slow-cooker. Add onions, paprika, salt, pepper and parsley. Cover with water. Cook 4 to 5 hours on **high**, or 8 to 10 hours on **low**. Add carrots and potatoes halfway through the cooking process.

"FOUR ALARM" CHILI

3 lbs. lean **beef** (chuck), diced
  or ground beef
¼ C. olive **oil**
4 C. **water**
6 T. **chili powder***
1½ t. **salt** (or less)
6 cloves **garlic**, minced
1 t. ground **cumin**
1 t. **marjoram**
1 t. red **pepper**
1 T. **sugar** or honey
3 T. **paprika**
3 T. **flour**
6 T. **cornmeal**
1 C. **water**
4 C. cooked **pinto beans**
  *(or 1 T. for "one-alarm" chili)

Heat oil in 6-qt. pot. Sear diced meat, stirring constantly, until no longer red. Add water, cover and cook 1½ to 2 hours, until tender. Or brown and drain ground beef. Add other ingredients to the beef through paprika. Cook 30 minutes. Mix flour, cornmeal and water. Add to chili. Cook 5 minutes. Stir and serve with cooked pinto beans.

This is true "4-alarm" chili and should be served with plenty of cold beverages.

PROTEIN: 259.4 grams; CALORIES: 4389
Deb Dewey
Rochester, New York

CHILI CON CASHEWS

1 clove **garlic**, minced
1 to 2 **carrots**, grated
2 **onions**, chopped
1 to 2 **green peppers**, chopped
1 to 2 T. **oil**
1 C. raw **cashews**
2 to 3 C. **kidney beans**, cooked
4 C. chopped **tomatoes**, with
their liquid
1 t. *each* **basil** and **oregano**
1 t. **chili powder**, or to taste
1 t. ground **cumin**
1 **bay leaf**

½ t. **salt** or less
dash of **pepper**
¼ C. **raisins**
½ C. grated **cheese**, Swiss
or Cheddar
¼ to ½ C. **sesame seeds**
1 recipe **cornbread** (p. 125) or
whole wheat pasta

Optional:
2 T. dry **wine** or vinegar
½ lb. **mushrooms**, sliced
1 medium **zucchini**, sliced

Saute garlic and vegetables (except tomatoes) in oil. Add nuts, beans, tomatoes, seasonings, raisins and wine if used. Simmer for at least 2 hours, until thick, in covered pot or slow-cooker. Serve topped with cheese and seeds, over cornbread or pasta.   *P.: 92.1 gms.; C.: 2072 + cornbread*

Lois Lake Raabe   Georgine Christensen   Chris Fletcher   Linda Springer
Easton, Connecticut   Peshastin, Washington   Alexandria, Indiana   Knoxville, Tennessee

CHILI CON CARNE

1 lb. ground **beef** or
ground turkey
1 C. chopped **onion**
1 C. chopped **green pepper**
4 C. **tomatoes** and ¾ C. **tomato
paste** *or* 2 C. tomatoes and
1 C. tomato sauce
2 t. **chili powder**
½ t. **salt** (or less)
pinch of **cayenne pepper**
pinch of **paprika**
2 to 3 C. cooked **kidney beans**

Brown meat with onion and peppers. Drain. Add remaining ingredients except beans. Cook, uncovered, for 45 minutes. Add beans and heat through. This dish is full of protein from the meat and beans, and freezes well. Great with grilled cheese sandwiches.

PROTEIN: 113.2 grams; CALORIES: 1532

Karen A. Barclay
Connellsville, Pennsylvania

SPICY HOPPIN' JOHN

2 C. dried **black-eyed peas**
or white navy beans
8 C. **water**
1 medium **ham hock**
2 C. chopped **tomatoes**
1 C. chopped **celery**
1 C. chopped **onion**
½ t. **salt** or less
2 t. **chili powder**
¼ t. crushed **basil**
1 **bay leaf**
1 C. raw **brown rice**

Rinse peas. Soak overnight (or boil 2 minutes, let stand 1 hour.) Do not drain. Add all of the ingredients except rice. Simmer 1¼ hours, or until peas are tender. Remove ham meat from bone. Add meat and rice to peas. Simmer until rice is tender, or longer. Serve with cornbread, green onions and sliced tomatoes.

PROTEIN: 150.3 grams; CALORIES: 2605

Jennifer Elam   Lynn Hicks
Huntsville, Alabama   Martinez, California

PASTA E FAGIOLE
("Pasta Fazool")

2 to 3 C. cooked **beans** (a good
   combination is red kidney,
   great northern and garbanzo)
1 medium **onion**, chopped
2 cloves **garlic**, minced
1 **carrot**, grated
½ stalk **celery**, sliced
2 T. **oil**
¼ C. **tomato puree**
¼ t. **oregano**
½ t. **salt** (or less)
dash of **pepper**
dash of **hot red pepper**
   (optional)
¼ C. chopped fresh **parsley**
   (2 T. dried)
liquid to make soup consistency
   (about 5 to 6 C.)
¼ C. chopped **green pepper**
1 C. grated **zucchini**
1 C. whole grain **pasta**,
   cooked and drained
grated Parmesan **cheese**
   (optional)

Saute onion, garlic, carrot and celery in oil. Add beans, tomato puree, seasonings and liquid. Simmer for 30 minutes. Add pepper and zucchini. Simmer 10 minutes longer. Add pasta. Sprinkle Parmesan on each serving, if desired.

This dish is a soup or stew, hearty enough for dinner with salad and homemade bread. The combination of whole grain pasta and beans ("fagiole") increases the protein value of both, and typifies traditional ways of achieving good nutrition and taste without animal protein.

PROTEIN: 73 grams; CALORIES: 1471

Lynn Ruggiero
Fitchburg, Massachusetts

AUTHENTIC INDIAN BEEF CURRY

1 to 1½ lbs. stewing **beef**
4 C. **water**
4 C. **tomatoes**
1 C. **tomato sauce**
1 to 3 T. **curry powder** (p. 286)
1 to 3 T. **cornstarch** to thicken
½ t. **salt** (or less)

Condiments:
4 C. cooked **brown rice**
2 C. *each*, in separate bowls:
   grated **cheese**
   chopped **tomatoes**
   chopped **green peppers**
   chopped hard-cooked **eggs**
   chopped **onions**
   chopped **peanuts**
   unsweetened **pineapple** chunks
   unsweetened, shredded **coconut**
   sliced **bananas**

Cube meat. Cover with water and cook until tender. Break up with a fork. Add remaining ingredients. Simmer 30 minutes, until thickened. While it is cooking, assemble the family to prepare the condiments. Amazingly delicious. My teenagers love to help prepare and serve it to friends, as well as to eat it. This is everyday fare where we lived in Africa.

PROTEIN: 321.3 grams; CALORIES: 7261

Wista Waldroop
Tahlequah, Oklahoma

NEW ORLEANS RED BEANS AND RICE

2½ C. dried **red kidney beans**
9 C. **water**
1 large **bay leaf**
2 to 3 T. tamari **soy sauce**
1 large **onion**, chopped
1 large clove **garlic**, minced
1 stalk **celery**, chopped
¼ t. **turmeric**
½ t. ground **cumin**
¾ t. ground **coriander**
3 T. **oil**
2 to 4 C. cooked **brown rice**

Rinse beans. Pour into water. Bring to boil; reduce heat to simmer. Add bay leaf and soy sauce. Saute vegetables and spices in oil until onions are soft. Add to beans. Simmer for about 2½ hours, until beans are soft and juices are creamy. Serve over rice.

This is a New Orleans favorite, and is traditionally served every Monday in homes and restaurants. The original is cooked with ham, pickled meat and sausage. This is my own "vegetarian" version—easy on the budget, and a complete protein without meat.

PROTEIN: 192.2 grams; CALORIES: 2515

Lulla K. Bell
Long Beach, Mississippi

KIMA

1 lb. ground **beef** or
   tofu, cubed
1 **onion**, chopped
1 clove **garlic**, minced
1 T. **butter**
1½ t. **curry powder** (p. 286)
½ t. **salt** (or less)
dash of **pepper**
2 to 3 t. **soy sauce**
2 **potatoes**, diced
2 **carrots**, diced
1 C. **peas**
1 stalk **celery**, diced
2 or 3 **tomatoes**, quartered

Saute onion and garlic in butter. Add beef or tofu and brown. Add seasonings and vegetables. Simmer 30 minutes.

This may be adapted to include any favorite foods. **Mushrooms** make a delicious addition. I've found toddlers love this meal as well as adults because all the food is in tasty, bite-sized pieces.

PROTEIN: 102.7 grams; CALORIES: 1314

Rose Isdale
Christchurch, New Zealand

BOEUF BOURGUIGNON STEW

6 strips nitrite-free **bacon**
2 lbs. **beef** (rump or chuck), cubed
1 medium **onion**, chopped
1 C. **water**
1 T. **tomato paste**
2 cloves **garlic**, minced
½ t. **thyme**
1 **bay leaf**
½ lb. tiny white **onions**
½ lb. **mushrooms**, sliced
½ C. **burgundy wine**
4 to 6 **potatoes**, quartered or
   8 to 10 **new potatoes**, peeled
½ to 1 lb. **green beans**

Fry bacon. Brown cubed meat in bacon drippings. Add onion and cook until soft. Add remaining ingredients except potatoes and beans. Cook in Dutch oven for 4 hours on low, or in slow-cooker for 8 to 10 hours on low. ½ hour before serving, add potatoes and beans. When potatoes are soft, dinner is ready. Great for company or a mother with a new baby.

PROTEIN: 201.3 GRAMS; CALORIES: 3021

Pam Dunne
Atwater, California

KA-WAHJ
(Baked Stew)

2 lbs. **beef** or lamb
(stew or ground)
1 large **onion**, sliced and cut
in half
8 large **tomatoes**, cubed
2 to 3 **zucchini** or summer
squash, cubed
4 **potatoes**, cubed
2 **eggplants**, cubed
½ lb. **okra**, tops removed
1 large **green pepper**, in strips
2 T. **oil**
½ t. **salt**
dash of **pepper**
ground **allspice** to taste
water
6 oz. **tomato paste** (optional)

Place stew meat and vegetables (except okra) in a 9 x 13 x 2" baking dish. (You may need 2 until vegetables cook down.) Drizzle some oil over all. Season with salt, pepper and allspice. Stir to coat. Add water to fill pan halfway. For thicker sauce, stir in tomato paste. Bake at 450° until half done, stirring occasionally. Add okra. (If using ground meat, form meat, salt, pepper and allspice into balls; brown and add now.) Continue to bake, at 350°, until tender. Total cooking time is 1½ to 2 hours.

This stew is traditionally eaten by dipping it up with pita bread, but you can use a fork and serve bread on the side. Leftovers freeze well. Alter the vegetables to suit your family's tastes. Those with fairly high water content work well. Green beans dry out too much.

Janet Nazif
PROTEIN: 204.1 grams; CALORIES: 4729   *High Bridge, New Jersey*

FRENCH ACADIAN CHICKEN STEW

2 to 3 lb. **chicken**, cut up
1 large **onion**, chopped
3 or 4 stalks **celery**, diced
2 t. **oregano**
1 t. **salt** (or less)
dash of **pepper**
water
3 or 4 **potatoes**, in chunks
3 or 4 **carrots**, in chunks

Dumplings:
2 C. whole wheat **flour**
¼ to ½ t. **salt**
water

Bring chicken, onion, celery and seasonings to boil in water to cover in a 4-qt. pot. Simmer about 2 hours. Remove and bone chicken, returning meat to stock. Add potatoes and carrots. Bring to a boil; reduce heat to simmer while you prepare dumplings.

For dumplings, mix flour and salt; add enough water to make a soft dough. Turn out on a floured surface and knead a few times. Roll out thinly (almost like pasta) and cut into 1" squares (a pizza cutter works well). Bring pot to boil and add dumplings while mixture is boiling. Simmer until done. Dumplings will puff a bit, but will be fairly firm—they are a cross between dumplings and homemade pasta.

This is a recipe handed down from my grandmother. My 5-year-old daughter already wants to know how to make it.   *P.: 384.1 gms.; C.: 1962*

Caroline Dube
Plaisted, Maine

AFRICAN CHICKEN AND SAUCE
(Groundnut Stew)

1 frying **chicken**, cut-up or
  1 lb. ground beef
½ C. **flour** to coat chicken
¼ C. **oil**
1 **onion**, chopped
2 C. stewed **tomatoes**
2 T. chopped, fresh **parsley**
2 cloves **garlic**, minced
tabasco sauce to taste
½ t. **salt** (or less)
dash of **pepper**
water
½ C. **peanut butter**
2 to 4 C. cooked **brown rice**

Dredge chicken with flour. Brown in oil. Remove and set aside. Saute onion; stir in tomatoes, parsley, garlic and seasonings. Add enough water to make a medium sauce. Return chicken to pan and simmer until tender, about 45 minutes. Add water as needed. Remove chicken; stir in peanut butter. Return chicken. Simmer 10 minutes to absorb peanut butter flavor. Serve over rice.

Sometimes I brown 1 lb. ground beef in place of chicken and *double* the remaining ingredients. This makes two nice meals for our family of 6. The peanut butter and rice complement each other to provide a more nearly complete protein, so you may stretch the meat a little further. Tastes great, too!

PROTEIN: 230.1 grams; CALORIES: 3123

Mary Baker
Yanfolila, Mali Republic, Africa

Esther Decker
Linwood, Kansas

NANCY'S CHICKEN STEW

3 to 4 lb. **chicken**, cut up, or
  4 to 6 chicken breasts
2 C. whole wheat **flour**
pinch of **salt**
¼ t. **pepper**
1 C. **orange juice**
4 to 6 T. **oil**
6 large **carrots**, in bite-sized sticks
6 stalks **celery** with leaves, cut into sticks
1 medium **onion**, sliced
¼ t. **poultry seasoning**
1 t. **salt** (or less)
dash of **pepper**
2 to 3 C. chicken **stock** or broth
4 oz. **egg noodles**, cooked
1 T. **butter**

Mix flour, salt and pepper to make coating mix. Dip chicken pieces in orange juice to moisten. Shake chicken in bag with half the coating mix, 2 or 3 pieces at a time. Add more coating as needed. Brown chicken well in oil over medium-high heat in large skillet. Add vegetables, seasonings and stock. Simmer, covered, until tender, about 1½ hours. Add more liquid if necessary. Thicken, if you wish, with 1 T. leftover coating mix. Serve with buttered noodles.

The whole wheat flour gives the dish a different flavor from traditional stews. I first served noodles as an afterthought; now they are a regular part of the meal. My family loves it!

P.: 571 gms.; C.: 3373

Nancy Schneider
Valatie, New York

CUTTING UP A CHICKEN

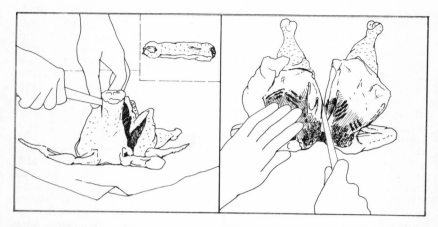

1. Hold chicken tail up, neck opening down, backbone toward you. Cut down each side of backbone (through ribs) and pull out backbone.

2. Open out chicken breast side down. Split breast bone.

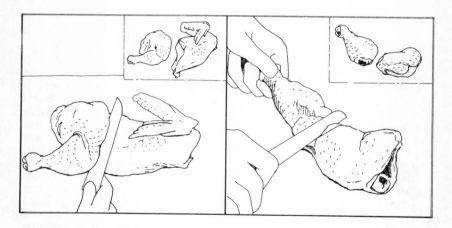

3. Dislocate thigh joint from back. Hold leg and thigh away from breast. Cut through joint and skin. Remove leg from breast. You now have quarters.

4. Bend backwards to dislocate joint between leg and thigh. Cut through meat and joint to separate.

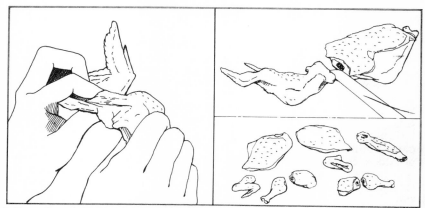

5. Bend wing backward and dislocate the wing at the joint where it joins breast. Cut through the joint to separate the wing from breast.

BONING A CHICKEN BREAST

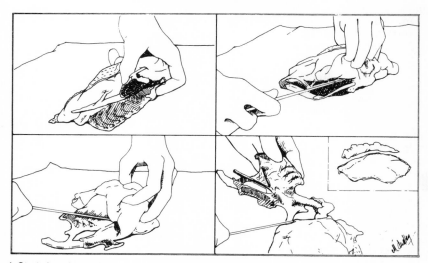

1. Start along breast bone. With thumb or fingers begin pulling meat away from bone.

2. Place the knife as close to the bone as possible. With a short sawing motion, cut away where the meat is connected.

3. Work back and forth—first pulling meat away from bone with fingers, then cutting and scraping close to bone with knife until entire fillet is removed. Turn chicken piece as needed for easy maneuvering.

4. Cut or pull out small piece of wishbone that remains. Save bones for soup pot.

5. The small fillet piece that separates from main breast meat is the "tenderloin" of the chicken. It can be saved for special use later or can be folded back into the rest of the breast-meat.

6. Remove skin if desired.

GRANNY'S EASY "BABY'S HERE" STEW
(Plus Even Easier Versions)

3 lbs. **beef stew meat** or
    chuck roast, in 1" cubes
2 C. **tomatoes**
2 C. **tomato sauce**
1 lb. fresh **green beans**,
    trimmed and halved (2 C.
    frozen), or peas or baby
    lima beans
6 **carrots**, cut in half
2 **potatoes**, cubed, or 1 white
    and 1 sweet potato
1 large **onion**, coarsely chopped
1 **turnip**, pared and cubed, or
    1 additional potato
½ t. **salt** (or less)
dash of **pepper**
3 T. quick-cooking **tapioca**
¼ C. cooking **sherry**
generous pinch of seasonings
    (mixed parsley, chives and
    tarragon(optional)
4 C. cooked **brown rice**

Additional seasonings to taste:

**oregano, bay leaf, allspice,
marjoram, cloves, lemon juice,
garlic, worcestershire sauce,
paprika, parsley, tarragon,
chives**

Carefully trim fat from meat. Brown
meat in 2 T. **oil** over medium heat.
Combine all ingredients, except
rice, in heavy 6 to 7-qt. pot. Stir gently. Cover tightly and simmer 2½ to 3
hours.   Or bake for 5 hours at 325°.
Or cook in slow-cooker 10 hours on
low. Serve over brown rice for a complete meal.

PROTEIN: 353 grams; CALORIES: 7424

Bonnie James Walther
Houston, Texas

HOPKINS COUNTY STEW

1 lb. **beef stew meat**
3 lb. **chicken**, cut up
2 to 4 C. **water**
2½ C. **corn**
2½ C. stewed **tomatoes**
4 or 5 medium **potatoes**
1 medium **onion**
2 to 3 C. mixed **vegetables**
    (peas, corn, green beans,
    lima beans)
2½ C. **tomato juice**
1 t. **poultry seasoning** or
    mixed thyme, sage, rosemary
    and nutmeg
½ t. to 1 t. **marjoram**
1½ t. **chili powder** (p. 286)
½ t. **sage**
½ to 1 t. **salt**
dash of **pepper**

In 10-qt. pot, cook beef and chicken
in water. Skin and bone meat and return meat to stock in pot. Add remaining ingredients, except corn;
cook 15 minutes. Add corn, cook 15
minutes, stirring occasionally. Fun
to cook in an iron pot over a wood
fire.

    This recipe won the Hopkins
County Cooking Contest in 1974.

PROTEIN: 651.3 grams; CALORIES: 4333

Wilma Townsend
Paris, Texas

LENTIL-VEGETABLE STEW

12 C. **water**, or part stock or
   vegetable-cooking water
2 C. **lentils**
1½ C. **tomato paste**
1 lb. **carrots**, sliced
3 stalks **celery**, sliced
3 medium **onions**, chopped
   or sliced
1 C. **corn**
1 C. **peas**
1 **green pepper**, chopped
½ C. **brown rice**
2 t. **basil** (or more)
2 cloves **garlic**, minced
2 **bay leaves**
2 C. additional **vegetables**
   (optional)

Put all ingredients in a 7-qt. pot.
Bring to a boil. Simmer 2 hours.
   This is one meatless recipe I've invented that my family loves! I make a double batch and freeze half. I keep a container in my freezer into which I throw all my leftover vegetables. When I make this stew, I toss them in. It's always a pleasant surprise as to what I will find. .

PROTEIN: 161.7 grams; CALORIES: 3006
Dorothy Turner
Centereach, New York

Lentil-Sausage Stew. 40 minutes before serving, add 1 lb. Italian sweet **sausage** (removed from casings, broken up, cooked in 1 T. olive **oil** for 10 minutes or until tender, and drained), and 2 lbs. fresh or frozen **spinach**. Add ½ C. **ditalini** (small macaroni) for the last 10 minutes. Garnish with grated Parmesan **cheese**. Corn, peas, garlic and rice may be omitted.

Mary Ann McMullen
Lancaster, Pennsylvania

ITALIAN BEEF STEW

2 lb. **beef** (chuck or round),
   cut in 1" cubes
2 T. **oil**
2 medium **onions**, chopped
2 to 6 cloves **garlic**, minced
4 **carrots**, sliced
4 stalks **celery**, sliced
3½ C. **tomatoes**, peeled
1 C. dry **red wine**
2 t. **oregano**
1 t. **basil**
1 t. **marjoram**
1 t. **salt** (or less)
dash of **pepper**
½ to 1 lb. **spaghetti**, cooked

Brown beef in oil. Add onion, then garlic. Cook until soft. Add remaining ingredients (except spaghetti). Simmer 2 hours, covered, stirring occasionally. Add water as needed. If sauce is too thin at the end of cooking, thicken with a little **flour** or **tomato paste**. Serve with hot spaghetti.
   This recipe is my own version of a roast in an Italian cookbook. I do not measure the vegetables, exactly. I just add what looks right.

PROTEIN: 213.8 grams; CALORIES: 3934
Gael Marshall Chaney
Martinsville, Virginia

STIFATHO
(Greek Stew)

2 lbs. stewing **beef**,
  lamb or venison
½ t. **salt** (or less)
dash of **pepper**
2 T. olive **oil**
2 T. cider **vinegar**
2 C. stewed or whole
  tomatoes, broken up
1 C. **tomato sauce**
4 rounded t. whole **allspice**
  (in teaball or cheesecloth)
1 **bay leaf**
10 small boiling **onions**

Brown meat in a little **water**. Salt and pepper to taste. Add oil and vinegar; stir to cover meat well. Add all ingredients except onions. Cook for 2½ hours on low to moderate heat. Add onions; cook 1 hour. May be doubled, but do *not* double allspice or bay leaf. *PROTEIN: 155.4 grams; CALORIES: 3630*

This makes up well the day before. The flavor is stronger upon reheating.
Deb Dewey
Rochester, New York

Stuffings

ROAST CHICKEN STUFFED A NEW WAY

1 roasting **chicken**
½ C. chopped **celery**
⅓ C. chopped **onion**
⅓ C. **brown rice**
¼ C. **butter** or margarine
1 C. chicken **broth**
1 t. **lemon juice**
½ t. **salt** (or less)
dash of **pepper**
½ to ¾ C. **raisins**, soaked
  until plump, then drained

Brown celery, onion and rice in butter until onion softens and rice browns lightly, about 10 minutes. Add broth, lemon juice, salt and pepper. Reduce heat, cover and cook slowly, until rice is tender and water absorbed, 35 to 45 minutes. Stir in raisins. Stuff chicken. Roast at 325° for 25 minutes per pound.

You may double or triple the recipe if your family likes the rice as much as mine does. My German great-grandmother, my grandmothers and my mother have made this family favorite for years. This is my variation, with the raisins for iron.

PROTEIN: 183.5 grams; CALORIES: 2091
Brenda Santer
Estevan, Sask., Canada

FRENCH CANADIAN PORK STUFFING FOR TURKEY

For a 20-lb. turkey:
2 lbs. lean ground **pork**,
  browned and drained
turkey giblets
broth from giblets
3 large **onions**
1 loaf dried **bread crumbs**
4 **eggs**, slightly beaten
½ t. **salt**
dash of **pepper**
poultry seasoning to taste

Cook giblets in a little water. Save the broth. Grind giblets together with the onions. Mix pork, giblets and broth together in a large bowl. Slowly add the crumbs, eggs and seasonings. Add water if the mixture is too dry, but not much as the stuffing absorbs turkey juices.

This recipe was handed down verbally from my husband's grandfather, "Pepere" Raymond Fortin. For special occasions the men did the stuffing.
Pat Guilmette
P.: 242.5 gms.; C.: 5298 *Albuquerque, New Mexico*

GREAT-GREAT GRANDMOTHER'S POTATO STUFFING

2 medium **potatoes**, boiled with skins on
7 slices **bread**, in small pieces
water to soak bread
2 stalks **celery**, chopped
2 small **onions**, chopped
4 T. **butter**
1 t. **poultry seasoning**
1 t. **marjoram**
½ t. **salt** (or less)
dash of **pepper**

Soak bread; set aside. Saute celery and onion in butter. Mash potatoes with skins. Squeeze water from bread; combine with potatoes. Add celery, onions and seasonings. This makes enough for a 10-lb. turkey. You may double or halve the amounts. This recipe is flexible. Modify it to suit what is in your pantry—more potatoes, less celery, a bit of **cornbread** or **rye bread**, etc. I make large quantities, cooking extra in a casserole with **giblets** on top. Bake at 350° for ½ hour covered, then ½ hour uncovered. This goes well with poultry and pork. Leftovers freeze well. PROTEIN: 27.9 grams; CALORIES: 1192

Eileen Wason
Sarasota, Florida

Variations: Omit potatoes. Use a loaf of **bread**. Try adding sauted **mushrooms,** cooked **sausage, raisins,** chopped **apples** and even some **nuts.** For another meal, layer leftover **meat** and stuffing in pan. Pour on **gravy** or meat juices. Bake at 350° until heated. Many LLL Contributors

NONA'S SPINACH DRESSING

2 C. chopped **celery** with leaves
4 small **onions**, chopped
4 T. olive **oil**
¼ C. **butter** or margarine
20 oz. chopped **spinach**, cooked
1 lb. **pork links**, chopped and fried, or bulk sausage (p. 282)
2 loaves **bread**, toasted and cubed
2 C. grated Swiss **cheese**
2 C. chicken or turkey **stock**
2 oz. **meat** from neck, giblets, chopped
½ t. **salt** (or less)
dash of **pepper**
1 **egg**, beaten
milk (optional)

Saute celery and onion in oil and butter until tender. Add spinach and pork links. Simmer 5 minutes. Add to bread cubes; mix thoroughly. Add cheese; mix. Add stock, meat, salt and pepper. Add some milk if needed. Just before stuffing, fold in egg. This makes enough to stuff 2 roasting chickens or a 10 to 12-lb. turkey. Bake extra dressing in greased casserole at 350° for 45 minutes. *For Appetizers:* roll mixture into small balls, bake as above.

My Italian grandmother also used this for stuffing ravioli, which she made by hand. Her dressing has always been the highlight of any holiday meal. P.: 283.6 gms.; C.: 6500

Angela Sicking
Cincinnati, Ohio

Mainly Meat

SWISS STEAK

2 lbs. **round steak**
2 T. **flour** (optional)
½ t. **salt** (or less)
dash of **pepper**
1 T. **oil**
1 medium **onion**, chopped
2 to 3 stalks **celery**, chopped
¼ C. chopped **green pepper**
1 C. peeled, chopped **tomatoes**
2 **carrots**, sliced (optional)
¼ to ½ lb. **mushrooms**, sliced
(optional)
2 C. **water**
8 boiled or mashed **potatoes**
(optional)

Pound flour, salt and pepper into meat. Cut into serving-sized pieces. Heat skillet to 375°; add oil and brown meat. Pour remaining vegetables and water over steak. Cover and reduce heat to 200°. Simmer 1 to 1½ hours or cook all day in slow cooker on low. Serve over potatoes, if desired.

PROTEIN: 188.7 grams; CALORIES: 2130
with potatoes: P.:205.5 gms.; C.: 2738

Lisa Newell
Phoenix, Arizona

Oven Swiss Steak. After browning meat, put it into a casserole or Dutch oven; add vegetables and water. Cover and bake at 300° for 3 to 4 hours. Add water as needed.

Hungarian Swiss Steak. Combine 2 t. **paprika** with flour, salt and pepper. Omit tomatoes; reduce water to ½ C. and add 2 T. **tomato juice.** Simmer or bake at 325° for 1½ hours. Remove meat. Mix 1 C. **yogurt** with 1 t. **flour** and a little **water.** Add to sauce slowly. Stir constantly. Add meat and reheat. *Carol Holthaus*   *Karen Renwick*   *Joyce G. Bliss*   *Charlotte Davis*
Decatur, Illinois   *Wheatley, Ont., Canada*   *Lawrenceville, Georgia*   *Atlanta, Georgia*

PEPPER STEAK

1 lb. **steak** (round, chuck or
flank), cut in 1½ x 3" strips
2 T. **worcestershire sauce**
1 T. **lemon juice**
1 T. tamari **soy sauce**
dash of **pepper**
1 T. whole wheat **flour**
1 T. **oil**
½ C. **water**
1 C. **green peppers**, cut in
slivers
2 **tomatoes**, cut in wedges
1 to 2 C. cooked **brown rice**

Optional:
1 C. chopped **onion**
¼ lb. **mushrooms**, sliced
½ C. chopped **celery**
½ to 1 C. mung **bean sprouts**

Combine Worcestershire sauce, lemon juice, soy sauce and pepper. Add meat, flour and optional vegetables (except sprouts) to sauce. Stir to coat. Saute in hot oil until meat is browned. Add water, cover and simmer until tender, about 1 to 1½ hours. When almost done, add green peppers and sprouts (if used); simmer gently until peppers are tender but still crunchy. Remove from heat; add tomatoes, mix and cook 5 minutes. Serve with rice.

PROTEIN: 102.8 grams; CALORIES: 1348

Christine Pando
Roselle, Illinois

Kathy Schneider
Sarasota, Florida

CHEESY LIVER STEAKS

1½ lb. baby beef **liver**
¼ C. whole wheat **flour**
6 slices nitrite-free **bacon**
   or 3 T. **butter**
½ lb. **mushrooms**, sliced
1 to 1½ C. thinly sliced **onion**
1 **bell pepper**, thinly sliced
4 oz. **cheese**, sliced

In large skillet, cook bacon until crisp. Remove from pan. Saute vegetables in bacon drippings until onion is transparent. Remove with slotted spoon. Dredge liver in flour; fry in remaining drippings until outside is crisp and inside is cooked. Top with cheese. Turn off heat; cover. Serve when cheese is melted, smothered with vegetables and crumbled bacon. Serve with **brown rice** and a **salad**.

This recipe is so delicious it could reform a liver-hater. The trick is to disguise the flavor of the liver with other flavors.   *PROTEIN: 186.9; CALORIES: 2585*

Stella Bock
Cranford, New Jersey

LIVER KAPAMA
(Greek-Style Liver)

1½ lb. calves' **liver**, sliced
¼ C. **oil**
2 medium **onions**, thinly sliced
¾ C. **tomato paste**
2 C. **water**
1 t. **salt**
1 t. ground **allspice**
1 t. ground **nutmeg**
¼ t. **pepper**
cooked **brown rice**, noodles,
   kasha or bulgur

Cut liver into 1" squares. Saute liver in oil until lightly browned. Add onion and saute for another minute. Add remaining ingredients and bring to a boil. Reduce heat, cover and simmer for 20 to 30 minutes, until liver is tender. Serve over **rice, noodles, kasha or bulgur.**

This is absolutely delicious. The spices make the sauce almost sweet. Goes well with a tossed salad.

Variation: Omit tomato paste; use 2 C. **tomato sauce.** Reduce water to ½ c.   *PROTEIN: 139 grams; CALORIES: 1651 + rice*

Anne Burton
Wanamassa, New Jersey

LIVER IN GREEN ONION SAUCE

1 lb. calves' **liver**, cut into
   ¼" slices
1 C. **white sauce** (p. 251)
2 bunches **green onions**, thinly
   sliced with tops
¼ t. **salt** (or less)
dash of **pepper**
dash of ground **nutmeg**
2 T. **oil** or melted butter

Prepare White Sauce, sauteing onions before adding flour. Season. Keep warm. Arrange liver on greased broiler pan. Brush with oil. Broil 3 to 4" from heat in preheated broiler. Cook 2 minutes per side, until browned. Cut liver into strips. Add liver and pan juices to onion sauce. Reheat quickly and serve.

PROTEIN: 98.8 grams; CALORIES: 1258

Alice Ziring
Mercer Island, Washington

ATLANTA LLLI CONFERENCE LIVER

As a special treat at the 1979 LLLI Conference, my roommate and I ate lunch in one of the restaurants in the hotel. On an elegant buffet table was a dish we didn't know was liver. It was so delicious, I was sure I could get my family to eat it. I came home and, after several experiments, sufficiently duplicated it so that now my family loves it!

1 lb. calves' **liver**, sliced
flour, seasoned with a dash of
   salt and **pepper**
1 C. (¼ lb.) sliced **mushrooms**
1 medium **onion**, sliced
   (optional)
2 T. **butter** or bacon grease
1 C. **brown gravy**

Lightly saute mushrooms and onions in butter. Remove from pan. Dredge liver in flour. Fry in same pan, 3 to 5 minutes per side, just until no longer pink inside. Remove from pan. In same pan, prepare brown gravy. Return vegetables and liver to pan. Warm through. Serve immediately.

PROTEIN: 97.9 grams; CALORIES: 1648

Kathie Hock
Geneva, New York

HINT FOR LIVER

If your family does not enjoy eating liver, grind it and cook with ground **beef**. Use in any recipe containing **tomatoes** or tomato sauce. Gradually increase the amount of liver as your family acquires a taste for it.

Sharen Littlefield
Shorewood, Minnesota

EASY-STYLE CHICKEN LIVER

1 lb. chicken **livers**
½ C. **flour**, seasoned with a
   dash of **salt** and **pepper**
3 T. **oil**
3 or 4 **green onions**, chopped
2 T. chopped, fresh **parsley**
¼ t. **salt**
dash of **pepper**
½ t. **thyme**
¼ C. cooked, crumbled **bacon**
2 C. cooked **brown rice**

Remove fat from livers. Dredge livers in flour. Heat oil in a skillet to medium-hot. Add livers, onion and parsley. Season with salt, pepper and half the thyme. Saute 8 to 10 minutes. Add crumbled bacon; adjust seasoning. Cook 5 minutes longer, until just done. Serve with rice.

Sometimes I stir the rice into the pan with livers to let the flavors blend. A green salad with more onions and parsley is a good side dish. *PROTEIN: 118 grams; CALORIES: 1337*

With rice—PROTEIN: 125.6 grams; CALORIES: 1693

Mardelle Baier
Brantford, Ont., Canada

HOMEMADE SALAMI
(Free of Preservatives)

4 lbs. ground **beef** (75% lean)
4 t. **sea salt** (uniodized)
1½ t. **garlic powder**
1½ t. **black pepper**
2 to 3 T. **steak sauce**
liquid smoke (optional)

Mix all ingredients thoroughly; cover and chill 24 hours. Divide into quarters. Shape each into a firm roll. Wrap snugly in nylon netting, 12 x 18". Tie ends securely. Place on a rack in pan. Bake at 225° for 4 hours. Allow to stand a few minutes. Unwrap and blot with towel to remove any excess fat. Freeze in foil or freezer wrap. Thaw and refrigerate when ready to use. Slice thinly. Yields about 3 lbs. of salami.

PROTEIN: 325.9 grams; CALORIES: 3403

Herb Recipe

3 T. dry **red wine**
1 t. **garlic powder**
½ t. **black pepper**
2 T. **mustard seeds**
1 T. **basil**
1 T. **oregano**
1 t. **onion powder**
½ C. grated Parmesan **cheese**

Spicy Recipe

*Joan D'Alessandro
Kent, Washington*

3 T. dry **white wine**
1 t. **garlic powder**
½ t. **black pepper**
2 T. **chili powder**
2 t. crushed **red pepper**
1 t. ground **cumin**

SOUTHERN MARYLAND STUFFED HAM

5-lb. cooked **ham**

Stuffing:
1 medium head **cabbage,**
  finely shredded
5 to 6 medium **onions,**
  finely chopped
1 bunch fresh **greens**
  (spinach, kale, collards)
1½ t. **salt** (or less)
dash of **pepper**
¼ t. **cayenne pepper**
1 t. **honey**

Combine stuffing ingredients. With a sharp knife, make a cut through the center of the ham, from one end to the other. Push stuffing into the hole. Do not force, as the ham might split open. Place the ham in a cloth bag. (I use an old pillow case, cut down to size, for this purpose.) Pile remaining stuffing on the top and sides. Tie shut. Set on a rack in a large pan with enough water to nearly cover the ham. Simmer 25 minutes per pound. Remove bag from water. Lift out contents. Serve.

This is the only way we like our ham now. I got this recipe over the telephone from my mother-in-law one Easter shortly after I was married. It sounds difficult, but it's easier than stuffing a turkey.

PROTEIN: 545.6 grams; CALORIES: 8524

*Beverly Morgan
San Jose, California*

SLOW-COOKER PORK ROAST

4 to 5-lb. **pork roast**
½ C. tamari **soy sauce**
½ C. **wine**
½ t. ground **ginger**
1 clove **garlic**, minced

Place roast in a slow-cooker. Combine remaining ingredients. Pour over roast. Cook on low for 10 hours. Turn meat every 3 hours.

PROTEIN: 304.3 grams; CALORIES: 5936

Nanci Ricciardi
Enon, Ohio

Sue Smith
Newport News, Virginia

PERFECT ROAST CHICKEN

3½ to 4 lb. whole **chicken**
2 or 3 cloves **garlic** or
   garlic powder to taste
1 **lemon**
½ t. **salt**

PROTEIN: 211.6 grams; CALORIES: 2785

Wipe chicken inside and out. Rub with cut cloves or garlic powder. Squeeze lemon juice inside and all over chicken. Rub with salt. Place on rack in roasting pan. Roast at 350°, 20 minutes for each pound. The last half hour, baste several times with pan juices. Let stand 10 minutes before serving to allow juices to set. Juicy and delicious.   Anne Burton
Wanamassa, New Jersey

West Indian Chicken. Omit garlic. Spread on whole or cut-up chicken a mixture of 1 T. butter, 1 T. **lemon juice**, 2 t. **curry powder**, 1 t. **thyme**, ½ t. **salt** and a dash of **pepper**. Bake at 375° for 1 to 1½ hours.

Susan Fortson Magee
Brownsville, Texas

BASIC BAKED CHICKEN

3 lb. **chicken**, cut up
½ t. **salt** (optional)
dash of **pepper**
garlic powder to taste
potatoes (optional)

Season chicken on both sides. Place in shallow baking pan, skin side up, for a crispy outside and juicy inside. Bake at 375° for 45 to 60 minutes. Accompany with baked potatoes, which may cook along with the chicken. This is low-calorie, simple and energy-efficient.

PROTEIN: 172.2 grams; CALORIES: 1146 + potatoes   Judy Earp
Louisville, Kentucky

Mrs. Kersey's Baked Chicken. Squeeze a **lemon** over the chicken. Sprinkle with **paprika** and **celery seed**. It may be mild or spicy, depending on your taste. Drizzle some **oil** over all. Bake at 500° for 20 to 25 minutes. Reduce heat to 350°. Continue baking for 35 to 45 minutes, or until chicken is tender.   Marcia Casais
Chatham, New Jersey

STEAMED CHICKEN

2 to 3 lbs. **chicken** parts or
   whole fryer
½ C. **soy sauce** (optional)
4 C. **water**
2 to 4 C. cooked **brown rice**

Put soy sauce and water into a 6 to 8-qt. pot. Bring to a boil. Place chicken in steamer basket in pot. Cover tightly. Steam until tender, about 45 to 60 minutes. Serve over rice or use the boned meat in vegetable or chicken salads, as steamed chicken is more moist than roasted chicken. You can cook even a frozen chicken this way, just cook it longer, about 1¼ hours.

PROTEIN: 132.8 grams; CALORIES: 1208

Helen Palmer
Edgewater Pk., New Jersey

Lisa Brown-Tsai
Friendswood, Texas

BULK COATING MIX

4 C. whole wheat **flour**
1 t. **salt** (or less)
½ t. **pepper**
2 T. **paprika**
½ t. **garlic powder**
1 T. ground **turmeric**
2 T. **herbs** (use any or all):
thyme, marjoram, basil,
oregano, parsley, sage
1 t. **celery seeds**

Combine ingredients and mix well. Store in airtight container in refrigerator. Use for breading chicken, fish or chops. Makes enough for 6 chickens. Try substituting **wheat germ**, rolled **oats, bread crumbs, cornmeal, matzo meal** or crushed **wheat crackers** for part of the flour.

PROTEIN: 65.9 grams; CALORIES: 1652

Susan C. Huml
Great Lakes, Illinois

Kathy Szymanski
Clear Lake, Iowa

OVEN-FRIED CHICKEN

1 frying **chicken**, cut up
½ C. whole wheat **flour** or
¼ C. flour and
¼ C **wheat germ**
½ t. **garlic powder**
1 t. **curry powder** (optional)
1 t. ground **allspice** (optional)
2 T. **oil**, to coat pan

Shake flour and garlic powder in a bag. Add chicken pieces; shake to coat. Bake in an oiled pan at 400° for 1 hour, turning once. For a spicier coating, add curry powder and allspice to the flour mixture. Curry turns leftover chicken yellow.

PROTEIN: 180.8 grams; CALORIES: 1611

Kathy Mead
Leland, Michigan

EASY MUSHROOM CHICKEN BAKE

3 lbs. **chicken**, cut-up, or
pork or lamb chops
1 C. medium-thick **white sauce**
½ C. chopped **onions**, sauteed
2 beef **bouillon cubes**, crushed,
or 2 heaping t. beef bouillon
powder
¼ lb. (4 oz.) **mushrooms**, sliced
and sauteed
¼ C. **milk**, dry sherry or
white wine

Arrange chicken in baking pan. Add onions, bouillon, mushrooms and liquid to white sauce. Mix well and pour over meat. Bake at 375° for 1 hour. Serve with **rice, noodles** or mashed **potatoes.**

PROTEIN: 195.8 grams; CALORIES: 1742

Bryanna Clark
Union Bay, B.C., Canada

FUSSY DAY CHICKEN

1 whole **chicken**
1½ C. **barbecue sauce** (p. 251)

Put chicken, legs up, into slow-cooker. Pour barbecue sauce over and inside chicken. Cover and forget about dinner while you tend to your fussy baby. It is not even a good idea to check it, as steam escapes and it takes quite a while to reheat. At low temperatures, dinner will not burn. Cook 8 to 10 hours on low. Dinner will be hot whenever you choose to eat. Meat falls easily from bones and sauce makes gravy for rice or potatoes. All that remains to do is to have Dad fix a salad.

PROTEIN: 55.8 grams; CALORIES: 1470

Karen L. Elkins
Minot AFB, North Dakota

BAKED CHICKEN BREASTS

4 medium **chicken breasts**
½ C. **breadcrumbs**
½ C. grated Parmesan **cheese**
1 t. **salt** (or less)
1 **egg**, beaten
2 t. **oil**
1 C. grated Cheddar **cheese**

Skin and bone chicken. Combine breadcrumbs, Parmesan and salt on a plate. Beat egg and oil in a bowl. Dip chicken in egg, then breadcrumbs. Bake at 350° for 30 to 35 minutes, on a cookie sheet or baking pan, until tender and slightly browned. Sprinkle with Cheddar cheese. Bake 5 minutes to melt cheese. For variety, substitute **wheat germ** for part of the breadcrumbs. To crumbs, add herbs such as **thyme, basil, marjoram, oregano, garlic powder** or **parsley.** Try substituting **romano** or grated **Swiss** for Parmesan, and **Monterey Jack** for Cheddar. Or use **chicken parts** and bake for 1 to 1½ hours.   *P.: 153.4 gms.; C.: 2012*

Donna Peebles
Grand Prairie, Texas

ISLAND-STYLE CHICKEN

5 to 8 pieces of **chicken**
1 to 2 T. **oil**
1¼ C. chicken **broth**
2½ C. unsweetened **pineapple** chunks, with juice
¼ C. apple cider **vinegar**
2 t. **soy sauce**
1 to 2 large cloves **garlic**, minced
1 medium **green pepper**, cut in bite-sized squares
2 **carrots**, sliced in julienne strips (optional)
1 to 3 T. **cornstarch** or arrowroot
¼ C. **water**
2 to 4 C. cooked **brown rice**

Brown chicken in oil. Add broth, pineapple with juice, vinegar, soy sauce, garlic, pepper and carrots. Bring to a boil, cover and cook on low heat 40 minutes, stirring occasionally. When done, remove chicken, pineapple, pepper and carrots. Combine cornstarch and water. Gradually stir into sauce and cook until thickened, about 1 minute. Serve over chicken and brown rice.

PROTEIN: 97.5 grams; CALORIES: 1562

Patricia T. Klein
Atlanta, Georgia

BAKED FISH FROM TURNING ISLAND

1½ to 2 lbs. **fish fillets**
1 T. minced **onion**
½ C. **mayonnaise** (p. 48)
½ t. **marjoram**
½ t. dry **mustard**
1 t. fresh **lemon juice**
dash **pepper**
paprika

Place fish in oiled baking dish. Mix remaining ingredients except paprika. Spread over fish. Bake at 500° for 17 to 20 minutes, until browned. Sprinkle with paprika.

This pleases even my "fish-hater." I found this tattered and worn recipe in our cottage kitchen on an island in Georgian Bay. It must have been used on many fish brought out of the clean Canadian waters of Lake Huron.   *PROTEIN: 122.1 grams; CALORIES: 1357*

Martha Sears
Hilton Head, S. Carolina

NAPA VALLEY FISH

¾ to 1 lb. fresh **fish fillets**
1 **lemon**, thinly sliced
1 **tomato**, thinly sliced
¼ t. **thyme**
2 T. **white wine** (optional)

Lay fillets in single layer in baking dish. Bake at 500° for 3 to 5 minutes, until they start to draw up and turn white. Remove from oven. Alternate slices of lemon and tomato on fish. Sprinkle with thyme and wine. Bake 3 to 5 minutes longer, until fish flakes with a fork. This quick cooking in a hot oven produces a very moist, flavorful dish.

This recipe was given to me by the chef-owner of a fine French restaurant. It is quick to prepare, fat-free and delicious *PROTEIN: 62.7 grams; CALORIES: 341*

Gwennyth Trice
Napa, California

DOROTHY'S FISH

1 lb. **fish fillets**
½ C. whole wheat **flour**,
  seasoned with **salt, pepper**
  and **paprika**
2 T. **butter**
1 C. medium **white sauce** (p. 251)
dash of ground **nutmeg**
⅓ C. grated Parmesan **cheese**
1 lb. fresh or frozen **spinach**,
  chopped and cooked
dash of **paprika**

Cut fish into bite-sized pieces. Roll in flour. Brown in butter. Prepare white sauce. Add nutmeg and cheese. Drain or squeeze excess water from spinach. Oil a 2-quart baking dish. Arrange fish along the sides; mound spinach in the middle. Cover with sauce. Sprinkle with paprika. Bake at 400° for 15 to 20 minutes. *PROTEIN: 124.2 grams; CALORIES: 1437*

Nancy Stevens
Cuyahoga Falls, Ohio

BUSY DAY FISH FILLETS

1 lb. frozen **fish fillets**
½ C. **wheat germ**
¼ t. **salt**
dash of **pepper**
oregano or dill weed (optional)
¼ C. grated Parmesan **cheese**
  (optional)
¼ C. melted **butter**
lemon slices

Cut frozen blocks of fish into 8 to 12 pieces. Combine wheat germ, seasonings and cheese. Dip fish into butter; coat on all sides with wheat germ mixture. Place on ungreased baking sheet. Bake at 400° for 20 to 25 minutes. Serve with lemon.

I double this to serve our family of seven. Any leftovers make an excellent sandwich with whole wheat bread, sliced tomato, mayonnaise and sprouts. *PROTEIN: 107.5 grams; CALORIES: 1145*

Diana Reardon
Dallas, Texas

WINE ROAST

3 to 4 lb. shoulder **roast**
½ to 1 C. dry **white wine**
1 t. **salt** (or less)
dash of **pepper**
½ to 1 C. **water**

Marinate meat in wine, salt and pepper for 4 to 5 hours in the refrigerator. Transfer everything to slow-cooker. Add water. Cook 8 to 10 hours on low or 4 to 5 hours on high. Reheat leftovers in sauce.

PROTEIN: 236.6 grams; CALORIES: 1442

Susan Renes
Moscow, Idaho

BAKED FISH FILLETS

2 lbs. **white fish fillets**
½ C. whole wheat **flour,**
  seasoned with **garlic powder**
3 **eggs,** beaten
½ C. **milk**
1 T. melted **butter**
½ t. **salt** (or less)
dash of **pepper**
1 medium **onion,** diced

Garnish:
1 T. chopped fresh **parsley**
lemon wedges

Roll fish in flour. Place in an oiled baking dish. Combine remaining ingredients. Pour over fish. Cover and bake at 400° for 30 minutes. Garnish. Delicious served with tartar sauce, green salad and baked potato.

PROTEIN: 205.4 grams; CALORIES: 2090

Catherine Andre
Wheaton, Illinois

UNSHISHED KABOBS

1 lb. well marbled **beef** or lamb,
  cut in cubes
2 to 3 **tomatoes,** in eighths
1 or 2 **green peppers,** sliced
1 medium **onion,** thickly sliced
1 small **zucchini,** sliced and
  quartered
1 C. unsweetened **pineapple**
  chunks
10 or more **mushrooms** (optional)
1 to 2 C. cooked **brown rice**

Marinade (Optional):
1 medium **onion,** sliced and
  separated into rings
1 T. **oil**
¼ t. **salt**
dash of **pepper**
2 T. **lemon juice** (fresh is best)

Mix marinade ingredients together. Marinate meat for 2 to 4 hours, if desired. Scatter meat and vegetables on broiler pan. Use onions from marinade, as well. Broil 5 to 6" from heat for about 20 minutes. Turn frequently to cook evenly. Serve with pan juices and rice. Be creative—try other vegetables and meats. Also good on skewers.

Kabobs—PROTEIN: 87.1 grams; CALORIES: 1503
Marinade—P.: 1.7 gms.; C.: 170

Constance Whitman   *Helen Palmer*
Turnersville, New Jersey   *Edgewater Park, New Jersey*

MEAT ON A SKEWER

2 lbs. **veal,** beef or chicken,
  cut in 1" chunks, or
  large shrimp

Marinade:
⅓ C. **soy sauce**
⅓ C. **lemon juice**
⅓ C. **oil**
onions, quartered
mushrooms
green peppers, sliced
water chestnuts, sliced
carrots, sliced
3 to 4 C. rice **pilaf** (p. 184) or
  cooked barley

Combine marinade ingredients. Add meat and marinate 5 to 6 hours in the refrigerator. Alternate meat with choices of vegetables on a skewer. Broil 10 to 15 minutes in oven, or 15 to 20 minutes over the grill. Serve over pilaf.

Eileen Fischer Goodrich
Bethel, Connecticut

SCRAPPLE

4 to 6 lbs. **pork meat** and **bones** (backbones and feet are good to include along with some meaty pieces from any cut)
1 C. **flour** (buckwheat improves flavor)
2 C. (or more) **cornmeal**
about 1 t. *each:* **parsley, sage, rosemary** and **thyme** (allow sage to predominate), *or* 4 t. mixed sausage or poultry seasoning
3 t. **salt**
1 t. **pepper**

Cook meat covered with water until it falls from bones. Get 6 cups of stock, either by boiling it down to reduce volume, or by adding more water. Chop or grind the meat (you should have 3 C. more or less). Strain the stock; bring to a boil. Stir in the flour. While still boiling, stir in cornmeal. Cook until thickened. Add herbs, salt, pepper and meat. Simmer about 15 minutes. Pour into three wet loaf pans and chill.

To serve, slice, dip in **wheat germ**, flour or crumbs and fry on hot, greased griddle or pan. Be patient for slices to brown before turning or they may break up. Pork stock made with bones will set into a firm jelly which aids slicing and frying. If the scrapple did not slice easily, use more bones the next time around.

PROTEIN: 266.9 grams; CALORIES: 5784

Joann S. Grohman
Dixfield, Maine

ROAST IN SPANISH SAUCE

2 to 3 lb. chuck **roast**
1 large **green pepper**, chopped
1 medium **onion**, chopped
3 or 4 **tomatoes**, chopped
½ t. **salt** (or less)
dash of **pepper**
¼ t. **garlic salt**
¼ t. **garlic powder**
1 T. **vinegar**

Tenderize meat by piercing with knife. Mix other ingredients. Place meat on top of half the vegetables in baking dish or Dutch oven. Pour the rest on top. Cover. Bake for 2 to 2½ hours at 350°. The vegetables cook down to a terrific sauce. Don't be tempted to try improve this dish by using wine or a better cut of meat— it works best with vinegar and less expensive meat. This can be prepared hours ahead.

PROTEIN: 173.5 grams; CALORIES: 2467

Barbara Vasquez
Metairie, Louisiana

CHINESE BARBECUE SAUCE

½ C. **honey**
1 C. **catsup** (p. 252)
½ C. tamari **soy sauce**
4 cloves **garlic**, minced

Blend all ingredients. Refrigerate. Great on **chicken** or **pork chops**.

PROTEIN: 11.2 grams; CALORIES: 833

Mary P. Ross
Merrickville, Ont., Canada

HERBED POT ROAST WITH VEGETABLES

3 to 4 lb. **roast**
pepper, garlic powder and
 paprika to taste
¼ t. **basil**
½ t. **thyme**
1 t. **oregano**
1 t. **marjoram**
1 to 2 T. **butter**
4 to 5 **mushrooms,** sliced
1 small **onion,** diced
½ to ¾ C. **water,** red wine
 or consumme
10 large **carrots,** quartered
10 small **potatoes,** quartered
2 to 3 T. **cornstarch**
water

Season meat with herbs and spices. Dot with butter. Put into large casserole; add mushrooms, onion and liquid. Bake, covered, at 325° for 2½ to 3 hours. Add carrots and potatoes. Cover and return to oven for 30 to 45 minutes. Remove meat and vegetables; keep warm. Mix cornstarch with water. Stir into juices; bring to a boil, stirring constantly.

PROTEIN: 238.8 grams; CALORIES: 4944

Kris Kluck
Zweibrucken, W. Germany

WHITE BOUDIN

4 lbs. boneless fresh **pork**
1 lb. pork **liver** or heart
3 **onions**
1½ **green peppers**
6 stalks **celery**
3 cloves **garlic**
1 C. chopped **green onions**
½ C. chopped, fresh **parsley**
6 C. raw **brown rice,** cooked
 (makes about 12 C.)
8 C. meat **broth**
1 t. **salt**
dash *each* red and black **pepper**
1 pkg. **pork casing** for stuffing
 (optional)

Cover pork and liver with water. Simmer about 2 hours, until tender. Run meat and vegetables through grinder. Mix in a large bowl with rice. Season well to taste.

To make boudin, place pork casing on a sausage stuffer. Fill with dressing. Tie ends. Boudin may be frozen. To heat, place in boiling water, reduce heat and simmer ½ hour. Or, bake frozen, foil-wrapped boudin at 350° for ½ hour. May also be eaten as dressing or made into patties. Makes twenty 18" links.

I often stuff a few links of lightly seasoned boudin for the children prior to adding more seasoning for the adults.

My in-laws have done their own butchering for many years. They have prepared delicious Cajun dishes such as this one. From time to time, I have been in my mother-in-law's kitchen learning and helping to prepare some of these recipes so this heritage may be passed along to our children.

PROTEIN: 487.3 grams; CALORIES: 11,651

Janie Daicet
Iowa, Louisiana

HAWAIIAN SPARE RIB SAUCE

3 T. **brown sugar** or honey
2 T. **cornstarch**
¼ C. **vinegar**
½ C. **catsup** (p. 252)
1 C. unsweetened, crushed
 pineapple

Combine sugar and cornstarch in saucepan. Stir in remaining ingredients. Cook until thickened, about 5 minutes, stirring constantly. Pour on spare ribs and bake as in Barbecued Spare Ribs (p. 221). *P.: 4.7 gms.; C.: 514*

◢◢◢◢◢◢Sauces◢◢◢◢◢◢◢

WHITE SAUCE
(My Mother's Technique)

	Thin	Med-Thin	Medium	Thick
Butter	1 T.	1½ T.	2 T.	3 T.
Flour or	1 T.	1½ T.	2 T.	3 T.
Cornstarch	1½ t.	¾ T.	1 T.	1½ T.
Milk	1 C.	1 C.	1 C.	1 C.

¼ t. **salt**(or less)
dash of **pepper**

Melt butter over low heat. **Off heat**, blend in flour until smooth. *Gradually* add milk, stirring constantly. Cook over medium heat until sauce thickens and comes to a boil. Reduce heat, simmer 2 to 3 minutes to remove floury taste. This same method may be used to thicken stock or any other liquid. This method avoids lumps, but sauce may burn if the saucepan is a poor heat conductor.

With flour—Thin—PROTEIN: 9.5 grams; CALORIES: 294
Marcia Casais   Med-Thin—PROTEIN: 10 grams; CALORIES: 361
Chatham, New Jersey Medium—PROTEIN: 10.6 grams; CALORIES: 427
Thick—PROTEIN: 11.7 grams; CALORIES: 560

Quick Low Calorie Medium White Sauce. Heat ¾ C. skim milk to boiling. Gradually stir in 1 T. cornstarch mixed with ¼ C. cold milk. Mixture will thicken quickly. Season as you wish.

PROTEIN: 8 grams; CALORIES: 125

Roberta Bishop Johnson

BARBECUE SAUCE

1 C. **tomato sauce**
¼ C. **water**
2 T. **butter**
¼ C. **lemon juice**
2 or 3 T. chopped **onion**
1 or 2 T. **honey**
3 shakes **worcestershire sauce**
1½ t. **salt** (or less)
dash of **pepper**
1½ t. **paprika**
½ t. **chili powder**
2 t. **garlic powder**
½ t. ground **cinnamon**
½ t. ground **allspice**
¼ t. ground **cloves**
(optional)

Combine all ingredients in a saucepan. Stir over medium-low heat until well blended. This sauce may seem spicy when tasted before use, but it is not as spicy on the meat. The seasonings may be adjusted to your own taste. Good on **chicken** and **spare ribs**.

PROTEIN: 5.4 grams; CALORIES: 421

Kris Kluck
Zweibrucken, W. Germany

QUICK 'N EASY CATSUP

2 C. **tomato puree**
½ to 1 t. **salt**
4 T. cider **vinegar**
2 T. **honey**
¼ t. **garlic powder**
¼ t. **basil**
¼ t. **nutmeg**
¼ t. dry **mustard**
dash **pepper**
dash ground **mace**
dash ground **cinnamon**

Using a blender or a wire whisk, combine all ingredients. Simmer for 5 to 10 minutes. Store in a covered container in the refrigerator.

This has less sweetening than the commercial varieties, so you may want to start with a bit more honey and gradually reduce the amount as your family's taste adjusts to the less sweet product.

PROTEIN: 11.1; CALORIES: 377
1 T. = P.: 3 gms.; C.: 11
Jan Foulk
Elwin, Illinois

CATSUP

1¼ C. **tomato paste**
   (12 oz. can)
1¼ C. **water**
¼ to ½ t. ground **cinnamon**
¼ t. ground **nutmeg**
¼ t. ground **mace**
1 t. **salt**

1 **bay leaf**, split
¼ t. **garlic powder**
⅓ C. **cider vinegar**
1 t. **blackstrap molasses**
1 T. **sugar** or honey
1 t. **celery seed**
¼ t. dry **mustard**

Simmer in a skillet long enough to get it as thick as you like it, about 40 minutes. Makes 2 cups.

PROTEIN: 12.5 grams; CALORIES: 363
1 T. = P.: 2.7 gms.; C.: 7.7
Barbara Horan
Indianapolis, Indiana

SALSA
(Mexican Hot Sauce)

1 medium **tomato**
1 medium **onion**
4 oz. **green chilies**
pinch of **salt** and **pepper**
dash of **vinegar**

Chop, blend or process the tomato, onion and chilies. Add salt, pepper and vinegar. Store covered in refrigerator. May be used as topping for **tacos, tostados, eggs, steak, hamburgers, hot dogs.** Be creative.

PROTEIN: 4.1 grams; CALORIES: 101
Tina Pulice
Redlands, California

TAMARI-GINGER SAUCE FOR FISH

1 C. tamari **soy sauce**
2 T. grated, fresh **ginger**
1 **green onion**, sliced
½ to 1 C. **water**
1 T. **honey** (or less)
1 T. **sesame seeds** (or more)
2 cloves **garlic**, crushed

Combine all ingredients. Marinate **fish** in sauce for several hours. Bake or broil fish in liquid. Sprinkle additional sesame seeds over fish while cooking—adds flavor.

PROTEIN: 24.1 grams; CALORIES: 352
Dot Buck
Lahaina, Maui, Hawaii

EASY ONION SAUCE

6 to 8 large **onions,**
   thinly sliced
oil for sauteing
⅓ C. **soy sauce**
3 T. **water**
2 t. **honey**
4 oz. grated **cheese**
   (Monterey Jack or Cheddar)

Saute onions in oil until browned. Add soy sauce, water and honey. Stir well. Turn off heat; add the grated cheese. Serve.

This is a favorite of ours for **tofu, potatoes, brown rice,** mixed steamed **vegetables,** etc.

PROTEIN: 44.8 grams; CALORIES: 910

Barbara Dick
Seattle, Washington.

TAHINI SAUCE

1 large **onion,** chopped
2 T. **oil**
1 C. **water**
5 T. **tahini** (ground sesame seeds)
2 t. tamari **soy sauce**
1 C. sliced **mushrooms**
¼ t. **miso** (soy paste)

Saute onion in oil until tender. Add remaining ingredients. Stir over low heat until thickened. Especially delicious over brown **rice** or bulgur. Garnish with toasted **sesame** and **sunflower seeds.**

PROTEIN: 27.9 grams; CALORIES: 971

Sherry Wiltsey
Fort Richardson, Arkansas

MARINADE

½ C. **oil**
6 T. tamari **soy sauce**
2 T. **worcestershire sauce**
1 T. dry **mustard**
1 t. **pepper,** coarsely ground
¼ C. wine **vinegar**
¾ t. (or more) chopped, fresh
   parsley
1 clove **garlic,** minced
3 T. **lemon juice**

Combine ingredients. Marinate **steak, hamburgers** or **chicken** for 2 to 24 hours. Baste meat while cooking. Use leftover marinade in stew.

Without meat—PROTEIN: 11 grams; CALORIES: 1147

Lois Lake Raabe
Easton, Connecticut

HORSERADISH SAUCE

1 C. **mayonnaise** (p. 48) and/or
   yogurt
juice of 1 **lemon**
1½ t. chopped, fresh **parsley**
2 T. **horseradish**
1 t. **worcestershire sauce**
2 hard-cooked **eggs,** chopped
   (optional)

Combine all ingredients and refrigerate until used. This is delicious on **vegetables,** especially green beans. Try it as a dip for raw vegetables. Also good on roast **pork** and **ham.** Makes about 1½ cups.

PROTEIN: 16.5 grams; CALORIES: 1800

Jean Hengge
N. Ft. Meyers, Florida

Desserts

QUICK FRUIT SALADS OR DESSERTS

Quick fruit salads can be prepared by combining bite-sized pieces of just a few fruits. A dressing (below) may be added if desired. Use your imagination and you have a simple but elegant salad or dessert for family or company. When little voices start chanting "I want dessert," these are so nutritious that you can always say "Yes." The children can help make them too!

Try these for "starters" and then create your own:

*oranges, bananas or pineapple, and unsweetened, shredded **coconut**
*cantaloupe, honeydew, peaches and blueberries
*cantaloupe, honeydew, bananas and strawberries tossed with orange juice
*watermelon, apples, bananas, pears and oranges tossed with pineapple juice
*blackberries, apples, oranges and bananas tossed with lemon juice
*bananas, blueberries and pineapple tossed with pineapple juice
*apples, bananas, sunflower seeds and peanuts with a frozen orange juice topping
*oranges and bananas with a honey dressing
*apples and seedless grapes with a yogurt dressing
*bananas, pineapple, strawberries and walnuts with a cooked pineapple dressing

Margaret MacPherson	*Barbara Vasquez*	*Marilynn Berry*	*Joanna Deslauriers*
Hudson, Massachusetts	*Metairie, Louisiana*	*Lawrenceville, Georgia*	*Willowdale, Ont., Canada*

DRESSINGS

#1 **Citrus fruit juice** or thawed concentrate will help prevent fruit from discoloring.

#2 Slightly frozen **fruit juice** or sherbet may be used as a topping.

#3 Mix ½ C. plain **yogurt** with ½ t. ground **cinnamon** and sweeten with 2 t. **honey** or fruit juice concentrate.   *PROTEIN: 6.2 grams; CALORIES: 196*

#4 Cook 1 C. **pineapple juice**, 1 T. **honey**, 1 T. **cornstarch** and 1 beaten **egg** over low heat, or in microwave oven, until thickened. If desired, **whipped cream** may be added to the cooled sauce and tossed with the fruit salad just before serving.   *PROTEIN: 7.3 grams; CALORIES: 314 + cream*

Barbara Becker Nelson	*Barbara Upton*	*Dianne Jeffries*	*Adrienne Archambault*
Eugene, Oregon	*Aurora, Colorado*	*Boulder, Colorado*	*Dauphin, Man., Canada*

RHUBARB PIE

9" double **pie crust,** unbaked (p. 266)
4 C. **rhubarb,** chopped
¾ C. **raisins**
½ t. ground **cinnamon**
dash of **salt**
2½ T. **cornstarch**
⅓ C. **honey,** sorghum molasses or barley malt syrup

Combine all filling ingredients and fill crust. Put top crust on and cut slits so steam can escape. Bake at 400° for 35 to 45 minutes.

PROTEIN: 37.3 grams; CALORIES: 2600

Lynn Ruggiero
Fitchburg, Maine

LUSCIOUS FRUIT SALAD

1 C. **cottage cheese**
1 C. **yogurt**, plain or flavored
1 unpeeled **apple**, diced
20 oz. unsweetened, crushed or chunk **pineapple**, drained
1 **banana**, sliced
½ C. **raisins**
½ C. chopped **walnuts**, pecans or almonds
seasonal **fruits** (berries, grapes, etc.) (optional)

Mix all ingredients well. (If smoother consistency is desired, whip cottage cheese with a little pineapple juice.) Chill 1 hour. Serve plain, or on **lettuce** or **waffles**.

This recipe has been handed down for several years at LLL gatherings. No one seems to remember who first made it, but everyone loves it! It's an especially good, easy dish to bring to a new mother for her lunches for a few days.

PROTEIN: 56.1 grams; CALORIES: 1478 + seasonal fruits

Lorrie Koslow-Green
Greensboro, N. Carolina

EAST INDIAN BANANA YOGURT SALAD

1 C. plain **yogurt**
2 C. unsweetened chunk **pineapple**, drained
½ C. unsweetened, shredded **coconut**
½ t. ground **coriander** or nutmeg
6 medium **bananas**, thinly sliced

Mix yogurt and pineapple in a 2-quart bowl. Stir in coconut and coriander. Gently fold in bananas. Refrigerate 2 to 4 hours before serving.

PROTEIN: 24.9 grams; CALORIES: 1389

Eugenia Spady
Hays, Kansas

FRUIT GELATIN WITH YOGURT

1½ T. (envelopes) unflavored **gelatin**
1 T. **lemon juice**
2 T. **water**
1 C. plain **yogurt**
4 oz. **cream cheese**
2 **bananas**, sliced
few drops **lemon juice**
2½ C. unsweetened, crushed **pineapple**, drained

Soften gelatin in 1 T. lemon juice and 1 T. of the water. Dissolve over low heat. Cool by adding remaining T. of water. Blend yogurt and cream cheese in blender. Blend in gelatin mixture. In serving bowl, fold in bananas which have been tossed with lemon juice and pineapple. Pour into oiled 4-cup mold if desired. Refrigerate 1 or 2 hours.

PROTEIN: 31.2 grams; CALORIES: 992

Crisanne Forsythe
Sandwich, Illinois

PEANUT BUTTER SATIN

½ C. **peanut butter**
½ C. **butter**
¼ C. **honey** or brown sugar
1 t. **vanilla**
3 or 4 **eggs**

Cream butters, sweetener and vanilla together. Add eggs, one at a time, beating on high speed at least 5 minutes after each addition. If mixture doesn't whip up well, be sure you are beating the full 5 minutes, or chill well, then finish beating.

Serve ¼ C. in an attractive glass, or use as a pie or torte layer filling. May be sprinkled with **carob chips**. It takes only a small serving to quench the withdrawal symptoms of a dessert-lover.

Roberta Johnson

PROTEIN: 53 GRAMS; CALORIES: 2042

Puddings & Custards

SIMPLE VANILLA PUDDING

2 C. **milk**
3 T. **honey,** malt syrup or
   ¼ C. brown sugar
3 T. **cornstarch** or 6 T. flour
2 **eggs,** well beaten
1 T. **vanilla**

Garnish:
fruit, nuts, coconut,
   and/or whipped **cream**

Quick Method: Heat 1½ C. milk and sweetener to simmer in a heavy saucepan over low heat. In a measuring cup, mix remaining ½ C. milk and cornstarch; stir into hot milk. Stir constantly over medium heat until thickened and starting to boil, about 2 to 3 minutes.
   Stir about ½ C. of the hot mixture into beaten eggs. Dribble egg mixture into pan and stir over low heat for one minute. Remove from heat and stir in vanilla. Serve warm or chilled in 4 dishes. This is less sweetened than commercial pudding and additive-free.   *PROTEIN: 29.4 grams; CALORIES: 814 + garnish*

Double Boiler Method: Gradually stir milk into cornstarch. Add sweetener. Cook over boiling water until thickened, stirring constantly, about 10 minutes. Cover and cook 10 minutes more, stirring 2 or 3 times. Add eggs and vanilla as in Quick Method.

Microwave Oven Method: Combine milk, sweetener and cornstarch in a 2-quart dish. Cook at high power for 6 minutes, stirring after 3 minutes, then after each minute. Beat in eggs and cook 30 seconds more. Remove from oven and add vanilla.

Variations:
Eggless. Use any cooking method and proceed as directed, omitting the eggs.   *PROTEIN: 17 grams; CALORIES: 658.* Other variations can also be made without eggs. For extra protein, add ½ C. dry **milk powder** with the milk.
                                          PROTEIN: 42.1 grams; CALORIES: 910

Butterscotch. Use brown sugar as sweetener, *or* add 2 T. **molasses** to honey. Stir in 2 T. **butter** after removing from heat. Reduce vanilla to 1 t.
                                          PROTEIN: 29.4; CALORIES: 973

Carob. Mix ¼ C. **carob powder** with 3 to 4 T. hot **water** until smooth. Stir into finished pudding. Reduce vanilla to 1 t.   *PROTEIN: 34 grams; CALORIES: 847*

Lemon. Substitute 3 to 4 t. **lemon juice** for vanilla, and add either 1 t. grated **lemon rind** *or* 1 t. lemon extract.   *PROTEIN: 29.8 grams; CALORIES: 781*

Vanilla and Fruit. Fold 1 to 2 C. sliced **bananas** or unsweetened berries (drained, if necessary) into finished pudding.   *PROTEIN: 31 grams; CALORIES: 941*

Rice. Increase milk by ¼ C. Add 1 to 1½ C. cooked **rice** to finished pudding.   *PROTEIN: 35.3 grams; CALORIES: 1032* Top with ground **nutmeg** and/or **raisins.**

Coconut. Add ½ to 1 C. unsweetened, shredded **coconut** to finished pudding.   *PROTEIN: 30.5 grams; CALORIES: 986*

Peach-Yogurt. When finished pudding is cool, add ½ C. **yogurt** or sour cream and 2 C. unsweetened, sliced **peaches** (drained, if necessary).

PROTEIN: 36.8 grams; CALORIES: 1014

Soy Milk. A milk substitute may be used for the pudding or variations.

PROTEIN: 30.4 grams; CALORIES: 666

Jean Baker White   *Bryanna Clark*   *June Benson*   *Melinda Carner*
Van Buren, Maine   *Union Bay, B.C., Canada* *Ovid, New York*   *Midvale, Utah*

BAKED HONEY CUSTARD

3 **eggs**
¼ C. **honey** or maple syrup
1 t. **vanilla**
2½ C. **milk**
ground **nutmeg** or cinnamon

Beat eggs, honey and vanilla with a wire whisk. Stir in milk. Pour into glass baking dish or six custard cups. Sprinkle with a spice. Set in a pan of hot water. Bake large dish at 325° for 1 hour; bake cups at 350° for 40 to 45 minutes. The custard is done when a knife inserted off-center comes out clean. Serve warm or cold. This contains lots of protein with only minimal sweetening.

PROTEIN: 39.8 grams; CALORIES: 902

Coconut Custard. Mix ¼ to ½ C. unsweetened, shredded **coconut** with other ingredients. Garnish cooled, baked custard with whole fresh or unsweetened, frozen **strawberries**, if desired.

Eileen Ward   *Janet Glover*   *Lorrie Koslow-Green*
Mililani, Hawaii   *Russiaville, Indiana*   *Greensboro, N. Carolina*

"I OUGHT TO FEEL GUILTY" CHEESECAKE

24 oz. **cheese** (use one, or a mixture, of the following white cheeses: cottage cheese, tofu, cream cheese, yogurt cheese or white Cheddar)
¾ C. **eggs** (3 to 5)
¼ C. **sweetener** (honey, barley malt syrup, molasses, etc.)
1 to 2 T. grated **lemon rind**
¼ C. **lemon juice** and pulp
Optional:
1 to 2 T. **cornstarch**
    (use if mixture is thin or you wish a finger food)
1 T. **rum** extract

Dump everything into food processor and process until smooth. Pour into 10" spring form pan with graham cracker crust. Bake at 350° for 45 to 60 minutes—until the top puffs lightly all the way to the center.

All-tofu cheesecake: Add ¼ to ½ C. softened **butter** for extra creaminess. Use maximum flavoring since tofu is so mild.

I feel I ought to feel guilty accepting compliments for this cake since it is so easy to make with a processor. I ought to feel guilty eating it but the cottage cheese and tofu versions are so low calorie, I don't.

PROTEIN: 110.5 grams; CALORIES: 1228   *Roberta Bishop Johnson*
                                                 Champaign, Illinois

BREAD PUDDING

4 eggs
2 C. milk
⅓ C. **honey** or brown sugar
½ t. **vanilla**, lemon or almond
extract
3 T. **butter**, melted (optional)
1⅓ C. **bread cubes** (2 to 3 slices)
⅓ C. **raisins** or other dried fruit,
chopped
½ C. **sunflower seeds**, sesame
seeds or nuts (optional)
dash of ground **cinnamon** and/or
ground **nutmeg** (optional)

Optional Toppings:
milk, melted butter, or maple syrup

Beat, blend or process together eggs, milk, honey, vanilla and butter. Stir in bread, fruit and seeds. The spices may be stirred in or sprinkled on top. Pour into a buttered 2-quart casserole. Set in pan of water (1" deep). Bake 45 to 55 minutes at 350°. Pudding is done when knife inserted halfway between center and edge comes out clean. Serve warm with topping, if desired.

Tastes good cold for breakfast, and is a good way to use up stale bread.

PROTEIN: 47.3 GRAMS; CALORIES: 2387, plus topping

Variations:

#1 Use 1 less **egg** and increase **bread** to 2 C. Bake 40 to 50 minutes.

#2 Add one **fruit** before baking: 1 grated **apple**, or 1½ C. chopped   **rhubarb**, or 1 or 2 mashed or blended **bananas**. Omit **dried fruit** and **seeds** if desired.

Polly J. Mertens
Harrison, Ohio

Marsha Foral
Vista, California

Carol Britton
Columbus, Ohio

Wanda Rezac
Marlboro, Massachusetts

FRUIT AND CUSTARD PUDDING

2 **eggs**, slightly beaten
1/8 to 1/4 C. **honey**
2 t. **vanilla**
1 C. plain **yogurt**
1 C. **cottage cheese**
2 C. diced **fruit**, fresh or
canned, drained (apples,
pears, peaches or apricot
halves)
⅓ C. **raisins**

Topping:
¼ C. light **brown sugar**
⅓ C. whole wheat **flour**
2 T. **butter**, softened
½ t. ground **nutmeg**

Garnish (optional):
cream, plain or whipped

Mix the eggs and honey thoroughly. Add the vanilla, yogurt and cottage cheese and mix well. Butter a 1½-quart casserole. Arrange diced fruit or apricot halves (rounded side down) in the bottom. Add the raisins and pour the egg mixture over all. Bake, uncovered, at 350° for 25 minutes. Mix topping ingredients with a fork until mixture resembles coarse meal. Sprinkle on top and return to oven. Bake 15 minutes longer.

This is good warm, topped with cream or unsweetened whipped cream. It's also delicious cold. It is full of protein and makes a very good breakfast. I have often cut the topping recipe in half, and it tastes every bit as good.

Connie Berkey
Chagrin Falls, Ohio

PROTEIN: 62.6 grams; CALORIES: 1854 + cream

BROWN RICE PUDDING

1⅓ C. raw **brown rice**, cooked
3 **eggs**
⅓ C. **honey** or maple syrup
3 C. **milk**
1 t. **vanilla**
½ t. **cinnamon**
¼ t. *each* **nutmeg** and **cloves**
½ C. **raisins**
½ C. unsweetened shredded
  coconut
½ C. finely chopped **almonds**
1 C. unsweetened crushed
  pineapple, drained (optional)
½ C. **wheat germ** (optional)

Beat eggs with honey until smooth. Stir in other ingredients. The wheat germ may be stirred in or sprinkled on top. Pour into greased 2½-quart casserole. Set in a pan of water (1" deep) if desired. Bake at 350° for 45 to 60 minutes, or until knife inserted in the center comes out clean. Serve warm or cold.

The raisins, coconut and almonds make this delicious as well as nutritious and it is just sweet enough. Kids love it cold for breakfast!

PROTEIN:103.5 grams; CALORIES: 3302

Variation: Omit nutmeg, cloves, coconut, almonds and pineapple. Use ⅔ to 1 C. raw **brown rice**, cooked. Add 1 grated **apple**, if desired.

Cherie Wolfe Parsons   Aggie Sanders   Sally Jo Bongle   Janet Glover
Morgan Hill, California   Eldersburg, Maryland   Kewaunee, Wisconsin   Russiaville, Indiana

ANNIE'S APPLE-STRAWBERRY PUDDING

¾ C. (6 oz. can) **apple juice
  concentrate**, thawed
2 cans **water** (1½ C.)
1 to 2 T. **honey** (optional)
¼ to ⅓ C. **cornstarch**
2 C. chopped, fresh or
  unsweetened, frozen
  strawberries

Stir together juice concentrate, water, honey and cornstarch. (Use larger amount of cornstarch if fruit is very juicy.) Cook over medium heat, stirring until thickened. Add strawberries and continue stirring for one minute. Remove from heat and cool. Good warm or cold.

PROTEIN: 2.7 grams; CALORIES: 578

Variations:
Apple-Pineapple. Use unsweetened, crushed **pineapple, raisins** and ground **cinnamon** to taste.
Apple-Peach. Use diced **peaches**.
Apple-Apple. Use diced **apples** (or a lesser amount of dried apples) plus ground cinnamon to taste.

*Suzie Crayton
Cedar Rapids, Iowa*

RUSSIAN CHEESE BLINTZES

crepes (p. 13)⁄)

Filling:
12 oz. **cottage cheese** or
  farmers' cheese
1 **egg yolk**
¼ C. **honey**
¼ t. **salt**
dash of **pepper**

Topping:
yogurt or sour cream (optional)

Combine filling ingredients. Fill crepes with cottage cheese mixture and roll. Arrange in pan and bake at 350° for 10 to 20 minutes, or until warmed.

Filling—PROTEIN: 25.7 grams; CALORIES: 422

*Sadie Doresh
Carnegie, Pennsylvania*

Cookies

POLYNESIAN BARS

Filling:
2 C. chopped **dates**
1 T. **vanilla**
2½ C. unsweetened crushed
pineapple with juice

Base:
1 C. whole wheat **flour**
1 C. unsweetened, shredded
coconut
½ C. chopped **nuts**
3 C. rolled **oats**
1 C. **orange juice**
¼ C. **brown sugar** or honey
¼ C. **oil** or butter

Cook dates, vanilla and undrained pineapple until thick. Mix together the base ingredients and press half this mixture into a greased 9 x 12" pan. Spread filling on top. Cover with the rest of the base mixture. Bake at 350° for 30 to 40 minutes.
PROTEIN: 65.3 grams; CALORIES: 4169

Variation: Substitute grated raw **apple** for part of the pineapple in the filling.
Milly Stevens
Boulder, Colorado

NO-BAKE DATE BARS

1 lb. pitted **dates**, chopped
1½ C. unsweetened, shredded
coconut
½ C. **butter**
½ C. **water**
¼ C. **honey** or other sweetener
2½ C. rolled **oats**
⅔ C. chopped **nuts**
1 t. **vanilla**

Combine dates, coconut, butter, water and honey. Cook 3 to 4 minutes, stirring often, until mixture is thick and blended. Add oats, nuts and vanilla. Spread into buttered 9 x 9" pan. Chill about 2 hours. Cut into 18 bars. Refrigerate in airtight container. *PROTEIN: 55.3 grams; CALORIES: 3972*

Phyllis K. Collins
Medina, Ohio

DATE DROPS

½ lb. **dates**, cut up
2 **eggs**
2 t. **vanilla**
½ C. **butter**
¼ C. whole wheat **flour**
⅓ C. dry **milk powder**
1 C. rolled **oats**
½ C. **raisins**
¼ C. **carob chips**
½ C. **sunflower seeds**
½ C. chopped **pecans**

Grind dates. Blend with eggs and vanilla to make a paste. Cream in butter. Stir in the rest of the ingredients. Drop by spoonfuls close together on greased cookie sheet. Bake at 325° for 10 to 15 minutes, or until peaks begin to brown. This recipe was created to help fight the "sugar monster." It is great for trips.
PROTEIN: 65.1; CALORIES: 3128

Susan Mitchell
Charlottesville, Virginia

GOODIE BALLS
(Unbaked)

3 oz. **cream cheese**, softened
3 T. **peanut butter**
2 T. **honey**
2 T. dry **milk powder**
¼ C. **sunflower seeds**
2 T. chopped **nuts**
½ C. unsweetened, shredded **coconut**

Optional:
wheat germ or coconut

Mix all ingredients together. Shape into small balls. May be rolled in wheat germ or coconut. Refrigerate. Vary the amounts in the recipe according to your family's taste.

PROTEIN: 40.2 grams; CALORIES: 1244 + wheat germ

Jean Ann Merrill
Southgate, Kentucky

PEANUT BUTTER BARS

½ C. **butter**, softened
½ C. **honey**
1 **egg**
1 C. whole wheat **flour**
½ t. **baking soda**
⅓ C. **peanut butter**
1 t. **vanilla**
1 C. rolled **oats**, soaked in 1 C. very hot **water**
Topping (optional):
⅓ C. **peanut butter**
2 to 3 T. **milk**
1 C. **carob chips**

Cream butter, honey and egg. Add remaining ingredients. Bake in greased 9 x 13" pan at 350° for 10 to 15 minutes. Cool.

For topping, mix peanut butter, milk and carob chips in a double boiler until chips melt. Spread over cooled bars.

PROTEIN: 57.8 grams; CALORIES: 2701

With topping—P.: 101.6 gms.; C.: 4176

Carolyn Baird
Sault Ste. Marie, Michigan

CHUNKY GRANOLA BARS

1 **egg**
½ C. **peanut butter**
2 T. **honey**
2 C. **granola** (p. 285)

Combine egg, peanut butter and honey in a small saucepan. Cook over medium heat, stirring constantly, until mixture starts to bubble. Remove from heat; add granola and mix well. Spread evenly in a greased 8" square pan. Chill until firm; cut into bars. Store in refrigerator. *PROTEIN: 76.4 grams; CALORIES: 1780*

Kristi Zimmerman
Englewood, Colorado

PUMPKIN BARS

½ C. **oil**
⅓ C. **honey**
2 **eggs**
1 C. + 2 T. whole wheat **flour**
1 t. **baking powder**

½ t. **baking soda**
1 C. cooked, mashed **pumpkin**
¾ t. ground **cinnamon**
⅓ C. chopped **nuts**

cream cheese frosting (p. 279)
(optional)

Mix all ingredients together. Spread in 9 x 13" pan. Bake at 350° for 25 to 30 minutes. Frost when cool, if desired. *P.: 39.1 gms.; C.: 2246 + frosting*

Carol Benoy
Medway, Ohio

WHOLE WHEAT PEANUT BUTTER COOKIES

½ C. **butter,** softened
½ C. **peanut butter**
½ C. **brown sugar** or honey
1 **egg**
½ t. **vanilla**
1 C. whole wheat **flour**
1 t. **baking soda**
½ C. dry **milk powder**

Optional:
Add ½ C. of *one* of the following:
wheat germ
rolled **oats**
seeds (sunflower or sesame)
chopped **peanuts**

Cream butter, peanut butter and sugar. Add egg and vanilla. Stir in flour, soda, dry milk powder and one optional ingredient. Drop by teaspoonfuls onto greased cookie sheets and flatten with a fork. Bake at 350° for 8 to 10 minutes. Makes about 3 dozen cookies.

This cookie recipe has half the sugar and twice the protein of ordinary cookie recipes.

PROTEIN: 81 grams; CALORIES: 2724

Karen Morris
St. Cloud, Minnesota

Christina Pinkerton
Loveland, Colorado

Linda Helminiak
W. Chicago, Illinois

Sheila Terrill
Kinsman, Ohio

OATMEAL COOKIES

½ C. **oil** or butter
1 C. **brown sugar** or ¾ C. honey
1 **egg**
¼ C. **water,** juice or milk
1 t. **vanilla**
1 C. whole wheat **flour**
½ C. dry **milk powder**
¼ t. **salt** (optional)

½ t. **baking soda**
1 t. ground **cinnamon** (optional)
2 C. rolled **oats**
1 C. **wheat germ**
¼ C. **bran** (optional)
½ C. chopped **nuts,** seeds, coconut, dried fruit, or carob chips (optional)

Thoroughly beat oil, brown sugar, egg, water and vanilla. Add flour, dry milk powder, salt, soda and cinnamon. Beat well. Mix in oats, wheat germ and optional bran, nuts, seeds, etc. Drop by teaspoonfuls onto greased cookie sheets. Bake at 350° for 10 to 12 minutes, or until lightly browned.

PROTEIN: 47.3 grams; CALORIES: 2551

Helen Brown
Fairmont, West Virginia

Vicki Gordon
New Orleans, Louisiana

Jeanie Donaldson
Ridgecrest, California

Judy Savage
Northford, Connecticut

HAMENTASHEN COOKIE DOUGH

¾ C. **oil** or butter
¾ C. **honey** or brown sugar
4 **eggs**
4 C. whole wheat **flour**
4 t. **baking powder**

Cream the oil and sugar together. Add eggs; gradually add flour and baking powder. Refrigerate for 24 hours or more.

Divide cold dough into 4 sections. Knead one section at a time on a floured surface, leaving the others in the refrigerator to keep cold. Roll out with slightly floured rolling pin. Cut round shapes and fill center with Prune Filling (Lekvar). Fold over, forming 3 corners and pinch closed. Bake on greased pan at 350° until lightly browned, 15 to 20 minutes. Makes about 60 small Hamentashen.

This dough recipe has been handed down from generation to generation in my family. These delicious pastries are eaten during the Jewish holiday Purim and are named for the villain Hamen.

Judy Savage
Northford, Connecticut

PROTEIN: 94.8 grams; calories; 4194

TOFU SPICE COOKIES

1½ C. whole wheat **flour**
¾ C. **raisins**
¼ C. chopped **dates** or prunes
½ C. chopped **nuts**
½ t. **baking soda**
½ C. **honey**
½ lb. **tofu**
1 **egg**
½ C. soft **butter** or oil
1 t. ground **ginger**
1 t. ground **cinnamon**
1 t. ground **nutmeg**
½ t. **salt**
1 t. **vanilla**

In a 2-qt. bowl, mix flour, raisins, dates, nuts and baking soda together. In a blender or food processor, blend the remaining ingredients. Mix wet and dry ingredients together. Drop by teaspoonfuls onto oiled cookie sheet. Bake at 400° for 10 to 15 minutes.

These cookies can be made ahead of time and frozen, or kept in a tin box for a few days.

I really like this recipe because I feel my son is getting a nice treat that is good for him, too.

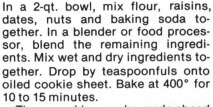

PROTEIN: 62.2 grams; CALORIES: 3080

Kathy Quinones
W. Amherst, New York

SESAME SUN "REFRIGERATOR" COOKIES
(Slice and Bake)

½ C. **butter**, softened
½ C. **honey**
1 **egg**
1 t. **vanilla**
¾ C. whole wheat **flour**
1½ C. rolled **oats**
¼ C. **wheat germ**
½ t. **baking soda**
¾ C. **sunflower seeds**
¾ C. **sesame seeds**

Cream together butter, honey, egg and vanilla. Mix dry ingredients and stir into creamed mixture, along with seeds. Shape dough into 2 logs about 2" in diameter. Wrap each in a sheet of waxed paper and refrigerate about 4 hours (or freeze for 2 hours) for easier slicing. Cut into ¼" slices. Place on ungreased baking sheets. Bake at 375° for 10 minutes, until lightly browned. Cool. Makes about 4 dozen.

Hint: Double recipe and freeze 2 logs to slice and bake later or to give to a friend.   *PROTEIN: 84.4 grams; CALORIES: 3419*   *Carol Tag*   *Kathy McAnally*
                                                                Springfield, Missouri   *Newark, Ohio*

SOURDOUGH DROP COOKIES

½ C. **sourdough starter** (p. 164)
½ C. **butter**, softened
¾ C. **brown sugar** or honey
1 **egg**, beaten
½ t. **baking soda**
2 C. whole wheat pastry **flour**
½ t. **baking powder**
½ t. ground **nutmeg**
½ t. **vanilla**
½ C. **raisins** or cut up prunes
¼ C. chopped **nuts**

Cream butter and sugar; add egg. Dissolve soda in sourdough. Sift dry ingredients together and add alternately with sourdough to the creamed mixture. Add vanilla, raisins and nuts. Drop by teaspoons on greased cookie sheet. Bake at 375° for 8 to 10 minutes.

PROTEIN: 52.7 grams; CALORIES: 3035

Marie Lundstrom
Cambridge, Wisconsin

GELATIN

1 T. (envelope) unflavored
  gelatin
½ C. cold **juice** or water
1½ C. **fruit juice**

Optional:
diced **fruit**
chopped **vegetables**
seeds or chopped **nuts**

Sprinkle unflavored gelatin over ½ C. cold juice or water. Stir constantly over low heat (or heat in microwave oven for 30 seconds) until gelatin is completely dissolved. Combine with 1½ C. juice. Add fruit immediately and stir again when slightly set, or add fruit after prepared gelatin has thickened.

Using juice instead of cold water will produce a stronger flavored gelatin which some people prefer and others think is too tart. Experiment to find your family's preference. **Honey** may be added (and then gradually decreased) if your family is used to sweetened gelatin mixes.

Any juice or fruit may be used except for fresh or frozen pineapple, mangoes, papayas or figs, which all contain an enzyme which prevents the gelatin from setting. Canned fruit works fine.

Double or triple the recipe and pour into a mold, if desired. To make a firmer gelatin for use in a large mold, increase the amount of unflavored gelatin by ½ to 1 T.

Try juices and matching fruits, such as apple juice or cider with diced apples. Try mixing flavors, such as grape juice with sliced bananas, or pineapple juice with chopped, unsweetened strawberries and bananas. Try combining juices, such as orange and pineapple, or peach and apricot. Make the salad or dessert more interesting by adding fruits plus grated carrots, chopped celery, sunflower seeds or chopped nuts. Be creative and experiment!

Yogurt Gelatin. Add 1 C. **yogurt** to prepared gelatin and mix with a wire whisk until smooth. Chill until set.

"Light-As-Air" Gelatin. Chill prepared gelatin until very thick. Beat with mixer or blender until frothy. Chill until set.

Or for an even fluffier texture, add 1 or 2 **egg whites** to thickened, prepared gelatin and beat with mixer about 5 minutes. Or beat egg whites separately and fold into the thickened, prepared gelatin. Chill until set.

Norene Schulenberg   *Kathy Schneider*   *Kathy Mead*
Silver Creek, New York   *Sarasota, Florida*   *Leland, Michigan*

YOGURT PIE

9" **graham cracker crust** (p. 266)
1 C. **cream cheese**
1 C. **yogurt**
¼ C. dry **milk powder**
½ C. (or less) **honey**
1 C. fresh **strawberries** or
  peaches, sliced (optional)

Mix cream cheese and yogurt. Add dry milk and honey. Pour into crust. Freeze. Remove 30 minutes before serving. Top with fresh strawberries or peaches, if desired.

This is a very easy, quick dessert.

PROTEIN: 68.8 grams; CALORIES: 2801

Kristi Zimmerman
Englewood, Colorado

GRANDMA'S "HALF-MOONS"

2 C. **dried fruit** (apricots, peaches, plums, apples)
water
¼ C. (or less) **honey**
ground **allspice** (optional)
double pie crust dough (p. 266)

Cover dried fruit with water in a medium saucepan. Bring to a boil, then cook on low heat for 30 to 40 minutes, until tender. Drain. (Save liquid for a beverage.) Mash fruit with a potato masher. Sweeten to taste; sprinkle with allspice, if desired. Cool.

Roll out dough. Cut 8 circles using a lid approximately 5" in diameter as a pattern. Place circles on cookie sheet. Spoon cooled fruit onto half of each circle, fold over, and pinch edges together. Prick holes in top with a fork. Bake at 400° for 30 minutes or until lightly browned.

My husband can remember his mom making "half-moons" for the men to take on elk-hunting trips. They were prepared with love and added to the special memories of weeks in the mountains. They are a finger food that can be packed so conveniently in lunches or backpacks!

PROTEIN: 45.2 grams; CALORIES: 2726

Variation: Substitute very ripe, **fresh fruit** or applesauce for cooked dried fruit.

Marion K. Marchant
Grandview, Wisconsin

APPLE CRISP

6 to 8 **apples**, sliced
½ C. **raisins** (optional)
⅓ C. **water**
1 C. rolled **oats**
½ C. whole wheat or rye **flour**
½ C. **wheat germ**
½ C. **butter** or oil
½ C. **brown sugar** or honey
2 t. **cinnamon**

Put sliced apples in buttered 9 x 13" pan. Sprinkle with raisins and water. Combine the rest of the ingredients. Sprinkle evenly over apples. Bake at 350° for 30 to 40 minutes, or until apples are soft. Serve warm or cold, plain or with a topping.

PROTEIN: 46.2; CALORIES: 3236 + topping

Topping:
Milk, yogurt or vanilla ice cream

Variation: Substitute 3 to 4 C. chopped **rhubarb** for the apple slices.

Joanna Deslauriers
Willowdale, Ont., Can.

Sandy Wozniak
Idna Station, Ont., Can.

Linda McConnell
Regina, Sask., Can.

Carol Kehler
Quesnel, B.C., Can.

COCONUT CRUST

1 C. unsweetened, shredded **coconut**
½ C. **wheat germ** (optional)
2 T. **oil** or butter
2 T. **honey** (optional)

Combine all ingredients and press into 8 or 9" pie pan. Bake at 325° for 5 to 8 minutes. Cool and fill.

PROTEIN: 23.9 grams; CALORIES: 1002

Granola Crust. Substitute 1½ C. **granola** for coconut and wheat germ.

Kathy Szymanski
Clear Lake, Iowa

Mary Dalpiaz
Berwick, Pennsylvania

Pies

GRAHAM CRACKER CRUST

⅔ C. **graham cracker crumbs**
¼ C. **wheat germ**
¼ C. dry **milk powder**
½ t. ground **cinnamon**
⅓ C. melted **butter**
1 T. **molasses** or honey

Combine crumbs, wheat germ, milk powder and cinnamon; mix thoroughly. Stir in melted butter. Add molasses and mix well. Grease a 9" pie pan and press the mixture firmly into the bottom and sides to make a crust 1/8" thick. Bake about 10 minutes in a 300° oven. Allow to cool.

PROTEIN: 26.1 grams; CALORIES: 1168   *Marcia Casais*
Chatham, New Jersey

PROCESSOR PASTRY

1¼ C. whole wheat pastry **flour**
½ t. **salt**
1 T. **wheat germ**
7 T. cold **butter**, cut into 7 pieces
(unsalted preferred)
1 **egg yolk**
2 T. **ice water**

Using steel blade of food processor, put flour, salt and wheat germ in the bowl. Turn on and off a few times to blend. Put in pieces of butter; process until it is well cut in and mixture looks evenly coarse. Add egg yolk and water while processor is running—dough ball will form on top of blade. Remove dough from bowl, wrap in waxed paper and chill at least 30 minutes. You may make this a day ahead or freeze airtight. Makes enough for a 10" pie shell.

I used to hate to make pastry until this recipe evolved.

PROTEIN: 26.2 grams; CALORIES: 1351

Diana Reardon
Dallas, Texas

EASY OIL CRUST

2 C. whole wheat **flour**
1 t. **salt** (optional)
½ C. **oil**
¼ C. cold **water**

Stir flour and salt in a bowl. Combine oil and water and mix into flour with a fork. Form into 2 balls with your hands and let sit, covered with a cloth, for 5 minutes. Roll out between sheets of waxed paper. Place rolled dough into pie plate; fill and bake. For prebaked pie shell, prick with a fork and bake at 375° for 10 to 12 minutes. Makes one 10" or two 9" crusts.   *PROTEIN: 32 grams; CALORIES: 1792*

Variation: Substitute ¾ C. **soy oil shortening** or sesame tahini for oil. Mix together well, using hands if necessary. Press into two 8 or 9" buttered pie pans.

Charlene Erikson   *Maureen Curry*   *Cathy Wirick*   *Barbara Bahun*
Lindenwold, New Jersey   *Kutztown, Pennsylvania* *London, Ont., Canada*   *New Carlisle, Ohio*

MALTED NUT PIE

9" **pie crust**, unbaked (p. 266)
2 C. **pecans** and/or walnuts
2 T. **butter**
1 C. **barley malt syrup**
4 **eggs**
1 t. **vanilla**
½ t. **salt**
½ to 1 t. ground **nutmeg**

Fill crust with pecans and/or walnuts. Bake in 425° oven for 5 minutes. Remove from oven and turn oven down to 350°. Combine remaining ingredients and mix well. Pour over nuts. Bake 40 to 50 minutes.

PROTEIN: 71.8 grams; CALORIES: 3737

Marty Hardy
Park Ridge, Illinois

FUDGE PIE

¾ C. **carob powder**
½ C. **honey**, Barley Malt Syrup, or other sweetener
½ C. **butter**, softened
3 **eggs**
1 t. to 1 T. **vanilla** (optional)

Beat or process everything together and pour into greased 8" pie pan. Bake at 350° for 20 to 25 minutes or just until the wet look is gone from the center of the pie. Cut into wedges. May be eaten as finger food.   *PROTEIN: 24.5 GRAMS; CALORIES: 1818*

Rocky Road Pie. Sprinkle ½ C. roasted peanuts on top before baking.

PROTEIN: 37.7 GRAMS; CALORIES: 2104   Roberta Bishop Johnson
Champaign, Illinois

COTTAGE CHEESE PIE

9" **graham cracker crust**
2 **eggs**, separated
2 T. **lemon juice** or orange juice
1 T. unflavored **gelatin**
¼ C. hot **milk**
⅓ C. **honey**
2 C. creamed **cottage cheese**
½ C. unsweetened, crushed **pineapple**, drained

Beat egg whites until stiff. Set aside. Put egg yolks, lemon juice and gelatin into blender. Cover and blend at low speed a few seconds; remove feeder cap and gradually pour in hot milk and honey. Replace feeder cap and continue blending until gelatin is dissolved, about 1 minute. Switch blender to high speed; gradually add cottage cheese, processing until smooth and well blended. Pour into large bowl and stir in pineapple. Fold in beaten egg whites. Pour into prepared crust. Chill until set.

PROTEIN: 108.5 grams; CALORIES: 2287

Mary Jo Johnson
Shavertown, Pennsylvania

TOFU-BANANA CHEESE PIE

1 C. **tofu**
1 C. **cottage cheese**
1 C. plain **yogurt**
1 to 2 ripe **banana(s)**
2 **eggs**
⅓ C. **honey** or less
1 T. **lemon juice** and/or **vanilla**
sprinkle of ground **nutmeg**
9" **pie crust**

Blend ingredients in blender until very creamy. Pour into pie crust. Bake at 350° for 55 minutes or until a knife inserted comes out clean.

If your family does not eat it all for dessert, try it for breakfast!

PROTEIN: 70.6 grams; CALORIES: 1376 + crust

Pat Harvey
Evergreen, Colorado

FRESH FRUIT PIE

9 inch pie **crust**, baked and
  cooled
4 C. fresh **fruit** (peaches,
  plums, berries, apples,
  pears, bananas, etc.)
1 or 2 T. **honey** or lemon juice
  (optional)
Optional Topping:
½ t. unflavored **gelatin**
1 T. cold **water**
1 C. **heavy cream** or plain
  yogurt
1 T. **honey** (optional)

Slice fruit. Sweeten with honey to taste if fruit is not fully ripened. If unsweetened, toss fruit with a small amount of lemon juice to prevent discoloration. Cover and refrigerate.

Soften gelatin in water and heat until dissolved. Add to cream or yogurt with honey and whip. Cover and refrigerate.

Immediately before serving, put prepared fruit into crust; top with whipped cream or yogurt, if desired.

When I was growing up this was the favorite summertime "company" dessert. Some people prefer using all soft fruits, while others like a combination of soft and crunchy fruits.

PROTEIN: 20.1 grams; CALORIES: 1213 + topping

Mary L. Moulton
Bristol, Connecticut

EASY APPLE PIE

9" double **pie crust**, unbaked
  (p. 266)
6 to 8 **apples**, washed and cut
  into eighths
1/8 t. **salt**
½ to 1 C. **raisins**
dash of ground **cinnamon**

Pile apple slices into pie pan lined with crust. Sprinkle with salt, raisins and cinnamon. Cover with top crust. Poke holes or cut some slits in the top crust. Trim the edges and pinch them to seal. Bake in 425° oven for 20 to 30 minutes until the crust is golden and the apples are steaming.

All fall and winter I keep the apple basket in the kitchen filled with apples from a nearby orchard. Day or night any child who wants a snack is always allowed to have an apple. I rarely get around to cooking apples (it destroys some of their nutritional value anyway), but when I do, the children and my husband always love this pie. Guests are surprised to find out that there is no sweetener added, just salt to bring out the natural sweetness of the apples.

Cathy Wirick
PROTEIN: 35.6 grams; CALORIES: 2519 *London, Ont., Canada*

TOFU YAM CUSTARD

2 C. steamed, mashed **yams**
  or sweet potatoes
1 lb. **tofu**
3 T. **orange juice concentrate**
½ C. **butter**
4 **eggs**
2 t. grated **lemon rind**
1 t. ground **cinnamon**
½ t. ground **nutmeg**
¼ t. *each* ground **allspice** and
  cloves
1 t. **vanilla**
½ C. **milk**

Combine yams with the other ingredients in a blender or food processor until smooth. Turn into a 2-quart casserole and bake at 350° for 1 hour, or until set. Chill before serving.

This dessert treat is naturally sweet, 100% nutritious and kids love it! *PROTEIN: 77 grams; CALORIES: 2193*

Barbara Becker Nelson
Eugene, Oregon

FRENCH STRAWBERRY PIE

9" **pie crust**, baked (p. 266)

Glaze Mixture:
4 C. fresh **strawberries**,
   washed and hulled
¾ C. **water**
⅓ C. **honey**
dash of **salt**
2 T. **cornstarch**
1½ T. **water** (approximately)

Cream Mixture:
3 oz. **cream cheese**
1 T. **honey**
2 t. **lemon juice**
½ t. **vanilla**
dash of **salt**

Garnish:
1 C. whipped **cream**

Glaze Mixture: Pick out 2 C. of best berries and set aside. Place remaining berries in saucepan and chop. Add ¾ C. water, honey and salt. Bring to a boil and boil hard for 2 minutes. Strain. Make a paste with cornstarch and water; add to strained juice. Return to heat and cook until thickened. Set aside to cool slightly.

Cream Mixture: Mix all ingredients together. Turn into baked crust. Place 2 C. reserved strawberries on top of cream cheese mixture. Pour cooled glaze carefully over the berries. Garnish with whipped cream.   *PROTEIN: 29.4 grams; CALORIES: 2328*

Josie Ettinger
Notasulga, Alabama

PUMPKIN PIE

9" **pie crust**, unbaked (p. 266)
2 C. cooked, mashed **pumpkin**
2 **eggs**, beaten
¼ to ⅓ C. **honey**
2 T. **molasses** (optional)
1 t. ground **cinnamon**
½ t. ground **ginger**
¼ t. ground **cloves**
1 C. light **cream** or half-and-half
   or milk plus 2 T. melted butter
   or yogurt
½ t. **vanilla**

Blend filling ingredients with beater or blender. Pour into pie crust. Bake at 400° for 45 to 55 minutes, or until knife inserted halfway between center and crust comes out clean. Cool on rack.

PROTEIN: 40 grams; CALORIES: 2043

Karen Nelson
Dickinson, North Dakota

Variation: Replace pumpkin with 2 C. cooked **sweet potatoes** or winter squash. Add ½ t. ground **nutmeg** and ½ C. unsweetened, shredded **coconut**, if desired. Bake at 350° for about 1 hour.   *PROTEIN: 44.1 grams; CALORIES: 2509*

Lois Lake Raabe
Easton, Connecticut

FROZEN FRUIT

Never toss out uneaten wedges of apple, melon, pineapple, oranges, peaches, or a few berries or grapes left on a child's plate. Freeze them! Stored in a bag, they're ready to pop frozen into any blend for 'sicles or shakes, giving surprise flavor and extra goodness that would otherwise be thrown away.   *Mary Margaret Coates*
Wheat Ridge, Colorado

FRUITRITIOUS

3 large **apples**
3 firm, ripe **bananas**
2 **oranges**, peeled
1 ripe **pear**
1 ripe **avocado**
1 ripe **papaya** (optional)
½ C. **raisins**
8 dried **apricots**
12 **dates**
8 **prunes**
⅓ C. **currants**
3 T. unsweetened, shredded
   coconut
2 T. raw **wheat germ**
2 T. raw, ground **almonds**
3 T. raw **peanuts**
3 T. raw **cashew** pieces
2 T. **sesame seeds**
heavy cream or soy cream
   (optional)

Cut fresh fruit into bite-sized pieces. Cut large dried fruit into small pieces. Combine all fruit in a 3-quart bowl. Mix raw nuts and seeds in a bowl before sprinkling over the fruit. (If preferred, toast the nuts and seeds in a cast-iron frying pan over medium-high heat, stirring constantly. Toast the sesame seeds, peanuts and cashews together first, as they toast more slowly. Hold a lid above the pan to prevent the sesame seeds from "popping" out. Then add the coconut, wheat germ and ground almonds. When cooled, sprinkle the nuts and seeds over the fruit.) Serve with cream at the table.

I won an honorable mention in an Ohio newspaper contest with this recipe.   *P.: 59.7 gms.; C.: 3490 + cream*

Barbara Dick
Seattle, Washington

YOGURT YUMSICLES

1 to 2 C. plain **yogurt**
1 C. unsweetened **fruit juice**
   or 6 oz. frozen concentrate,
   thawed (orange, apple, grape
   or pineapple)
1 t. **vanilla**
1 T. **honey**

Optional:
1 ripe **banana**
10 or 12 **strawberries**
1 T. (envelope) unflavored
   gelatin
¼ to ½ C. cold **water**

Yogurt and orange juice make dandy popsicles. A 2-year-old, a bowl and a fork are all the equipment necessary (plus towels for mopping up!). If using whole fruit, puree everything in a blender or food processor. Gelatin in the mixture retards melting on a hot day. Soften it in water, heat slightly to dissolve; blend with yogurt mixture. Pour into molds or small paper cups. Plastic spoons make good handles; stick them in when yogurt is partially frozen.

PROTEIN: 13.7 grams; CALORIES: 330
Many LLL Contributors

FROZEN YOGURT SANDWICHES

yogurt yumsicles (above)
18 **graham cracker** squares (p. 100)

After blending, pour yumsicle mixture about 1" thick into an 8" square pan. Freeze until very firm. Cut into nine 2½" squares and serve between graham cracker halves.

Bobbie Jarvinen   *Barbara Upton*
Howell, Michigan   *Aurora, Colorado*

MAKE-AHEAD FROZEN YOGURT SALAD

1½ C. diced fresh **fruit** (or
  unsweetened canned, drained)
4 C. flavored **yogurt**
⅓ C. **sunflower seeds** or
  chopped nuts (optional)
lettuce (optional)

Mix all ingredients except lettuce. Line muffin pans with paper baking cups, if desired. Fill cups; freeze until firm. Store in plastic bags. Thirty minutes before serving, remove the number needed for a quick, special salad treat. (Or put them in the microwave oven for 15 to 20 seconds.) Serve on lettuce leaves, if desired.   *PROTEIN: 49.1 grams; CALORIES: 1173*

Try this salad with orange yogurt and apricots. It can be varied according to your family's preferences and the availability of fresh fruit. It is perfect to prepare ahead for a baby's arrival, or for a special occasion. Young kitchen helpers enjoy stirring the ingredients together and spooning them into the cups. This makes 16 to 18 salads, depending upon how much is eaten by your helpers before it is frozen.

Martha Campbell   *Paula Janssen*
Mobile, Alabama   *Midlothian, Illinois*

ORANGE-FRUIT SLUSH

12 oz. **orange juice
  concentrate**, thawed
1½ C. (12 oz. can) **water**
6 to 10 small **bananas**, diced
2 to 4 C. unsweetened **pineapple**,
  crushed or tidbit
2 C. fresh or unsweetened
  canned **apricots**, diced
2 T. **lemon juice**
1 to 2 C. fresh **fruit** (optional)
  (strawberries, cherries,
  apples, pears, oranges)

Variation:
Omit pineapple and apricots.
Use only 6 bananas and add
2 C. **peaches**, diced.

Mix all ingredients, including all of the juice from the canned fruit. Spoon into parfait glasses or small paper cups. Cover each with foil and freeze. Thaw for 30 minutes before serving. Keeps in the freezer for one month or more.   *P.: 27.7 gms.; C.: 1790*

Popsicles. Blend some of the mixture and freeze in popsicle molds.

For Baby: Freeze in an ice cube tray. A cube or two thawed to a mushy consistency is a good snack or dessert for a baby who's had all of these fruits. A frozen cube will help ease teething pain.

Susan Reed   *Linda Miller*   *Debbie Wack*   *Patsy Reed*
Anderson, Indiana   *McPherson, Kansas*   *Clairton, Pennsylvania*   *Waverly, Iowa*

SNOW ICE CREAM

2 **eggs**, well beaten (optional)
2 C. **milk**
1 C. **sugar** or ¾ C. **honey**
1 T. **vanilla**
¼ t. **salt**
flavoring to taste (optional)
bucket of fresh, clean **snow**

In a 2-qt. bowl, mix beaten eggs and milk. Blend in sugar, mixing well. Add vanilla, salt and flavoring, if desired. Put into a gallon container and gradually add snow, mixing well, until of desired consistency. Serve immediately (it melts fast!) or freeze. This makes about a gallon of ice cream.   *Karen Elkins*
P.: 29.2 gms.; C.: 1293   *Minot AFB, N. Dakota*

FRESH PINEAPPLE SHERBET

1 ripe **pineapple**
1 pint **strawberries**, hulled
  or 2 C. peeled, cut up
    oranges or orange juice
  or 1 to 2 C. oranges or
    juice *plus:* ¼ C. rhubarb,
    2 apples, cored and cut up,
    or other fruits (plums,
    cherries, nectarines,
    apricots, mangoes, papaya)
½ C. unsweetened, shredded
  coconut (optional)

Garnish:
ground **walnuts**, almonds
  or pecans

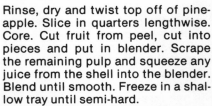

Rinse, dry and twist top off of pineapple. Slice in quarters lengthwise. Core. Cut fruit from peel, cut into pieces and put in blender. Scrape the remaining pulp and squeeze any juice from the shell into the blender. Blend until smooth. Freeze in a shallow tray until semi-hard.

Blend the strawberries. Fold into the pineapple slush. Fold in coconut. Refreeze. Cut chunks of frozen sherbet and serve, or put into a food processor or blender to make more like a soft sherbet.

If in a hurry, the fruits can be blended together right away. A fluffier sherbet will result if the mixture is blended again when semi-hard.

PROTEIN: 6.3 grams; CALORIES: 636 + garnish

Peach Frost. Use 2 C. **peaches** and 2 C. orange juice or peeled, cut up oranges.

Jo Ann Ploeger
Alexandria, Kentucky

INSTANT BANANA ICE CREAM

1 to 6 T. **apple juice**, water
  or milk
2 very ripe **bananas**, peeled,
  sliced and frozen
1 t. **vanilla**

Optional:
½ C. cold fresh **fruit** (peaches,
  strawberries or blueberries)
honey to taste, if fruit is tart

Put 1 T. juice, frozen banana slices and vanilla in blender or food processor and blend, turning on and off, until smooth. Add more juice if necessary. (While the machine is off, you may need to stir the frozen slices towards the blades of the blender.) If desired, blend in cold fruit and honey. Serve immediately, as it melts quickly.

Everyone enjoys this for a quick snack or dessert. It is easily prepared for unexpected company and may be a milk-free treat. *PROTEIN: 3.7 grams; CALORIES: 308*

Variations: Omit cold fruit. Add 3 pitted **dates** and ¼ C. raw **cashews** *or* 2 T. **carob powder.**

Suzanne Parker   *Rose Yonekura*
Griffin, Georgia   *Lincoln, Nebraska*

INSTANT BLUEBERRY ICE CREAM

1 C. frozen **blueberries**
½ C. **milk**
1 T. **honey** (optional)

Put everything in blender or food processor. Blend and serve immediately. *P.: 5.4 gms.; C.: 229*

Marge Wright
Richland, Pennsylvania

WATERMELON SHERBET

Seed and puree any amount of **watermelon**. Freeze in large shallow pans. Stir every hour until desired consistency.
This is a big hit with kids and adults alike.

Lauren Pohn
Wheeling, Illinois

HONEY VANILLA CUSTARD ICE CREAM

6 **egg yolks**
1 C. **honey**
3 T. **cornstarch**
4 C. **milk**
4 C. **heavy cream** or milk
2 T. **vanilla**
6 **egg whites**

Beat egg yolks, lightly. Gradually add honey and cornstarch until smooth. In 3-quart heavy saucepan, combine the milk with the egg mixture. Cook over medium heat, stirring constantly, until mixture is thickened. Refrigerate for several hours. When mixture is thoroughly chilled, stir in heavy cream and vanilla. Beat the egg whites until stiff and gently fold into the custard mixture. Process in an ice cream freezer until thick and creamy. Harden in freezer. This ice cream is creamy, delicious, and just sweet enough.

Try this even if you don't have an ice cream freezer. Stir to break up the egg whites and freeze. Stir every hour or so until it hardens. It won't be as creamy this way, but it will still be delicious. *PROTEIN: 79.5 grams; CALORIES: 3752*

Quick and Easy. Use eggs without separating. Use all milk, no cream.

PROTEIN: 93.9 grams; CALORIES: 2732

Cherie Wolfe Parsons   *Josie Ettinger*
Morgan Hill, California   *Notasulga, Alabama*

Cakes

EGGLESS, SUGARLESS CARROT CAKE

½ C. grated **carrots**
1¼ C. chopped **dates**
1⅓ C. **water**
1 C. **raisins**
¼ C. **butter**
1 t. *each* ground **cinnamon,
cloves** and **nutmeg**
2 C. whole wheat **flour**
1 t. **baking powder**
1 t. **baking soda**
¼ t. **salt**
½ C. chopped **nuts**

Place carrots, dates, water, raisins, butter and spices in a pan. Bring slowly to a boil and simmer for 5 minutes; cool. Meanwhile, stir together dry ingredients and add with nuts to the first mixture. Stir until blended. Pour into a well greased and floured 9" ring mold. Bake at 375° for 45 to 50 minutes. To fill a large Bundt pan, make a double recipe.

PROTEIN: 52 grams; CALORIES: 2532

Donna Weifert
Kings Beach, California

CARROT OR ZUCCHINI CAKE
(With Pineapple)

2 C. whole wheat **flour**
2 t. **baking powder**
1½ t. **baking soda**
1 t. **salt**
2 t. ground **cinnamon**
¾ C. **oil**
¾ C. **honey**
4 **eggs**
2 C. grated **carrots** or zucchini
1 C. unsweetened, crushed
  pineapple, drained
½ C. chopped **nuts**

cream cheese frosting (p. 279)

Mix dry ingredients together in a large bowl. Add oil, honey and eggs; mix well. Stir in remaining ingredients. Turn into 3 greased and floured 9" layer pans, or one 9 x 13" pan. (Dust pans with **wheat germ** for extra nut flavor.) Bake at 350° for 35 to 40 minutes. Cool a few minutes in pan; turn out and thoroughly cool on racks. Fill layers and frost with Cream Cheese Frosting.
  This is a big favorite for family and for company.

PROTEIN: 68.6; CALORIES: 3227 + frosting

Jean McNertney   *Polly J. Mertens*   *Stephanie Carlquist*   *Meredith Hoare*
Ft. Worth, Texas   *Harrison, Ohio*   *Burbank, California*   *Toronto, Ont., Canada*

TROPICAL DELIGHT CAKE

2 **eggs**, beaten
½ C. **honey**
2 C. whole wheat pastry **flour**
½ t. **salt**
2 t. **baking soda**
¾ C. chopped **walnuts**
2½ C. unsweetened, crushed
  pineapple, with juice
1 C. diced **dates**
½ C. unsweetened, shredded
  coconut
¼ C. dry **milk powder**
¼ C. **wheat germ**

Mix all ingredients together. Pour batter into an oiled and floured tube pan. Bake at 350° for 35 to 40 minutes. Cool. Frost with **banana-nut cream cheese frosting** (p. 279).
  This cake gets rave reviews wherever it goes. It's a cake that can be made well ahead of time and frosted at the last minute. Very moist! It's one cake I don't mind serving my family and friends because it is wholesome and nutritious, yet meets their criteria for being good too! Is this what they call having your cake and eating it too?

PROTEIN: 83.3 grams; CALORIES: 3335   *Linda Studer*
  Avon, Ohio

ORANGE-COCONUT FROSTING

1 T. **arrowroot** or cornstarch
6 oz. **orange juice concentrate,**
  thawed
1 C. unsweetened, shredded
  coconut

Stir arrowroot into concentrate. Heat until thickened, stirring constantly. Remove from heat and stir until slightly cooled. Dip muffins in frosting and then in coconut.
  Plain bran muffins and other "health loaves" always seemed to be left over at bake sales until I discovered this easy way to make them more attractive.

P.: 7.2 gms.; C.: 647

Nancy Johnson
Greeley, Colorado

SERENITY'S PUMPKIN CAKE

1 C. boiling **water**
1 C. **currants** or raisins
½ C. **butter**
¾ C. **honey**
¼ C. **molasses**
2 **eggs**, beaten
1 t. **vanilla** or maple extract
1 C. cooked, mashed **pumpkin**
2 C. whole wheat pastry **flour**
1 C. soy **flour**
⅔ C. dry **milk powder**
pinch of **salt**
¼ t. **baking soda**
4 t. **baking powder**
1 t. ground **cinnamon**
¼ t. *each* ground **cloves,**
   allspice and **nutmeg**
½ C. **milk**
1 C. chopped **walnuts** or pecans

Pour boiling water over currants; set aside. Cream together butter and sweeteners until light and fluffy. Beat in eggs and vanilla, then pumpkin. In another bowl, sift together flours, dry milk, salt, soda, baking powder and spices. Drain plumped currants and toss with fork in 1 C. of the flour mixture to coat. Add the rest of the flour mixture alternately with the milk to the creamed mixture, stirring after each addition. Lastly, fold in floured currants and nuts. Turn the batter into greased and floured layer pans (for "fancy"), Bundt or tube pan. Bake at 350° for 25 minutes, or until it tests done.

This cake is very moist and nutritious, especially with home-cooked pumpkin. Kids can have all they want and Mama can relax and enjoy the party! This cake was created for Serenity's October birthday.

PROTEIN: 140.1 grams; CALORIES: 4452

Diana Lewis
San Antonio, Texas

DATE-NUT CAKE
(Egg- and Milk-free)

1 C. coarsely chopped **dates**
½ C. chopped **walnuts**
⅓ to ½ C. **sugar** or honey
1¼ C. whole wheat **flour**
1 t. **baking soda**
½ t. **salt** (optional)
1 C. boiling **water**
1 T. **butter**
1 t. **vanilla**
2 C. unsweetened, whipped
   cream as garnish

In a 6-cup bowl, mix dates, walnuts and dry ingredients. In a small bowl, mix boiling water, butter and vanilla; add to date mixture and stir until all ingredients are moistened. Bake in a greased and floured 8" or 9" square pan at 350° for 30 to 40 minutes. Serve warm or cold, plain or topped with whipped cream.

This recipe is quite old, and is traditionally a Christmas dessert. I have taken it to several LLL meetings and always get requests for the recipe.

PROTEIN: 79.5 grams; CALORIES: 2541

Janice Trevail
Catskill, New York

GOLDEN NUGGET ICING

8 oz. **cream cheese**, softened
1 C. unsweetened, crushed
   pineapple, drained, and
   reserved **juice**
½ C. finely chopped **walnuts**
   (optional)

Mix cream cheese with pineapple. Add juice to achieve desired consistency. Try this on carrot cake with walnuts sprinkled on top.

PROTEIN: 26.8 grams; CALORIES: 1322

Polly J. Mertens
Harrison, Ohio

FRESH APPLE GINGERBREAD

½ C. **butter**
2 to 3 large **eggs**
⅔ C. **molasses**
2 C. whole wheat **flour**
1½ t. **baking soda**
1 t. ground **ginger**
½ t. *each* ground **cinnamon**
and **nutmeg**
¼ t. ground **cloves**
⅓ C. **milk**
1¼ C. grated **apple**

Cream butter, eggs and molasses well. Combine the dry ingredients and add alternately with the milk to the butter mixture. Stir in grated apple. Pour into a greased and floured 9" square pan. Bake at 350° for 40 to 45 minutes. Cool 10 minutes in pan, then remove and cool on wire rack. Top with sweetened **whipped cream**, if desired.   *Patty Holtz*

PROTEIN: 48.9 grams; CALORIES: 2570   *Geneva, Illinois*

GOOD-FOR-YOU BANANA CAKE

1⅔ C. whole wheat pastry
flour
⅓ C. soy **flour**
¼ C. **nutritional yeast**
1 C. **honey**
1¼ t. **baking powder**
1½ t. **baking soda**
1 t. **salt**
⅔ C. **butter**, softened
⅔ C. **buttermilk**
2 to 3 **eggs**
1½ C. mashed, ripe **banana**
⅓ C. **wheat germ**
⅓ C. finely chopped **nuts**

Measure all ingredients into a large bowl. With mixer, blend for ½ minute on low speed, scraping the bowl constantly. Beat for 3 minutes at high speed, scraping occasionally. Pour into greased and floured 9 x 13" pan. Bake at 350° for 45 to 50 minutes. This is good with **cream cheese frosting** (p. 279).

PROTEIN: 97.9 grams; CALORIES: 3991
Sue La Leike
Cape Coral, Florida

CAROB "DEVIL'S FOOD" CAKE

⅔ C. **honey**
¼ C. **butter**, softened
1 **egg**
½ C. **buttermilk**
1 t. **vanilla**
1 C. whole wheat pastry **flour**
1 T. **nutritional yeast**
1 T. soy **flour**
½ t. **salt**
1 t. **baking soda**
2 T. **carob powder**
½ C. hot **water**

Cream together honey and butter. Beat in egg, buttermilk and vanilla. Sift together dry ingredients and add to honey mixture alternately with water. Pour into a greased and floured 9" square pan. Bake at 350° for 30 to 40 minutes. May be easily doubled for a 9 x 13" pan, and baked a little longer.

I developed this recipe from a cocoa and sugar-laden version that used to be a family favorite. It's a big help in winning my husband over to carob.   PROTEIN: 34.6 grams; CALORIES: 1738

Sue LaLeike
Cape Coral, Florida

LISA'S WEDDING CAKE
(Apple Spice Cake)

½ C. **butter**
¾ C. **honey** or brown sugar
2 **eggs**
2½ to 3½ C. chunked **apples**
2 C. whole wheat pastry **flour**
1½ t. **baking powder**
½ t. **baking soda**
1½ t. ground **cinnamon**
¼ t. ground **cloves**
½ t. grated **nutmeg**
½ t. ground **allspice**
½ t. **salt**
¾ C. golden **raisins**
¾ C. black **walnuts**

Cream butter and honey together in food processor. Add eggs and 2 C. apples and process until smooth. Mix flour with other dry ingredients and add gradually to mixture.

Beat briefly, then add the rest of the apples, processing only until the pieces are ¼" chunks—or size you prefer. Stir in raisins and nuts (of your choice) by hand. Pour into greased and floured 9" cake pan or 8 x 8" baking pan. Bake at 350° 45 to 60 minutes. Frost with maple flavored butter frosting.

To make without a food processor, omit the chunked apples; use 1½ C. applesauce and 1 C. chopped apples.   *PROTEIN: 65.1 grams; CALORIES: 3888*

This was recipe #11 developed over a summer of recipe testing for Lisa's wedding—a special cake for a daughter who shares an October 1956 birthdate with La Leche League.

Roberta Bishop Johnson
Champaign, Illinois

OAT CAKE

1 C. **water**
½ C. **butter**
¾ to 1 C. **honey** or maple syrup
2 C. **oat flour***
½ C. whole wheat **flour**
1 t. **baking soda**
½ t. **salt**
1½ t. ground **cinnamon**
2 **eggs**, beaten
½ C. **buttermilk**, yogurt, sour cream or soured milk

Combine water, butter and honey in a 3-quart pan. Heat to boiling; remove from heat. Stir together dry ingredients and add to heated mixture, mixing until well blended. Add eggs and buttermilk; mix well. Bake in greased 9 x 13" pan at 375° for 30 to 40 minutes.

If I assemble the ingredients, my 4-year-old can make this cake himself. It's great because you can use what's on hand and have your treat ready to go in less than an hour. I don't usually frost it, but for special occasions I add a Cream Cheese Frosting.

*Make oat flour by grinding rolled oats in a blender or food processor.

PROTEIN: 74.2 grams; CALORIES: 3379 + frosting

Variations:

#1 Add about 1 C. chopped **fruit**. Especially good are apples, peaches, bananas, pears or dried fruits.

#2 For a gingerbread-like cake, substitute ½ C. **molasses** for ½ Ç. honey; add about 1 t. ground **ginger** and ¼ t. ground **cloves**.

#3 For a carob cake, add   ½ C. **carob powder** to water before boiling. Omit cinnamon.

Renee Chalfant-Bednark
Boulder, Colorado

VANILLA YOGURT TOPPING

1 **egg**, separated
1 C. plain **yogurt**
½ t. **vanilla**
3 T. liquid **honey**

Optional:
1 t. unflavored **gelatin**
2 T. cold **water**

Beat egg yolk in a medium bowl. Add yogurt and vanilla and whip smooth. In another bowl beat the egg white until stiff peaks form. Beat in honey.
Soften gelatin in water and heat until dissolved. Stir into yogurt and mix well. Fold in beaten egg white.

If the topping is to be used immediately, the gelatin may be omitted; if it is to be kept in the refrigerator for several hours, the gelatin will help prevent separation.   PROTEIN: 18.3 GRAMS; CALORIES: 411   *Bryanna Clark*
Union Bay, B.C., Canada

HONEY FROSTING

⅓ C. **honey**
2 to 4 **egg whites**
dash of **cream of tartar**
a few grains of **salt**
1 t. **extract** (vanilla, almond, anise, lemon or other)

Combine all ingredients. Beat at high speed until fluffy. Use as frosting for 9 x 13" or 2-layer cake.
A good way to use extra egg whites after you start feeding yolks to the baby.

Meringue Kisses. Drop by teaspoonfuls onto brown paper-lined cookie sheet. Dry in very low (200°) oven for 1 hour. Turn off oven and leave until dry. Remove from paper with sharp knife or by moistening the underside of the brown paper.

Torte Layer or **shell.** Spread frosting into circles or shape into shells. Dry as above. Fill with crushed **fruit.** Or form torte by layering with fruit or **peanut butter satin** (p. 255). For special occasions, pipe through decorating tube.   PROTEIN: 7 grams; CALORIES: 391

Roberta Bishop Johnson
Champaign, Illinois

FRUITY CAKE TOPPING

1 C. non-instant dry **milk powder**
2 T. **honey**
¼ C. **pineapple juice**
1 C. unsweetened, crushed **pineapple**, drained
¼ C. **juice** (pineapple, orange or apple)
1 T. (envelope) unflavored **gelatin**
1 pint fresh **strawberries**, sliced

Mix dry milk, honey and ¼ C. pineapple juice in a blender until smooth. Put in a bowl and mix in the pineapple. Set aside. Soften gelatin in the other ¼ C. juice. Heat to boiling, stirring to dissolve. Dribble the gelatin into the icing mixture, stirring constantly. Refrigerate until thick. Spread either on top of a 9 x 13" cake or on bottom layer of a round cake. Arrange strawberries on top of icing. You may wish to save

some strawberries to put on the top of a double layer cake. Try this topping on cheesecake too.   PROTEIN: 33.5 grams; CALORIES: 1104

Patti Adamski
Hometown, Illinois

POWDERED MILK FROSTING

¼ C. **butter**, softened
¼ C. **honey** or maple syrup
2 to 3 T. **milk** or cream
1 t. **vanilla**, almond or
   lemon extract
⅔ to 1 C. instant or ½ C.
   non-instant dry **milk powder**

Cream together butter and honey. Beat in milk and vanilla. Add dry milk powder and continue beating until light and fluffy. Add more liquid or milk powder to achieve proper consistency. For use on breads or rolls, the butter may be omitted, if desired, and the frosting thinned. If a smoother frosting is desired, add a little more butter.

The frosting may be naturally colored by using **fruit juice**, such as cranberry or grape, or juice from a raw beet or carrot which has been grated and squeezed in cheesecloth. The frosting may be left uncolored and decorated with fresh **flowers** which would not hurt baby in case one is eaten, such as sweet peas, pansies, violets, calendulas or nasturtiums.

PROTEIN: 35.1 grams; CALORIES: 1058

Carob Frosting. Add ¼ C. sifted **carob powder** before adding ⅔ C. instant or ⅓ to ½ C. non-instant dry milk powder.   *P.: 36.7 gms.; C.: 1121*

Fruit Frosting. Substitute **fruit juice** for milk. Add grated **orange rind**, lemon rind, raisins or chopped dates.

Bryanna Clark   *Joann Grohman*   *Karen Wedman*
Union Bay, B.C., Canada *Dixfield, Maine*   *Alberta, Canada*

GLAZE

¼ C. **juice** (lemon or orange)
2 T. **honey**
1 T. **butter**

Combine ingredients in saucepan. Boil for 2 to 3 minutes. Pour over cooled **cake**. This may be used to "dress up" any cake or **bread**, and is especially good on applesauce cake.   *PROTEIN: .6 grams; CALORIES: 246*

Jackie Diachun
Lexington, Kentucky

CREAM CHEESE FROSTING

8 oz. **cream cheese**, softened
8 T. **butter**, softened
2 to 4 T. **honey**
1 t. **vanilla**
½ C. chopped **nuts** (optional)

Beat cream cheese and butter until fluffy. Beat in honey to taste. Add vanilla and nuts. Keep refrigerated. Delicious on carrot cake!

PROTEIN: 26.7 grams; CALORIES: 2183

Variations:

Banana-Nut. Omit the honey, or use only 2 T. Beat in one small ripe **banana**. Add nuts. Chill to spreading consistency. Decorate frosted cake with banana chips or **raisins**.

Tinted. Add ¼ to ½ C. unsweetened crushed **raspberries, blueberries** or **strawberries**. If desired, arrange whole berries or fresh sliced strawberries in a design on top of the cake.

Butterless. Omit butter. Thawed **orange** or **apple juice concentrate** may be substituted for the honey. Omit vanilla.

Jean McNertney   *Linda Studer*   *Barb Muehlhausen*   *Judith A. Gubala*
Ft. Worth, Texas   *Avon, Ohio*   *Schaumburg, Illinois*   *Rocky Hill, Connecticut*

Making Your Own

COTTAGE CHEESE

Cottage cheese is made from milk which has stood until sour and formed a solid curd. If you are able to use untreated (raw) milk, simply stand the container of milk, loosely covered, in a dark place at about 75 degrees until set. This may take one or two days. If you use pasteurized milk, starter must be added. Cultured buttermilk or yogurt that is known to contain an active culture may be used; add 1 T. per quart of milk. Cottage cheese curd may also be formed by using a junket rennet tablet. Plain junket tablets are now rarely available in grocery stores but may be obtained from a pharmacy. Only pasteurized or raw milk may be used with junket. Boiled, canned or longlife milk cannot be used as high heat has reduced the soluability of the calcium upon which the action of the rennet depends.

After the milk has set, either by the action of rennet or by natural acid formation (natural souring) heat it slowly, stirring frequently, to about 120 degrees. Pour off the whey through a cheesecloth. The curds of commercial cottage cheese are then washed and cream or thickened milk added. This step is unnecessary and somewhat wasteful. You need only drain the curds, adding a little salt if desired.

Joann S. Grohman
Dixfield, Maine

CIRAK or EASTER CHEESE
(Traditional Czechoslovakian Easter delicacy)

1 dozen **eggs**
4 C. **milk**
1 t. **salt**

Use a heavy saucepan but not aluminum or cast iron, as they tend to discolor egg mixtures. Non-stick, glass, stainless steel or vitrified porcelain are best. Keep heat low or use pad heat diffuser to avoid sticking. Pour milk in pan, add salt, break eggs in one at a time, breaking yolks. Cook, stirring slowly, until mixture resembles scrambled eggs. Line a bowl with four layers of cheesecloth and pour in egg mixture. Tie up corners and drain one hour, suspended over bowl. Place on wire mesh rack or reed mat and weight with heavy object; press and drain about two hours. Carefully remove cheese from bag to avoid breaking; chill. Delicious with whole wheat toast and ham. Can be sliced.

Mary Jo Heinen
Woodbine, Maryland

Before draining—PROTEIN: 108 grams; CALORIES: 1580

YOGURT

4 C. **milk**
1 C. dry **milk powder**
2 to 4 T. plain **yogurt** with active cultures
2 t. unflavored **gelatin** softened in ¼ C. cold water (optional)

Scald milk. Cool to temperature of 95° to 115°. Check with candy or outdoor thermometer to be sure. Stir in milk powder and yogurt. Add softened gelatin for a firmer yogurt. Pour into sterilized jars, a baking dish with a cover or a thermos rinsed with very hot water. Put on lids or cover. Place into or on yogurt maker or use other heat source. Just wrap thermos with a towel and it does not need an outside heat source. Put it in a warm place. Incubate at 95° to 115° until yogurt sets. It can take from 3 to 9 hours depending on your heat source. After 3 hours check to see if it is set by tilting jar or by tapping the jar with the heel of your hand. When set, refrigerate immediately. Makes 4 C.

The heat source is the most critical factor for successful yogurt making. Too low a temperature will incubate sour milk bacteria rather than yogurt bacteria; too high a temperature will kill the bacteria. There are other alternatives to commercial yogurt makers or a thermos. You can put the dish or jars in a water bath (95° to 115°) in an electric fry pan or crock pot, in a gas oven with pilot light on, in an electric oven preheated at its lowest temperture setting then turned off, in a box with a light bulb, or in a box set on a heating pad. Or you can wrap the dish or jars in a heating pad set on low. All of these sources work well, so experiment and see what works best for you. Once you establish your heat source yogurt making will be simple. *PROTEIN: 81.3 grams; CALORIES: 1113 Many LLL Contributors*

MAKE-YOUR-OWN BUTTERMILK

¼ to ½ C. **buttermilk**
3½ to 4 C. fresh **milk** or reconstituted dry milk powder

Leave ¼ to ½ C. commercial or homemade buttermilk in bottom of its container. Fill with milk, leaving ½ to 1" head space. Close container and shake well. Let sit in warm place all day or overnight. It will take about 10 hours in winter, 5 to 10 hours in summer. When slightly thickened, refrigerate. Save some for the next batch.

This buttermilk is very sweet-smelling, higher in quality than store-bought and it tastes much better! *With whole milk—PROTEIN: 31.6 grams; CALORIES: 586*
With skim milk—PROTEIN: 30.2 grams; CALORIES: 334

Debbie Guy   *Lenora Hedin*
Hattiesburg, Mississippi   *Askov, Minnesota*

BUTTER

Use either cream which you have skimmed off of fresh milk or cartons of whipping cream; any quantity. Bring the cream to about 60° F. in your mixing bowl. Turn on the mixer and beat at medium speed until cream separates into clumps of butter the size of wheat grains or larger. Sometimes the cream whips before becoming butter; simply keep beating until it "breaks." Drain off the buttermilk and rinse the butter under cold water. Press with a wooden spoon or cold fingers to remove all water. Add salt if desired, ½ t. to ½ lb. butter. Small quantities of cream may be churned in a blender at lowest speed. *Joann S. Grohman*
Dixfield, Maine

SUPER BUTTER

½ t. **salt**
2 t. warm **water**
1 T. **lecithin**
1 lb. **butter**, softened
2 C. vegetable **oil**
4 T. dry **milk powder**

Dissolve salt in water. Add lecithin to soften. Add this mixture to the remaining ingredients. Process in mixer, blender or food processor until smooth. Refrigerate. Yields 4 C.

PROTEIN: 12.6 grams; CALORIES: 5865

Barbara Becker Nelson
Eugene, Oregon

HOMEMADE SAUSAGES

Easy Breakfast Sausage
1 lb. ground **pork** or beef
¼ to 1 t. **sage**
¼ to ½ t. **marjoram** (optional)
¼ to ½ t. **thyme** (optional)
¼ to ½ t. **coriander** (optional)
1 t. **salt**
1/8 t. **pepper**
1 to 3 T. **water**
3' of sausage **casings** (optional)

PROTEIN: 68.5 grams; CALORIES: 1566

Italian Sausage
1 lb. medium ground **pork** or ½ lb. pork and ½ lb. beef
1 medium **onion**, minced
1½ t. **salt**
1 clove **garlic**, minced
1 **bay leaf**, finely crumbled
½ t. **pepper**
½ t. **fennel seed**, crushed
¼ t. **paprika**
1/8 t. **thyme**
1/8 t. **cayenne pepper**
3' of sausage **casings** (optional)

PROTEIN: 70.5 grams; CALORIES: 1613

Polish Kielbasa
2 lb. coarsely ground **pork** butt
¾ lb. finely ground **beef**
1½ t. coarse **salt**
1½ t. crushed **peppercorns**
1½ t. **marjoram**
1 T. **paprika**
2 cloves **garlic**, minced
1 t. **honey** (optional)
½ t. ground **nutmeg**
6' of sausage **casings** (optional)

PROTEIN: 198.5 grams; CALORIES: 4081

Sausage casings are available from your butcher. Refrigerated they will keep for 2 years. If using casings, soak in water for 2 hours or overnight in the refrigerator.

Choose the sausage you want to make. Sprinkle the seasonings over the ground meat. Knead until thoroughly blended. Make into patties, a meatloaf or stuff into sausage casings by hand or with a sausage horn. Make a large roll or tie off in 5 to 18" links with string. Refrigerate in airtight containers for 2 or 3 days to allow flavors to blend. If you plan to use the sausage immediately, the spices will not be as strong.

Cooking instructions
Patties: Fry until golden brown.
Loaf: Set loaf pan in another pan of hot water in oven. Bake at 350° for 1½ hours or until meat thermometer reaches 160°.
Roll or **links:** Cover with water in fry pan. Simmer for 20 to 30 minutes. Drain water and fry until golden brown. Or use in other recipes.

Making your own sausage allows you to choose the freshest ingredients available and to avoid the use of nitrites. Use only fresh ground meat since the refrigerator life of nitrite-free sausage is 4 to 5 days. Curing takes 2 to 3 days. If you cannot use all of the sausage, freeze it. It will keep for 1 or 2 months in the freezer.

Chorizo (Hot Spanish Sausage)
1½ lbs. ground **pork** or beef or
   ¾ lb. of each
2 t. **chili powder** or cayenne
1 large **onion**, minced
2 t. **oregano**, crushed
½ t. ground **cumin**
¼ t. ground **cinnamon**
½ t. **garlic powder**
5 T. **vinegar** or red wine
1 t. **salt**
4' of sausage **casings** (optional)

Pork shoulder and beef chuck contain enough fat. If using leaner meat add fat in a ratio of 3 parts lean to 1 part fat. Curing and the addition of salt preserve the meat. Extra spices actually shorten the freezer life of the sausage. Sage will make the meat bitter if it is frozen. So season lightly and let the curing process extend the flavors.

PROTEIN: 105 grams; CALORIES: 2415

Nancy Yant
East Aurora, New York

Barbara Becker Nelson
Eugene, Oregon

Karen Barclay
Connellsville, Pennsylvania

PEANUT BUTTER

1 lb. raw shelled **peanuts**

Place peanuts in large flat pan, such as a jelly roll pan, one layer deep. Roast in 325 to 350° oven for 10 to 40 minutes. Keep out a few peanuts to use for color check. The peanuts roast so gradually, you may think they aren't roasting at all and be tempted to turn up the oven or leave them longer before checking them again, so it appears they burn suddenly. When checking the roasting peanuts, pull the pan all the way out of the oven to be sure that the peanuts are roasting evenly. Many ovens have a hot spot at the back, so you should stir or shake the peanuts to rearrange them, then rotate the pan. Remove a few peanuts and compare them away from the oven light with the unroasted peanuts. Taste one. When they are done to your taste, remove from the oven and pour into a food processor at once. The warm peanuts liberate oil easily and the job is soon done. If using a blender, pour in only ¼ C. peanuts and process until butter begins to form around the blender blades. Push peanuts down into this forming butter. **Do not scrape the butter away from the blades.** It serves as the liquid vehicle for the rest of the peanuts. Add more peanuts about 2 T. at a time. To keep from overloading the motor, remove the peanut butter after you have processed about one cup and start a new batch. Using hot peanuts and small batches, you should be able to make creamy peanut butter without the addition   of any other oils. You'll have scrumptiously fresh tasting and peanut-ty smelling peanut butter.

—Roberta Johnson

FRUIT LEATHER

1 to 1½ lbs. (or more) ripe
  fruit
1 T. to ¼ C. **water**, if needed

Optionals:
1 T. to ½ C. **honey**
ground **spices** (cinnamon, allspice,
  cloves, ginger)
flavorings (vanilla or grated lemon
  or orange rind)

An enormous variety of fruit can be pureed and dried to leather-like consistency.

Soft-type fruits, such as peaches, plums, nectarines, and strawberries, can be pureed without cooking. Peel, pit, cut-up (or hull) fruit. Puree in blender or food processor. Add water if necessary. Add options to taste.

Firmer fruits, such as apples and pears, are best if cooked. Core and slice the unpeeled fruit. Steam, or boil fruit in ¼ C. water while stirring to prevent scorching, for 3 to 5 minutes. Puree with skins in blender, or cool and force through a sieve. Add options to taste.

Citrus fruits are best combined with other less juicy fruits such as cranberries. Try combining other fruit purees, such as banana with rhubarb, apricot, or pineapple. Canned or frozen fruits can be used if the juice is drained or boiled down. Dried fruits can be pureed after plumping in water. The puree should be of an applesauce-like consistency; if it is too thin it can be boiled down.

Use baking sheets with non-stick surface or line baking sheets or drying screen with heavy plastic wrap, securing the corners. About 1 to 1½ lbs. fruit will make 2 C. puree which will cover a 10½″ x 15½″ sheet; use this as a guide to determine how many drying sheets you will need. Spread cooled puree evenly over plastic, about 1/8″ inch thick.

Cover the sheets with cheesecloth or fine mesh to keep out insects; dry outside in the sunshine on warm days. (Bring inside at night.) Drying can also be done in a turned off oven with pilot light or in an electric oven that is occasionally heated to 120° to 140°. Open the oven door periodically to let out moisture. The top of a wood stove works nicely, as does the rear window of a closed car parked in the sun. A food dehydrator is ideal.

Drying takes 1 to 2 days, depending upon humidity and moisture of fruit. The puree should be thoroughly dried with no wet or sticky spots

Remove from baking sheets and plastic and roll. Store airtight in a cool, dry place. Refrigerate, or freeze in rigid containers, for long-term storage. If fruit becomes brittle, crack into small bits and sprinkle on cereal or yogurt.

This age-old treat satisfies the sweetest tooth, requires a minimum of preparation time, and lasts as long as you can hold off the snackers! Just cut off a piece and enjoy!

Pumpkin Leather. Puree cooked pumpkin, add options, and proceed as directed.

Leather with Toppings. Sprinkle crushed granola, shredded coconut, chopped nuts, chopped dried fruit, or seeds on puree before drying.

Creamy Roll-Ups: Spread sheets of dried fruit with creamy fillings, such as peanut butter, cream cheese, or fruit butter. Sprinkle with chopped dates and nuts, if desired. Peel dried fruit from plastic, roll, and cut into 1″ pieces. Wrap separately to store.

Judith Hardin   *Norene Schulenberg*   *Ellen Clagett*   *Vicki Ruggiero*
Lubbock, Texas   *Silver Creek, New York* *Littleton, Colorado* *Jewell, Kansas*

YOGURT "CREAM CHEESE"

Dump 1 qt. homemade **yogurt** (make without gelatin) into a colander lined with 2 to 4 layers of cheesecloth, suspended over a bowl. (If possible, tie up the corners of the cheesecloth and suspend the "bag" from a faucet.) In the morning, you'll have creamy yogurt cheese!

ONE-PAN GRANOLA

A recipe for granola is as good as your imagination and the ingredients on your pantry shelf.

Start with:
5 to 6 C. old-fashioned **rolled oats**
Add 6 C. total of any or all of these:
soy flour
whole wheat flour
wheat germ
rolled wheat flakes
sunflower, pumpkin, sesame seeds
non-fat dry milk powder
shredded coconut
unsalted nuts (almonds, peanuts, cashews, walnuts, pecans)

Options for dry mixture:
1 C. **bran**
½ C. **millet**
¼ C. **soy grits**
2 T. nutritional **yeast**
2 t. **cinnamon**
1 t. **salt**

Heat in large roasting pan:
½ to 1 C. **oil** or 2 sticks butter
½ to 1 C. **honey**, molasses or maple syrup or any mixture of these

½ C. **water**
2 t. **vanilla** or almond extract

When liquid mixture is warm and thinned, begin adding dry ingredients; stir each in well with a large wooden spoon. Here's one situation where "too many cooks" are an asset—let all helpers have a turn!

Granola may be toasted right in the roasting-mixing pan! Set oven at 250°; bake approximately 2 hours, stirring every 20 minutes. You may spread mixture on cookie sheets, too, for shorter baking time (about 30 minutes at 325°). Turn with pancake turner at 10 minute intervals. Watch carefully until done to your family's taste; remember granola becomes crisper as it cools in the pan. If you have difficulty getting the mixture to taste cooked, you might try toasting the flours lightly in the oven or by stirring in an iron skillet for a few minutes.

When the cereal is cool, mix in up to 2 C. of dried **apricots, apple,** or **pineapple, raisins, dates,** or **prunes.** Serve "as is" for a snack, with milk or yogurt for breakfast, or create your own granola bars. It makes a thoughtful gift for the mother of a new baby with older children at home, or for friends at holiday time, packed in a decorative tin. Carry along for camping and hikes in little paper bags. Share with squirrels! Quantities of granola are easily adjusted up or down, according to family size. This recipe makes about 14 cups.   *PROTEIN: 242.2 grams; CALORIES: 6189*

SEASONING MIXTURES

Greek Seasoning:
oregano
lemon juice
cinnamon
nutmeg
garlic
parsley
fennel

Italian Seasoning:
oregano
marjoram
basil
rosemary
savory
thyme

Curry Powder
coriander
cumin
mustard powder
turmeric
foenugreek
cardamom
black pepper

Chili Powder
garlic
oregano
cumin
chili pepper, optional
cayenne, optional

Pickling Spice
coriander seeds
allspice
cinnamon
mustard seeds
bay leaves
ginger
cloves
black peppercorns
chilis, optional

MISO

Miso is a traditional Japanese food made from soybeans, various grains and salt. Available in many varieties (and colors!) its flavors range from sweetish to salty. Basically, it is a pasty soy sauce and can be used in much the same way tamari is to enhance flavors. In addition, it makes a good instant soup stock (in Japan, such a miso soup is a breakfast staple) and used sparingly, a sandwich spread. Like tofu, it is easily digested: in fact, traditionally, it is reputed to be an aid to better digestion!

JBW

TOFU

Tofu, also known as soybean curd or soy cheese, is a staple food of high quality vegetable protein. To make it, soybeans are soaked, then ground. Water is added to this resultant pulp, and the mixture is cooked before being strained. Once all the pulp, known as okara, has been removed, the soymilk is curdled by the addition of a salt such as Nigari (extracted from seawater), calcium sulfate or Epsom salts.

The curds are pressed into creamy-white blocks and are packed in water, ready for use. Tofu is high in protein, making it an ideal food for those trying to replace animal protein soundly and inexpensively, or for those allergic to milk products. Because of its bland flavor and its great digestibility, tofu can be added unobtrusively to many dishes, increasing their nutritional value. It comes in two basic types: silken and firm. The silken tofu is soft, making it ideal for soft spreads, dips, and for adding general creaminess to a dish, much as the cottage cheese or ricotta cheese, sour cream or yogurt which it replaces do. Firm tofu, being denser, is best where a recipe calls for marinating, cubing, slicing, crumbling, frying or broiling. Given such versatility, it is not surprising that tofu has such a long history in the Far East — or that its popularity is growing so rapidly in the Western world.

—Jean Baker White

SPROUTS
Introduction, Methods, and Reference Chart

Sprouts, used for thousands of years elsewhere in the world, are finally becoming known in this country. In these potentially gloomy days of high priced, heavily treated vegetables, sprouts are sure to play an increasingly important role in our diets—and for many good reasons!

A sprout is just that—a newly germinated seed, bean or grain. The most popular are alfalfa, mung, lentil, soy, garbanzo and wheat sprouts. In their original unsprouted form, each of these is respectably nutritious, but when sprouted become even more so. Soybeans for example show a 500% increase in vitamins after 3 days sprouting time! One cup, raw is a mere 48 calories, providing 6.5 grams of protein. (A large egg has about 82 calories to the same amount of protein and has the cholesterol that sprouts do not!) Sprouted mung beans come in at a whopping 37 calories per cup!

These little morsels are versatile. The tiny alfalfa sprouts, or chopped up mung and lentil sprouts add a delightful, delicate crunch to sandwiches. Try mixing a cupful in your next tuna or egg salad mixture. Whole lentil, mung and soy sprouts are nothing short of wonderful added to pilaf, stir-fries, soups and stews in the last few moments of cooking time. Salads get a new lift and crunch when any sprouts are tossed in with them, while sprouted wheat berries, thrown into bread dough along with the first cups of flour ensure a sweet bread, without any extra sweetener added. As if all these uses aren't enough—well consider taking beans or seeds to sprout on your next camping trip! Lightweight and occupying little space, they are easily sprouted while on the trail. Imagine fresh vegetables 3 days out! And then lest we forget—they have a great taste and bite to them. Toddlers with enough teeth to chew properly will love the raw mung and lentil sprouts especially well—and get a good dose of vitamins, minerals and protein at the same time. Larger sprouts—soy and garbanzo—should not be eaten raw but rather steamed 10 minutes first.

Such paragons should be expensive, but here is the real surprise. A pound of mung beans, soy beans, lentils or wheat berries, or a half pound of alfalfa seeds, will produce a good gallon or more of fresh vegetables for you!

Some supermarkets now stock fresh sprouts in their produce sections as well as canned mung bean sprouts, but growing them is child's play. In fact this is a good job for the 3-and-ups in your house. Remember what seeds need to germinate in a garden; darkness (under the soil), moisture (watering cans and rain) and warmth (the sunny growing months). These requirements are easily mimicked in your kitchen. Some evening, after the dishes are done, pour a small amount of seeds into a wide mouthed quart jar or shallow bowl. Fill the container with tepid water and ignore it until the morning. Seeing it then, tip the water out into a bowl. It contains water soluble vitamins and minerals and so is a good addition to soups or your houseplants! Fill the jar or bowl with tepid water again, but this time, strain it all out, leaving only what clings to the potential sprouts. In order to provide the essential warmth, humidity and dark, you now must place a piece of plastic (a bag or piece of wrap) loosely over the mouth of the container and place it in one of your kitchen cupboards or in a bread box. If using a jar, place it on its side, lying down. Twice a day, repeat the business of filling the jar with tepid water and draining it all out. This will prevent mold and fermentation from occurring. Keep up this twice-a-day schedule until sprouts are the size indicated by the following chart. If you tend to be an out-of-sight, out-of-mind person, keep the sprouts on your counter top, but allow an extra 24 hours sprouting time.

Should you meet problems—rotting sprouts, sourness, spotty germination, or mold, consider the following—and try again!

1. Were the seeds/beans top quality and unbroken ones from a reputable natural food store? Broken seeds cause n. d and rot. Old ones don't sprout well.

2. Did you oversoak the seeds? Did you leave too much water in the sprouting vessel? In both cases, rot and mold can again set in.

3. Did you underwater or undersoak the seeds? If so, germination will be poor.

4. Did you keep sprouts at too low a temperature? Rate of sprouting will be slowed down encouraging spoilage.

5. Did you keep sprouts at too high a temperature? This causes sourness and fermentation of sprouts.

If you do not want the fiber rich hulls on your sprouts, although they are perfectly edible, tip the fully grown sprouts into a large basin of warm water. Gently rub them between your hands for a minute or so and the hulls will rise to the water's surface ready to be scooped out. Drain the sprouts well and return them to their jar. Set it in a sunny spot for a few hours—this will further enhance their vitamin C and chlorophyll content, for free!

Store the mature sprouts, in a loosely tied plastic bag in the refrigerator for up to a week. If you think of it, rinse them every day or two to prolong their freshness—but they are bound to be so popular in your home that the last thing you need worry about is losing them!   *—Jean Baker White*

SPROUT	DAYS OF SPROUTING TIME *	HARVEST LENGTH	YIELD
Alfalfa mildly sweet-nutty, very delicately crisp	3-4	1¼-1¾"	¼ C. = 2 C., plus
Lentils slightly peppery, crisp	3-4	½"-1"	½ C. = 3 to 4 C.
Mung beans like sweet raw peas; crunchy and crisp	3-4	1"-1¾"	½ C. = 3 to 4 C.
Radish seeds very hot; use sparingly!	2-4	½"-1"	2 T. = 1 to 2 C.
Wheat berries very sweet, chewy	2-4	¼"-¾"	½ C. = 2½ to 3 C.
Garbanzo beans (Chickpeas), and Soybeans somewhat nutty, vaguely crunchy	2-4	¾"-1¼"	½ C. = 2 to 3 C.
Aduki beans very crisp	3-5	½"-1"	½ C. = 2 to 3 C.

*Time depends on age of bean or seed used, the temperature they are kept at (66°-74° works well), and the frequency of rinsing.

LEGUMES
(dried beans and peas)

Legumes are versatile and nutritious. They appear in the cuisines of many cultures (for instance: black beans in Cuban cooking, pinto beans in Mexican, garbanzos in Spanish, black-eyed peas in foods of the American South, soybeans in Oriental dishes), and can be used in salads, dips and spreads, and, of course, main dishes.

Although legumes lack some of the eight essential amino acids, when eaten with grains, dairy products or nuts and seeds, the food combination provides a complete meatless protein. Dishes such as Tamale Pie (p. 24) provide this protein with kidney beans, cornbread, and cheese; Beans in Pita (p. 65) combines garbanzos, grain (whole wheat pita bread) and cheese or yogurt to achieve a complete protein.

"Ethnic" recipes are a good way to begin eating meatless meals. Virtually every nation has at least one traditional meatless dish. Italian and Mexican recipes are particularly easy to serve meatless because you seldom miss the meat in flavorful concoctions which contain beans, cheese, cottage cheese, ricotta or tofu. Oriental dishes are also good material. Japanese sukiyaki is great without the beef if you use tofu, which is often eliminated from North American versions altogether. East Indian dishes, from a traditionally vegetarian culture, are wonderful. Middle Eastern recipes are great, too. In Egypt, for instance, even wealthy people who can afford meat enjoy the peasant bean dishes. Russian, German and Scandinavian cultures abound in dairy dishes. In fact, you could eat meatless meals for years and never repeat a recipe.

LEGUME COOKING TABLE

LEGUME (1 C. dry)	Minimum Am't Water	Approximate Minutes of Cooking Time	Approximate Yield
Black Beans	4 C.	90-120	2 to 2½ C.
Black-eyed Peas	3 C.	90-120	2 to 2½ C.
Garbanzos (chickpeas)	4 C.	180	2 to 2½ C.
Great Northern Beans	3½ C.	120	2 to 2½ C.
Kidney Beans	3 C.	120-150	2 C.
Lentils (no soaking necessary)	3 C.	30-45	2¼ C.
Lima Beans	2 C.	120	1¼ to 1½ C.
Pinto Beans	3 C.	120-150	2 to 2½ C.
Navy Beans and other small white beans	3 C.	60-90	2 C.
Soybeans	4 C.	180 +	2 C.
Soy Grits	2 C.	15	2 C.
Split Peas (no soaking necessary)	3 C.	45	2¼ C.

HINTS FOR COOKING LEGUMES

- Presoaking (except lentils and split peas): Method I—Rinse and pick over every legume. Soak each cup of legumes in 3 to 4 C. water for 8 hours, *or* Method II—Bring beans and water to a boil. Cook for 2 minutes. Remove from heat. Let stand for at least 1 hour. (In warm weather, refrigerate beans while soaking, to avoid fermentation.)

- Cooking: Add to water 1 T. oil (and up to 1 t. salt if desired for each cup of legumes). Bring water and legumes to a boil. Reduce heat and simmer for time listed in table below. (Legumes which are old will take longer to cook.) Check occasionally while cooking to add more water as legumes cook, always keeping the level of water covering the legumes. (Hint: cooking beans with seaweed makes the beans more digestible.)

- Testing for doneness: The length of cooking time will depend on the type of bean or pea used, and also on the age and freshness of the legume. For salads and casseroles, legumes should be firmer than for recipes calling for mashed beans. Legumes are nearing doneness when you blow on a few beans in a spoon and the bean or pea skins slip off, and/or when your tongue will easily mash a legume against the roof of your mouth.

- Freezing: To save time and energy, cook double batches of legumes. Freeze them and some of their cooking water in airtight containers. To thaw, set container in hot water. Or put frozen legumes in hot soup or stew. Simmer until legumes are hot. Also, by freezing presoaked soy beans and soaking water, you can cut their cooking time by ⅓ to ½.

- Refried beans: In a hot, oiled skillet, mash and stir cooked beans and a little of their liquid.   *—Lois Lake Raabe*

READY TO USE DRIED BEANS

2 lbs. dry **beans**: navy, soy, kidney, etc.

8 to 10 **pint jars** and **lids**

Wash beans and place in 3 quart bowl. Cover with water and soak overnight. In the morning, fill the jars ⅔ full of beans. Add **salt, pepper** or **seasonings** if desired. (Try ¼ t. **chili powder** for your own Chili Beans.) Add boiling water to within one inch of jar top. Adjust lids and process in pressure canner or pressure pan for 1 hour and 15 minutes at 10 pounds pressure. Have your own supply of ready to use beans for quick-fix recipes.

PROTEIN: 202.4 grams; CALORIES: 3084

GRAINS

Grains can make a delicious morning porridge—but they aren't *just* for breakfast! They can appear in salads, stuffings, and side dishes, and can form the basis of any number of main dishes. Although grains lack two essential amino acids, you can remedy this by serving a grain with

- a legume
- eggs
- a dairy product (milk, cheese, yogurt)
- nuts, seeds, or *ground* sesame seeds
- tofu
- nutritional yeast
- 1/8 C. soy grits per cup of grain.

Thus, you can provide a complete, high-quality protein without serving meat. In Texas Rice (p. 217), rice and dairy products are combined, and in Arroz con Frijoles (p. 188), rice and black beans provide the complete protein.   *—Lois Lake Raabe*

TIMETABLE FOR COOKING GRAINS

Length of cooking time will depend on age of the grain.
Check after shortest time for tenderness.

GRAIN (1 C. dry)	Cups of Liquid	Approximate Minutes of Cooking Time	Approximate Yield
Barley	3 C.	75	3½ C.
Brown rice	2 C.	30-45	3 C.
Bulgur	4 C.	15-20	4 C.
Cornmeal (mix with 1 C. cold water first)	4 C.	25-30	2½ to 3 C.
Cracked Wheat	1 C.	5-15	2 C.
Hominy Grits	3 C.	60-120	3½ C.
Millet	2 C.	40-60	3 C.
Oats, Rolled (Oatmeal)	2 C.	5-10	3 C.
Oats, Steel Cut	3 C.	35-45	3 to 3¼ C.
Rye (Berries) Kernels	3 to 5 C.	60-120	2½ to 2¾ C.
Rye Flakes	2 C.	10-15	2½ to 3 C.
Wheat (Berries) Hard (drain later)	3 to 5 C.	120-150	2½ to 2¾ C.
Wheat (Berries) Spring (drain later)	3 to 5 C.	90	2½ to 2¾ C.
Wheat Flakes	2 C.	10-15	2½ to 3 C.

GRAIN COOKING METHODS

Brown Rice (Medium or Long Grain)

1 C. **brown rice**
2 C. boiling **liquid**
1 T. **butter** or oil
1 t. **salt** (or less)

Rinse and sort rice. In skillet, over medium high heat, toast rice, stirring constantly, or saute in butter. Add liquid, butter if not already used, and salt if desired. Return to a boil. Stir once. Cover tightly. Simmer for 30 to 45 minutes, until liquid is absorbed.

P: 15; C: 812   *Cindy Butler*   *Sally Jo Bongle*   *Laurie Carroll*
Ottawa, Ontario, Canada *Kewaunee, Wisconsin* *Suttons Bay, Michigan*

Brown Rice (Short Grain)—especially good for Oriental meals

1 C. short grain **brown rice**
1-7/8 C. **water** or broth
1 to 2 T. tamari **soy sauce**

Rinse and sort rice. Bring all ingredients to a boil, stirring once. Cover and simmer for 45 to 60 minutes or until liquid is absorbed. Spread rice on plastic wrap-lined cookie sheet. Cool. Cover with more wrap. Refrigerate for 24 hours, to allow rice kernel to shrink inside its shell. Now it will stir fry well. Rice may be refrigerated for up to one week, or frozen.

P: 15 ; C: 704

Leslie Doney
Nazareth, Pennsylvania

Cracked Wheat

Wash, rinse wheat. Bring liquid to a boil. Stir in wheat (and ½ t. or less salt, optional). Cover. Remove from heat. In 5 to 10 minutes, liquid will be absorbed and grain tender.

Wheat Berries

1 C. **wheat berries**
5 C. **water**

Rinse and sort berries. Soak overnight, or bring ingredients to a boil for 2 minutes, and let stand for 1 hour. Bring to a boil again. Cover. Simmer for 1½ to 2½ hours, or until tender. Spring wheat will cook more quickly than hard (durum) wheat. (In a slow cooker, cook for 8 to 10 hours on low.) Drain and serve. For breakfast, serve as a hot cereal with butter, milk, and honey. For dinner, use cold in pilaf or grain salad, or hot with gravy. For a quick complete protein meal, combine with equal parts cooked kidney (or other) beans, leftover vegetables, and grated cheese. Serve hot. *PROTEIN: 12.7 grams; CALORIES: 361*

Rhoda Taylor
Duncan, B.C., Canada

Carol Lyons
Monroeville, Pennsylvania

Basic Grain Pilaf

1 C. **cracked wheat**, brown rice or millet
1 medium **onion**, chopped
1 T. **oil**
2 C. **liquid**

Wash grain. Saute grain and onion in oil until onion is golden. Add liquid (water with 1 T. tamari soy sauce, *or* broth, *or* part fruit juice or wine, etc.?. Simmer until liquid is absorbed. Cracked wheat will cook in 15 to 20 minutes, other grains will take longer (see table above).

Variation: Saute additional vegetables (mushrooms, celery, etc.) with onions, and/or stir in sprouts, leftover vegetables, or cooked cubed meat, fish, or poultry after grain is cooked. Warm through.

PROTEIN: 15.5 grams; CALORIES: 534

Basic Method for Cooking Other Grains

(See table above for amounts and cooking times.)

Rinse and sort grain. (For cornmeal, mix with 1 C. *cold* water.) Bring liquid to a boil. (Add 1 T. butter and ½ t. or less salt, if desired.) Slowly stir the grain in, stirring constantly. Reduce heat to lowest setting. Cover. Simmer for length of time in chart (check for tenderness after shortest time).

To vary, substitute milk, stock, broth, or tomato juice for all or part of water, or add 1 T. tamari soy sauce to water.

Fried Mush ("Pauper's Breakfast")

Cook a batch of any fine-textured grain such as cornmeal or hominy grits, according to table above. Pour into buttered pan. Chill until firm. Cut into squares. Brown in butter. Serve with honey or syrup for breakfast, or with gravy or tomato sauce and cheese at dinner.

Hints for Using Leftover Grains:

- in tuna salad
- in a cheese omelette or scrambled eggs
- in pancake batter
- in meatloaf

—Lois Lake Raabe

Out of the Cupboard and Onto the Table

Once your kitchen is finally stocked with all kinds of wonderful whole foods, you may find yourself facing another problem. How do you go about combining those foods into tasty, nutritious and appealing meals? Meal planning was so much simpler when you followed the meat-potato-vegetable-and-sometimes-a-salad routine, you think? It *is* true it is hard to miss the nutritional mark that way, *but* if you are one of the many people worried by the high cost of animal protein on your plate, or are trying, for various personal, health or moral reasons, to reduce or eliminate that meat from your diet, then please take time to study what you are under-taking. Your health, and your family's, is at stake.

Everyone probably knows that it is vitally important to eat a variety of whole foods regularly. This is because by doing so you stand a good chance of obtaining all needed nutrients—even from the most unexpected sources. Did you know, for example, that 3½ oz. of Brussels sprouts or green pepper contain more vitamin C than the same amount of orange juice? Or that 1 cup of cooked cabbage contains 86% of the calcium in a cup of milk? Half a cup of ground sesame seed contains nearly twice as much calcium as a cup of milk! Keeping these and other comparative food values in mind can be a big help to you, especially given the vagaries of cost and supply in the market place.

The need for protein has been drummed into us since grade school. Nowadays, we have scientific proof that a low-meat/no meat diet does contain adequate protein to sustain human life, as many other peoples have known for generations. Protein, after all, is found in plants as well as in animals.

The human body does not store protein, so must obtain it daily. Its value to the human body depends on its use-ability; that is, how well the body can digest it and extract its constituent amino acids, which are re-quired for basic protein synthesis. Meat and eggs are considered com-plete proteins: their amino acids are present in ideal balance. Not so plant proteins which are termed "incomplete." Because an amino acid or two is missing from their protein make-up, the nutritive value of plant pro-tein is usually less than that from animal sources, *unless* the missing amino acids can somehow be replaced. This is where protein comple-mentarity comes in. If you were to eat a meatless meal of chili and corn-bread, the amino acids missing from the cornmeal would be supplied by the "extras" in the beans and vice versa. The plant protein has thus be-come complete through this basic complementation or combination.

In practical terms, back in your kitchen, this means you must learn the various complementary groups of food in order to extract as much nutrition as possible from what you eat. The following chart gives you the basic food combinations, along with suggested recipes to get your meal planning started.

PROTEIN COMPLEMENTS

Food Group	Combined With	Quick Suggestions	Sample Recipes

Milk
Cheese
Yogurt
Butter
etc.
	Grains
	Legumes (peanuts,
	peas, lentils,
	beans)
	Seeds/Nuts
		1 Glass of milk
		  with toast
		2 Yogurt sprinkled
		  with granola
		3 Pizza with lots
		  of cheese
		4 French toast
			1 Quesadillas
			2 White Sauce
			  Casserole
			3 Macaroni and
			  Cheese
			4 Manicotti
			5 Welsh Rarebit
			6 Bread and
			  Cheese Souffle
			7 Cheesecake

Grains
Rice
Wheat
Millet
etc.
	Milk and its
	  products
	Legumes
	Seeds/Nuts
		1 Grilled cheese
		  sandwich
		2 Peanut butter
		  sandwich
		3 Oatmeal cookies
		  and milk
		4 Cake with cream-
		  cheese frosting
		5 Nutty granola
		  bars
		6 Cheese fondue
		  with bread
		7 Roasted nuts
		  sprinkled on
		  grains
			1 Brown Rice
			  Pudding
			2 Soyburgers
			3 Bean Soup (with
			  fresh bread)
			4 Texas Rice
			5 Pastina
			6 Cheese
			  Quesadillas
			7 Peanut Butter
			  Bars
			8 Roasted Grain
			  Cereal

Legumes
Beans
Lentils
Peas
Peanuts
etc.
	Seeds/Nuts
	Grains
	Milk and its
	  products
		1 Trail mix of
		  roasted soy-
		  beans, nuts
		  and sunflower
		  seeds
		2 Peanut Butter
		  icing on cakes
		  and bar cookies
		3 Peanut butter on
		  crackers
		4 Stir-fried or
		  steamed lentil,
		  mung, or soy
		  sprouts on rice
		5 Bean dips/
		  spreads with
		  bread or cracker
		  "dippers"
		6 Bean tacos
			1 Chili Con
			  Cashews
			2 Sweet and Sour
			  Sprouted
			  Soybeans on
			  Rice
			3 Arroz Con Frijoles
			4 Peas and Cheese
			  Salad
			5 Tamale Pie
			6 Whole Wheat
			  Peanut Butter
			  Cookies
			7 Bean Dip
			8 New Orleans Red
			  Beans and Rice

Seeds/Nuts
Sunflower
Sesame
Walnuts
Pecans
Cashews
etc.

Legumes
Milk and its
  products
Grain

1 Roasted nuts/
  seeds, chopped
  or ground,
  sprinkled on
  grains and beans
  or on yogurt
2 Cheese Ball
  covered with
  nuts, served
  with bread
  and crackers
3 Nutty granola

1 Hummus
2 Felafel
3 Chinese Style
  Broccoli-on-Rice
4 "Unmeat" Balls
5 Vegetable Nut Loaf
6 Sesame
  Vegetables with
  Rice

Any of the above

Eggs
Tofu
Nutritional Yeast
Small amounts
  (leftovers?) of
  meat, poultry or
  fish
Wheat Germ

1 Any pilaf type
  dish—add all
  those left-
  overs!
2 Extra eggs added
  to bread
3 Extra milk
  powder added to
  baked goods

1 Fried Rice
2 Oriental Oats
3 Lentil Soup
4 Split Pea Soup
  for Busy Mothers
5 Chili, using tofu
  or low-meat
  options

In addition to planning meals around the complementary proteins above, use the same theory to pack as much nutrition as possible into whatever you cook. In baking, stir a tablespoon of milk powder into every cup of flour or cornmeal your recipe requires. Grind a pound of sunflower or sesame seeds in your blender, storing the resultant meal in your refrigerator. It will be easy to scoop out a few tablespoons to add to bread, cookies and other baked goods or granolas. Make it a habit to add protein and mineral rich wheat germ to everything you bake—as well as to scrambled eggs, quiches, cheese sauces, casseroles, lasagnas and on pizzas.

By following these guidelines you should have no worries about meeting your daily protein requirements. What about needed vitamins and minerals though? This again is where variety is critical to getting enough of the nutrients you need. Go for a colorful array of vegetables on your plate and you are bound to succeed. White potatoes are great for potassium and vitamin C; and sweet potatoes and carrots for vitamin A, along with greens. Yellow rutabagas are good for vitamin C as are red beets and tomatoes, and white cauliflower. Broccoli and leafy greens are as terrific for calcium as they are for iron. (Mind you, simply cooking in plain black cast iron pots ensures you will get your daily ration of iron without even trying!) In planning accompaniments to your entrees then, remember the significance of color and you won't go wrong. Remember too, that there is no law to say vegetables must be cooked. In fact, it is a very sound idea to serve raw vegetables often. This can be as simple as a platter of scrubbed veggies, or mung, lentil, alfalfa and radish sprouts tossed in a tangy salad dressing, or any of the various salads listed in this book.

Desserts can be a boon to your daily nutritional package—or a real disaster. Keeping in mind the protein combinations discussed earlier, you can see that a simple clean-out-the-fridge fried rice or pilaf meal could be well complemented by a yogurt dessert, or an egg custard. A simple quiche and salad meal might be given substance by being followed by a whole wheat gingerbread or fruit bread. In these examples, dessert is in its rightful place, rounding out a meal, not being something completely extraneous to it. You see, with proper planning, it is very possible to have your cake—and benefit from it too!   —*Jean Baker White*

NATURAL EASTER EGG DYES

TO GET: **USE:**

Yellow   yellow onion skins, turmeric (½ t. per C. water), chamomile, sage, celery leaves.
Orange   any yellow dye plus beet juice.
Red   beets, safflower seeds, paprika, rose hips tea.
Blue   blueberries, grape juice concentrate, red cabbage.
Brown   black tea, white oak, juniper berry, coffee, barberry.
Light Purple blackberry, grapes, violets.
Green   alfalfa, spinach, kale, violet blossom plus ¼ t. baking soda, tansy, nettle, chervil, sorrel, parsley, carrot tops, beet tops. Or dip yellow egg in blue dye.
Khaki-Green red onion skins.

Hard cook eggs with 1 T. vinegar in water. Place dying materials in non-aluminum pans, cover with water and boil 5 minutes to extract the color or until darker than you like. Some things like grapes may take as long as an hour. Use enough material to make at least one cup of dye. Crush ingredients as they boil to extract as much color as possible. Strain the dye. Most dyes should be used hot. Temperature of the egg does not matter. Leave egg in dye until it reaches the desired color. Some dyes will take longer than others to color the eggs. Then remove and let dry. Experiment with mixing dyes to get different colors.

Jan Foulk   *Kay Hoover*   *Kathy Siddons*   *Nancy Johnson*
Elwin, Illinois   *Media, Pennsylvania* *Manchester, Connecticut* *Greeley, Colorado*

BEEF JERKY

1½ to 2 lbs. very lean flank **steak** or brisket

Optional:
⅓ C. tamari **soy sauce**
1 clove **garlic**, minced

Trim fat off meat. Cut across grain into 2 pieces; slice lengthwise with grain into 4" strips ¼" thick. Combine soy sauce and garlic in mixing bowl. Add meat. Marinate for 15 to 20 minutes, stirring occasionally. Drain and arrange in single layer on cooling rack set in baking pan. Bake overnight at 150° for 12 hours until dried. Blot meat on paper towel to absorb excess fat. Store in tightly covered container. Will keep for several weeks. Does not require refrigeration. Compare with store prices and see how inexpensive beef jerky can be.   *PROTEIN: 121 grams; CALORIES: 1010*   *Kathy Schneider*
Sarasota, Florida

Baby's First Foods

Breast milk is the superior infant food.

For the healthy full-term baby breast milk is the only food necessary until baby shows signs of needing solids, about the middle of the first year after birth.

Good nutrition means eating a well-balanced and varied diet of foods in as close to their natural state as possible.

— *from* "What La Leche League Believes . . . Concepts"

Our belief that human milk is the superior source of nourishment for our babies leads to a commitment to good nutritional practices for the benefit of the entire family as well.

In the beginning, both carrying, then nursing a baby require an increase in mother's nutritional needs. After that, the introduction of solid foods for baby initiates the weaning process.

Thus, an interest in all aspects of food—from purchase to preparation—is a natural outgrowth of La Leche League's purpose of promoting good mothering through breastfeeding.

When to Begin Solids

The exact time to start baby on solid foods varies because, as individuals, babies vary in appetite, readiness and temperament. However, La Leche League mothers and other* experts agree that the general time to consider introducing new foods is around the mid-year mark. That timing makes sense, too, since that's about when little teeth are able to chew, little hands are able to grab and little bodies are able to sit. Waiting until this time also helps mother maintain a plentiful milk supply and aids baby in staving off possible allergic reactions as well.

In What Order?

New foods should be introduced one at a time, allowing a week between each new food. After nursing the baby, give about a quarter-teaspoon of a new food once the first day. Increase it little by little until by the end of the first week baby is getting as much as wanted two or three times a day.

Commercial baby foods are not necessary since they are relatively expensive and some contain undesirable fillers such as sugar, excessive salt and other preservatives. Instead, make your own; all you need is the back of a fork.

• Start with raw mashed **banana**, a wholesome fruit that contains more food value than cereals. Or try cooked, mashed **sweet potato**, a good alternative for the first food in your little one's diet.

• Next, add **meat** because of its high protein and high iron content. Chopped chicken or mashed stew beef are easy to prepare. **Fish** is another high-protein food. But watch for bones and hold off on the smoked and pickled varieties.

• **Whole wheat bread** is a good item to add next, especially for babies who enjoy chewing. Besides, you can spread other nutritious foods on them (like peanut butter, liverwurst and soft cheeses) later on. **Whole-grain cereals** are included in this category as well.

• **Potatoes**—easily cooked and quite tasty—are ideal as a first vegetable, as are yams.

• Next, add **fresh fruits**. Scrape raw apple with a spoon or hand baby a piece of soft mushy peach or pear. Seasonal fruit, like berries, are best given with caution (because of possible allergies) after baby is eight months old or older. Wait on citrus fruits, too, for the same reason.

• Other **vegetables**, like finely-grated raw carrots, can be given gradually, although even cooked vegetables are harder to digest than other foods.

• **Eggs** should wait until baby is at least a year old since egg white is one of the more common causes of allergies.

• **Cow's milk** is another popular grocery staple that should stay in the background. The only milk your baby really needs is yours, of course, until weaning.

Julie E. Hopson

*Nutrition Committee of the American Academy of Pediatrics, October 1978.

Planning Ahead

(and for when you can't!)

Food Shower

Instead of a baby shower, why not a food shower? The recipes below are particularly appropriate to make ahead to stock an expectant mother's freezer. These are one-dish meals that provide a balance of nutrients. Choose a bread to go along with the main dish and she will have a complete and filling meal. All she will have to do is to thaw and heat the bread and heat the main dish. If time permits, Dad can put a salad together. Add a dessert for her to freeze to have on hand for company or a special treat.

Main Dishes
Chicken Pot Pie
Cornish Pasties
Mighty Meatloaf
Stuffed Peppers
Cabbage Rolls
Stuffed Jumbo Shells
Texas Quiche
Kathy's Lasagne
Island Style Chicken
Canneloni
Kitchener Special
Classic Quiche
Strata
Spinach Mushroom Crepes
Vegetable Soup
Italian Escarole Soup
Pizza
Piroshki
Zucchini-Potato Soup
Manicotti
Salmon Croquettes
Chili Con Carne
Turkey Loaf
Rice-Lentil Custard
Bean Dip

Breads
Pumpkin Pan Rolls
Cheese Bread
Refrigerator Rise Italian Bread
Potato Rolls or Bread
Two Way Oatmeal Bread
Sesame Cottage Cheese Bread
Pumpkin Corn Bread
No Knead Yeast Rolls
High Protein Wheat Bread
Couldn't Be Easier Slow Cooker
    Bread
Heidelberg Rye Bread

Desserts
Surprise Kugel (Noodle Pudding)
Tropical Delight Cake
Applesauce Cake
Orange Fruit Slush
Make Ahead Frozen Yogurt Salad
Carrot Cake
Good For You Banana Cake
Pumpkin Bread and Cupcakes
Yogurt Pie
Fantastic Carob Fudge

Breakfast (pop in toaster)
Waffles
French Toast
Whole Wheat English Muffins

Don't Fret, New Mother

You'll have some busy days, soon,
with your baby's care.
You'll stroke
    her tender body
and kiss her downy hair.
You'll nurse and hug and rock her
and sing her many a tune—
and then you'll note
    with worried frown
that dinnertime is soon!

No need to fret, new mother,
or take your babe from breast.
Your friends have made
    these dinners
to help when you feel pressed.
Just warm them in the oven;
then, with your family there,
all eat with calm
    and loving hearts,
rememb'ring that we care.

—*Lois Lake Church*

Foods that Keep Well

If you stop by to see the new baby, you can bring along some fresh fruits, vegetables or other foods that keep well in the refrigerator or on the shelf. Your gift of love gives the new mother more time to care for her baby.

In the Refrigerator
Tabouli
Marinated Vegetables
Potato Salad
Apple-Carrot-Raisin Salad
Gazpacho
Sunshine Salad
Unbelievable Jam
Yogurt
Whole Wheat English Muffins
Dandy Candy
Celestial Chicken Salad
Crunchy Chicken Salad
Cheese Leather
Meat Spread
Lekvar (Prune Butter)
Applesauce
Brown Rice Pudding
Bread Pudding
Pita Bread

On the Shelf
One Pan Granola
Bulk Coating Mix
Roasted Grain Cereal
Pancake Mix
Dry Dip Mix
Graham Crackers
Whole Grain Soft Pretzels
Croutons
Toddler-on-the-Run Breadsticks
Digestive Biscuits
Bread Stix Snack Mix

Fresh Baked Goodies
Muffins
Yeast Breads
Quick Breads
Cookies
Cakes
Pies

It's Four O'Clock !

These recipes require little time to prepare and will be ready to eat within an hour. In addition to these selected recipes most **muffins, quick breads, French toast, pancakes, waffles** and **salad dressings** are quick to make.

Main Dishes
Sally's Beef Teriyaki
Healthburgers
Sloppy Joes
Mou-Far-Rah-Kay
Kima
Easy Beef Stroganoff
Fried Rice
Steamed Chicken
Oven Fried Chicken
Baked Fish from Turning Island
Baked Fish Fillets
Calico Fish
Salmon Loaf
Crab Cakes
Super Summer Tuna
Hot Tuna Sandwiches
Busy Day Fish Fillet
Liver Teriyaki
Kitchener Special
Pork Chop 'N Cabbage Casserole
Pizza Pie
Zucchini Pizza
White Pitza
Vegetable Nut Loaf
Live Longer Casserole
Salmon Croquettes
Tunaburgers
Napa Valley Fish
Cold Salami Salad
Green Spaghetti
Creamy Soups
Individual Pizzas
Variable Zucchini Casserole
Texas Quiche
Tofu-Cheese-Egg Quiche
Easy Broccoli Souffle
Strata
Quick Soup
Gazpacho

Side Dishes
Orange Romaine Salad
Tomatoes Oregano
Fancy Vegetable Medley
Spaghetti Squash
Summertime Salad
Curried Rice
Indian Style Green Beans
Mushrooms and Cheese
Dilly Carrots
Chinese Style Broccoli
   or Spinach
Steamed Veggies
Pastina
Wilted Salad
Sesame Vegetables
Party Peas
Parsnips and Savory Sauce
Zucchini Boats
Galloping Galuska

Sweet Things
Luscious Fruit Salad
Simple Vanilla Pudding
Fruit and Custard Pudding
Quick Fruit Salads or Desserts
Instant Banana Yogurt Salad
No-Bake Cookies
Applesauce Crazy Cake
Wacky Carob Cake

Bean Dip
Hummus
Invent-A-Dip
Toasty Tofu

Easy to Make

These recipes are very simple for those times when you have only 10 or 15 minutes to prepare a meal or a snack.

Main Dishes
Steamed Chicken
Perfect Roast Chicken
Oven Fried Chicken
Busy Day Fish Fillet
Super Summer Tuna
Baked Fish Fillets
Salmon Patties
Calico Fish
Baked Fish from Turning Island
Cold Salami Salad
Cottage Cheese Salad
Chili Con Cashews
Picky Eater's Baked Cabbage
Cheese and Potato Puff Pie
Easy Broccoli Souffle
Strata
Individual Pizzas
Pita Bread Sandwiches

Side Dishes
O'Brien Potatoes
Sideshow Potatoes
Indian Style Green Beans
Dilly Carrots
Sprout Salad
Baked Fresh Asparagus
Oriental Oats
Pastina
Yorkshire Pudding
Orange Romaine Salad
Tomatoes Oregano
Daddy's Favorite Salad
Cheese Spread
Galloping Galuska

Sweet Things
Malted Nut Pie
Unbelievable Jam
Banana Boats
Summer Ice
Instant Ice Cream
Fantastic Carob Fudge
Applesauce Crazy Cake
Wacky Carob Cake
Fudge Pie
Simple Vanilla Pudding

Leftovers

Many recipes provide an option for use of leftovers; other recipes reheat very well. Use leftovers in **quiches, souffles, soups, meat salads** and **meat spreads**; reheat **soups, stews, casseroles** and **quiches**.

Use of Leftovers
Fried Rice
Two Way Tofu Parmesan
Meatless Hash from Leftovers
Pasta E Fagiole
White Sauce Casserole
Leftover Grains, Leftover Rice
Skillet Dinner
Green Turkey
Feijoada
Bubble and Squeak
Strata
Chicken and Bulgur Casserole
Aunt Mary's BBQ
Bean Bread
Rice Lentil Custard

Reheats Well
Cabbage Rolls
Texas Rice
Burros
Pierogi
Piroshki
Macaroni and Cheese
Creamy Noodle Bake
Brisket and Sweet Potatoes
Aunt Mary's BBQ
Manicotti Filling
Fried Rice
Veggie-Rice Bake
Island Chicken
Mighty Meatloaf
Stroganoff

Make Ahead

These recipes may be prepared early in the morning or the night before. Refrigerate until ready to use. In addition to these selected recipes most **breads, pancakes, spaghetti sauces, souffles, stratas, meatloaves, pizza, soups, stews, pies** and **cakes** are easy to make ahead of time.

Main Dishes
David's Favorite Casserole
Cornish Pasties
Piroshki
Kathy's Lasagne
Healthburgers
Chicken Pot Pie
Stir Fry
Fried Rice
Crunchy Chicken Salad
Chili Con Cashews
Vegetable Pie
Super Six Layer Casserole
Pierogi
Macaroni and Cheese

Side Dishes
Bean Salad
7 Layer Salad
Tabouli
Peas and Cheese Salad
Cucumber Salad
Texas Rice
Potato Salad
Daddy's Favorite Salad
Potato-Veggie Salad
Susan's Cole Slaw
Stuffed Veggie-Take Alongs

Sweet Things
Simple Vanilla Pudding
Brown Rice Pudding
Bread Pudding

Easy to Freeze

When you have some extra time, double or triple one of these recipes and freeze part of it for a "rainy" day. When ready to use, thaw or pop into the oven to reheat. In addition to these selected recipes most **breads, muffins, pancakes, waffles, French toast, soups, stews, spaghetti sauces, pizzas, quiches, meatloaves, meatballs, cakes** and **cookies** freeze well.

Main Dishes
Stroganoff
Chili Con Carne
Cabbage Rolls
Stuffed Jumbo Shells
Cornish Pasties
Piroshki
Stuffed Green Peppers
Tamale Pie
Chicken Pot Pie
Island Style Chicken

Side Dishes
Katie's Noodles
Cream Puff Miniatures
Texas Rice
Easy Beans

Main Dishes
Canneloni
Salmon Croquettes
Homemade Sausages
Kitchener Special
Pierogi
Burros
Macaroni and Cheese
Spinach Mushroom Crepes
Strata

Sweet Things
Blueberry Jam
Unbelievable Jam
Dried Fruit Jam
Processor Pastry
Baked Doughnuts
Orange Fruit Slush

IN A PARTY MOOD

Trays of cut up **fruits** and **vegetables, quick breads, muffins, cakes, pies** and **cookies** are standard fare. How about a loaf of fresh baked **bread** with homemade **butter** and **jam?** Homemade **yogurt** with **granola** topping? Or **quiche** cut in bite-sized pieces? Try a **dip** with the fruit and vegetables. Just about any wholesome food can be a snack, so why not try some of these more unusual ideas.

Puddings
Brown Rice Pudding
Bread Pudding
Fruit and Custard Pudding
Simple Vanilla Pudding
Surprise Kugel (Noodle Pudding)
Baked Honey Custard

Frozen Treats
Orange Fruit Slush
Make Ahead Frozen Yogurt Salad
Yogurt Yumsicles
Cinnamon 'Sicles

Salads
Tabouli
Sunshine Salad
Susan's Cole slaw
Apple-Carrot-Raisin Salad

Pancakes
Puffed Oven Pancake
Texas Quiche

Soup
Zucchini-Potato Soup
Gazpacho

Snacks
Bread Stix Snack Mix
Graham Crackers
Whole Grain Soft Pretzels
Crispy Crackers, Breadsticks
Teething Biscuits
Baked Doughnuts
Dough Dabs
Bean Dip
Tofu Cheesecake
Hummus
Invent-A-Dip
Toasty Tofu
Ants on a Log
Apple Goodie
Banana Boats
Peanut Butter Apples
Frozen Bananas

Drinks
Winter Meeting Cider
Fruit Punch
Homemade Apple Juice
Hot Cup O'Carob
Summer Ice

Hands

Mother's hands, patient hands,
measure, reach, and show.
They guide the small ones
    at her side
though cooking's sometimes slow.

        Father's hands, loving hands,
        willing to learn how
        to slice and stir when
            Mother can't,
        for Baby needs her now.

Children's hands, helping hands,
peel and sort and mash,
mix and pour
    (oops! the floor!)
pat and knead and splash.

        All the hands, family hands,
        round the table share.
        Our food is spiced
            with smiles and love—
        a joyous feast is here.

                Lois Lake Church

Thank You

to our Recipe Testers

A special thank you to the 1,400 families who tested recipes—too many to list—but very important!

♡

Thank You also to our Typists

Fifty-six volunteer mothers from all over the United States and Canada typed the recipes for us.

Thank You to our Recipe Contributors

Over 500 LLL members sent recipes that were used as resource material for a recipe which was selected and rewritten for inclusion in the cookbook.

Thank You to

OUR OWN FAMILIES

Thank You also
to these Artists:

Judy Espensheid
Richland Center, Wisconsin

Ruth Friedman
Eau Claire, Wisconsin

Debby Thielking
Syracuse, New York

Mary Vizer
Ozark, Alabama

Marilyn Barry
Logansport, Indiana

Jan Foulk
Elwin, Illinois

Andrea Larmor
Islip, New York

Karen Williams Burdette
Tullahoma, Tennessee

Patty Lack
Mountainview, Oklahoma

Chrissy Lombardi
Danbury, Connecticut

Linda Foreman
New Ellenton, South Carolina

Debbie Smollen
Middlefield, Connecticut

Anthony Rizzo
Palm Springs, Florida

Manuscript Assistance: Madelon Gauer

Thank You also

A special thanks to these friends. Their help at crucial times was invaluable.

Allan S. Church
Meriden, Connecticut

Betty Hale
Pomfret Center, Connecticut

Jean Howell
Champaign, Illinois

Laura Mohrbacher
Champaign, Illinois

Renny Northrop
Summit, New Jersey

Gerri Perkins
Chatham, New Jersey

Janet Reynolds
Chatham, New Jersey

Linda Ritter
Mt. Holly, New Jersey

Notes and Recipes

Notes and Recipes

Notes and Recipes

Notes and Recipes

Notes and Recipes

Index